Wergild, Compensation and Penance

Medieval Law and Its Practice

Edited by

John Hudson (*St Andrews*)

VOLUME 31

The titles published in this series are listed at *brill.com/mlip*

Wergild, Compensation and Penance

The Monetary Logic of Early Medieval Conflict Resolution

Edited by

Lukas Bothe
Stefan Esders
Han Nijdam

BRILL

LEIDEN | BOSTON

DFG Collaborative Research Centre 700 – Governance in Areas of Limited Statehood (2010–2017)

Cover illustration: Heidelberg, Universitätsbibliothek, Cod. Pal. germ. 164, fol. 11v. With kind permission of the Universitätsbibliothek Heidelberg.

The Library of Congress Cataloging-in-Publication Data is available online at http://catalog.loc.gov
LC record available at http://lccn.loc.gov/2021941435

Typeface for the Latin, Greek, and Cyrillic scripts: "Brill". See and download: brill.com/brill-typeface.

ISSN 1873-8176
ISBN 978-90-04-31510-5 (hardback)
ISBN 978-90-04-46612-8 (e-book)

This book is printed on acid-free paper and produced in a sustainable manner.

Contents

Preface and Acknowledgments

The present volume is the result of an initial observation that the theme of wergild, although immensely important in (early) medieval culture and prominent in numerous sources, has been understudied in the last decades. Although wergild might at first sight appear as a very special aspect of medieval law, it becomes soon obvious that it can provide a key to understanding medieval societies — their modes of conflict settlement, but also their social cohesion and mentalities. With its focus on the payment of wergild, the volume thus documents a process of reflecting this topic that evolved over the years. The editors first met at the International Medieval Congress in Leeds in 2011 to organize two sessions titled 'Establishing a Person's Worth: Approaches to Wergeld and Composition'. The positive feedback we received inspired us to convene an international conference on the same topic, but in an extended perspective. Thus, 'Wergild, Compensation and Penance. The Monetary Logic of Early Medieval Conflict Resolution' was held 29 and 30 September 2014 at the Freie Universität Berlin, in a collaborative effort of the DFG Collaborative Research Centre 700 — Governance in Areas of Limited Statehood (Stefan Esders and Lukas Bothe) and the Frisian Academy (Han Nijdam). Having engaged in lively discussions at the conference, most of the speakers were willing and able to convert their presentations into contributions to this present volume. We hope that it can stimulate further research on what still seems to be a fairly neglected topic.

A few remarks need to be made on the scope and content of this volume. The main focus of its contributions is on the legal history of wergild and on monetary conflict resolution in the early medieval period, sometimes in relation to the late antique predecessors of the cases described. In a number of cases a comparative approach is taken, which often leads to the use of the very inspiring studies of later medieval Scandinavia that have been written lately. However, even though legal texts from later medieval Scandinavia have been considered, the large body of Icelandic saga literature remains immaterial to this volume. Moreover, a comparative approach that extends beyond Christian Europe remains to be taken. As legal and technical language figures prominently on numerous occasions, a final remark concerns the use of Latin in the contributions: for the sake of accessibility, we have tried to provide as many translations of the Latin quotations as possible. Being well aware of our aim's limitations, we cited existing translations where available and provided our own where necessary.

A great number of people helped in the various phases of this project and deserve our gratitude. First of all we would like to thank our contributors for their patience and endurance. Getting this volume done took us more time than we had ever hoped or feared. In chronological order we would further like to thank the moderators of the IMC sessions, Arnoud-Jan Bijsterveld and Alice Rio, and also Christophe Camby, who contributed to one of the Leeds sessions. Our thanks go also to the participants of the Berlin conference for their contributions and participation in an intense discussion: especially Jenny Benham, Christoph Meyer, Nurit Tsafrir, the late Miriam Czock, Ludger Körntgen, Marianne Elsakkers and Miriam Tveit.

Our special thanks go to John Hudson for allowing this volume to find a fitting place in the series "Medieval law and its practice". The people at Brill Publishers were extremely helpful and supportive, in particular we would like to thank acquisition editor Kate Hammond and Marcella Mulder. We would also like to express our gratitude to the unknown peer reviewer for the beneficial review and constructive critique of the volume.

Finally, we are extremely grateful to our student assistants Michael Eber, Felix Fischer, Anna Gehler-Rahůnek, Gerd Krause, Friederike Michel and Victor Wagner who helped us in various stages of the project. In the course of producing this book, Courtnay Konshuh and Keith Ruiter accurately checked and revised the contributions by authors who are not native speakers of English, while Albert Fenton created the index. Without all their help, this volume would not have come into being.

Lisi Oliver, an inspiring scholar of early medieval law and a wonderful colleague, contributed hugely to bringing people together at the symposium in Berlin. Both her talk and her overall presence were absolutely stimulating and remain unforgettable for those who were present. Lisi sadly passed away suddenly on June 7, 2015 in a tragic traffic accident and is greatly missed by everyone who knew her. We would like to extend our huge gratitude to Lisi's close colleagues Andrew Rabin and especially Stefan Jurasinski for their help with asking permission from Lisi's heirs to have her contribution to this volume published and with finalizing the article. It is to the memory of Lisi Oliver that we would like to dedicate this volume.

Figures and Tables

Figures

Tables

Abbreviations

CCSL	Corpus Christianorum, Series Latina
MGH	Monumenta Germaniae Historica (and its following subseries)
AA	Auctores antiquissimi
Capit.	Capitularia regum Francorum
DD	Diplomata
EE	Epistolae
Fontes iuris	Fontes iuris Germanici antiqui in usum scholarum separatim editi
LL	Leges (In Folio)
LL nat. Germ.	Leges nationum Germanicarum
SS	Scriptores
HRG	Handwörterbuch zur Deutschen Rechtsgeschichte
LexMA	Lexikon des Mittelalters
RGA	Reallexikon der Germanischen Altertumskunde
Transactions of RHS	Transactions of the Royal Historical Society
ZRG	Zeitschrift der Savigny-Stiftung für Rechtsgeschichte
GA	Germanistische Abteilung
KA	Kanonistische Abteilung
RA	Romanistische Abteilung

Bibliographical note:
Throughout the footnotes and bibliographies superscript numbers before years mark the edition of the work cited (e.g. Heinrich Brunner, *Deutsche Rechtsgeschichte* vol. 1, Leipzig ^{2}1906 = second edition, Leipzig 1906).

Contributors

Lukas Bothe
Freie Universität Berlin

Warren Brown
Californian Institute of Technology, Pasadena

Stefan Esders
Freie Universität Berlin

Wolfgang Haubrichs
Universität des Saarlandes, Saarbrücken (Emeritus)

Paul Hyams
University of Oxford (Emeritus)

Tom Lambert
Sidney Sussex College, Cambridge

Ralph W. Mathisen
University of Illinois, Urbana-Champaign

Rob Meens
Universiteit Utrecht

Han Nijdam
Fryske Akademy, Leeuwarden

Lisi Oliver†
Lousiana State University, Baton Rouge

Harald Siems
Ludwig-Maximilians-Universität München (Emeritus)

Karl Ubl
Universität zu Köln

Helle Vogt
Københavns Universitet

Contributors

[illegible]
Freie Universität Berlin

[illegible]
California Institute of Technology, Pasadena

[illegible]
Freie Universität Berlin

[illegible]
[illegible]

[illegible]
University of Oxford

[illegible]
Sidney Sussex College, Cambridge

[illegible]
University of Illinois at Urbana-Champaign

[illegible]
[illegible]

[illegible]
[illegible]

[illegible]
[illegible]

[illegible]
Ludwig-Maximilians-Universität München

[illegible]
Universität Zürich

[illegible]
Københavns Universitet

CHAPTER 1

Wergild and the Monetary Logic of Early Medieval Conflict Resolution

Stefan Esders

One of the rare medieval depictions illustrating the payment of wergild comes from an illuminated manuscript of Eike von Repgow's *Sachsenspiegel*, a famous law-book from 13th-century Germany.[1] The illumination serves to elucidate a provision on the facing page that deals with the culpability of a child under age who has killed a person:

> No underage child can do anything that would exact the death penalty. If he kills or injures a man, his guardian shall pay compensation in the amount of that person's wergild if it is proven against him. Whatever damage the child causes shall be compensated from the child's property by the guardian according to his estimation.[2]

On the left, an under-age male is denoted standing in a yellow tunic with an axe almost equaling his size. The axed victim is portrayed lying on the ground in blood-stained clothes with his head covered in blood and also having received

---

1 *Der Sachsenspiegel. Die Heidelberger Bilderhandschrift Cod. Pal. Germ. 164. Kommentar und Übersetzung*, ed. Walter Koschorrek and Wilfried Werner, Frankfurt/Main 1989, fol. 11^{r} (Facsimile) and 157–159 (transcription of the text). The following article, which serves as an introduction here, grew out of a project on "Law, Security and Order in Early Medieval Kingdoms" conducted from 2010 to 2017 as part of the Collaborative Research Centre 700 "Governance in Areas of Limited Statehood", funded by Deutsche Forschungsgemeinschaft. Further discussion on wergild and its role in societies engaging in military values took place within the project "The Militarisation of early medieval Societies. Nature, Control and Perception in a west-European Comparison", funded by Fritz Thyssen-Foundation from 2016 to 2019. — I should like to thank in particular Lukas Bothe for constant support and helpful criticism on the topic of wergild over the years.

2 *Sachsenspiegel, Landrecht* II, 65.1, ed. Karl August Eckhardt, Göttingen 1955, 93: *Nen kint ne mach binnen sinen jaren nicht dun, dar it sinen lif mede verwerke. Sleit it enen man oder belemt it ene, sin vormunde scal it <buten unde> beteren mit jenes wergelde, of it op ene vulbracht wert. swelken scaden it dut, den scal he gelden na sime werde mit des kindes gude*; *Saxon Mirror. A "Sachsenspiegel" of the Fourteenth Century*. Translated by Maria Dobozy, Philadelphia 1999, 112 (cited as *The Saxon Mirror*. Translated by Dobozy).

 | DOI:10.1163/9789004466128_002

FIGURE 1.1 Heidelberg, Universitätsbibliothek, Cod. Pal. germ. 164, fol. 11[v] (early 14th cent.)

a further injury on his arm, while his closed eyes indicate that he was dead.[3] The person standing in the middle of the scene is the under-age perpetrator's ward, wearing a tunic with green stripes and turning towards a third person standing to his left. This person, wearing a white tunic with stripes, probably is a close relative of the victim, to whom the child's guardian is handing over a large sum of money. As is made clear by the oath-gesture performed with his left hand, this person had convincingly made a case for claiming the wergild, and possibly also promised to abstain from taking further revenge.[4]

The figure's virtue is to epitomize a fairly complex bundle of legal action and thought by combining two scenes into one sequence. This might explain why only few illustrations have come down to us that illustrate what must have been an ever-present phenomenon in the earlier Middle Ages. Indeed, from the early medieval period onward, wergild figures very prominently in our sources — most notably in legal texts, of course — but also to some extent in historiographical and hagiographical narratives and in royal and private charters. Most famous is Gregory of Tours' account of the feud between Sichar and Chramnesind in the 580s which, though not typical in every respect, illustrates how difficult it was to arrive at a lasting settlement and how the church came into play through the mediation of the bishop, but also by lending money so that the wergild was paid.[5] The illumination from the *Sachsenspiegel* also

3 The figure insofar seems to reflect the text's provision that deals with homicide as well as with injury.

4 If the latter is true, the illumination, in putting emphasis on these gestures, would have made a point that was not contained in the wording of the text. On such discrepancies between text and illumination in this law-book see Ruth Schmidt-Wiegand (ed.), *Text-Bild-Interpretation. Untersuchungen zu den Bilderhandschriften des Sachsenspiegels*, Munich 1986.

5 Gregory of Tours, *Decem Libri Historiarum* 7.47 and 9.19, ed. Bruno Krusch and Wilhelm Levison, MGH SS rerum Merovingicarum 1, 1, Hanover 1951, 366–368 and 432–434. On this

encapsulates an extended process in which the payment of wergild finalized a longer series of actions and negotiations that transformed a violent conflict into a peaceful settlement. This process involved several intermediate actors and various steps of formal procedure so that the parties came to accept an agreement or a judicial decision. Its ultimate success, however, depended on a large sum of money being at hand, and no less on the ability and willingness of the conflicting parties to pay and accept it.

Wergild thus can open a window that allows for a closer look at how early medieval societies settled their conflicts. But it also enables us to get closer to early medieval mentalities and some of their underlying concepts. Posing a challenge to scholars, the large number of legal texts that relate to wergild — in particular the long lists of wergild tariffs and composition fees as contained in the law-codes — call for a complex contextualization. Despite such obvious features, wergild has been a widely neglected topic for a long time. It is only very recently that research interest in this topic has increased significantly.[6] As the present volume aims to carry this discussion further, in what follows a more general framing of the topic will be given that also seeks to delineate some fields of future research, proceeding from the contributions contained herein.

1 The Breakthrough of Blood-Money in Western Europe: A Paradigmatic Shift around 500

Around 500, a legal compilation was drafted at the behest of the Burgundian king Gundobad, probably in Lyons. The objective of this *liber constitutionum*, also often called *Lex Burgundionum* or *Lex Gundobadi*, was to establish peace and justice in the kingdom of Burgundy with its mixed population composed

episode see Philippe Depreux, 'Une faide exemplaire? A propos des aventures de Sichaire: Vengeance et pacification aux temps mérovingiens', in: *La vengeance 400–1200* (Collection de l'École française de Rome 357), ed. Dominique Barthélemy, François Bougard and Régine Le Jan, Rome 2006, 65–85, and the article by Rob Meens in this volume.

6 An important starting-point is provided by Patrick Wormald, *The Making of English Law: King Alfred to the Twelfth Century, Volume I, Legislation and its Limits*, Oxford 1999, 374–378; moreover Id., 'The *Leges Barbarorum*: Law and Ethnicity in the Post-Roman West', in: *Regna and Gentes: The Relationship Between Late Antique and Early Medieval Peoples and Kingdoms in the Transformation of the Roman World*, ed. Hans-Werner Goetz, Jörg Jarnut and Walter Pohl, Leiden 2003, 21–53. See also, for instance, the contributions by Camby, Depreux, Esders, Faulkner, Oliver, Tyszka and Ubl quoted in the following footnotes, none of which antedates the year 2009.

of Romans and Burgundians.[7] In its second title, devoted to homicide (*De homicidio*), it prescribed what should happen if someone killed "a native freeman of our people of any other nation (*ex populo nostro cuiuslibet nationis*) or a servant of the king, in any case a man of barbarian tribe (*natione barbarum*)". The punishment envisaged for such crime was somewhat boldly called "bloodshed" (*sanguinis effusio*), most likely meaning the death penalty, while the provisions that follow allowed for the possibility to pay a blood-money if such deed had not been committed "with boldness or rashness bent on injury". The chapter goes on to explain that for the killing of a person in self-defence or revenge, half a wergild should be paid varying according to the status of the person (*secundum qualitatem personae*) from 150 *solidi* for a noble man, to 100 *solidi* for a middle-class person, to 75 *solidi* for a minor person.[8] While these

7 On the *Liber constitutionum* and its purpose see David Gene Frye, 'Gundobad, the *Leges Burgundionum*, and the struggle for sovereignty in Burgundy', *Classica et Mediaevalia* 14 (1990), 199–212; Patrick Amory, 'The meaning and purpose of ethnic terminology in the Burgundian laws', *Early Medieval Europe* 2 (1993), 1–28; Peter Heather, 'Law and society in the Burgundian kingdom', in : *Law, Custom, and Justice in Late Antiquity and the Early Middle Ages*, ed. Alice Rio, London 2011, 115–153; Ian N. Wood, 'The Legislation of *Magistri Militum*: the laws of Gundobad and Sigismund', *clio@themis. Revue électronique d'histoire du droit* 10 (2016) (thematic issue *La forge du droit. Naissance des identités juridiques en Europe, IVe–XIIIe siècles*): http://www.cliothemis.com/IMG/pdf/5-_Wood-2.pdf.

8 *Leges Burgundionum, Liber constitutionum* 2 (*De homicidiis*), ed. Ludwig Rudolf von Salis, MGH LL nationum Germanicarum 2, 1, Hanover 1892, 42–43: *Si quis hominem ingenuum ex populo nostro cuiuslibet nationis aut servum regis, natione duntaxat barbarum, occidere damnabili ausu aut temeritate praesumpserit, non aliter admissum crimen quam sanguinis sui effusione conponat. Illud sane huic legi rationabili censuimus provisione subiungi, ut si cui forte a quocumque inlata vis fuerit, ut aut ictibus verberum aut vulneribus urgeatur, et dum sequitur percutientem dolore aut indignatione conpulsus occiderit, atque ita factum re ipsa aut idoneis, quibus credi possit, testibus fuerit conprobatum, medietatem pretii secundum qualitatem personae occisi parentibus cogatur exsolvere, hoc est: si obtimatem nobilem occiderit, in medietatem pretii* CL *solidos, si aliquem in mediocri,* C *solidos, pro minore persona* LXXV *solidos praecipimus numerari.* [...] *Hoc specialiter in huiusmodi causa universitas noverit observandum, ut interfecti parentes nullum nisi homicidam persequendum esse cognoscant, quia sicut criminosum iubemus extingui, ita nihil molestiae sustinere patimur innocentem.* — 'Of murders. If anyone presumes with boldness or rashness bent on injury to kill a native freeman of our people of any nation or a servant of the king, in any case a man of barbarian tribe, let him make restitution for the committed crime not otherwise than by the shedding of his own blood. We decree that this rule be added to the law by a reasonable provision, that if violence shall have been done by anyone to any person, so that he is injured by blows of lashes or by wounds, and if he pursues his persecutor and overcome by grief and indignation kills him, proof of the deed shall be afforded by the act itself or by suitable witnesses who can be believed. Then the guilty party shall be compelled to pay to the relatives of the person killed half his wergild according to the status of the person: that is, if he shall have killed a noble of the highest class, we decree that the payment be set at one hundred fifty solidi, i.e., half his wergild; if a person of middle class, one hundred solidi; if a person of the lowest

regulations clearly aimed at the Burgundian or barbarian part of the population, it was only shortly later that a separate law-code was compiled for the Romans living under Burgundian rule. This code, the so-called *Lex Romana Burgundionum*,[9] deliberately paralleled the *Liber constitutionum* in structure. In its second title, also dealing with homicide (*De homicidio*), it confirmed that according to Roman law, homicide should in general be punished by the death penalty, if a perpetrator was found outside a church; if a freeborn homicide took refuge in a church, however, he should wait for the king's judgment. And, since Roman law had nothing fixed on the price of killed persons, the king decided that he, who committed homicide, should be transferred with one half of his property to the service of the heirs of the person killed, while the other half of his goods would be directly associated to the fortune of his own heirs. Moreover, a freeborn person who killed a slave, would have to pay according to the latter's status, that is for an estate manager 100 *solidi*, a retainer 60 *solidi*, a peasant or a swineherd 30 *solidi*, a goldsmith 100 *solidi*, a blacksmith 50 *solidi* and a carpenter 60 *solidi*.[10]

---

class, seventy-five solidi. [...] In such cases let all know this must be observed carefully, that the relatives of the man killed must recognize that no one can be pursued except the killer; because just as we have ordered the criminals to be destroyed, so we will suffer the innocent to sustain no injury.' (*The Burgundian Code. Book of constitutions or Law of Gundobad. Additional enactments*. Translated by Katherine Fischer Drew, Philadelphia 1976, 23–24). It should be noted that the prime intention of these provisions was to limit feud by only allowing to take revenge on the culprit alone and by sanctioning intentional killing with the death penalty.

9 On this law-book, see Wilfried Roels, *Onderzoek naar het gebruik van de aangehaalde bronnen van Romeins Recht in de Lex Romana Burgundionum*, Antwerp 1958.

10 *Leges Burgundionum, Lex Romana constitutionum* 2 (*De homicidiis*), ed. von Salis, MGH LL nat. Germ. 2, 1, 125–127: *Homicidam, tam ingenuum quam servum, si extra ecclesiam inveniatur, morte damnari. Si vero homicidium casu vel vitande mortis causa forte dicatur admissum, ad principis notitiam per relationem iudicis est referendum, et eius sententia expectanda, secundum legem ex corpore novellarum Theudosii et Valentiniani ad Maximum patricium datam. Si vero ad ecclesiam servus homicidii reus forte confugerit, quia lex Theudosiani libro nono ad Antiochum data ab ecclesia nullum inermem permittit abduci, indulta vita, pro eo, quem occidit, ipse deserviat.* [...] *De ingenuo vero homicida intra ecclesiam posito de interempti precio principis est expectanda sententia; et quia de preciis occisorum nihil evidenter Lex Romana constituit, dominus noster statuit observandum: ut si ingenuus ab ingenuo fuerit interemptus, et homicida ad ecclesiam confugerit, is ipse, qui homicidium admisit, cum medietate bonorum suorum occisi heredibus serviturus addicatur; reliqua medietas facultatis eius homicidae heredibus derelinquatur. Si vero servus cuiuscumque occisus fuerit ab ingenuo, et ipse homicida ad ecclesiam convolaverit, secundum servi qualitatem infra scripta domino eius precia cogatur exsolvere, hoc est: pro actore C solidi, pro ministeriale LX solidi, pro aratore aut porcario XXX, pro aurifice electo C, pro fabro ferrario L, pro carpentario XL solidi inferantur. Hoc ex praecepto domini regis convenit observari.* — 'A killer, whether free-born or slave, if found outside of a church, shall be

Both regulations point to what appears as a new phenomenon in the legal texts written around 500 AD. The payment of money in compensation of homicide, the *wergild*, is a characteristic trait in almost all law-codes that were drafted henceforth.[11] It has often been assumed that monetary tariffs for homicide in the barbarian law-codes derived from Germanic law and were introduced as a consequence of the "Germanic invasions", but it should be noted that the practice of blood-money payment can be found in many, if not most societies past and present.[12] Here, as always, the question of origins could tell only part of the story anyway. Its larger, and surely much more interesting part is to tell how these regulations were used, and adapted, in the much more complex and heterogeneous societies of the post-Roman kingdoms, and what role they played in early medieval conflict settlement. Here again, the Burgundian case appears as highly instructive, as it seems to shed light on a paradigm-shift in a crucial moment. The Burgundian kings had established their kingdom in the mid-5th century near Lake Geneva, and from there extended their realm to the highly Romanized Rhône valley shortly after. To stabilize their rule, they

condemned to death. If however, the homicide is said to have been committed by accident or to evade death, it shall be brought to the notice of the king by report of the judge and his judgment shall be awaited, according to the law given to the patricius Maximus, as contained in the corpus of the novels of Theodosius and Valentinian. If, however, a slave charged with homicide happens to take refuge in a church, as the Theodosian Law in book nine given to Antiochus forbids removing an unarmed person from a church, he is to be granted his life and will personally perform service [in compensation] for the person he killed. [...] In case a freeborn homicide is situated within a church, the king's judgment on the price of the killed person should be awaited; and as Roman law apparently has nothing fixed about the prices of killed persons, our lord has decreed the following to be observed: if a freeborn man has been killed by a freeborn man, and the killer took refuge in a church, he who committed the homicide, shall be transferred with half of his belongings to the heirs of the killed person to serve them; the remaining half of his property shall be consigned to the heirs of the killer. If, however, the slave of someone is killed by a freeborn person, and the killer takes refuge in a church, he shall be forced to pay the slave's price according to the quality of the slave as written below, that is: for an estate agent 100 solidi shall be paid, for a servant 60 solidi, for a ploughman or swineherd 30, for a chosen goldsmith 100, for a blacksmith 50, for a cartwright 60 solidi. It was agreed that this should be observed according to the precept of the lord king.' (trans. S. E.).

11 Noteworthy is the absence of wergild lists from the Ostrogothic *Edictum Theoderici* and the Visigothic *Liber iudiciorum* which seems to correspond to both codes' infiltration by Roman law and should not be considered as reflecting a typical feature of "Gothic" law.

12 See, e.g. for ancient Crete Hans-Joachim Gehrke, 'Gewalt und Gesetz. Die soziale und politische Ordnung Kretas in der Archaischen und Klassischen Zeit', *Klio* 79 (1997), 23–68, at 43–44 and 50–51. In a more general perspective, see Philip Grierson, 'The Origins of Money', *Research in Economic Anthropology* 1 (1978), 1–35, at 12–19 (repr. in Id., *Scritti storici e numismatici*, Spoleto 2001, 69–106, cited as Grierson 'The Origins of Money').

issued several laws and eventually had two law-codes compiled from which the above quotations were taken. Their maintaining the notion that murder was to be punished by the death penalty, points to a late Roman penal tradition which they had adapted. However, their introduction of money compensation for several other categories of homicide points to something new.

We are dealing here with the transition from ancient to medieval statehood, and from Roman to "barbarian" law. It was only less severe types of homicide that the Burgundian lawgiver integrated into the system of money compensation. However, when his legal advisers sought to apply these rules to their Roman subjects, they realized that "Roman law apparently had nothing fixed on the price of killed persons" (*quia de preciis occisorum nihil evidenter Lex Romana constituit*). This observation points indeed to a remarkable moment of legal transformation. To be sure, Roman jurists committed a great deal of thought to concepts such as personal damage and the monetary consequences the killing of a person could have, but it was clear that in Roman law homicide could not be compensated for with money. Rather, it called for a publicly inflicted sanction in late Roman law, with corporal and capital punishment being the typical sanctions imposed for homicide.[13] In Burgundy, it was thus in the reign of king Gundobad (480–516) that new regulations had to be introduced for the Romans who, up to then, had hardly been accustomed to the concept of wergild. Such an adjustment of law was not uncharacteristic, as new kingdoms were established on Roman provincial soil in Gaul which became more and more independent and where Romans constituted the majority of the population. Nearly contemporary with these developments, in the Frankish kingdom under King Clovis (486–511), we find in the *Lex Salica* a wergild introduced for the Romans. However, in so doing, the Franks downgraded the wergild of a Roman to half the worth of a free Frank.[14] It seems the Franks were the first to introduce wergilds that were differentiated according to ethnic status. Interestingly, some marginal glosses recently detected by Karl Ubl in a 9th-century Roman law manuscript added the wergild tariffs for killing different categories of Romans as known from the Frankish law-codes to

13 On late Roman punishments see Theodor Mommsen, *Das römische Strafrecht*, Berlin 1899, 897–1040.

14 *Lex Salica* 41 (*De homicidiis ingenuorum*), 8–10, and 42 (*De homicidiis a contubernio factis*), 4, ed. Karl August Eckhardt, MGH LL nationum Germanicarum 4, 1, Hanover 1962, 157 and 164. See Karl Ubl, *Sinnstiftungen eines Rechtsbuches. Die Lex Salica im Frankenreich*, Ostfildern 2017, 74–75 and 93; also Lukas Bothe, 'From Subordination to Integration: Romans in Frankish Law', in: *Transformations of Romanness. Early Medieval Regions and Identities*, ed. Walter Pohl, Clemens Gantner, Cinzia Grifoni and Marianne Pollheimer-Mohaupt, Berlin 2018, 345–368.

various groups of Romans as defined by the Roman jurist Gaius.[15] This points to the practice of using wergild as a means to define the status of ethnic groups. By comparison, the carefully calibrated Burgundian tariffs for different sorts of freemen and for the killing of qualified and skilled slaves, such as craftsmen and smiths, betray a policy of protecting relevant functional groups within a society that was apparently characterized by a high degree of social mobility and violence.

2 Wergild and the Logic of Money in Sociological Theory and Early Medieval Practice

It was, above all, money that could make such legal policies work. The logic of money appears as highly relevant to understand how early medieval conflict resolution actually functioned. While there has been a long tradition to interpret monetary fines for homicide as an expression of Germanic legal thought, in particular in German scholarship, the first to place this feature into a wider perspective was the sociologist Georg Simmel (1858–1918). In his "Philosophy of Money", published in 1900,[16] Simmel emphasized that it was not societies that organized the monetary economy, but rather the other way round: the monetary economy organized society and transformed its mentality. This could happen, as money in principle was such an indifferent accounting unit that it could define equivalences between goods and services on the one hand and a certain value on the other. Money thus also entails, as was already detected by ancient philosophers and jurists, the remarkable quality of understanding things in an abstract way that went far beyond its economic dimension: it enables a society to put very different things into a relation to one another, to classify and systematize them.

Interestingly, in his study Simmel devoted considerable space to discussing wergild, as he was interested in "the way in which money provided a quantitative concept of the value of human beings".[17] Simmel regarded this tendency as critical, which he did in accordance with other sociologists of his time who were interested in the relationship between capitalism and processes of

15 Paris, Bibliothèque nationale, lat. 4416, fol. 50r. These findings will be dealt with in more detail in a future publication.

16 Georg Simmel, *Philosophie des Geldes*, Berlin 1900, 365–454; English translation (quoted thereafter): Georg Simmel, *The Philosophy of Money*. Translated by Tom Bottomore and David Frisby, London 1978, 355–428 (cited as Simmel, *The Philosophy of Money*).

17 Simmel, *The Philosophy of Money*, 355.

rationalization. This becomes clear from his analysis of the decline of wergild in modern times:[18]

> the rising value of human life and the declining value of money conspired to render wergild impossible. The same cultural process of differentiation that gives to the individual a special significance which renders him relatively unique and irreplaceable makes money the standard and equivalent of such a divergent range of objects that the growing indifference and objectivity makes it increasingly less suitable as an equivalent of personal values.[19]

As is highlighted by this passage, Simmel was primarily interested in building a concise theory about the origin of the free individual and the role played by money as a generalized exchange value. Within this context, wergild served him as a starting point for the formation of the modern subject or 'self', because he saw it as some sort of nuclear constellation that already contained decisive elements for future evolution. This was the idea of the material worth of a human life as an entity, and the two kinds of its entire substitution — namely, in the original form, the 'utilitarian' valuation of a sum of goods, and the equivalent 'objective' monetary value.

The transition from the utilitarian to the objective and absolute valuation of the human being constitutes a decisive step in this concept.

> The origin of wergild is obviously purely utilitarian, and even though it does not altogether pertain to civil law it none the less belongs to that state of indifference with regard to private and public law with which social development begins. The tribe, the clan and the family demanded a substitute for the economic loss which the death of one of its members implied and was willing to accept it instead of an impulsive vendetta.[20]

For Simmel, a new step in the development was only taken when

> the State or the Church takes over the responsibility for the expiation of the crime. Because the damage to the victim is now no longer a personal

18 I owe this information on the background to Simmel's work and thought to an inspiring conference contribution by Ludolf Kuchenbuch (Berlin), who kindly handed over to me the manuscript of his paper.

19 Simmel, *The Philosophy of Money*, 380.

20 Simmel, *The Philosophy of Money*, 357.

> event but rather a disturbance of public order or a violation of an ethical-religious law, the condition of the criminal becomes the final purpose of the action taken, whereas formerly his situation was only an indifferent accident for the person who sought compensation. Only here can we talk about punishment in the full sense of the word. The purpose is now to affect the subject himself, and any penalty as practical action is merely a means towards this end. Money fines thus take on a totally different meaning from the former monetary compensation for wounding and killing. They are not supposed to compensate for the damage done, but to inflict pain upon the culprit.[21]

The shift from material damage to mental pain thus is the leading idea of the proceeding text. But it should be added, that at the same time Simmel conceives this shift as a splitting, an opening of the scissor between body and soul as signs of the growing incalculability of the value of a person.

Simmel's analysis shows many interesting aspects and ideas,[22] though a modern reader will feel bewildered by its underlying evolutionism and its focus on the emergence of the individual. In fact, Simmel's entire book is not on history, but aims at a philosophy of history as some sort of prehistory, or, in modern terms, as an archaeology of the present.[23] Nonetheless, his approach to take money and wergild as a vehicle to analyze societies can still be relevant for historians working on societies of the distant past. For the closer we get to our texts, the more it becomes clear that, in early medieval legal life, money could fulfil manifold political, social and legal functions. This can tell us a lot about the character of early medieval conflict resolution and also about the possibilities to stem the problem of violence in this period. One may arguably state that monetary compensation was superior to other modes of conflict settlement in this period. For instance, against the background of early medieval societies' social structures, it may have been more effective if a Count safeguarded the payment of blood-money between two groups rather than if he executed a perpetrator, thereby being at risk to become personally involved in

21 Simmel, *The Philosophy of Money*, 364.

22 Most relevant is his focus on the value of the free man (*liber homo*), the woman and the slave, for in other sections of his book, Simmel analyses slavery and marriage by purchase in this respect. See also, without reference to Simmel, Emanuel Seitz, 'Der Wert des Menschen und sein Preis. Das Verhältnis von Person und Eigentum bei Brautpreis, Wergeld und Sklaverei', in: *Embodying value? The transformation of objects in and from the Ancient World*, ed. Anabel Bokern and Clare Rowan, Oxford 2014, 11–22.

23 For some more recent approaches to the uses of money mirroring social practices see the contribution by Han Nijdam in this volume.

a feud and being regarded as belonging to one of the conflicting groups. His business remained an extraordinarily difficult task anyway. The Ripuarian law-code's provision calling a scribe of a disputed charter into a judicial combat should serve as a warning in this respect.[24]

The totalizing quality of money to introduce an overall neutralizing convertibility and pure quantification, allowed it to fulfil diverse functions. Tariffs such as wergild could be designed to give satisfaction and to move away from a violent situation and to introduce a business-like and unemotional way to balance the value of a human life by an amount of money. This must have always been vulnerable as emotions could not be suppressed but often only be redirected into a different field. The lists of commutable goods to be paid for wergild, as contained in the 7th-century Ripuarian law-code, illustrates well how the Merovingian kings sought to establish clear value equivalents that could be given instead of money — that is ox or cow, stallion and mare, sword, byrnie, helmet, shield etc.[25] Against this background, it is telling that Louis the Pious had to forbid any payment of wergild by giving a falcon or a *spatha* because this increased the danger of perjury.[26]

24 *Lex Ribuaria* 62 (59) (*De venditionibus*), 4, ed. Franz Beyerle and Rudolf Buchner, MGH LL nationum Germanicarum 3, 2, Hanover 1954, 115.

25 *Lex Ribuaria* 40 (36) (*De diversis interfectionibus*), 11, ed. Beverle and Buchner, MGH LL nat. Germ. 3, 2, 94–95: *Si quis weregildum solvere coeperit, bovem cornutum videntem et sanum pro duos solid. tribuat. Vaccam cornutam videntem et sanam pro uno solido tribuat. Equum videntem et sanum pro septem soli. tribuat. Equam videntem et sanam pro tres solid. tribuat. Spatam cum scoligilo pro septem solid. tribuat. Spatam absque scoiliglo pro tres solid. tribuat. Brunia bona pro duodecim solid. tribuat. Helmo condericto pro sex solid. tribuat. Scuto cum lancia pro duos solid. tribuat. Bagnbergas bonas pro sex solid. tribuat. Aucceptorem indomito pro 3 solid. tribuat. Conmorsum gruarium pro sex solid. tribuat. Aucceptorem mutatum pro 12 solid. tribuat.* — 'If anyone begins to pay a wergild, let him give a horned ox, able to see and healthy, for two solidi. Let him give a horned cow, able to see and healthy, for one solidus. Let him give a stallion, able to see and healthy, for seven solidi. Let him give a mare, able to see and healthy, for three solidi. Let him give a sword with a sheath for seven solidi. Let him give a sword without a sheath for three solidi. Let him give a metal tunic in good condition for twelve solidi. Let him give a helmet in good condition for six solidi. Let him give a shield with a lance for two solidi. Let him give [a pair of] leggings in good condition for six solidi. Let him give an untrained hawk for six solidi. Let him give a trained hawk for twelve solidi.' (*Laws of the Salian and Ripuarian Franks*. Translated with an Introduction by Theodore John Rivers, New York 1986, 185–186).

26 *Capitula legibus addenda*, a. 818/819, c. 8, ed. Alfred Boretius, MGH Capitularia regum Francorum 1, Hanover 1883, 282: *Quid in conpositione wirgildi dari non debeat. In compositione wirgildi volumus ut ea dentur quae in lege continentur* (= L. Rib. 36,11), *excepto accipitre et spata, quia propter illa duo aliquoties periurium conmittitur, quando maioris pretii quam illa sint esse iurantur.* — 'What should not be given as payment for wergild.

Again, we are getting close here to another peril of wergild: it served to calculate the value of a human life in an abstract way. However, once these high amounts were imagined and commuted as precious items within a militarized peasant society, these amounts could raise the temptation to infringe the "legal order". Notwithstanding, one should have the many positive and flexible features of wergild in mind when considering its efficiency, especially being without alternatives. Money could represent the honour of a person numerically, be preventive in a deterrent manner and provide an incentive for officials to arrange the peaceful settlement of a conflict, while it could to some extent be also regarded as a fine. Early medieval societies understood money exceedingly well in order to use it to calculate in both an abstract and more concrete manner. As Philippe Depreux has emphasized, the amounts of money to be paid as wergild did not only derive from tradition but were subject to regulation and indeed legislation.[27] Only recently, the late Lisi Oliver[28] and Przemysłav Tyszka[29] have analyzed systematically the innumerable finely graded tariffs of compensation of early medieval law, which had to be paid for wounding a person, cutting off a thumb, nose and so on. Dealing with these tariffs as part of a history of the human body, they scrutinized the knowledge of anatomy and natural health, as well as some practical considerations that were lying behind this classification, such as the capacity to work, economic considerations, and embodied honour. Both studies showed that we are not dealing here with seemingly "archaic" modes of retaliation, which should compensate for seriously affected manpower or the loss of one's honour. Rather, the closer we look at these measures, the more obvious it becomes that these tariffs were mechanisms of social engineering, to define personal status, to provide for social cohesion and to allow for solving as well as preventing conflicts. These monetary tariffs, at least to some extent, could even allow for the complex numerical rendering of some juristic reasoning, for instance by taking into account if

For wergild payments we want to be given what is included in the law, except for hawk and sword, as often for these two, perjury is committed, while it is sworn that those are of a higher price.'

27 Philippe Depreux, 'Wergeld, composition et rachat dans le capitulaires des rois francs', in: *La victime*, t. 2: *La réparation du dommage*, ed. Jacqueline Hoareau-Dodinau, Guillaume Métairie and Pascal Texier, Limoges 2009, 345–362 (cited as Depreux, 'Wergeld, composition et rachat').

28 Lisi Oliver, *The Body Legal in Barbarian Law*, Toronto 2011.

29 Przemysłav Tyszka, *The Human Body in Barbarian Laws, c. 500–c. 800*, Frankfurt/Main 2013.

a crime was committed in public, or at night,[30] though this is not to deny that this capacity appears to have been fairly limited.[31]

Even when emphasizing the importance of money to express different sorts of crimes and personal statuses, one should take into account that wergild is particularly significant to differentiate these societies' capabilities to cope with the omnipresent problem of homicide. It has to be emphasized that in the Frankish kingdom, for instance, certain political and religious crimes — for instance treason, infidelity, incest, certain pagan practices, but also robbery — often continued to be sanctioned by corporal or even capital punishment during the early medieval period.[32] This observation suggests that it was only in the sector of "ordinary homicide" — that is killing a person without an imminent political or religious motive — where we see a transition from corporal to monetary punishment. It seems it was in this sector that, from around 500 onward, the state withdrew its persecution of these crimes through the infliction of corporal punishments. Instead, the law-codes sought to have things mediated through local officials, thereby handing over conflict resolution to local family groups and their social networks who also were the main actors addressed by wergild. The situation in many post-Roman societies thus may resemble that in modern states such as Georgia or Albania where, following the end of the Soviet Empire, bloodfeud became accepted as a legal form to demand and pursue one's right, while the same states continued to raise taxes, finance armies etc.[33] Compared with the late Roman period, in post-Roman Gaul there was undoubtedly a significant reduction and regional transformation of Roman state structures, which allowed for a reappreciation of wergild as an instrument of steering early medieval societies at a significantly reduced grade of statehood. We are dealing here with mixed societies, composed of Romans and/or various groups of non-Romans, in which family-based and other groups feature prominently.

Moreover, it deserves to be emphasized that the success of monetary conflict resolution in the case of wergild depended on the fact that the use of

30 See Stefan Esders, 'Wergeld und soziale Netzwerke im Frankenreich', in: *Verwandtschaft, Name und soziale Ordnung (300–1100)*, ed. Steffen Patzold and Karl Ubl, Berlin and New York 2014, 141–160, at 150 (cited as Esders, 'Wergeld und soziale Netzwerke').

31 See the contribution by Harald Siems in this volume.

32 See Hermann Nehlsen, 'Entstehung des öffentlichen Strafrechts bei den germanischen Stämmen', in: *Gerichtslauben-Vorträge. Freiburger Festkolloquium zum 75. Geburtstag von Hans Thieme*, ed. Karl Kroeschell, Sigmaringen 1983, 3–16, and more recently the contributions in Jürgen Weitzel (ed.), *Hoheitliches Strafen in der Spätantike und im frühen Mittelalter*, Cologne 2002.

33 See, e.g., Jan Köhler, *Die Zeit der Jungs. Zur Organisation von Gewalt und der Austragung von Konflikten in Georgien*, Münster 2000.

money tends, as is well known, to develop its own logic. Discussing wergild as part of medieval conflict resolution inherently requires talking about solidarity, social cohesion and networks,[34] and this for a number of reasons. First, wergild was usually paid to a group of persons — in most, but by no means all, cases to the closest relatives of a victim. In addition to relatives, also wards and seniors could have a right to receive wergild for the killing. Second, a person who had committed murder or manslaughter would most likely not be able to afford paying a wergild easily from his personal wealth. They would require financial support. In fact, the whole wergild system is centered on the idea that the killing of a person was not something that one could easily afford. The sums fixed for a killing had to be so high that they deliberately overcharged an individual, making it dependent on support by its family or social group. This, in turn, would most likely also exact some preventive measures, making this kind of misdeed less likely to happen. Indeed, the payment of wergild will often also have involved the engagement of sureties and institutions, such as churches and monasteries, who could lend money or commute in kind payments into cash. Thirdly, the perpetrator and his group would have to activate further networks in order to persuade the victim's side to accept the wergild. This part of the process anteceding the payment of wergild is particularly hard to reconstruct, but its importance can hardly be underestimated if the party of the victim had some power and some honour to defend. And fourthly, one should also take into account that the whole procedure to arrive at an agreement, if it was conducted by formal institutions, involved a number of legal experts in the community with judicial authority and experience in such valuations, but who also had some social standing within the community.

Thus, the closer we get into social practice involving wergild, it becomes more obvious that the process required involvement and interlocking of different groups, some of whom were kin groups while others were not. Accordingly, the dry lists of tariffs to compensate for homicide so ubiquitous in the early medieval law codes, require a more or less precise idea of how early medieval societies functioned in order to understand why the provisions given in the law-codes could actually make sense.

---

34 For what follows, see in more detail Esders, 'Wergeld und soziale Netzwerke'; Id., '*Wergild* and social practice in the early middle ages: A 9th-century Reichenau fragment and its context', in: *Entre texte et histoire. Études d'histoire médiévale offertes au professeur Shoichi Sato*, ed. Osamu Kano and Jean-Loup Lemaître, Paris 2015, 117–127.

3 New Fields and Avenues of Research

Each article contained in this volume makes an important contribution to a better understanding of particular societies and texts. Generalizing from these contributions, the aim here is to delineate more generally some fields of research in which a focus on wergild can yield new results and improve our understanding of how early medieval societies worked.

3.1 *Wergild and the Question of Roman Continuities*

The practice of paying money for homicide directly to the group of the victim clearly marks a break with Roman legal tradition and its clear distinction between "public" and "private" law. Both Harald Siems and Ralph Mathisen in their contributions present a very clear case for arguing that there was indeed nothing comparable to wergild in Roman law. This should also be read as a cautionary note against a recent hypothesis put forward by Christophe Camby who, in a controversial book on wergild, believed that he could detect Roman continuities almost everywhere.[35] Indeed, a lot of differentiation seems to be at place here. Ralph Mathisen refers, among other texts, to a law given by the Roman emperor Honorius against the Donatists which threatened perpetrators with different monetary fines according to their status, while this law later became repeated by the Vandal king Hunerich. Such classification according to social status is indeed a feature of Late Roman law. Thus, already in late Roman law, monetary sanctions could be imposed according to the status of a person (*pro qualitate personarum*) which reminds one of different penal sanctions inflicted on *honesteriores* and *humiliores*.[36] However, most if not all such monetary punishments as contained in Theodosian Code refer to regulations that could be attributed to "public law", and thus were fiscal in nature, while there is no evidence that these amounts of money were directly paid to private persons. Any blunt claim for Roman continuities thus pushes aside the very problem why wergild became so important and so prevalent in the early medieval period and why it also emerged in regions that had never been under Roman control.

Denial of direct Roman precursors does not mean, however, that there may not have been relevant Roman influences below the surface. In particular,

---

35 Christophe Camby, *Wergeld ou uueregildus. Le rachat pécuniaire de l'offense entre continuités romaines et innovation germanique*, Geneve 2013 (cited as Camby, *Wergeld ou uueregildus*).

36 See Rolf Rilinger, *Humiliores — Honestiores. Zu einer sozialen Dichotomie im Strafrecht der römischen Kaiserzeit*, Munich 1988.

when looking at legal developments in former Roman provinces Roman law often exercised a considerable influence on the definition of crimes and even in some procedural elements.[37] The legal advisers on whose experience barbarian kings drew when compiling law-codes often were well acquainted with Roman law. A complicated task was to express subtle differences regarding various types of crimes and the status of individuals and groups through carefully calibrated monetary tariffs and sanctions. This not only required intimate knowledge of customary law and legal tradition, but also the capacity to conceive of this as some sort of consistent "system". Such expertise was most likely to be expected from someone versed in another legal tradition, too. This might explain why some Roman influences can be detected in the shaping of wergild, although wergild itself was not a Roman concept.

An important starting point for adjusting the value of a human being was undoubtedly provided by the price one had to pay for a slave;[38] although the wergild was centered around the value of a free man, there could have been a direct link between the Roman value and the early medieval wergild of a slave.[39] Also, where wergild acquires the character of a punishment so that certain offenses were sanctioned by the payment of extraordinarily high amounts, this perhaps has to be attributed to some Roman influence, at least in Gaul. The range of "unemendable crimes" — often associated with treason, arson and grave religious offenses — also points to a tradition or notion of Roman public law, though its impact can often be only explained by assuming indirect influence. Another field in which Roman influence may have been indirect, is what Harald Siems calls the "perpetrator wergild", which refers to those cases in which a culprit pays his own wergild as a fine to the state. However, as is shown by Lisi Oliver, this meaning of wergild can also be found in Anglo-Saxon

---

37 See, e.g. Harald Siems, 'Bemerkungen zu *sunnis* und *morbus sonticus.* Zum Problem des Fortwirkens römischen Rechts im frühen Mittelalter', *ZRG RA* 103 (1986), 409–446; Wulf Eckart Voss, 'Vom römischen Provinzialprozeß der Spätantike zum Rechtsgang des frühen Mittelalters', in: *Recht im frühmittelalterlichen Gallien. Spätantike Tradition und germanische Wertvorstellungen*, ed. Harald Siems, Karin Nehlsen-von Stryk and Dieter Strauch, Cologne 1995, 73–108; Stefan Esders, 'Late Roman Military Law in the Bavarian Code', *clio@themis. Revue électronique d'histoire du droit* 10 (2016) (thematic issue *La forge du droit. Naissance des identités juridiques en Europe, IVe–XIIIe siècles*): http://www.cliothemis.com/IMG/pdf/3-_Esders-2.pdf.

38 See François Bougard, '*Culpabilis iudicetur*: réparation et châtiment des crimes et délits dans les lois "barbares"', in: *Les lois barbares. Justice et société dans les royaumes post-romains*, ed. Sylvie Joye, Marcelo da Silva Candido and Bruno Dumézil (in press, cited as Bougard, '*Culpabilis iudicetur*').

39 On slavery as a "bridge" see also Grierson, 'The Origins of Money', 15.

England. Though it figures in some sources,[40] this use of wergild should not be regarded as typical or "original", but rather as one of a number of secondary adaptations of the term wergild.

The main problem in the field of Roman continuities is that the question where it all came from has exhausted itself. Today, it seems more rewarding to look at hybrid phenomena which show how legal experts drew on a variety of available legal resources to cope with the immediate problems of their day. The more such phenomena become evident and the availability of different legal resources is considered, the more refinement and sophistication we might detect behind those seemingly monotonous tariff lists.

3.2 *Terminology and Concepts of Wergild*

One striking feature of wergild is that it takes the value of a man as its very starting point. In this way, we can speak of a masculinization of legal status within society as "wer-", the first part of the compound, refers to a man and seems to be related to the Latin word *vir*. However, Wolfgang Haubrichs makes clear how differentiated the vernacular vocabulary in the lexical field of *compositio* was and that most of the vernacular terms used here do not derive from Latin, but probably from older legal language.[41] His paper also illustrates that the vernacular terminology of wergild, including *leodi, leudis* as synonyms, had as an ultimate reference point the adult man in his military capacity. From there, the term was also assigned to women and children, and could be scaled into different directions, for instance, according to the status of a woman. Within such a vast field of application, the concept of wergild could also be applied to serfs and slaves.[42] More often, however, it was calibrated up, extending to nobles, clerics and officials, as is demonstrated by Lukas Bothe with regard to the social and functional differentiation engineered by wergild tariffs.[43] Application of wergild as a category thus was quite flexible, for it could also build up hybrid

---

40 This is what the study of Camby, *Wergeld ou uueregildus*, deals with at greater length.

41 It may be noted here that certain uses of wergild as a category seem rather to echo a Roman concept of *persona* as a social role than an actual legal institute. On this concept see e.g. Manfred Fuhrmann, '*Persona*, ein römischer Rollenbegriff', in: *Identität*, ed. Odo Marquard and Karlheinz Stierle, Munich 1979, 83–106.

42 See Hermann Nehlsen, *Sklavenrecht zwischen Antike und Mittelalter. Germanisches und römisches Recht in den germanischen Rechtsaufzeichnungen, 1: Ostgoten, Westgoten, Franken, Langobarden*, Göttingen 1971.

43 On wergild tariffs for clerics, see also Edvard van Hartingsveldt, 'De "Zeven Zaken" en de frankische bisschop', *Revue belge de philologie et d'histoire* 67 (1989), 677–694, and Thomas Faulkner, *Law and Authority in the Early Middle Ages. The Frankish leges in the Carolingian period*, Cambridge 2016, 155–159.

numeric compounds such as *novigild* for more serious offenses, indicating a shift away from the subject to the payment itself. A more general perspective, and comparable to a nuclear definition, is also given in the articles by Han Nijdam and Lisi Oliver. This could perhaps be described as a more or less radical transition from the Roman legal system, in which being a citizen or a subject had played a defining role, to an androcentric legal system, in which a man's value, his honour, his body, his family and his property functioned as a sort of point of departure.

The legal concept conveyed by this terminology seems to be related to our notion of "crimes", although this seems to impose modern (or indeed, Roman) categories on what one could more appropriately describe as grave or serious offenses. It seems clear that from an ecclesiastical point of view, such misdeeds were regarded as grave "crimes" or, more correctly, as "sins", but one should be hesitant to conflate these concepts all too easily. For at the same time, wergild terminology could entail notions that had been categorized as *damnum* or *iniuria* in Roman legal terminology. Moreover, the earliest occurrences of *wergildum* (as distinct from *leod* which is attested earlier) point to a concept of paying one's own personal worth as a man for a grave misdeed. Our sources display a great variety in extending the term wergild by applying it to different meanings and by using it as a unit of measuring amounts of money.[44] This demonstrates that wergild must really have been a key concept applicable to very different phenomena within societies in which money payments mattered very much.

Having a personal wergild marked an important dividing line within society. However, this status was not sacrosanct, as for a free man, entering penal servitude meant the (temporary) loss of his wergild. In a general perspective, wergild depended on the killed person's individual status, hence Simmel's interest in it. This status was acknowledged by the society he was a member of. Paying respect to this principle was what societies regarded as just or what at least should be regarded as being in accordance with certain notions of justice. That early medieval societies' social stratification and functional differentiation was reflected in the wergild tariffs, is demonstrated in Lukas Bothe's contribution for the Frankish kingdom. Wergild markers ascribed status such as gender, age, freedom, ethnic affiliation, and office-holding. Though Frankish law appears to be keen on maintaining status differences, the wergild tariffs suggest a high degree of social mobility that needed to be reflected in the process of drafting legal compilations. This becomes particularly clear in case of manumission,

44 See Depreux, 'Wergeld, composition et rachat'.

as is dealt with in Lisi Oliver's paper. The manumitter as patron had a claim to obtain his freedman's wergild in case the latter was killed, while in Francia, as observed by Lukas Bothe, this principle was adapted in favour of churches and monasteries, whose manumitted slaves came to form a new social group. A Frankish feature is the handling of ethnic diversity, as reflected in divergent wergilds for Ripuarians, Bavarians, Romans etc., which sought to encourage horizontal elite mobility by protecting foreigners (*advenae*). It is here as in other examples that the influence of royal legislation can be directly felt.

3.3 *Wergild as a "Legal System"*

It may thus seem tempting to interpret the differentiated tariffs as contained in the law-codes as a "legal system". This term is here, as most often, perhaps a bit misleading. For it should not be seen as a complete framework of internal references. Indeed, wergild as a system can mean very different things. First, lists of wergild tariffs as contained in several law-codes betray an influence of (royal) legislation, as these lists often were based on several layers of provisions of different age. What makes the quest for a system interesting here is the issue of proportion: do these tariffs for different offenses appear as reasonably calculated? To what extent, as asked by Tom Lambert and Han Nijdam, do they respond to values such as honour? Do they reflect attitudes and perceptions of justice held within a society? Were they anticipating conflicts and thus preventive in character? Where do they echo royal interest? If we think that the compilation and application of law-codes presupposed some idea of a *consensus*, these questions seem to be extremely relevant.[45]

One may also add here that in the Frankish *Lex Ribuaria*, but also in Bavarian law and certain Anglo-Saxon law-codes, certain crimes were subsumed under a special category (such as treason), which were explicitly excluded from monetary compensation by wergild and composition. This emphasized the special quality of certain crimes which were perceived as directed against the community, the political elite or essential religious values. However, by the same token it could preserve the character of the other parts of the law that were indeed based on wergild and compensation alone. Interestingly, we can see here some self-reflection on the "system" of wergild, inasmuch the crime of treason, for instance, was marked as a deliberate break with the system of wergild. One could solve the problem of protecting the king in two different ways,

45 Stefan Esders, 'Zwischen Historie und Rechtshistorie. Der *consensus iuris* im frühen Mittelalter', in: *Recht und Konsens im frühen Mittelalter*, ed. Verena Epp and Christoph H. F. Meyer, Ostfildern 2017, 427–474.

that is either by raising the king's wergild to a rate which was hard to imagine in cash, or by introducing capital punishment: the first option extended the system to arrive at incredibly high amounts of money, the second broke with it and more actively maintained a notion of "public offense". Where did those crimes start which could not be compensated for with money, but called for different sanctions such as corporal punishment, outlawry or exile? Indeed, the "non-emendable crimes", which can be found in Anglo-Saxon England, in Frankish Gaul and also in medieval Denmark, seem to point to the fact that some notion of "public law" was retained and should find an expression in monetary classification.

The threefold wergilds to be paid for persons of eminent functional or social status or for very serious offenses appear as a deliberate attempt to preserve the standard units by simply multiplying them, a practice that can be traced back to Roman law with its *duplum*, *quadruplum* etc. This leads to another aspect of wergild as a "system", namely its adaptability and potential for development. Features such as the perpetrator's wergild, as dealt with in the papers by Harald Siems and Wolfgang Haubrichs, attest to an extension of the concept of wergild to the area of punishment. This and the rise of wergild sums point to the possibility that wergild could acquire a more penalizing character. However, as is shown by Harald Siems in his contribution, there were also serious limits inherent in the "wergild system". For instance, if a crime was committed by several people, these could share in paying one wergild, although they were all involved in committing the crime — individual guilt could hardly be expressed in terms of wergild alone. Another revealing case was if someone repeatedly attempted to commit a crime: here the wergild system, as confined to the "effect" of a misdeed alone, could not prescribe anything to compensate for, as there was no damage. The fixation of a wergild could only proceed from the effect of a crime.

3.4 *Wergild and Public Authority*

The relationship between wergild and public authority is perhaps one of the most intriguing topics. It is a wide-spread belief among scholars to interpret the rise of wergild as resulting from a process in which "private" justice prevailed over "public" administration of justice. As fines were reduced, state officials withdrew from prosecuting crimes, organizing the payment of huge sums of money between the groups of the perpetrator and the victim instead. To be sure, there was a reduction of statehood in the transition from late Roman provinces to early medieval kingdoms. But does that mean that the king was completely out of the game?

Any answer to this question implies a consideration how much sophistication one is inclined to attribute to the seemingly monotonous catalogues of wergild tariffs. We know from several texts coming from Francia that one third of the wergild obviously was not destined for the surviving relatives of the victim, but was classified as peace money under the category of the Latin word *fredus*. This *fredus* had to be exacted by a royal official who through his action had provided a judicial settlement of the conflict and sought to enforce the judicial decision. A passage in the 7th-century Ripuarian code made clear that no judge should exact peace-money (*fredus*) for any lawsuit whatsoever before a definite settlement was achieved: no peace-money should be given to that judge by the person who committed this crime, but by him who received the wergild; and one third of it should be given to the public treasury in the presence of witnesses so that peace may be permanently maintained.[46] It seems that the enormously high amounts of wergild, like fiscal fines as we often find them in early medieval charters,[47] functioned as some sort of monetary "incentive", which sought to instigate the local officials to intervene in conflicts by giving them the prospect that they could earn revenues from providing for a peaceful settling of such a conflict. The inclusion of fines within a wergild, or their addition to it, thus introduced a third party's interest in the settlement of conflicts.[48] The *fredus* thus makes visible a more complex calculation behind these tariffs, which by no means was directed at the conflicting parties and their kin groups alone. Rather, it betrays some sort of "public" dimension of the monetary mode of conflict resolution. At the same time, the regulation makes clear where the danger lies: if the perpetrator was mighty enough to find his separate and direct arrangement with the count, the victim's side would have little chance to receive compensation, as there would be little chance to settle the conflict permanently in the sense of a perpetual peace. Wergild thus was more than mere compensation, but to some extent also included preventive and penal elements, which make it very hard to find appropriate terms here to describe this intermingling of "private" and "public" aspects more precisely.

46 *Lex Ribuaria* 88 (*Ut nemo munera in iudicio accipiat*), ed. Beyerle and Buchner, MGH LL nat. Germ. 3, 2, 133–134: *Ut nemo munera in iudicio sedens aliquando accipiat*; 89: *Ut iudices sive missi fiscales freda non exigant, priusquam facinus conponatur.*

47 Hans Werle, 'Gold und Silber. Die Geldstrafen in den Pönformeln frühmittelalterlicher Urkunden des Klosters Lorsch', in: *Recht und Wirtschaft in Geschichte und Gegenwart. Festschrift für Johannes Bärmann zum 70. Geburtstag*, ed. Marcus Lutter, Helmut Kolhosser and Winfried Trusen, Munich 1975, 53–63.

48 It may be added that this was also vital when jurisdiction and the right to collect *fredus* etc. was transferred to ecclesiastical institutions through grants of immunity.

Also, the formularies mentioning wergild and granting security, as investigated by Warren Brown, make clear that a dividing line between compensation, fine and punishment is not always easily drawn. It should be noted that in the Frankish law-codes the typical wording *culpabilis iudicetur*, most often used for assigning to a culprit the obligation to pay wergild or composition, is occasionally replaced by *culpabilis multetur*, which suggests that a notion of punishment and fine could be included in wergild as well.[49]

As is shown by Lisi Oliver for Kent and Wessex, a person who formally entered into a relationship with a patron created the base for the patron's claim to his man's wergild. The king's protection (*mundiburdium, munt* etc.), also known from Francia, is a very prominent type of this, which could become spatially extended to the king's palace or a royal assembly. So wergild or *man bot* was indeed connected to a notion of peace centered on the king and those to whom he granted his protection. Increasing or multiplying the wergild of those who were in the king's service and protection was a means by which to arrive at more complex expressions of what should be regarded as "public" law. The notion of breaking the king's peace, leading to a share of wergild going to the king, can also be found in Denmark, as is shown by Helle Vogt. Here, as in the other examples, wergild payment seems to have gone beyond compensation paid to a victim's group, but implied a fine. Vogt's study of Denmark is particularly illuminating in this respect, as she questions the widely held notion that wergild was primarily a means to interrupt a vicious circle of continuous revenge and feud. Compensation was often effective, but by no means for this reason alone. As Vogt demonstrates in her paper, there is much to say about royal legislation on wergild. It becomes clear that an increasing importance of the king as a protector of peace and administrator of justice played a key role in the calibration of wergild. The same tendency is observed by Lukas Bothe in his study of seventh-century Francia and by Lisi Oliver for Anglo-Saxon England, where the concept of wergild was applied to a number of officials who held positions in the king's service. The tripling or multiplication of the wergild of certain officials moved towards deterrence and increased the visibility of public authority. Although the development from wergild to punishment largely took place in the high and later middle ages,[50] one should be cautious already

49 Bougard, '*Culpabilis iudicetur*'.

50 See Ernst Schubert, 'Vom Wergeld zur Strafe: Die übersehene Bedeutung der friesischen Rechtsquellen zur Interpretation eines epochalen mittelalterlichen Wandels', in: *Tota Frisia in Teilansichten. Hajo van Lengen zum 65. Geburtstag*, ed. Heinrich Schmidt, Wolfgang Schwarz and Martin Tielke, Aurich 2005, 97–120.

for the early medieval period, as the concept of wergild includes notions that do not lend themselves to a precise attribution to modern categories.

3.5 *Wergild as a Crucial Step within an Extended Process of Conflict Settlement*

As said before, the payment of wergild was a decisive step within a longer process of attributing satisfaction and arriving at peace. The formularies, studied by Warren Brown, that document the payment of blood-price and often come as a result of judgment in court seem to attest to some efficiency of the regulations we gather from the law-codes. They also show some sort of intervention on the part of public authority, as they make clear that once wergild was paid, anyone who tried to revive the conflict was threatened with severe sanctions. Thus, seeking to give security to the perpetrator after having made his payment, these documents show the involvement of families, kin and further laypeople, but leave any role of kings unmentioned, despite referring occasionally to penalties going to the royal fisc.

In fact, not only blood-revenge, but also compensation creates groups. Private charters often record the process of borrowing money and of commuting payments in kind into cash, a process in which ecclesiastical institutions seem to have played a major role.[51] At least to the person or institutions that lended the money, it would usually have been repaid in instalments — that credit played a major role not only in the Roman period, but continued to do so in the early middle ages has only been shown recently.[52] Indeed, as the payment of such a fine could easily ruin the offender, there were different rituals to urge his relatives to pay for him — such as the famous *chrenecruda* ritual in Lex Salica by which an impecunious offender could oblige his relatives to stand in for him.[53] As is shown by Lukas Bothe, law-givers could also envisage different solutions to this problem, by imposing the debt on the next generations of an offender's heirs. Forms of "vertical" and "horizontal" payment have

---

51 See the examples discussed in Stefan Esders, '"Eliten" und "Strafrecht" im frühen Mittelalter. Überlegungen zu den Bußen- und Wergeldkatalogen der *Leges barbarorum*', in: *Théories et pratiques des élites au haut Moyen Âge*, ed. François Bougard, Hans-Werner Goetz and Régine Le Jan, Turnhout 2011, 261–282, at 272–280.

52 François Bougard, 'Le crédit dans l'Occident du haut Moyen Âge: documentation et pratique', in: *Les élites et la richesse au Haut Moyen Âge*, ed. Jean-Pierre Devroey, Laurent Feller and Régine Le Jan, Turnhout 2011, 439–478. For the Roman period see Matthias Bange, *Kreditgeld in der römischen Antike. Ursprünge, Entstehung, Übertragung und Verbreitung*, Rahden/Westphalia 2014.

53 *Lex Salica* 58 (*De chrenecruda*), ed. Eckhardt, MGH LL nat. Germ. 4, 1, 218–221.

also been observed by Lisi Oliver in Anglo-Saxon records. Such lending could also become dysfunctional, as Helle Vogt shows how restrictive regulations on collective payment of wergild were introduced by royal legislation in Denmark around 1200.

It should also be emphasized that the payment itself and the use of coins or metal equivalents — something which is often hard to reconstruct and not dealt with in this volume — is another important aspect of the process of conflict settlement.[54] As money has important implications relating to time,[55] it is essential to also consider the instant payment, and the practice of money-lending often including installments for repaying the debt, as part of this process. In the law codes, we often find the judgment formula *culpabilis iudicetur*, indicating that a debt was imposed on the perpetrator.[56] Debt plays an important role in conflict settlement,[57] and the history of the concept of debt in the early middle ages, visible in the omnipresence of Latin terms like *debere* and *solvere*, yet remains to be written.[58]

3.6 *Wergild and Christian Religion*

Seeing wergild as a step within a larger process also allows for its connectedness to religious issues to become more clearly visible, which usually is not very obvious in the law-codes which focus on the more "secular" aspects of compensation. It was observed a long time ago by Cyrille Vogel that the penitential books, with their long lists of penitential tariffs, resemble strongly the secular law-codes with their lists of wergild and composition fees.[59] Can these be compared? If we have discussed possible Roman continuities, it has to be mentioned that blood-money payment, which had been common in the Ancient Near East,[60] was also to some extent part of the Jewish tradition as

54 See on this Grierson, 'The Origins of Money', 12–19, and Dagfinn Skre, 'Monetary Practices in Early Medieval Western Scandinavia (5th–10th Centuries AD)', *Medieval Archeology* 61 (2017), 277–299.

55 See Axel T. Paul, *Theorie des Geldes zur Einführung*, Hamburg 2017, 106–108 and 211–212 (cited as Paul, *Theorie des Geldes*).

56 See Bougard, '*Culpabilis iudicetur*'.

57 Compare David Graeber, *Debt: The First 5,000 Years*, New York 2011, 133–145.

58 On the notion of an early medieval "debitive climate", as becomes evident in the concept of wergild and the vocabulary used in the polyptyques, see Ludolf Kuchenbuch, *Versilberte Verhältnisse. Der Denar in seiner ersten Epoche*, Göttingen 2016, 57–66.

59 Cyrille Vogel, 'Composition légale et commutations dans le système de la pénitence tarifée', *Revue de droit canonique* 8 (1958), 289–318; 9 (1959), 1–38 and 341–359.

60 Pamela Barmash, 'Blood Feud and State Control: Differing Legal Institutions for the Remedy of Homicide during the Second and First Millennia B.C.E.', *Journal of Near Eastern Studies* 63, 3 (2004), 183–199.

inherited in the Christian Old Testament.[61] However, in a Christian context, there were, as is emphasized by both Harald Siems and Rob Meens, clear functional differences between penance and wergild. Penitence served to repair a perpetrator's damaged relationship to God, as killing a person was also regarded a serious religious sin, while wergild-centric legal reasoning, as we have seen, arises out of the effect of a crime and is aimed at satisfying an earthly counterpart: namely, the social group of the victim.

So, were these resemblances just by chance or does their shared casuistic style betray a general trait of early medieval legal thought? Rob Meens, focusing on the Frankish kingdoms, emphasizes that it would be misleading to see the payment of wergild as a purely secular affair. Religious attitudes on violence and reconciliation became not only evident in churches' lending of money to pay wergild, but also in their involvement as asylum places, for instance. Indeed, the penitential books, with their intention to reconcile the sinner with God, also served to reintegrate a culprit into a community that shared essential religious values. Compensation for an offense thus would have often comprised different parts that, along with the payment of wergild, could include the performance of religious acts. Paying alms to the poor, or as observed by Helle Vogt for Denmark, self-humiliation and the giving of religious gifts for the soul of the departed were only three possibilities. After all, it was Christian communities in which the payment of wergild was appreciated, and the ways in which satisfaction with a wergild payment was attained had not only to reflect the hard "legal" and "economic" aspects of such a deal, but also had to be accommodated by these societies' mentalities and emotional values.

Such a perspective offers a new view of wergild and penance as complementing one another. The amoral, almost mechanical attitude of the wergild system, and its focus on the damage rather than on individual guilt could be counterbalanced by the penitentials. As the penitentials were much more interested in an individual's responsibility and reconciliation, in repeated sin, and ultimately also in conscience and guilt when facing the last judgment, it is here where we can trace the process that Peter Brown once called "la sinification" or "la peccatisation du monde".[62]

Intentionally killing a person is a bigger issue here. According to Meens, from the Carolingian period onward, the treatment of several sins suggests that confession and penance became a part of regular Christian life centered around the idea of receiving the Eucharist. A great number of 9th and 10th-century

61 On this, see also Bougard, '*Culpabilis iudicetur*'.

62 Peter Brown, 'Vers la naissance du purgatoire: Amnistie et pénitence dans le christianisme occidental de l'antiquité tardive au haut moyen âge', *Annales HSS* 52 (1997), 1247–1261.

manuscripts contain both *leges barbarorum* and capitularies on the one hand and penitential books on the other. This can be linked to an important observation made earlier by Meens that within the Frankish kingdom, the penitentials loom large exactly in those areas of Gaul in which Roman law was not prevalent.[63] While in Roman law ethical reasoning was perhaps more present, in the more Northern and Eastern parts of Gaul we can not only observe a call for a close cooperation between counts and bishops,[64] but also between secular punishment and ecclesiastical penance which can also be seen in Anglo-Saxon England.[65] Indeed, the increasing importance attributed to monastic exile points to a different approach to crime and to reform, suggesting an educative agenda was applied to a perpetrator.[66] In Denmark, as is shown by Helle Vogt, ecclesiastical doctrine on individual guilt and penance also left its mark on wergild practice and on the definition of offenses and "crimes". Still, many aspects of this multifaceted and complex interplay of wergild and religious law yet remain to be uncovered and explored — not least in comparison to societies dominated by other religions such as Islam, where the practice of paying blood-money also underwent significant changes introduced by religious considerations and motivations.[67]

3.7 *Wergild and Texts*

Since 1977, when Patrick Wormald[68] and Hermann Nehlsen,[69] interestingly without taking notice of each other, for the first time denied the practical function of the barbarian law-codes and voted for their more ideological importance as symbolizing royal authority and a people's civilization, these texts'

63 Rob Meens, *Penance in Medieval Europe 600–1200*, Cambridge 2014.

64 See Paul J. Fouracre, 'Carolingian Justice: The Rhetoric of Improvement and Contexts of Abuse', in: *La giustizia nell'alto medioevo (secoli V–VIII)*, Spoleto 1995, vol. 2, 771–803.

65 Thomas P. Oakley, 'The Cooperation of Medieval Penance and Secular Law', *Speculum* 7 (1932), 515–524; Catherine Cubitt, 'Bishops and Councils in late Saxon England: the intersection of secular and ecclesiastical law', in: *Recht und Gericht um 900*, ed. Wilfried Hartmann, Munich 2007, 151–168.

66 On this development, framed in a more general perspective, see also Julia Hillner, *Prison, Punishment and Penance in Late Antiquity*, Cambridge 2015.

67 See, e.g., Hend Gilli-Elewy, 'Soziale Aspekte frühislamischer Sklaverei', *Der Islam* 77 (2000), 116–168, at 121 and 123; for a modern example of blood-money (*diya*) see, e.g., Aharon Layish, 'Interplay between Tribal and Sharʿī Law: A Case of Tibbāwī Blood Money in the Sharīʿa Court of Kufra', *Islamic Law and Society* 13, 1 (2006), 63–75.

68 Patrick Wormald, 'Lex Scripta and Verbum Regis: Legislation and Germanic Kingship, from Euric to Cnut', in: *Early Medieval Kingship*, ed. Peter H. Sawyer and Ian N. Wood, Leeds 1977, 105–138.

69 Hermann Nehlsen, 'Zur Aktualität und Effektivität germanischer Rechtsaufzeichnungen', in: *Recht und Schrift im Mittelalter*, ed. Peter Classen, Sigmaringen 1977, 449–502.

functions have been a matter of some debate. Did the long lists with fixed tariffs of wergild and compensations not fulfil any practical function at all? Or did they intend to give some orientation as regards certain standards? Or could they form the base for the judges memorizing the provisions contained therein? And if there was an unsurmountable gap between the law-codes and legal practice, to what extent was negotiation on payments possible or even necessary?

Concentrating on the laws of King Æthelberht of Kent, Tom Lambert explores more nuanced ways to understand the relationship between law-code and legal practice. Following observations made by Lisi Oliver that many legal regulations are formulated in an elevated prose style and through the use of alliterations became more easily memorable, he focuses on the people's willingness to recognise the importance of peace for the wider community as an essential message to be conveyed by a law-code. These laws' authority was enhanced by the fact that they did not even envision the possibility of revenge but present detailed catalogues of compensations as the only possible, and by tradition acceptable, way to settle a conflict. Moreover, the laws transmitted the notion that the community had access to legal knowledge. Lambert's conclusions draw our attention to the ideological and idealistic implications of law-giving on wergild, as these texts signaled that it was alright to accept compensation, while anything else would have caused damage to the community. The law-code thus presents a vision of a world that was not non-violent, but one where violence and conflict could be sorted out, as the preservation of honour and the monetary valuation of a human life were presented as not incompatible.

A focus on wergild might also improve our understanding of texts where scholars always felt less comfortable with the ideas put forward by Wormald and Nehlsen. For instance, some of the lists of wergild tariffs presented in law-books imply that they were added later. Often it was different layers of legal material that were assembled within one law code. The existence of innovations suggests that the symbolic meaning of a law-book and its practical use should not be seen as alternative explanations that exclude one another. Adding new laws, including new tariffs, would have been irrelevant in symbolic terms had it not implied some intention to adjust law and to impact legal practice. Any revision implied some sort of consensus and, interestingly, Charlemagne and Louis the Pious issued new prescriptions to be inserted into the barbarian law-codes (*capitula legibus addenda*) within a particular chapter.[70] Louis the Pious

70 Steffen Patzold, 'Die Veränderung frühmittelalterlichen Rechts im Spiegel der "Leges"-Reformen Karls des Großen und Ludwigs des Frommen', in: *Rechtsveränderung im*

and his advisors also prepared legal reforms and considered the limit of the highest and lowest amounts of money to be paid for killing a person.[71]

But was there a kind of "wergild policy" or some sort of social engineering with the help of wergild? This again touches on the issue of legislation. In his contribution on Charlemagne's policy of having written down the laws of the Saxons, Frisians, Thuringians and Chamavian Franks, Karl Ubl observes a very limited endeavour to impose uniform standards of wergild within the Frankish realm. Although some sort of standardization can be observed in case of the *bannus* for public crimes such as arson and gang assault, Ubl observes certain tensions between local custom and royal law-giving. While the law-codes drafted shortly after 800 show the recognition of a separate nobility by attributing a higher wergild to it, Ubl sees Charlemagne reacting here largely to aspirations from among the local aristocracies and elites. Direct intervention of the ruler through his officials is rarely mentioned in the law-codes, which is why Ubl does not see here a governmental strategy of unification, as varying monetary systems and divergent wergild tariffs were not subject to Charlemagne's otherwise attested attempts to unify silver coinage. This suggests that Charlemagne sought to have the wergild system written down and gather information about local customs at the royal court, but was not aiming to impose uniform standards. By contrast, in his contribution on Frisia, Han Nijdam points to legal texts documenting changing stages in the amount of wergild.

Does the very existence of written lists and innovations not speak exactly against the assumption that wergild tariffs were negotiable? Warren Brown's contribution sheds light on the prominence of wergild in charters and formularies, which give a rare insight into wergild as part of social practice. That the formularies often leave wergild amounts blank allowed them to cover a wide range of actions, from which one might cautiously conclude that wergild amounts may indeed, to some extent, have been negotiated, while other cases also make clear that they must have been regarded as fixed. Here, again, further differentiations appear as necessary, since in all likelihood not all cases

---

politischen und sozialen Kontext mittelalterlicher Rechtsvielfalt, ed. Stefan Esders and Christine Reinle, Münster 2005, 63–99.

71 *Capitula adhuc conferenda* (a. 819?), no. 19, Preface and c. 2, ed. Hubert Mordek, *Bibliotheca capitularium regum Francorum manuscripta. Überlieferung und Traditionszusammenhang der fränkischen Herrschererlasse*, Munich 1995, 1010: *De his capitulis interrogandum est:* [...] *De maxima et minima conpositione, quod solidorum esse debeat.* On this text see Hubert Mordek, 'Unbekannte Texte zur karolingischen Gesetzgebung. Ludwig der Fromme, Einhard und die *Capitula adhuc conferenda*', *Deutsches Archiv für Erforschung des Mittelalters* 42 (1986), 446–471.

and quantities of wergild payment could be expected to be referenced in law-code provisions.

On the other hand, one should resist the temptation to develop a model of conflict settlement that would render these masses of texts as merely symbolic or even written down without any practical purpose. After all, in a comparative global perspective on different legal cultures that are accustomed to the practice of paying blood-money, the long lists of precise tariffs of wergild as contained in the early medieval law-codes are unique in the world history of blood-money.[72] If we draw comparisons to the use of blood-money in other, particularly tribal, societies, we should be aware that in the post-Roman kingdoms there was a remarkably high social differentiation which needed to be expressed in terms of wergild. Historians of this period should be aware of this and not try to explain away the evidence as presented by the law-codes on an a priori assumption that texts containing general norms could only be symbolic while in practice things must have been altogether different. What they have to explain instead is why lists containing such detailed amounts at some time were written down, how they became part of larger law-codes and why these laws even came to be updated on certain occasions.

4 Conclusion

In a more general perspective, it may be said that wergild as a concept of early medieval law appears as very open. For this reason it cannot be studied in isolation, but has to be looked at in relation to other features and factors of these societies, be they economic, political or religious. Wergild points to the importance of money not just as a currency, but as a substantial transformative force. As money can express value in a very precise way, it has the potential to change ways of thinking fundamentally, which it does by comprising two aspects which only at first sight appear as paradoxical. In establishing a relation between the value of a human life and a specified amount of money, it allows for reducing a complex conflict to a quantitative dimension, thereby individualizing it and neutralizing further dimensions, emotional and otherwise. At the same time, the sheer amounts attributed to wergilds introduced a new logic that deliberately overcharged any individual, a logic according to which networks or social groups were activated or newly created as debtors,

72 An important point made by Paul, *Theorie des Geldes*, 71–72.

money-lenders, sureties, recipients and judgment finders. Thus, in a way, wergild was responsible for "communitizing" the settlement of a violent conflict.

Whereas in Roman times *iudex non calculat* was an axiom that served to characterize a typically Roman attitude towards law and jurisdiction as placed in the hand of a single judge, wergild and the monetary logic of early medieval conflict resolution are perhaps most adequately symbolized in the activity of the Frankish lay judges called *rachinburgi*. The term itself refers in a telling way etymologically to their task of calculating.[73] Numerical valuation of lives thus promised to be a blessing for early medieval societies in their endeavour to cope with homicide and violence.

Wergild may thus be characterized as a key concept of early medieval law and conflict settlement in a more general sense. It was centered in what one might, in comparison to Roman law, call a new legal anthropology. Rooted in the value of a man, it points to a certain "masculinization" in the definition of social status within society. The value of a man provided a point of departure which could be applied, by analogy and adjustment, to calculate the status and value of women, slaves, social groups, political and religious functionaries etc. In so doing, wergild tariffs could also be used to define functional positions and social groups. The variability of these tariffs attests to legislative attempts to anticipate and prevent potential conflicts within these societies, or even to protect endangered individuals and groups. The careful calibration of tariffs also shows that certain notions of what was regarded as "public" could find an expression, for instance in the distinction between amendable and non-emendable offenses or in the multiplication of certain payments.

Within this range of possibilities, wergild could be used to respond to a limited variety of legal differences in the assessment of homicide, while its fixation on compensation of damage also shows certain deficits not allowing for a more complex reasoning about concepts such as "criminality", "individual guilt" etc. But in the early medieval West, wergild could also be used as one component within a system of dual sanctions, as wergild could be combined with and complemented by ecclesiastical penance which placed more emphasis on ethical reasoning. Moreover, wergild could be used and adopted in flexible and differentiated ways to demarcate the amount a person had to pay according to his status in the sense of a fine (the perpetrator's wergild). Its adaptability as a concept is also demonstrated by the fact that already in the early middle ages, wergild became used as an abstract unit of measuring a certain amount of money.

---

73 As is also reflected by the Old High German word for calculating ("*rehhanon*").

In the course of the medieval period, its viability even allowed the concept of wergild to be applied to compensate for the killing of animals, as again is evidenced by the *Sachsenspiegel* from which our considerations started:

> Now hear about the wergild of birds and animals. A chicken is compensated with a half-penny, as is a duck; a goose with one penny; a broody hen or goose during their hatching period and a call duck with three pennies. The same compensation applies for a piglet and a kid while they are suckling. For a cat and a lamb four pennies shall be paid; six for a calf, one shilling for a foal during its suckling stage, and the same for the dog. The tariff for the dog called sheepdog is three shillings; for a horse, a yearling pig, and a cow it is four shillings; for a draft ox and a grazing horse eight shillings; and for a workhorse able to do a full day's work, the tariff is twelve shillings. Younger animals are valued according to their age. The tariff for a riding horse with which a man serves his lord is one pound. No tariff has been set for a knight's horse, charger, saddle horse, or for fattened pigs. Instead, one shall return them and all movable goods or make restitution according to the appraisal of the owner.[74]

Whereas in the early middle ages, law-givers were keen to specify which animals could be given in compensation so that they would provide an equivalent for a particular sum of money,[75] by the thirteenth century wergild had acquired the character of a universal concept of damage that was thought

74 *Sachsenspiegel, Landrecht* III, 51.1–2, ed. Eckhardt, 123–124: *Nu vernemet umme vogele unde dire weregelt. Dat hun gilt men mit enem halven penninge, de anet also. De gans mit enem penninge, de brut gans unde de brut henne mit dren penningen binnen erer brut tit, unde de stelle anet also; dat selve dut men dat verken unde dat zickelin binnen erme soge unde de katten. Dat lam vor vire; dat kalf vor sesse. Dat volen vor enen scilling binnen sime soge, unde den hofwart also. Den hunt, den man scaprode het, mit dren scillingen unde dat suert unde dat jarege swin. Dat rint mit vir scillingen. De soge, de verkene dreget oder tut, mit vif scillingen. Den vulwassen ber also unde den esel. Den mul mit achte scillingen unde den tochossen unde den veltsterken. Andere veltperde, de to vulleme arbeide dogen, mit twelf scillingen. De aver beneden eren jaren sin, de gilt men als en na erme aldere geboret. Dat rideperd, dar de rideman sime herren oppe denen scal, dat gilt men mit eneme punde. Riddereperde aver, ors unde teldere unde runciden, den n'is nen weregelt gesat, noch meste swinen; dar umme scal men se unde alle varende have weder geven oder gelden na des werderunge, de se verlos, jene ne minnere se mit sinem ede, de se gelden scal; The Saxon Mirror.* Translated by Dobozy, 128. Another passage (Landrecht III, 28.1) makes clear that, for the unintentional killing of an animal, only restitution without a fine had to be given, which seems to imply that wergild, as paid for intentional killing, included some sort of fine at that time.

75 See above, n. 25.

FIGURE 1.2
Wolfenbüttel, Herzog-August-Bibliothek, Cod. Guelf. 3.1 Auf. 2°, fol. 49r: Wergild for the killing of animals

to be applicable even to non-human beings.[76] This once more illustrates the enormous practical flexibility and conceptual adaptability that characterizes the monetary logic of law and conflict resolution from the early medieval period onward.

Bibliography

Manuscripts

Heidelberg, Universitätsbibliothek, Cod. Pal. germ. 164
Paris, Bibliothèque nationale, lat. 4416
Wolfenbüttel, Herzog-August-Bibliothek, Cod. Guelf. 3.1 Auf. 2°

Primary Sources

Capitularia regum Francorum I, ed. Alfred Boretius, MGH LL Sect. 2, 1, Hanover 1883.
Das Landrecht des Sachsenspiegels, ed. Karl August Eckhardt, Göttingen 1955.

76 See Peter Oestmann, 'Das Tier in der Rechtsgeschichte. Tierhalterhaftung und Wergelder', *Unipress: Forschung und Wissenschaft an der Universität Bern* 122 (2004), 17–20.

Der Sachsenspiegel. Die Heidelberger Bilderhandschrift Cod. Pal. Germ. 164. Kommentar und Übersetzung, ed. Walter Koschorrek and Wilfried Werner, Frankfurt/Main 1989.
Gregory of Tours, *Decem Libri Historiarum*, ed. Bruno Krusch and Wilhelm Levison, MGH SS rerum Merovingicarum 1, 1, Hanover 1951.
Leges Burgundionum, ed. Ludwig Rudolf von Salis, MGH LL nationum Germanicarum 2, 1, Hanover 1892.
Lex Ribuaria, ed. Franz Beyerle and Rudolf Buchner, MGH LL nationum Germanicarum 3, 2, Hanover 1954.
Lex Salica, ed. Karl August Eckhardt, MGH LL nationum Germanicarum 4, 1, Hanover 1962.
The Burgundian Code. Book of constitutions or Law of Gundobad. Additional enactments. Translated by Katherine Fischer Drew, Philadelphia 1976.
The Saxon Mirror. A "Sachsenspiegel" of the Fourteenth Century. Translated by Maria Dobozy, Philadelphia 1999.

Secondary Works

Amory, Patrick, 'The meaning and purpose of ethnic terminology in the Burgundian laws', *Early Medieval Europe* 2 (1993), 1–28.
Bange, Matthias, *Kreditgeld in der römischen Antike. Ursprünge, Entstehung, Übertragung und Verbreitung*, Rahden/Westphalia 2014.
Barmash, Pamela, 'Blood Feud and State Control: Differing Legal Institutions for the Remedy of Homicide during the Second and First Millennia B.C.E.', *Journal of Near Eastern Studies* 63, 3 (2004), 183–199.
Bothe, Lukas, 'From Subordination to Integration: Romans in Frankish Law', in: *Transformations of Romanness. Early Medieval Regions and Identities*, ed. Walter Pohl, Clemens Gantner, Cinzia Grifoni and Marianne Pollheimer-Mohaupt, Berlin 2018, 345–368.
Bougard, François, 'Le crédit dans l'Occident du haut Moyen Âge: documentation et pratique', in: *Les élites et la richesse au Haut Moyen Âge*, ed. Jean-Pierre Devroey, Laurent Feller and Régine Le Jan, Turnhout 2011, 439–478.
Bougard, François, '*Culpabilis iudicetur*: réparation et châtiment des crimes et délits dans les lois "barbares"', in: *Les lois barbares. Justice et société dans les royaumes post-romains*, ed. Sylvie Joye, Marcelo da Silva Candido and Bruno Dumézil (in press).
Brown, Peter, 'Vers la naissance du purgatoire: Amnistie et pénitence dans le christianisme occidental de l'antiquité tardive au haut moyen âge', *Annales HSS* 52 (1997), 1247–1261.
Camby, Christophe, *Wergeld ou uueregildus. Le rachat pécuniaire de l'offense entre continuités romaines et innovation germanique*, Geneve 2013.

Cubitt, Catherine, 'Bishops and Councils in late Saxon England: the intersection of secular and ecclesiastical law', in: *Recht und Gericht um 900*, ed. Wilfried Hartmann, Munich 2007, 151–168.

Depreux, Philippe, 'Une faide exemplaire? A propos des aventures de Sichaire: Vengeance et pacification aux temps mérovingiens', in: *La vengeance 400–1200* (Collection de l'École française de Rome 357), ed. Dominique Barthélemy, François Bougard and Régine Le Jan, Rome 2006, 65–85.

Depreux, Philippe, 'Wergeld, composition et rachat dans le capitulaires des rois francs', in: *La victime*, t. 2: *La réparation du dommage*, ed. Jacqueline Hoareau-Dodinau, Guillaume Métairie and Pascal Texier, Limoges 2009, 345–362.

Esders, Stefan, '"Eliten" und "Strafrecht" im frühen Mittelalter. Überlegungen zu den Bußen und Wergeldkatalogen der *Leges barbarorum*', in: *Théories et pratiques des élites au haut Moyen Âge*, ed. François Bougard, Hans-Werner Goetz and Régine Le Jan, Turnhout 2011, 261–282.

Esders, Stefan, 'Wergeld und soziale Netzwerke im Frankenreich', in: *Verwandtschaft, Name und soziale Ordnung (300–1100)*, ed. Steffen Patzold and Karl Ubl, Berlin and New York 2014, 141–160.

Esders, Stefan, '*Wergild* and social practice in the early middle ages: A 9th-century Reichenau fragment and its context', in: *Entre texte et histoire. Études d'histoire médiévale offertes au professeur Shoichi Sato*, ed. Osamu Kano and Jean-Loup Lemaître, Paris 2015, 117–127.

Esders, Stefan, 'Late Roman Military Law in the Bavarian Code', *clio@themis. Revue électronique d'histoire du droit* 10 (2016) (thematic issue *La forge du droit. Naissance des identités juridiques en Europe, IVe–XIIIe siècles*): http://www.cliothemis.com/IMG/pdf/3-_Esders-2.pdf.

Esders, Stefan, 'Zwischen Historie und Rechtshistorie. Der *consensus iuris* im frühen Mittelalter', in: *Recht und Konsens im frühen Mittelalter*, ed. Verena Epp and Christoph H. F. Meyer, Ostfildern 2017, 427–474.

Faulkner, Thomas, *Law and Authority in the Early Middle Ages. The Frankish leges in the Carolingian period*, Cambridge 2016.

Fouracre Paul J., 'Carolingian Justice: The Rhetoric of Improvement and Contexts of Abuse', in: *La giustizia nell'alto medioevo (secoli V–VIII)*, Spoleto 1995, vol. 2, 771–803.

Frye, David Gene, 'Gundobad, the *Leges Burgundionum*, and the struggle for sovereignty in Burgundy', *Classica et Mediaevalia* 14 (1990), 199–212.

Fuhrmann, Manfred '*Persona*, ein römischer Rollenbegriff', in: *Identität*, ed. Odo Marquard and Karlheinz Stierle, Munich 1979, 83–106.

Gehrke, Hans-Joachim, 'Gewalt und Gesetz. Die soziale und politische Ordnung Kretas in der Archaischen und Klassischen Zeit', *Klio* 79 (1997), 23–68.

Gilli-Elewy, Hend, 'Soziale Aspekte frühislamischer Sklaverei', *Der Islam* 77 (2000), 116–168.

Graeber, David, *Debt: The First 5,000 Years*, New York 2011.

Grierson, Philip, 'The Origins of Money', *Research in Economic Anthropology* 1 (1978), 1–35 (repr. in Id., *Scritti storici e numismatici*, Spoleto 2001, 69–106).

Heather, Peter, 'Law and society in the Burgundian kingdom', in: *Law, Custom, and Justice in Late Antiquity and the Early Middle Ages*, ed. Alice Rio, London 2011, 115–153.

Hillner, Julia, *Prison, Punishment and Penance in Late Antiquity*, Cambridge 2015.

Köhler, Jan, *Die Zeit der Jungs. Zur Organisation von Gewalt und der Austragung von Konflikten in Georgien*, Muenster 2000.

Kuchenbuch, Ludolf, *Versilberte Verhältnisse. Der Denar in seiner ersten Epoche*, Göttingen 2016.

Layish, Aharon, 'Interplay between Tribal and Sharʿī Law: A Case of Tibbāwī Blood Money in the Sharīʿa Court of Kufra', *Islamic Law and Society* 13, 1 (2006), 63–75.

Meens, Rob, *Penance in Medieval Europe 600–1200*, Cambridge 2014.

Mommsen, Theodor, *Das römische Strafrecht*, Berlin 1899.

Mordek, Hubert, 'Unbekannte Texte zur karolingischen Gesetzgebung. Ludwig der Fromme, Einhard und die *Capitula adhuc conferenda*', *Deutsches Archiv für Erforschung des Mittelalters* 42 (1986), 446–471.

Mordek, Hubert, *Bibliotheca capitularium regum Francorum manuscripta. Überlieferung und Traditionszusammenhang der fränkischen Herrschererlasse*, Munich 1995.

Nehlsen, Hermann, *Sklavenrecht zwischen Antike und Mittelalter. Germanisches und römisches Recht in den germanischen Rechtsaufzeichnungen, 1: Ostgoten, Westgoten, Franken, Langobarden*, Göttingen 1971.

Nehlsen, Hermann, 'Zur Aktualität und Effektivität germanischer Rechtsaufzeichnungen', in: *Recht und Schrift im Mittelalter*, ed. Peter Classen, Sigmaringen 1977, 449–502.

Nehlsen, Hermann, 'Entstehung des öffentlichen Strafrechts bei den germanischen Stämmen', in: *Gerichtslauben-Vorträge. Freiburger Festkolloquium zum 75. Geburtstag von Hans Thieme*, ed. Karl Kroeschell, Sigmaringen 1983, 3–16.

Oakley, Thomas P., 'The Cooperation of Medieval Penance and Secular Law', *Speculum* 7 (1932), 515–524.

Oestmann, Peter, 'Das Tier in der Rechtsgeschichte. Tierhalterhaftung und Wergelder', *Unipress: Forschung und Wissenschaft an der Universität Bern* 122 (2004), 17–20.

Oliver, Lisi, *The Body Legal in Barbarian Law*, Toronto 2011.

Patzold, Steffen, 'Die Veränderung frühmittelalterlichen Rechts im Spiegel der "Leges"-Reformen Karls des Großen und Ludwigs des Frommen', in: *Rechtsveränderung im politischen und sozialen Kontext mittelalterlicher Rechtsvielfalt*, ed. Stefan Esders and Christine Reinle, Muenster 2005, 63–99.

Paul, Axel T., *Theorie des Geldes zur Einführung*, Hamburg 2017.

Rilinger, Rolf, *Humiliores — Honestiores. Zu einer sozialen Dichotomie im Strafrecht der römischen Kaiserzeit*, Munich 1988.

Roels, Wilfried, *Onderzoek naar het gebruik van de aangehaalde bronnen van Romeins Recht in de Lex Romana Burgundionum*, Antwerp 1958.

Schmidt-Wiegand, Ruth (ed.), *Text-Bild-Interpretation. Untersuchungen zu den Bilderhandschriften des Sachsenspiegels*, Munich 1986.

Schubert, Ernst, 'Vom Wergeld zur Strafe: Die übersehene Bedeutung der friesischen Rechtsquellen zur Interpretation eines epochalen mittelalterlichen Wandels', in: *Tota Frisia in Teilansichten. Hajo van Lengen zum 65. Geburtstag*, ed. Heinrich Schmidt, Wolfgang Schwarz and Martin Tielke, Aurich 2005, 97–120.

Seitz, Emanuel, 'Der Wert des Menschen und sein Preis. Das Verhältnis von Person und Eigentum bei Brautpreis, Wergeld und Sklaverei', in: *Embodying value? The Transformation of Objects in and from the Ancient World*, ed. Anabel Bokern and Clare Rowan, Oxford 2014, 11–22.

Siems, Harald, 'Bemerkungen zu *sunnis* und *morbus sonticus*. Zum Problem des Fortwirkens römischen Rechts im frühen Mittelalter', *ZRG RA* 103 (1986), 409–446.

Simmel, Georg, *Philosophie des Geldes*, Berlin 1900.

Simmel, Georg, *The Philosophy of Money*. Translated by Tom Bottomore and David Frisby, London 1978.

Skre, Dagfinn, 'Monetary Practices in Early Medieval Western Scandinavia (5th–10th Centuries AD)', *Medieval Archeology* 61 (2017), 277–299.

Przemysław, Tyszka, *The Human Body in Barbarian Laws, c. 500–c. 800*, Frankfurt/Main 2013.

Ubl, Karl, *Sinnstiftungen eines Rechtsbuches. Die Lex Salica im Frankenreich*, Ostfildern 2017.

Van Hartingsveldt, Edvard, 'De "Zeven Zaken" en de frankische bisschop', *Revue belge de philologie et d'histoire* 67 (1989), 677–694.

Vogel, Cyrille, 'Composition légale et commutations dans le système de la pénitence tarifée', *Revue de droit canonique* 8 (1958), 289–318; 9 (1959), 1–38, 341–359.

Voss, Wulf Eckart, 'Vom römischen Provinzialprozeß der Spätantike zum Rechtsgang des frühen Mittelalters', in: *Recht im frühmittelalterlichen Gallien. Spätantike Tradition und germanische Wertvorstellungen*, ed. Harald Siems, Karin Nehlsen-von Stryk and Dieter Strauch, Cologne 1995, 73–108.

Weitzel, Jürgen (ed.), *Hoheitliches Strafen in der Spätantike und im frühen Mittelalter*, Cologne 2002.

Werle, Hans, 'Gold und Silber. Die Geldstrafen in den Pönformeln frühmittelalterlicher Urkunden des Klosters Lorsch', in: *Recht und Wirtschaft in Geschichte und Gegenwart. Festschrift für Johannes Bärmann zum 70. Geburtstag*, ed. Marcus Lutter, Helmut Kolhosser and Winfried Trusen, Munich 1975, 53–63.

Wood, Ian N., 'The Legislation of *Magistri Militum*: the laws of Gundobad and Sigismund', *clio@themis. Revue électronique d'histoire du droit* 10 (2016) (thematic issue *La forge du droit. Naissance des identités juridiques en Europe, IVe–XIIIe siècles*): http://www.cliothemis.com/IMG/pdf/5-_Wood-2.pdf.

Wormald, Patrick, 'Lex Scripta and Verbum Regis: Legislation and Germanic Kingship, from Euric to Cnut', in: *Early Medieval Kingship*, ed. Peter H. Sawyer and Ian N. Wood, Leeds 1977, 105–138.

Wormald, Patrick, *The Making of English Law: King Alfred to the Twelfth Century*, vol. I: *Legislation and its Limits*, Oxford 1999.

Wormald, Patrick, 'The *Leges Barbarorum*: Law and Ethnicity in the Post-Roman West', in: *Regna and Gentes: The Relationship Between Late Antique and Early Medieval Peoples and Kingdoms in the Transformation of the Roman World*, ed. Hans-Werner Goetz, Jörg Jarnut and Walter Pohl, Leiden 2003, 21–53.

CHAPTER 2

Observations Concerning the 'Wergild System': Explanatory Approaches, Effectiveness and Structural Deficits

Harald Siems

According to early medieval legal sources, especially the so-called 'Volksrechte', the *leges barbarorum*, wergild is a sum of money that must be paid to the relatives of the victim in the event of a homicide.[1] It means 'man payment', often amounts to 200 *solidi* and is part of the composition system of the *leges*, which details fixed compensation sums for all acts of wrongdoing. According to the *leges*, significant financial assets had to be raised as atonement for the loss of a human life in order to compensate and pacify the sides of both the perpetrators and the victims.[2]

1 Translated by Alissa Rubinstein, translation revised by Courtnay Konshuh. I am grateful for the translation as well as for helpful additions by Lukas Bothe and Stefan Esders.

2 For space reasons, the following evidence is limited to the essentials. In view of the large amount of literature available on the subject, readers are referred to the following articles in *HRG*, *RGA* and *LexMA*: 'Buße', Ekkehard Kaufman, in: *HRG* 1, Berlin 1971, col. 575–577; Harald Ehrhardt et al., in: *LexMA* 2, Munich and Zurich 1983, col. 1123–1151; 'Blutrache', Wolfgang Preiser, in: *HRG* 1, Berlin 1971, col. 459–461; Hartmut Böttcher, in: *RGA* 3, Berlin and New York 1978, 85–101; Hans-Rudolf Hagemann, in: *LexMA* 2, Munich and Zurich 1983, col. 289–250; 'Erfolgshaftung', Ekkehard Kaufmann, in: *HRG* 1, Berlin 1971, col. 989–1001; id., in: *RGA* 7, Berlin and New York 1989, 486–488; 'Fehde', Ekkehard Kaufmann, in: *HRG* 1, Berlin 1971, col. 1083–1093; Ekkehard Kaufmann and Eckhard Meineke, in: *RGA* 8, Berlin and New York 1994, 279–285; Andrea Boockmann, in: *LexMA* 4, Munich and Zurich 1989, col. 331–334; 'Friedlosigkeit', Michael Lundgreen, in: *RGA* 9, Berlin and New York 1995, 613–621; Karl Kroeschell, in: *LexMA* 4, Munich and Zurich 1989, col. 930–931; 'Handhafte Tat', Dieter Werkmüller, in: *HRG* 1, Berlin 1971, col. 1965–1973; id., in: *RGA* 13, Berlin and New York 1999, 614–616; Heinz Holzhauer, in: *LexMA* 4, Munich and Zurich 1989, col. 1902–1903; 'Kompositionensystem', Karl Scherner, in: *HRG* 2, Berlin 1978, col. 995–997; Ludger Körntgen, in: *RGA* 17, Berlin and New York 2001, 179–180; 'Peinliche Strafe', Ekkehard Kaufmann, in: *HRG* 3, Berlin 1984, col. 1574; 'Sippe', Ekkehard Kaufmann, in: *HRG* 4, Berlin 1990, col. 1668–1670; Stefan Saar and Dieter Strauch, in: *RGA* 28, Berlin and New York 2005, 473–498; Karl Kroeschell, in: *LexMA* 7, Munich and Zurich 1995, col. 1934–1935; 'Strafe/Strafrecht', Ekkehard Kaufman, in: *HRG* 4, Berlin 1990, col. 2011–2029; Stefan Saar, in: *RGA* 30, Berlin and New York 2005, 58–67; Ludwig Burgmann et al., in: *LexMA* 8, Munich and Zurich 1997, col. 196–207; 'Sühne', Ekkehard Kaufmann, in: *HRG* 5, Berlin 1998, col. 72–76; Heinrich Beck, in: *RGA* 30, Berlin and New York 2005, 107–109; Ludwig Hödl and Steffen Schlinker, in: *LexMA* 8, Munich and Zurich 1997, col. 295–298; 'Todesstrafe', Dieter Meurer, in: *HRG* 5, Berlin 1998, col. 264–270; Wolfgang Schild, in: *RGA* 31, Berlin and

 | DOI:10.1163/9789004466128_003

Scholars since the 19th century have conceptually detailed this phenomenon in the development of criminal legal history.[3] A picture with comprehensive explanatory claims for the social and legal conditions of the Germanic past arises — from peacelessness, i.e. outlawry and blood feuds, to the early medieval composition system, and finally to the beginnings of public criminal law in the high Middle Ages. Originally, the criminal act would have breached the general peace. Homicide in and of itself put the offender in a state of peacelessness. He would have been threatened with the death penalty, vengeance or blood feud, which were considered legal institutions legitimized by custom, and afforded the right to kill any perpetrator caught in the act. The function of the wergild payment therefore was to return the perpetrator to the protection of the general peace and thereby end the feud. The involvement of *propinqui* (relatives) in the raising and distribution of wergilds and, in the case of compurgation, could be used to draw conclusions about kinship structures and property obligations.

Many attempts have been made to create a universal theory for the evolution of wergild. However, it is not only the scarce source material that is methodologically difficult; it is equally problematic to generalize often uncertain individual examples from different time periods into a conceptually solidified overall vision of alleged Germanic law that has been correlated with the early medieval situation. More recent research is directed towards the development of public criminal law and concentrates on the evolution of capital and corporal punishment, as well as fines.[4] In contrast to the wergild and compensation system, those legal consequences are no longer seen as subject to a private settlement between the perpetrator and the victim. However, here too, the

New York 2006, 16–20; Jürgen Weitzel; in: *LexMA* 8, Munich and Zurich 1997, col. 836–838; 'Tötungsdelikte', Dieter Meurer, in: *HRG* 5, Berlin 1998, col. 286–290; 'Verklarung', Adalbert Erler, in: *HRG* 5, Berlin 1998, col. 741–743; Mathias Schmoeckel, in: *RGA* 32, Berlin and New York 2006, 213–215; and 'Wergeld', Wolfgang Schild, in: *HRG* 5, Berlin 1998, col. 1268–1271; Ruth Schmidt-Wiegand, in: *RGA* 33, Berlin 2006, 457–463; Norbert Angermann et al., in: *LexMA* 8, Munich and Zurich 1997, col. 2199–2204.

3 Jean-Marie Moeglin, 'Le "droit de vengeance" chez les historiens du droit au Moyen Âge (XIXe–XXe siècles)', in: *La vengeance 400–1200* (Collection de l'École française de Rome 357), ed. Dominique Barthélemy, François Bougard and Régine Le Jan, Rome 2006, 101–148; Carsten Bernoth, *Die Fehde des Sichar*, Baden-Baden 2008.

4 The yields of an interdisciplinary research project have been presented in the series: Klaus Lüderssen et al. (ed.), *Konflikt, Verbrechen und Sanktion in der Gesellschaft Alteuropas*, comprised of *Fallstudien* and *Symposien und Synthesen*. From the latter, the following are particularly relevant: vol. 1, *Die Entstehung des öffentlichen Strafrechts*, ed. Dietmar Willoweit, Cologne 1999; vol. 2, *Neue Wege strafrechtsgeschichtlicher Forschung*, ed. Hans Schlosser, Cologne 1999; vol. 7, *Hoheitliches Strafen in der Spätantike und im frühen Mittelalter*, ed. Jürgen Weitzel, Cologne 2002.

desire for distinction and conceptual rigor can be countered by the diversity of historical phenomena, and any grand vision is likely to fail due to the scarcity of the sources.

The following analysis compiles considerations regarding the rationality, function and shortcomings of wergild as a reaction to wrongdoings from legislative texts. This article's perspective on historical realities is hence restricted to the respective authors' point of view on pending conflicts, their controllability and management.

First of all, it does not seem entirely unreasonable to take a look at previous stages in the evolution of law in order to categorize wergild. The *Formulae Marculfi* show that a killer faced death, which could however still be averted through high level intervention resulting in wergild payment *ad pacis concordia* (to restore the harmony of peace).[5] King Rothari raised the fines of Lombard

5 *Marculfi Formulae* 2.18, ed. Karl Zeumer, MGH Formulae Merowingici et Karolini aevi, Hanover 1886, 88–89: *Securitas pro homicidio facto, si se pacificaverint. Domino fratri illo illi. Dum, instigante adversario, quod non debueras, germano nostro illo visus es interfecisse et ob hoc vitae periculum incurrere potueras, sed intervenientes sacerdotes et magnificis viris, quorum nomina subter tenuntur adnexa, nos ad pacis concordia, ob hoc visi fuerunt revocasse, ita ut pro ipsa causa solidus tantus in pagalia mihi dare debueras, quos et in presenti per wadio tuo visus es transsolsisse, et nos ipsa causa per fistuco contra te visus sum werpisse: propterea iuxta quod convenit hanc epistolam securitatis in te nobis conscribere conplacuit, ut de ipsa morte germano nostro nec a me nec ab heredibus meis aut suis nec de iudiciaria potestate nec a quemlibet nullo casu nec refragatione aliqua aut damnietate amplius habere non pertimiscas, sed in omnibus exinde ductus et absolutus appareas. Et fortasse ego ipse aut aliquis de heredibus meis vel quecumque te ob hoc inquietare voluerit, et a me defensatum non fuerit, inferamus tibi cum cogenti fisco duplum, quod nobis dedisti; et quod repetit quis vindicare non valeat, sed presens epistola securitatis a me facta firma permaneat.* — 'Security for a murder if they made peace. To my lord brother A, B. Since, at the instigation of the devil you were seen to kill our brother C, which you should not have done, you could have been in danger of [losing your] life because of this. But through the intervention of priests and great men, whose names are added below, we were seen to restore the harmony of peace in this matter, so that you were to give me n. solidi in compensation for this, which you were seen to deliver; by your pledge, and we were seen to relinquish this claim against you by the rod. Therefore, according to what was agreed, it pleased us to write this document of security for you, so that you should not fear any further claim or accusation or penalty regarding this death of our brother, whether from me or from my heirs or his, or from a judiciary power, or from anybody, but you will be seen as free and absolved from this in every way. And if perhaps I myself or one of my heirs or anyone else wants to trouble you regarding this and is not prevented by me, we will pay to you, the fisc compelling [us], twice what you gave us. And let him be unable to assert his claim. But let the present document of security made by me remain firm.' (*The Formularies of Angers and Marculf. Two Merowingian Legal Handbooks*. Translated with an introduction and notes by Alice Rio [Liverpool Translated Texts for Historians 46], Liverpool 2008, 203–204); See also *Formulae Salicae Lindenbrogianae* 19, ed. Zeumer, MGH Formulae Merowingici et Karolini aevi, Hanover 1886, 280–281.

law to halt *faida, quod est inimicitia* (feud, i.e. enmity)[6] and prohibited feuds for certain cases.[7] One could build upon this notion, if one wanted to view peacelessness and blood feud as a legal response to homicide. However, there could be no stringent path from the (by now justifiably) disbelieved peacelessness to wergild, since, in theory, anyone would have been allowed to kill an outlaw, while only the relatives of the victim could claim the wergild. It must also be said that the *Lex Frisionum* does not count a killer among those people whom one can kill without having to pay a fine.[8]

Hartmut Böttcher has already objected to the notion of blood feud as the primary reaction to homicide by raising the point that sources famously name violent retaliations, but no unending private wars.[9] Furthermore, concepts regarding feuds implicitly assume that the victim's side was more powerful and possessed superior means, which would push the perpetrator to pay the wergild. However, if a helpless victim's side were up against a powerful perpetrator, how would the former apply pressure on the latter? Moreover, in regard to blood vengeance, it is assumed that the cases in question concern intentional homicide. Should a deadly accident in everyday life initially have led to blood vengeance as well, and only later to the payment of wergild? In these cases, the public declaration of a killing can be interpreted as a demonstration of one's willingness to reconcile via the paying of a fine. However, this does not reveal anything about blood feud in earlier times.

Attempts to interpret the payment of wergild as substitution for feud or blood vengeance leave open questions regarding successive stages in an alleged legal development. However, it is undoubtedly the case that, no matter the time period, external pressure can encourage a willingness to negotiate between parties in conflict.

Further clues must be sought to explain wergild. As atonement for a homicide, wergild relates a monetary value, or, more realistically, a material value, to the value of a person. Given the natural uniqueness and irreplaceable character of every human being, human life cannot be valued in money and is therefore priceless. However, in earlier cultures, too, the necessity of atoning for a killing in a mutually satisfying and bearable manner could have called for

6 *Edictus Rothari* 74, ed. Friedrich Bluhme, MGH LL 4, Hanover 1868, 23–24.

7 *Edictus Rothari* 45, 75, 126, 138, 162, 326, 387, ed. Bluhme, MGH LL 4, 20, 24, 29–30, 31–32, 37, 75, 90.

8 *Lex Frisionum* 5, ed. Karl August Eckhardt and Albrecht Eckhardt, MGH Fontes iuris Germanici in usum scholarum seperatim editi 12, Hanover 1982, 46.

9 Hartmut Böttcher, Art. 'Blutrache', in: *RGA* 3, Berlin and New York 1978, 85–101.

compensation in tangible assets.[10] Yet, only a fictional path remains in order to arrive at the concept of the value of a human life being measured as wergild.

Distinct wergilds, scaled according to the status of the person who was killed, prompt us to look for connecting factors for the creation of value. Lombard law might suggest that the extent of people's land holdings was decisive. The word *angargathungi*, whose first component *angar* implies *Anger* in German (meaning a village green in the sense of commons) and is interpreted as a relation to the land, provides the sole point of reference. It is stated as follows in the *Edictum Rothari ... pro mortuum adpretietur, qualiter in angargathungi, id est secundum qualitatem personae* ...(composition shall be computed as if for death *angargathungi*, that is, according to the rank of the person), and is then repeated in a similar way two more times.[11] It seems as if the status of the person were being defined according to his land holdings. Can the origin of wergild therefore be traced simply from an assessment of real assets? Doubts are raised, as all three references to *angargathungi* in the *Edictum Rothari* technically add special regulations which indicate later legal development. Moreover, the inserted explanatory gloss, *id est secundum qualitatem personae* (that is, according to the rank of the person), hints at a lack of understanding of the word *angargathungi*.[12] Is the passage perhaps only intended to remedy a later need for explanation regarding how different wergild amounts came to be? It should also be considered that wergild sums are indeed assumed but not

---

10 P. Cornelius Tacitus, *Germania* 12.2, 21.1, ed. Allan Lund, Heidelberg 1988, 80, 86.

11 *Edictus Rothari* 48, ed. Bluhme, MGH LL 4, 21: *De oculo evulso. Si quis alii oculum excusserit, pro mortuum adpretietur, qualiter in angargathungi, id est secundum qualitatem personae; et medietas praetii ipsius conponatur ab ipsum, qui oculum excusserit.* — 'On gouging out eyes. In the case where someone gouges out another man's eye, composition shall be computed as if for death *angargathungi*, that is, according to the rank of the person: he who strikes out the eye shall pay half of the wergeld as composition.' (*The Lombard Laws*. Translated with an introduction by Katherine Fischer Drew, Philadelphia 1973, 61) See also c. 14 and 74, ibid. 15 and 23–24.

12 The glosses also do not establish a connection to land holding and land use: *Glossarium Matritense* 7, ed. Bluhme, MGH LL 4, Hanover 1868, 651: *Inangargathungin. Id est secundum arbitrium regis sicut appretiatum fuerit. Glossarium Cavense* 56, ibid. 654: *Gargathungin. Id. secundum qualitatem persone. Glossarium Vaticanum* 36, ibid.: *Gargathunchin. qualitate persone.* 51: *Ingargathugi. secundum arbitrium regis sicut appreciatus fuit iuxta qualitatem persone;* Huguccio, *Derivationes*, ed. Enzo Cecchini, Florence 2004, G29, 513: *Gargathungi, id est secundum qualitatem persone.* — On the words: Ingeborg Schröbler, 'Langobardisch-Deutsches Glossar', in: *Die Gesetze der Langobarden*, ed. Franz Beyerle, Weimar 1947, 501–502; Florus van der Rhee, *Die germanischen Wörter in den langobardischen Gesetzen*, Rotterdam 1970, 29–31; Ulrike Lade, *Flur und Feld: Volkssprachige Bezeichnungen in den frühmittelalterlichen Leges*, Muenster 1986, 139–145; Friedrich Kluge and Elmar Seebold, *Etymologisches Wörterbuch der deutschen Sprache*, Strasbourg [23]1999, 39 v. 'Anger'.

given, and a nobility is also not explicitly named in the *Edictum Rothari*,[13] even though said nobility might have possessed a significant amount of property.

In this context, subsequent determinations of property limits that entail military obligations do not lead us to any satisfactory conclusions.[14] These provisions are related in a different functional context. They do not correlate human life to material assets. Rather, they attach specific military obligations to respective private assets. The development of the wergild principle from land holdings[15] would thus require clearer sources or considerable auxiliary hypotheses.

Canon law penitential tariffs in the *libri paenitentiales* present an opportunity for a comparison with wergild.[16] Cyrille Vogel has investigated this and highlighted functional differences.[17] Nonetheless, it is conceivable that the gradation of church penance in cases of Christian misconduct and the formation of wergild and compensation tariffs for coincident secular offenses influenced each other. Both spheres are concerned with the re-establishment of a disturbed order and the reconciliation of the parties. Admittedly, if secular law were really based on an ecclesiastical system of rules, it would be surprising that the earlier *leges* lacked wergilds for clerics.[18] Ultimately, however, the differences predominate, especially in terms of intention. While the ultimate goal of the *libri paenitentiales* is the salvation of the sinner, the payment of wergild according to the *leges* aims to offer compensation between perpetrator and victim and thus restore peace. It is not the goal of the wergild taxes in the *leges* to reform the sinfulness of the perpetrator, and the penitentials do not aim to assign material value to human life.

Finally, the influences of Roman law should be borne in mind. After all, the *XII Tables* included monetary fines for assault and personal injury: for the *os fractum* (broken bone), 300 As had to be paid, and in cases of *cetera iniuria* (other injuries), 25 As. *Talio* threatened in cases of *membrum ruptum* (severed

13 *Nobilitas* in *Edictus Rothari* 75 and 378, ed. Bluhme, MGH LL 4, 24, 88 does not mean the 'nobility'.

14 *Leges Liutprandi regis* 83, ed. Bluhme, MGH LL 4, Hanover 1868, 140–141; *Capitulare* 44, c. 19, ed. Alfred Boretius, MGH Capitularia regum Francorum 1, Hanover 1883, 125; *Capitulare* 48, c. 2, ibid., 135.

15 Regarding the problem of earlier land holding and land use, see Tacitus, *Germania* 26, ed. Lund, 90.

16 Rob Meens, *Penance in Medieval Europe 600–1200*, Cambridge 2014 (cited as Meens, *Penance*).

17 Cyrille Vogel, 'Composition légale et commutations dans le système de la pénitence tarifée', *Revue de droit canonique* 8 (1958), 289–318; 9 (1959), 1–38, 341–359.

18 This applies to the *Lex Visigothorum*, *Lex Burgundionum*, *Leges Langobardorum* until Aregis, *Pactus Alamannorum*, *Pactus legis Salicae* A and C manuscripts.

limbs) if the concerned parties could not come to an arrangement. This information comes to us from Gaius, among others, in his *Institutes* from the middle of the second century AD. He concludes his historical memorandum with the following words: ... *sed nunc alio iure utimur* (the rule now in use is different).[19] According to a report by the Roman lawyer Labeo (a contemporary of Augustus), which was preserved by Aulus Gellius, a departure from the compensations, which were far too low by that point, can be traced back to the shameful behavior of one Lucius Veratius, who is said to have slapped free people in the face for fun. His slave followed behind him and gave the affected person a purse with 25 As, therefore immediately settling the compensatory debt according to the *XII Tables*. Furthermore, Labeo explains the *lex talionis* as a deterrent and form of pressure to get someone to pay a fine.[20] In the jurisdiction of the *Praetors* an estimate of the damages emerged in place of fixed compensation amounts, thereby ensuring that lost labour and expenditures for healing were also taken into account. However, scars and deformities were not included in estimates. The rationale for this is the following repeatedly used principle clause: *Librum corpus nullam recipit aestimationem.*[21] The body of a free person does not admit of appraisement. At first glance, this reveals differences between slaves and free men, since the value of a slave did decrease in the case of deformations. However, it also means that a free person was not reimbursed for such permanent injuries. In Roman law, the value of a free person's body cannot be expressed through pecuniary valuation.

---

19 Gaius, *Institutiones* 3.223–224, ed. Ulrich Manthe, Darmstadt 2004, 314: 223. *Poena autem iniuriarum ex lege XII tabularum propter membrum quidem ruptum talio erat; propter os vero fractum aut conlisum trecentorum assium poena erat, [veluti] si libero os fractum erat; at si servo, CL; propter ceteras vero iniurias XXV assium poena erat constituta. Et videbantur illis temporibus in magna paupertate satis idoneae istae pecuniariae poenae. 224. Sed nunc alio iure utimur.* — 'The penalty of outrage in the Twelve Tables for a limb broken was retaliation: for a bone broken or bruised three hundred asses, if the person injured was a freeman; one hundred and fifty, if he was a slave; for other injuries twenty-five asses: and in those days of excessive poverty such sums seemed an adequate reparation. The rule now in use is different.' (*Gai Institutiones or Institutes of Roman Law by Gaius*. With a Translation and Commentary by Edward Poste and E. A. Whittuck, Oxford 1904); See also Justinian, *Institutiones* 4.4.7, ed. Paul Krüger, Berlin [4]1921, 143; Sextus Pompeius Festus, *De verborum significatu*, v. *talionis*, lib. 20, ed. Wallace Martin Lindsay, Leipzig 1913, 496.

20 A. Gellius, *Noctes atticae* 20.1.12–13, 31–38, ed. Peter K. Marshall, vol. 2, Oxford 1968, reprinted 1990, 586, 589–590.

21 Justinian, *Digesta* 9.3.7, ed. Theodor Mommsen, vol. 1, Berlin 1870, 296: Gaius libro sexto ad edictum provinciale *Cum liberi hominis corpus ex eo, quod deiectum effusumve quid erit, laesum fuerit, iudex computat mercedes medicis praestitas ceteraque impendia, quae in curatione facta sunt, praeterea operarum, quibus caruit aut cariturus est ob id, quod inutilis factus est. cicatricium autem aut deformitatis nulla fit aestimatio, quia liberum corpus nullam recipit aestimationem.* See also *Digesta* 9.1.3, ibid. 277; Justinian, *Institutiones* 4.5.1, ed. Krüger, 145.

A passage in the *Digest* that is relevant for the wergild problem could perhaps signify something different.[22] The fragment stems from the lawyer Ulpian's (†223) second book on the *Edictum* of the *curulic Aedils*. It concerns the edict *de feris* (On wild animals).[23] The *Aedils* prohibit keeping wild animals on public streets (... *qua vulgo iter fiet* ... *where people are constantly passing* ...). When someone who is responsible for a wild animal violates this and a free person dies as a result, then the person responsible must pay a fine of 200 solidi! Here we have it: in the case of the killing of a free person, 200 s. must be paid (the standard wergild in the *leges*). But what is the legal construction in detail? It is not a matter of the *actio de pauperie* against the owner of a domestic animal,[24] which was the liability for damages caused by animals with the possibility of noxal surrender, *noxae deditio*. Unlike the latter, the *Aedilic* prohibition was

22 Justinian, *Digesta* 21.1.40–42, ed. Theodor Mommsen, Berlin 1899, 276: 40. Ulpianus libro secundo ad edictum aedilium curulium *hi enim non erunt separandi. Deinde aiunt aediles: 'ne quis canem, verrem vel minorem aprum, lupum, ursum, pantheram, leonem'* — 'For these should not be separated. Next, the Aediles say, 'That a dog, a hog, a small wild boar, a wolf, a bear, a panther, a lion'; 41. Paulus libro secundo ad edictum aedilium curulium *et generaliter 'aliudve quod noceret animal, sive soluta sint, sive alligata, ut contineri vinculis, quo minus damnum inferant, non possint.* — 'and, generally speaking, 'Or any other animal likely to commit injury, whether it be at large or tied, but incapable of being restrained so as not to cause damage'; 42. Ulpianus libro secundo ad edictum aedilium curulium *'qua vulgo iter fiet, ita habuisse velit, ut cuiquam nocere damnumve dare possit. si adversus ea factum erit et homo liber ex ea re perierit, solidi ducenti, si nocitum homini libero esse dicetur, quanti bonum aequum iudici videbitur, condemnetur, ceterarum rerum, quanti damnum datum factumve sit, dupli'* — 'Cannot be kept in a place where people are constantly passing, and where the said animal may injure anyone, or cause any damage. If these provisions should be violated, and a freeman lose his life in consequence, two hundred *solidi* shall be paid; and if a freeman should be injured, the party responsible shall have judgment rendered against him for a sum which may seem in the wisdom and justice of the judge to be proper; and where any other person or any property is injured, the said party shall be compelled to pay double the amount of the damage caused.' (*The Digest or Pandects of Justinian*. Translated by Samuel P. Scott, Cincinnati 1932).

23 Otto Lenel, *Palingenesia iuris civili* 2, Leipzig 1889, reprinted 1960, 898 (cited as Lenel, *Palingenesia* 2); Id., *Das Edictum perpetuum: Ein Versuch zu seiner Wiederherstellung*, Leipzig ^{3}1927, 566–567 (cited as Lenel, *Edictum*).

24 Max Kaser, *Das römische Privatrecht* 1, Munich ^{2}1971, 633; Ernst Levy, *Weströmisches Vulgarrecht: Das Obligationenrecht*, Weimar 1956, 348–350 (cited as Levy, *Obligationenrecht*); Lothar Müller, Art. 'pauperies', in: *Realencyclopädie der klassischen Altertumswissenschaft*, Supplement 10, Munich 1965, 521–529; Philipp Klausberger, 'Vom Tierdelikt zur Gefährdungshaftung: Überlegungen zur Haftungsstruktur bei der *actio de pauperie* und dem *edictum de feris*', *Teoria e Storia del Diritto Privato: rivista internationale on line* 4 (2011), 1–30 (cited as Klausberger, 'Tierdelikt').

intended to ensure the security of public streets and led to the strict liability of the animal keeper, enforceable through a penal suit (*actio poenalis*).[25]

The intricacies of legal construction need not be completely exhausted as to content in cases of appropriation processes. On the other hand, the obvious correlation — 'when a free person is killed, 200 solidi become due' — decreases when one takes into account that, originally, sesterces, perhaps some 200,000 of them, was stated.[26] The roots of wergild in Roman damages law is unlikely,[27] even if some influences, for example of the *actio de pauperie*, exist.[28]

As early as the sixth century, it was realized that no templates for wergild were to be found in the preserved Roman legal texts. In a remote version of Title 2 *De homicidiis* of the *Lex Romana Burgundionum*, one reads:

> *De interempti pretio principis est expectanda sententia. Quia de pretio occisorum nihil evidenter Lex Romana constituit, dominus noster Theodericus rex Francorum statuit observari* ... (On the price of a killed person the king's judgment is to be awaited. Since Roman law apparently had nothing fixed on the price of killed persons, our lord Theoderic, king of the Franks, decreed the following to be observed ...)[29]

Accordingly, the loss of half of one's assets, along with the obligation to render servile services for the victim's heirs, was ordered for the killing of a free person. The text's author explores the origins of wergild. He is looking for the *pretium* (price), primarily in the body of Roman law, and therefore has the conflicts of the Romans in mind. Furthermore, he naturally proceeds on the assumption that the payment of a *pretium* is an appropriate settlement for the offence and the loss of a person. His legal understanding is reflected in the fact that, for a determination of the *pretium*, a potential provision in the *Lex Romana* should be given priority over an authoritative ruling by the Frankish king, which was

25 Roland Wittmann, *Die Körperverletzung an Freien im klassischen römischen Recht*, Munich 1972, 74–75; Klausberger, 'Tierdelikt', 1–30.

26 Lenel, *Palingenesia* 2, 898; id., *Edictum*, 566–567.

27 The distinctive phrase: ... *qua vulgo iter fiet*, in Justinian, *Digesta* 21.1.42, ed. Mommsen, 615–616, was preserved in Justinian, *Institutiones* 4.5.1 and 4.9.1, ed. Krüger, 145, 158; *Lex Romana Visigothorum, Pauli Sententiae* 1.15.2, ed. Gustav Haenel, Leipzig 1849, reprinted 1962, 350: ... *qua populi iter est*, but both the liability according to the Edictum de feris and a 200 s. fine were lost. The same applies for *Lex Romana Burgundionum* 13.2, ed. Ludwig Rudolf von Salis, MGH LL nationum Germanicarum 2, 1, Hanover 1892, 137, which does after all speak of: ... *in viis publicis* ...; *Lex Burgundionum* 18.2, ibid. 56; *Lex Visigothorum* 8.4.17–18, ed. Karl Zeumer, MGH LL nationum Germanicarum 1, Hanover 1902, 336–339 with the general wergild taxes. Levy, *Obligationenrecht*, 341–342.

28 Levy, *Obligationenrecht*, 348–350.

29 *Lex Romana Burgundionum* 2.1 (version of the Codex Basiliensis C. III,1. XVI. saec.), ed. von Salis, MGH LL nat. Germ. 2, 1, 125.

only to be obtained in the case of the *Lex Romana*'s silence. A *consuetudo* (legal custom) or the involvement of other people to claim legitimacy and acceptance for the provision are not taken into account.

Previous considerations on the origins and potential reception of the relation of human life to money or material assets remain unsuccessful and are also methodologically problematic. The methodological caveat concerns the frequent expectation that the origins of a given phenomenon will also reveal its essentials, which is not necessarily the case. Changes over time, like the transformation of the respective phenomenon's function, are thus not perceived. Early cultures may have valued a relation between human beings and material assets in the form of goods that accrued to the bride's family in the case of marriage.[30] These values could reach the amount of wergilds.[31] However, theories on bride purchase and marriage-by-purchase are shaky.[32] Functionally, bride purchase is distinguished from wergild payment by the absence of an element of sanction. In search of earlier phenomena akin to wergild, there is a risk of alleging exactly what is to be proved by assuming processes of reception and appropriation. Assuming that the early *gentes* first became aware of and undertook the payment of wergild as a result of contact with other cultures, this is unlikely to have been immediately universally accepted. What kind of general mood would have to exist for people to say: 'a human life for 200 solidi, that is correct, fair, reasonable in every respect, and we shall adopt it'? The problem of acceptance should not be underestimated. Intellectually, acceptance may be given if e.g. a new legal rationale is recognized as the long-desired solution to a pending problem. Comparable phenomena alone are barely sufficient as proof of processes of reception and appropriation.

By focusing on the function of wergild instead of the origin, one might start with the conflict that is to be solved. The point of departure is the killing of a person. That signifies a disturbance of peaceful coexistence. Furthermore, an economic, emotional and mental loss occurs as well. In order to cope with this, a satisfactory resolution is sought. The *Formulae* and the well-known Feud of Sichar and Chramnesind show interventions undertaken by the church and eminent people in order to restore *pacis concordia* (the harmony of peace) by an arrangement between the involved parties.[33] On the one hand, the offence demanded a sanction that was not allowed to close the door on a bearable

30 Collection of material by Jacob Grimm, *Deutsche Rechtsaltertümer* 1, Leipzig [4]1899, 583–592.

31 *Aethelberht* 31, 77, *Ine* 31, ed. and trans. Felix Liebermann, *Die Gesetze der Angelsachsen* 1, Halle 1903, 5, 7, 103; *Lex Saxonum* 40, 49, ed. Claudius von Schwerin, MGH Fontes iuris Germanici in usum scholarum seperatim editi 4, Hanover 1918, 27–28, 30.

32 Friedmar Geißler, Art. 'Brautwerbung', in: *RGA* 3, Berlin and New York 1978, 423–424.

33 *Marculfi Formulae* 2.18, ed. Zeumer, MGH Formulae Merowingici et Karolini aevi, 88–89; The 'Feud of Sichar and Chramnesind': Gregory of Tours, *Decem Libri Historiarum*, 7.47;

coexistence. After all, the killing could concern not only intentional killings, but also slightly negligent acts in everyday life as well. On the other hand, the loss of a person had to be compensated. At all times, people probably sensed that the worth of an individual human being, with his or her variety of interpersonal relationships ranging from the emotional to the religious, could not be expressed in monetary terms. One might have compensated for this by forcing the perpetrator to serve as a substitute for the victim, for example, when a murderer took the victim's place, serving the man's parents as a replacement son. There is even evidence for this exact form of recompense.[34] However, self-surrender as a son could hardly have been the rule. There thus remains the loss of those services that the victim was to provide to the bereaved, to his relatives and *propinqui*, particularly welfare, protection and livelihood.

Such obligations can be estimated in money. In this case, the main focus is no longer the value of a human being, but rather the replacement of the loss of services and contributions of the killed person. Any disagreements that occurred in the attempt to place a value on the sanction and recompense were resolved by way of an agreement and with strong support from mediators who simultaneously served as witnesses to the reconciliation.[35] The generalization in the wergild tariffs of the *leges* intended to aid the affected parties in their attempt to come to a compromise without loss of reputation.

9.19, ed. Bruno Krusch and Wilhelm Levison, MGH SS rerum Merovingicarum 1, 1, Hanover 1951, 366–368, 432–434.

34 *Penitentialis Vinniani* c. 23, ed. Ludwig Bieler, *The Irish Penitentials*, Dublin 1963, 80, 82: *Si quis clericus homicidium fecerit et occiderit proximum suum et mortuus fuerit, .x. annis exterrem fieri de patria sua oportet et agat penitentiam vii annorum in alia urbe, tres ex his cum pane et aqua et sale per mensura et .iiii. abstineat se a uino et a carnibus et ieiunet xlmas cum pane et aqua et sal, et sic impletis .x. annis, si bene egerit et comprobatus fuerit testimonium abbatis siue sacerdotis cui commissus fuerit, recipiatur in patria sua et satis faciat amicis eius quem occiderat et uicem pietatis et oboedientie reddat patri et matri eius si adhuc in corpore sunt et dicat: 'Ecce ego uobis pro filio uestro; quecumque dixeritis mihi faciam.' Si autem non satis egerit, non recipiatur in aeternum.* — 'If any cleric commits murder and kills his neighbor and he is dead, he must become an exile for ten years and do penance seven years in another region. He shall do penance for three years of this time on an allowance of bread and water, and he shall fast three forty-day periods on an allowance of bread and water and for four years abstain from wine and meats; and having thus completed the ten years, if he has done well and is approved by testimonial of the abbot or priest to whom he was committed, he shall be received into his own country and make satisfaction to the friends of him whom he slew, and he shall render to his father or mother, if they are still in flesh, compensation for the filial piety and obedience [of the murdered man] and say: 'Lo, I will do for you whatever you ask, in the place of your son'. But if he has not done enough he shall not be received back forever.' (*Medieval Handbooks of Penance. A Translation of the principal Libri poenitentiales*. By John T. McNeill and Helena M. Gamer, New York 1938, 91). See also *Poenitentiale S. Columbani* B 1 and 13, ibid., 98, 102; Meens, *Penance*, 45–57.

35 See footnote 33 above.

Affiliated problems emerge from the relationship of the wergild amounts to the concrete material assets actually given. The amounts in the *leges* are mostly indicated in *solidi* and show a remarkable numerical consistency. The wergild of a free man totals around 200 s. everywhere, although up to 300 years separate the respective *leges*, and the economic conditions in Italy and on the North Sea coast differed as well. To be sure, there were adjustments in the coinage used for calculation in the Carolingian era, as the *Lex Frisionum* shows,[36] but even then, one concurrently calculated the fines in both *maiori* and *minori solidi* (apparently nominal coins worth three and only two *tremisses* respectively).[37] One should bear in mind that in the period during which the wergild for a free man was listed quite evenly at 200 s., a shift from the gold standard to the silver standard and a Carolingian coinage reform took place, while the goods-money relationship was also encountering significant fluctuation.[38] Correspondingly, the indication of 200 s. could result in very different material assets which had to be raised in payment. This was both prone to engender conflict and endangered the achievement of a satisfactory settlement between the affected parties. This becomes clear in the example of a catalogue of estimated material

36 See the details in *Lex Frisionum* Tit. 1 and 15, ed. K. A. Eckhardt and A. Eckhardt, MGH Fontes iuris 12, 34, 60.

37 *Lex Saxonum* 66, ed. Schwerin, MGH Fontes iuris 4, 33–34: *Solidus est dupplex: unus habet duo tremisses, quod est bos anniculus XII mensium vel ovis cum agno. Alter solidus III tremisses, id est bos XVI mensium; maiori solido aliae conposiciones, minori homicida conponuntur. Quadrimus bos duo solidi. Duo boves, quibus arari potest, V solidi. Bos bonus III solidi. Vacca cum vitulo solidi duo et semis. Vitulus anniculus solidus I. Ovis cum agno et anniculus agnus ei superadiunctus solidus I.* — 'There are two types of solidi: one has the value of two tremisses, that is of a one-year old ox of twelve months or a sheep with a lamb. The other solidus has the value of three tremisses, that is an ox of sixteen months. The solidus of minor value is used to compensate for homicide, the solidus of major value for other compositions. A four-year old ox is worth two solidi. Two oxen suitable for plowing are worth five solidi. A good ox three solidi. A cow with a calf two and a half solidi. A one-year old calf one solidus. A sheep with a lamb and with a one-year old lamb added one solidus' (trans. S.E.). See also *Capitulare* 39, c. 9; 134, c. 3; 135, c. 2, ed. Boretius, MGH Capit. 1, 114; 268; 269–270.

38 Sources and literature on this point: in *RGA* the articles: Peter Berghaus et al., 'Geld', in: *RGA* 10, Berlin and New York 1998, 616–636; Eckhard Meineke et al., 'Gold', in: *RGA* 12, Berlin and New York 1998, 304–312; Bernd Kluge, 'Karolingisches Münzwesen', in: *RGA* 16, Berlin and New York 2000, 314–317; Arent Pol, 'Merowingische Münzen', in: *RGA* 19, Berlin and New York 2001, 598–600; Harald Witthöft, 'Münzfuß', in: *RGA* 20, Berlin and New York 2002, 337–350; Stefan Krmnicek, 'Silbergeld', in: *RGA* 28, Berlin and New York 2005, 440–443; Jörg Jarnut and Jürgen Strohmann (ed.), *Die Merowingischen Monetarmünzen als Quelle zum Verständnis des 7. Jahrhunderts in Gallien* (Mittelalterstudien 27), Paderborn 2013; Waltraud Bleiber, *Naturalwirtschaft und Ware-Geld-Beziehungen zwischen Somme und Loire während des 7. Jahrhunderts*, Berlin 1981.

goods in *solidi* with which wergilds and fines were settled according to the *Lex Ribvaria*.[39] Louis the Pious later restricted the resulting practice since there were perjuries in cases of the concrete assessment of ceded hunting birds and swords.[40] The very fact that an oath was required regarding asserted values illustrates the importance of the matter. The settlement of a wergild payment had the potential to create new hostilities, although satisfaction was hoped for.

Detailed investigations that would allow for the appraisal of the real procedures are still lacking, particularly since the frequently-discussed Feud of Sichar and Chramnesind is a rather exceptional case.[41] Even the *Formulae* do not depict a genuine reality. Rather, they provide a prescient model for the composition of documents that record a formal homicide proceedings, including the compensation payment. Such documents, called *securitas*, were supposed to safeguard the perpetrator from any future claims from the victim's relatives.[42] The goal was a permanent pacification. Therefore, as a precaution, further claims were ruled out regarding both the killing and the compensation paid.[43] The manifest payments rendered and accepted in the process are only barely implied in the *Formulae*. The following are named: *argentum solidos tantos dedisti* (given so many silver solidi),[44] paid *leudis* (wergild),[45] material goods as *leudis ... quod eis bene conplacuit* (as wergild ... what pleases well)[46] or also only in pledge of a *solidi* amount.[47] It seems as if the homicide proceedings pursuant to the *securitas* formulae was not only intended to assess wergild, but also to ensure understanding and implementation of the specific payments to

39 *Lex Ribvaria* 40.11 (36.11), ed. Franz Beyerle and Rudolf Buchner, MGH LL nationum Germanicarum 3, 2, Hanover 1954, 94.

40 *Capitulare* 139, c. 8, ed. Boretius, MGH Capit. 1, 282. The mispriced *accipiter* mentioned here is not named in the *Lex Ribvaria* 40.11 (36.11), ed. Beyerle and Buchner, MGH LL nat. Germ. 3, 2, 94.

41 See footnotes 3 and 33 above.

42 *Marculfi Formulae* 2.18, ed. Zeumer, MGH Formulae Merowingici et Karolini aevi, 88–89, *Formulae Turonenses* 38, ibid. 156, *Cartae Senonicae* 11 and 51, ibid. 189, 207; *Formulae Salicae Bignonianae* 8 and 9, ibid. 230–231; *Formulae Salicae Merkelianae* 39, ibid. 256; *Formulae Salicae Lindenbrogianae* 19, ibid. 280.

43 *Formulae Salicae Bignonianae* 8 and 9, ed. Zeumer, MGH Formulae Merowingici et Karolini aevi, 230–231: *de ipsa leode nulla remalatione* (with no repeated prosecution concerning this wergild); just as *Formulae Salicae Merkelianae* 39, ibid. 256; *Formulae Salicae Lindenbrogianae* 19, ibid. 280: The *securitas* also guarantees, *si aliquis* [...] *de hac compositione remallare voluerit* (in case anyone ... intends to repeat prosecution concerning this composition).

44 *Formulae Turonenses* 38, ed. Zeumer, MGH Formulae Merowingici et Karolini aevi, 156.

45 *Cartae Senonicae* 11, ed. Zeumer, MGH Formulae Merowingici et Karolini aevi, 189.

46 *Cartae Senonicae* 51, ed. Zeumer, MGH Formulae Merowingici et Karolini aevi, 207.

47 *Marculfi Formulae* 2.18, ed. Zeumer, MGH Formulae Merowingici et Karolini aevi, 88–89.

be rendered. After the perpetrator's conviction, negotiations may thus have concentrated quite quickly not on abstract *solidi* amounts, but rather on real objects that were obtainable.

In terms of social history, it is above all the scaling of the wergilds according to status that is an important reference point for the structure of early medieval society. Occasionally, the rank of a person is explicitly characterized by wergild.[48] Despite the schematism, the gradation of wergilds, for example in the *Lex Francorum Chamavorum* of 600 s. for the *homo francus*, 200 s. for the *ingenuus*, 100 s. for the *lidus* and 50 s. for the *servus*, suggests insight into real circumstances, especially since similar gradations can be found in other *leges*.[49] However, it should give one pause that the wergilds follow a different regulatory intent. This becomes apparent if, in the same *lex*, other relations between the estates appear in the cases of injury tariffs and compurgators.[50] The lower wergild for Romans (living in the Frankish kingdoms) is also not a secure social indicator, particularly if it were also valid for the clergy.[51] Gregory of Tours refers to disputes between the Frankish aristocracy of the Merovingian period, yet it is common knowledge that the *Lex Salica* does not mention any aristocracy. What is more, the economic basis of this aristocracy is not discernible in the picture of Frankish everyday life sketched by the *Lex*, as if an aristocracy did not exist at all.[52] The *Lex Saxonum* gives the *nobilis* a remarkably high wergild, while the contemporaneous *Lex Frisionum* only sets the wergild of

48 *Marculfi Formulae* 1.18, ed. Zeumer, MGH Formulae Merowingici et Karolini aevi, 55; *Lex Frisionum* 6.2, ed. K. A. Eckhardt and A. Eckhardt, MGH Fontes iuris 12, 50.

49 *Lex Francorum Chamavorum* 3–6, ed. Karl August Eckhardt, *Lex Ribvaria II: Text und Lex Francorum Chamavorum* (Germanenrechte N.F., Westgermanisches Recht 6), Hanover et al. 1966, 89.

50 *Lex Francorum Chamavorum* 19, 21–23, ed. K. A. Eckhardt, 91. See also *Lex Burgundionum* 2.2 compared with 26, ed. Salis, MGH LL nat. Germ. 2, 1, 42, 63. On the missing synchronization of wergild levels and coniurators/compurgators *Lex Ribvaria* 7–11, ed. Beyerle and Buchner, MGH LL nat. Germ. 3, 2, 77–78.

51 *Pactus legis Salicae* 41.9, ed. Karl August Eckhardt, MGH LL nationum Germanicarum 4, 1, Hanover 1962, 157 gives the *Romanus possessor* a wergild of 100 s.; in accordance with *Lex Ribvaria* 40.3 (36.3), ed. Beyerle und Buchner, MGH LL nat. Germ. 3, 2, 92; on the wergild of *romani homines* in Raetien: '*Capitula Remedii*' c. 3, ed. Meyer-Marthaler, Die Rechtsquellen des Kantons Graubünden A,1: *Lex Romana Curiensis*, Aarau [2]1966, 646. The wergild of a *presbyter* according to *Lex Baiuvariorum* 1.9, ed. Ernst von Schwind, MGH LL nationum Germanicarum 5, 2, Hanover 1926, 280; of *solidos CCC auro adpretiatos* should be higher than that of the *genealogiae* Tit. 3, calculated in silver.

52 Harald Siems, 'La vie économique des Francs d'apres la *lex salica*', in: *Clovis, histoire et mémoire* 1, ed. Michel Rouche, Paris 1997, 607–630.

the *nobilis* at a third higher than that of the *liber*.[53] Were the circumstances in the neighboring territories really so different? The earlier *leges* lack wergilds for clerics. Only later do the Ripuarian, Alemannic and Bavarian laws cover graduated wergilds for clerics according to their hierarchical classification.[54] The elevation of secular functionaries by increased wergilds is similarly patchy in the *leges*. In the Frankish laws *graphio*, *iudex* and *comes* are protected by a threefold wergild.[55] In Bavarian and Alemannic law the tasks of *comes* and *iudex* are detailed indeed but — like in other *leges* — their specific wergild is not given.[56] Apparently, by means of the graduated wergilds, the *leges* do not want to reflect the complexity of society with its functionaries and holders of power. This complicates the question concerning to what extent wergild were supposed to reflect social reality.

The problem of the assumed addressees which the wergild regulations supposed, has apparently not yet been examined. In the literature one encounters arbitrary assumptions as to affordability: it is said that the amounts of money are so high that almost no one would have been able to raise them; or, one imagines that it was definitely possible with the help of relatives. 'Imaginations' of social networks for the provision of wergilds based on assumptions of this sort remain unsure.[57] According to the catalogue of the *Lex Ribvaria*, material assets in the amount of 100 oxen or 33 decorated helmets or 66 swords without sheaths would have been required for a wergild of 200 s.[58] The poor devil in the *Chrenecruda* proceeding, who cannot raise the wergild even with the help of his *proximi* (next of kin) and thus loses his life, was not really without

---

53 *Lex Saxonum* 14, ed. Schwerin, MGH Fontes iuris 4, 21; *Lex Frisionum* 1.1–3, ed. K. A. Eckhardt and A. Eckhardt, MGH Fontes iuris 12, 34.

54 *Lex Ribvaria* 40.5–9 (36.5–9), ed. Beyerle and Buchner, MGH LL nat. Germ. 3, 2, 93–94; *Lex Alamannorum* 11–15, ed. Karl August Eckhardt, MGH LL nationum Germanicarum 5, 1, Hanover ²1966, 76–79; *Lex Baiuvariorum* 1.8–10, ed. Schwind, MGH LL nat. Germ. 5, 2, 278–283; *Lex Salica*, D-Manuscripts 78, E-Manuscripts 77, ed. K. A. Eckhardt, MGH LL nat. Germ. 4, 2, 124–126.

55 *Pactus legis Salicae* 54, ed. K. A. Eckhardt, MGH LL nat. Germ. 4, 1, 203; *Lex Ribvaria* 54 (53), ed. Beyerle and Buchner, MGH LL nat. Germ. 3, 2, 103; *Lex Francorum Chamavorum* 7, ed. K. A. Eckhardt, 89. — Wergilds graduated according to function are named in the *Capitula Remedii* 3, ed. E. Meyer-Marthaler, 646.

56 *Lex Baiuvariorum* 2.5, 2.14–18, 9.17–20, ed. Schwind, MGH LL nat. Germ. 5, 2, 297–299, 307–311, 380–383; *Lex Alamannorum* 28.2, 36, 41, 81 (84), ed. K. A. Eckhardt, MGH LL nat. Germ. 5, 1, 87, 94–97, 100–102, 145–147. — Yet, special wergilds are lacking for *comes* and *iudex*. The same is true for Burgundian, Lombard, Saxon, Frisian and Thuringian law.

57 Stefan Esders, 'Wergeld und soziale Netzwerke im Frankenreich', in: *Verwandtschaft, Name und soziale Ordnung (300–1000)*, ed. Steffen Patzold and Karl Ubl (Ergänzungsbände zum Reallexikon der germanischen Altertumskunde 90), Berlin et al. 2014, 141–159.

58 See footnote 39 above.

means, since he did have property.[59] His situation adds to the economically tough circumstances of the *Lex Salica*.[60] It was even worse for those vagabonds from far away, who roved about in the forest without blowing a horn. King Ine of Wessex allows his subjects to kill such vagabonds, but also allows for the vagabonds to ransom themselves.[61] The concession seems an insincere mockery, since how was such an uprooted person supposed to raise the necessary resources in an honest way in the first place? Charlemagne's worries that such bandits would be summarily executed without any proceedings whatsoever were likely more realistic.[62] We are well acquainted with significant assets from the Merovingian testaments,[63] and one can reasonably assume that considerable funds at the disposal of those families were involved in the feud of Sichar and Chramnesind.[64] However, both parties seem to show little interest in a settlement via compensation payment. In the end, in order to create peace, the bishop paid the half wergild that the judges imposed on Sichar. Sichar and Chramnesind each expected the dispute to be settled in their favour respectively, not via a court decision and compensation payment.

Rather, they capitalized on their relationship with the Merovingian court, where they already had contacts with the interest groups surrounding the king and queen. Receiving wergild was also welcome in these circles, but one did not let oneself be domesticated in terms of power interests as a result. The editors of the *Lex Salica* could have had that constraint in mind when they overlooked the nobility in composing the *Lex*. The question of who was imagined as the addressee in each case when compensation and wergild norms were being conceived therefore becomes all the more pressing. Without more specific reference points for the intended effects, a measure for assessing effectiveness is lacking.

All the same, the system of wergilds and fines shows some superiority with respect to other forms of legal consequences. In addition to the dominant compensation function of the wergilds, their significant amount also had

59 *Pactus legis Salicae* 58, ed. K. A. Eckhardt, MGH LL nat. Germ. 4, 1, 218–221.

60 See footnote 51 above.

61 *Ine* 20, ed. Liebermann, vol. 1, 99; see also *Wihtraed* 28, ibid. 28; *Das Rechtsbuch des Frostothings* 40, ed. Rudolf Meißner, Germanenrechte 4, Weimar 1939, 83.

62 *Capitulare* 52, a. 808, c. 2, ed. Boretius, MGH Capit. 1, 139.

63 Margarete Weidemann, *Das Testament des Bischofs Berthramn von Le Mans vom 27. März 616: Untersuchungen zu Besitz und Geschichte einer fränkischen Familie im 6. und 7. Jahrhundert*, Mainz 1986.

64 See footnote 33 above; for literature see footnote 3 above; Philippe Depreux, 'Une faide exemplaire? A propos des aventures de Sichaire: vengeance at pacification aux temps mérovingiens', in: *La vengeance 400–1200* (Collection de l'École française de Rome 357), ed. Dominique Barthélemy, François Bougard and Régine Le Jan, Rome 2006, 65–85.

a sanction effect, so that both elements of the offence, the wrong itself and the tort, were taken into account. The payment of wergild as the result of a homicide appears to fundamentally correspond to the legal possibilities and the necessities of justice of the time. In contrast, the death penalty,[65] corporal punishment,[66] prison, and exile were considerable repercussions for the perpetrator, and one might hope that any of these would serve as enough of a deterrent. However, they had no effect on the loss adjustment for the victim and could even make compensation more difficult to attain. Therefore, the obligation to pay compensation was required in addition to any corporal punishment or imprisonment.[67] Simple monetary fines that were to be directed to the king himself rather than the victim also function accordingly. Feuds, understood as private wars between victim and perpetrator, do not provide satisfaction; only, at best, the willingness to reach a settlement due to exhaustion. It was already a common notion in the ancient world, that such pressure may evoke a willingness to communicate.[68] The respective wergild tariffs of the *leges* provided orientation for this kind of enforced conflict solution. However, the king's efforts to contain feuds wind their way through the entire early Middle Ages.[69]

The wergild amounts become the central measure in the composition system. Injury tariffs were fractions of wergild, especially in cases of major damages, and in the case of multiple injuries, total compensation could not exceed the wergild.[70] In addition, the wergild becomes an independent parameter for gauging fiscal fines paid to the king as a sanction of thievery, without connection to the victim and the damages incurred, and thus is entirely oriented on the perpetrator.[71]

---

65 *Pactus pro tenore pacis* 1 and 2, ed. Boretius, MGH Capit. 1, 4–5; *Decretio Childeberti* 5, ed. Wilhelm Alfred Eckhardt, *ZRG GA* 84 (1976), 38; *Edictus Rothari* 1.3–7, ed. Bluhme, MGH LL 4, 13.

66 *Liutprand* 80, ed. Bluhme, MGH LL 4, 139–140.

67 Ibid.

68 A. Gellius, *Noctes atticae* 20.1.31–38, ed. Marshall, vol. 2, 589–590; *Lex Saxonum* 18, ed. Schwerin, MGH Fontes iuris 4, 22.

69 *Lex Visigothorum* 6.1.8, ed. Zeumer, MGH LL nat. Germ. 1, 256; *Lex Burgundionum* 2.7, ed. Salis, MGH LL nat. Germ. 2, 1, 43; *Edictus Rothari* 45, 74, 75, 138, 143, 162, 326, 387, ed. Bluhme, MGH LL 4, 20, 23–24, 31–32, 37, 75, 90; *Liutprand* 13, 119, 135, ibid. 112, 156–157, 166; *Lex Frisionum*, Additio 1, ed. K. A. Eckhardt and A. Eckhardt, MGH Fontes iuris 12, 80; *Lex Saxonum* 19, ed. Schwerin, MGH Fontes iuris 4, 23; *Capitulare* 20, c. 22; 33, c. 32; 44, c. 5; 139, c. 13, ed. Boretius, MGH Capit. 1, 51; 97; 123; 284.

70 *Lex Frisionum*, Additio 3.58 (Addendum for West Friesland), ed. K. A. Eckhardt and A. Eckhardt, MGH Fontes iuris 12, 94.

71 *Lex Frisionum* 3.3, ed. K. A. Eckhardt and A. Eckhardt, MGH Fontes iuris 12, 44: *Thiubda. […] et ad partem regis pro fredo weregildum suum.* — Theft. […] and for the king's part as peace money his wergild.

The wergild is also a trusted unit in aspects of life other than homicide atonement. In the particular case of a donation to the Abbey of Fulda, it was agreed that the heir could repurchase the goods for two wergilds.[72] Military obligations are linked to minimum assets, usually measured by the number of manorial holdings (*mansi*). In 866, however, Louis II names a man's own wergild as the lower limit for movable assets required for the respective man's military duty.[73]

General fine increases,[74] special high fines, for example for women,[75] and combination with corporal punishments, incarceration and the death penalty were intended increase the efficiency of the wergild and composition system in regards to the inclusion of particular previously uncompensated effects of an offense, general crime prevention and hindrance of feuds.[76] An additional fiscal fine, for example the *fredus* ('peace money'), which was to be paid to the king, appears to have been common. This involvement of the king changes the assessment of the offence through to the legal proceedings. The adjustment of the settlement process was no longer the responsibility of the perpetrator and victim with bilateral procedure, as shown in the *securitas* formulae, in which there is no talk of a fine payable to the king.[77] The payment of a fine to the king turns the offence and its consequences into a matter of public concern. In addition to serving fiscal interests, the payment is made public and unconscionable acts against the weak are prevented. Even the *Lex Burgundionum* and the *Pactus pro tenore pacis* forbid a theft's clandestine atonement, *occulte sine iudice* (secretly without a judge).[78]

The perpetrator wergild required new legitimation, and its imposition was structurally even more serious.[79] The victim wergild, which has been the topic of this paper up until now, is justified as compensation for the loss of a person. This does not apply with regard to the perpetrator wergild. It may be related to the ransom of the perpetrator's forfeited life, a notion that was conceivable

72 *Urkundenbuch des Klosters Fulda*, No. 176, a. 788, ed. Edmund Stengel, vol. 1, Marburg 1958, 269–270.

73 *Capitulare* 218, a. 866, c. 1, ed. Alfred Boretius and Viktor Krause, MGH Capitularia regum Francorum 2, Hanover 1897, 94–95; see footnote 13.

74 *Edictus Rothari* 74, ed. Bluhme, MGH LL 4, 23–24.

75 *Edictus Rothari* 200–201, ed. Bluhme, MGH LL 4, 49–50; see also c. 14 *De morth*, ibid. 15.

76 *Liutprand* 80, ed. Bluhme, MGH LL 4, 139–140.

77 See footnote 42 above.

78 *Pactus pro tenore pacis* 3, ed. Boretius, MGH Capit. 1, 5; *Lex Burgundionum* 71, ed. Salis, MGH LL nat. Germ. 2, 1, 96.

79 Philippe Depreux, 'Wergeld, composition et rachat dans le capitulaires des rois francs', in: *La victime: II. La réparation du dommage*, ed. Jacqueline Hoareau-Dodinau, Guillaume Métairie and Pascal Texier, Limoges 2009, 345–362.

early on.[80] In essence, the following basic principle again comes into effect: wergild in place of an inherently priceless human life. Certainly, however, there is a significant shift. The victim wergild is determined based on the concept of *compensation* as regards the loss of services that would have been provided by the killed person. When it comes to perpetrator wergild, the element of *sanction* shifts to the foreground.[81] This new focus enables an expansion of the protection of legal rights to include community interests for whose violation, like for example in cases of treason, there was no directly injured party in terms of the composition system.[82] As early as the *Decretio Childeberti,* the payment of perpetrator wergild was imposed for a breach of the royal ban.[83] Since the prestige and interests of victims do not present any obstacles, a new legal development towards further scopes of protection could emerge. The consideration of the gravity of the offense, and even the chance of pardon, became possible.

Already very early on, a juxtaposition of legal consequences emerges. The victim and compensation-oriented wergild and composition system dominate the *leges*, and the relevance is reflected in their overwhelming manuscript dissemination. At the same time, and often blending with the former, there are other sanctions, all of whose development hints at proximity to the king: death penalties and corporal punishment, perpetrator wergild, and fiscal fines.[84] In order to avoid the hardships of corporal punishments, offenders who had confessed would ask for the privilege of paying wergild instead. Letters detailing the intervention of important dignitaries attest to this,[85] church asylum

80 *Pactus pro tenore pacis* 1 and 2, ed. Boretius, MGH Capit. 1, 4–5; *Liutprand* 20, ed. Bluhme, MGH LL 4, 117; *Lex Frisionum*, Additio 1.3, ed. K. A. Eckhardt and A. Eckhardt, MGH Fontes iuris 12, 80.

81 *Liutprand* 135, ed. Bluhme, MGH LL 4, 166. It is not the violation of honour for a woman whose clothes were stolen while she was bathing that must be atoned for, since the wergild that must be paid in that case is not based upon her status, but rather upon the status of the perpetrator. Liutprand's threat of punishment is intended to prevent acts of feud that could potentially ensue from the humiliation of the woman.

82 *Edictus Rothari* 4, ed. Bluhme, MGH LL 4, 13; *Lex Baiuvariorum* 2.1, ed. Schwind, MGH LL nat. Germ. 5, 2, 291–293.

83 *Decretio Childeberti* 5, ed. W. A. Eckhardt, 38.

84 *Liutprand* 80, ed. Bluhme, MGH LL 4, 139–140.

85 Einhard, *Epistolae* 48 and 49, ed. Karl Hampe, MGH EE 5, 133–134: [...] *ut eis liceat solvere illum weregildum pro fratre suo* — 'They ask that they be allowed to pay the proper wergild for their brother'; 49: *ut indulta membrorum integritate verberumque pena liceat illi solutione pecuniae componere atque emendare* — 'I pray your holiness to deign to spare him ..., and remitting punishment in limb and by scourging, to allow him by a payment of money to compound and repair' (*Carolingian Civilization. A Reader*, ed. by Paul Edward Dutton, Peterborough/Ontario 1993, 304); *Formulae Salicae Bigonianae* 23, ed. Zeumer,

provides the opportunity for relevant negotiations, and some imminent death penalties are redeemable. However, the tendency was to enforce death penalties, as the possibility of redemption was restricted to the *parentes*[86] or was even prohibited for them in cases of punishment, *ut qui noverit occidere discat morire*.[87] An aggravated sentence could also occur when one's own wergild must be paid in order to redeem a forfeited hand.[88]

The limited efficiency and deficits of the wergild system are the consequences of its orientation towards compensation for actual damages and limitation of judicial conciliation to the victim and perpetrator sides. It revolves around strict liability (*Erfolgshaftung*). If there was no damage, there was nothing to compensate for. If an injury or some sort of damage occurred that was not guided by an impulse requiring sanction, a need for compensation between the involved parties still remains. This applies to compensation in the case of an unintentional offense,[89] as well as for a killing in self-defense.[90] Alemannic law follows strict liability and grants the relatives of a victim killed by a dog the full wergild, but decrees that the dog must be hung over their door until it decomposes.[91] To avoid this, the injured party had to forgo half the wergild. When strict liability seemed inappropriate in cases of accident, a humiliating ordinance forced the injured party to withdraw their right to full pecuniary compensation. In principle, the *misericordia* (mercy) lends itself to the alleviation of strict liability. In accordance with psalm 100, one claims *primum quidem iudicium postea misericordia* (first judgment, and mercy later on).[92] Extralegal categories are intended to correct the severities of the wergild system.

MGH Formulae Merowingici et Karolini aevi, 236; *Formulae Salzburgenses* 64, ibid. 454; *Collectio Pataviensis* 2, ibid. 457.

86 *Pactus pro tenore pacis* 2, ed. Boretius, MGH Capit. 1, 4–5.

87 *Decretio Childeberti* 5, ed. W. A. Eckhardt, 38; *Laws of the Salian and Ripuarian Franks*. Translated with an Introduction by Theodore John Rivers, New York 1986, 146: '[…] that [he] who knows how to kill should learn how to die.'

88 *Lex Frisionum* 10, ed. K. A. Eckhardt and A. Eckhardt, MGH Fontes iuris 12, 52.

89 *Edictus Rothari* 387, ed. Bluhme, MGH LL 4, 90; *Lex Ribvaria* 73 (70), ed. Beyerle and Buchner, MGH LL nat. Germ. 3, 2, 124; *Ælfred* 19.3, 36, ed. Liebermann, 60–61, 68–69.

90 *Liutprand* 20, ed. Bluhme, MGH LL 4, 117.

91 *Pactus Alamannorum* 28.2, ed. Karl Lehmann, MGH LL nationum Germanicarum 5, 1, Hanover ²1966, 31.

92 *Concilium Ascheimense* a. 756, c. 12, ed. Albert Werminghoff, MGH Concilia 2, 1, Hanover 1906, 58; Isidore of Seville, *Sententiae* 3.52.4, ed. Pierre Cazier, CCSL 111, Turnhout 1998, 305: *per iustitiam reddet peccati sententiam, per misericordiam peccati temperat poena* — 'by justice he renders his judgment on the sin, by mercy he mitigates the punishment for the sin.' Taken up by Alcuin, *De virtutibus et vitiis* 20, ed. Jacques-Paul Migne, PL 101, Paris 1863, 628; *Capitulare* 40, a. 803, c. 13, ed. Boretius, MGH Capit. 1, 116.

The composition system's concern with accomplished facts causes seemingly insurmountable difficulties when it comes to punishing attempt. Without the successful fulfilment of a crime or violation, there is no injury or damages needing to be compensated. Only in isolated incidents are preparations for crimes set aside as distinct offenses, like for example plotting against the life of the king, which was punishable by death and confiscation.[93]

Another deficit of the composition system results from the standardization of the compensation tariffs, which are not capable of accounting for individual damages or particularly reprehensible methods. A poisoning was therefore atoned for through wergild, exactly like any other homicide.[94] Subsequent legal developments attempted to include distinct characteristics of an injury. King Rothari, for example, endeavored to incorporate aggravated damages, like lasting injury.[95] His compensation of doctor's fees and absenteeism could be based on Roman legal example.[96] The more intense suffering of the one-eyed man whose only eye was plucked had a higher fine than otherwise.[97] Similarly, Frisian law reinforced the protection of specialized craftsmen.[98] The *Lex Baiuvariorum* doubled the fines for injuries done to draft animals when the injuries occurred out of *inimicitia* (enmity).[99] These cases remain infrequent and did not become principles that led to a complete overhaul of the composition system. The incorporation of special misconduct by the perpetrator in the settlement remained an exception to the functioning of the law. This also concerns repeat offenses. The amount of the wergild to be paid did not change for repeat offenders. Corporal punishment for repeat offenders were the norm only in isolated cases.[100]

The final shortcoming of the wergild system was for offenses involving several parties. If a number of people committed homicide, only the death of one person needed to be compensated. The Lombards remain firm in this

---

93 *Edictus Rothari* 1, ed. Bluhme, MGH LL 4, 13; *Lex Baiuvariorum* 2.1, ed. Schwind, MGH LL nat. Germ. 5, 2, 291–293.

94 *Pactus legis Salicae* 19.1, ed. K. A. Eckhardt, MGH LL nat. Germ. 4, 1, 81; *Edictus Rothari* 141, ed. Bluhme, MGH LL 4, 32.

95 *Edictus Rothari* 112 and 127, ed. Bluhme, MGH LL 4, 28 and 30.

96 *Edictus Rothari* 128, ed. Bluhme, MGH LL 4, 30. In addition see Justinian, *Institutiones* 4.5.1, ed. Krüger, 145; *Digesta* 9.1.3, 9.3.7, ed. Mommsen, vol. 1, 277, 296. *Leges Longobardorum cum argutissimis glosis Caroli de Tocco*, Venice 1537, fol. 16rb; see footnote 20.

97 *Edictus Rothari* 377, ed. Bluhme, MGH LL 4, 87–88.

98 *Lex Frisionum, Iuditia Wlemars* 10 and 11 (taken from *Lex Thuringorum* Tit. VI), ed. K. A. Eckhardt and A. Eckhardt, MGH Fontes iuris 12, 90, 92.

99 *Lex Baiuvariorum* 14.16, ed. Schwind, MGH LL nat. Germ. 5, 2, 419.

100 *Liutprand* 80, ed. Bluhme, MGH LL 4, 139–140; '*Capitula Remedii*' 4, 7, 8, ed. Meyer-Marthaler, *Lex Romana Curiensis*, 647–648; *Capitulare* 20, a. 779, c. 12, 23, ed. Boretius, MGH Capit. 1, 9, 51.

assessment and permitted perpetrators to raise the wergild together.[101] This practice reduces the deterrence factor but increases the chance that the necessary sum could be reached. There were some attempted remedies to this issue. In the case of an uprising against the duke, the Bavarian *Lex* made a distinction between the leading perpetrator and those *qui secuti sunt* (who followed).[102] The graded fines could then surpass even a duke's wergild.[103] The management of the problem is particularly remarkable in the *Lex Frisionum*. In the case of a homicide committed *in turba* (in a riot), different elaborate proceedings are provided in the three parts of the country in order to fix on one single perpetrator out of all the involved parties, even though the offense took place *in turba populi* (in a riot of the people).[104] A downright capitulation in face of the problem of multiple accomplices can be found in the *Lex Frisionum*, Title II *Forresni*.[105] It concerns a case in which someone does not kill the intended victim himself, but rather causes the victim to be killed by another (*ad occidendum exposuerit*, literally: exposes to be killed). Nothing is said about the relationship between killer and *expositor*. An alternative consequence is determined: if the killer flees the country, then the *expositor* pays one third of the wergild. If the perpetrator does not flee, then the *expositor* does not have to pay anything, probably because the perpetrator was responsible for raising the wergild. The need to sanction the *expositor* is therefore taken into account in the sense that he is *faidosus* (threatened with feud) and *inimicitias propinquorum hominis occisi patiatur, donec quomodo potuerit, eorum amicitiam adipiscatur* (shall bear the enmity of the killed man's relatives, until he manages to win their friendship). The payment of a *fredus* fine to the king would also have made sense. However, the threat of imminent feud was the basis chosen to force reconciliation, relying upon the regulatory force of private compensation between the involved parties. In this case where the composition system lacked a solution, the threat of otherwise constrained feud was the legal basis for sanction.[106] Lombard law, with its selective provision *cessante faida*, sug-

101 *Edictus Rothari* 12, ed. Bluhme, MGH LL 4, 14.

102 *Lex Baiuvariorum* 2.3, ed. Schwind, MGH LL nat. Germ. 5, 2, 294.

103 *Lex Baiuvariorum* 3, ed. Schwind, MGH LL nat. Germ. 5, 2, 314, the wergild of the duke amounts to 960 s.

104 *Lex Frisionum* 14, ed. K. A. Eckhardt and A. Eckhardt, MGH Fontes iuris 12, 56–60.

105 *Lex Frisionum* 2.1 and 2, ed. K. A. Eckhardt and A. Eckhardt, MGH Fontes iuris 12, 38: 1. *Si nobilis nobilem per ingenium alio homini ad occidendum exposuerit, et is qui eum occidit patria relicta profugerit, qui eum exposuit tertiam partem leudis comp(onat). 2. Si vero homicida non fugerit, nihil solvat, sed tantum inimicitias propinquorum hominis occisi patiatur, donec quomodo potuerit eorum amicitiam adipiscatur.*

106 *Lex Frisionum*, Additio 1.1, ed. K. A. Eckhardt and A. Eckhardt, MGH Fontes iuris 12, 80 and as a matter of principle, footnote 69 above.

gests the threat of feud may lurk behind the wergild system as a method of enforcement to meet contemporaries' sense of justice.[107]

In place of a succession of systems of legal consequences, from blood feud to wergild and fines and then again followed by public punishments, a complex picture of simultaneous and different reactions to offences in the Early Middles Ages emerges. The various sources provide their own perspectives and stimuli in regards to anticipated and enacted wrongs: narratives tell of private extreme acts of violence being triggered, letters contain requests for exemption from corporal punishments, administrative ordinances demand the building of dungeons,[108] charter formulae are supposed to secure the final establishment of peace after a homicide, royal edicts establish death penalties, but also their commutability, and the *leges* solidify an itemized composition system arranged around the wergild and supplemented by fiscal fines. These phenomena cannot be treated separately. Even the *leges*, which dominate the picture because of their substantial manuscript dissemination, show in their juxtaposition the diversity of answers to offences at the time and seek a general pacification between compensation and sanction. Be that as it may, a relationship of rules and exceptions according to the legal consequences (if there had even ever been such a relationship) cannot be determined, as there are not enough sources to substantiate the claim. Even the apparent semblance of reality of a specific petition letter leaves open whether just anyone could hope for the intercession of a bishop. Irrespective of how many material goods a compensation was actually 'paid' with, the meaning of wergild as a central orienting factor of early medieval law emerges from its position in the composition system, in the redemption of corporal punishments, in the perpetrator wergild, and from its ability to serve as a neutral reference point enabling negotiations on compensation payments that did not lead to the loss of reputation for any of the involved parties. However it arose, 'wergild' was indispensable.

Bibliography

Primary Sources

A. Gellius, *Noctes atticae*, ed. Peter K. Marshall, 2 vols., Oxford 1968, reprinted 1990.

Alcuin, *De virtutibus et vitiis*, ed. Jacques-Paul Migne, PL 101, Paris 1863, 613–638.

107 *Edictus Rothari* 45, 75, 138, 362, ed. Bluhme, MGH LL 4, 20, 24, 31, 75.

108 *Liutprand* 80, ed. Bluhme, MGH LL 4, 139–140; *Capitulare* 77, a. 801–813, c. 11, ed. Boretius, MGH Capit. 1, 171.

Capitularia regnum Francorum 1, ed. Alfred Boretius, MGH Capitularia regnum Francorum 1, Hanover 1883.

Capitularia regnum Francorum 2, ed. Alfred Boretius and Viktor Krause, MGH Capitularia regnum Francorum 2, Hanover 1897.

Concilia aevi Karolini [*742–842*], ed. Albert Werminghoff, MGH Concilia 2, Hanover 1906–1908, reprinted 1997–2003.

Das Rechtsbuch des Frostothings, ed. Rudolf Meißner, Germanenrechte 4, Weimar 1939.

'Die Decretio Childeberti und ihre Überlieferung', ed. Wilhelm Alfred Eckhardt, *ZRG GA* 84 (1976), 1–71.

Die Gesetze der Angelsachsen, ed. Felix Liebermann, 3 vols., Halle 1903–1916.

Epistolae Karolini aevi (III), ed. Ernst Dümmler, Karl Hampe et al., MGH EE (in Quart) 5, Hanover 1898.

Formulae Merowinigici et Karolini aevi, ed. Karl Zeumer, MGH Formulae Merowinigici et Karolini aevi, Hanover 1886.

Gaius, *Institutiones*, ed. Ulrich Manthe, Darmstadt 2004.

Gai Institutiones or Institutes of Roman Law by Gaius. With a Translation and Commentary by Edward Poste and E. A. Whittuck, Oxford 1904.

Gregory of Tours, *Decem Libri Historiarum*, ed. Bruno Krusch and Wilhelm Levison, MGH SS rerum Merovingicarum 1, 1, Hanover 1951.

Huguccio, *Derivationes*, ed. Enzo Cecchini, Florence 2004.

Isidore of Seville, *Sententiae*, ed. Pierre Cazier, CCSL 111, Turnhout 1998.

Justinian, *Digesta*, ed. Theodor Mommsen, Berlin 1899.

Justinian, *Institutiones*, ed. Paul Krüger, Berlin ^{4}1921.

Laws of the Salian and Ripuarian Franks. Translated with an Introduction by Theodore John Rivers, New York 1986.

Leges Alamannorum, ed. Karl August Eckhardt, MGH LL nationum Germanicarum 5, 1, Hanover ^{2}1966.

Leges Burgundionum, ed. Ludwig Rudolf von Salis, MGH LL nationum Germanicarum 2, 1, Hanover 1892.

Leges Langobardorum, ed. Friedrich Bluhme and Alfred Boretius, MGH LL (in Folio) 4, Hanover 1868.

Leges Saxonum und Lex Thuringorum, ed. Claudius von Schwerin, MGH Fontes iuris Germanici antiqui in usum scholarum separatim editi 4, Hanover 1918.

Leges Visigothorum, ed. Karl Zeumer, MGH LL nationum Germanicarum 1, Hanover 1902.

Lex Baiwariorum, ed. Ernst von Schwind, MGH LL nationum Germanicarum 5, 2, Hanover 1926.

Lex Frisionum, ed. Karl August Eckhardt and Albrecht Eckhardt, MGH Fontes iuris Germanici antiqui in usum scholarum separatim editi 12, Hanover 1982.

Lex Ribvaria II: Text und Lex Francorum Chamavorum, ed. Karl August Eckhardt, Germanenrechte N. F., Westgermanisches Recht, Hanover 1966.

Lex Ribvaria, ed. Franz Beyerle and Rudolf Buchner, MGH LL nationum Germanicarum 3, 2, Hanover 1954, reprinted 1997.

Lex Romana Curiensis, ed. Elisabeth Meyer-Marthaler, Die Rechtsquellen des Kantons Graubünden A,1: Lex Romana Curiensis, Aarau ²1966.

Lex Romana Visigothorum, ed. Gustav Haenel, Leipzig 1849, reprinted 1962.

Lex Salica, ed. Karl August Eckhart, MGH LL nationum Germanicarum 4, 2, Hanover 1969.

Medieval Handbooks of Penance. A Translation of the principal Libri poenitentiales. By John T. McNeill and Helena M. Gamer, New York 1938.

P. Cornelius Tacitus, *Germania*, ed. Allan Lund, Heidelberg 1988.

Pactus Alamannorum, ed. Karl Lehmann, Leges Alamannorum, MGH LL nationum Germanicarum 5, 1, Hanover 1888, 21–33.

Pactus legis Salicae, ed. Karl August Eckhardt, MGH LL nationum Germanicarum 4, 1, Hanover 1962.

Sextus Pompeius Festus, *De verborum significatu quae supersunt cum Pauli epitome*, ed. Wallace Martin Lindsay, Leipzig 1913.

The Digest or Pandects of Justinian. Translated by Samuel P. Scott, Cincinnati 1932.

The Formularies of Angers and Marculf. Two Merowingian Legal Handbooks. Translated with an introduction and notes by Alice Rio (Liverpool Translated Texts for Historians 46), Liverpool 2008.

The Irish Penitentials, ed. Ludwig Bieler, Dublin 1963.

The Lombard Laws. Translated with an introduction by Katherine Fischer Drew, Philadelphia 1973.

Urkundenbuch des Klosters Fulda, ed. Edmund Stengel, vol. 1, Marburg 1958.

Secondary Works

v. Amira, Karl, *Die germanischen Todesstrafen: Untersuchungen zur Rechts- und Religionsgeschichte*, Munich 1922.

Bernoth, Carsten, *Die Fehde des Sichar*, Baden-Baden 2008.

Beyerle, Franz, *Das Entwicklungsproblem im germanischen Rechtsgang: 1. Sühne, Rache und Preisgabe in ihrer Beziehung zum Strafprozeß der Volksrechte*, Heidelberg 1915.

Bleiber, Waltraud, *Naturalwirtschaft und Ware-Geld-Beziehungen zwischen Somme und Loire während des 7. Jahrhunderts*, Berlin 1981.

Böttcher, Hartmut, Art. 'Blutrache', in: *RGA* 3, Berlin and New York 1978, 85–101.

Brunner, Heinrich, *Deutsche Rechtsgeschichte*, vol. 1, Berlin ²1906, vol. 2., ed. Claudius Freiherr von Schwerin, Berlin et al. 1928.

Depreux, Philippe, 'Une faide exemplaire? A propos des aventures de Sichaire: vengeance et pacification aux temps mérovingiens', in: *La vengeance 400–1200*

(Collection de l'École française de Rome 357), ed. Dominique Barthélemy, François Bougard and Régine Le Jan, Rome 2006, 65–85.

Depreux, Philippe, 'Wergeld, composition et rachat dans les capitulaires des rois francs', in: *La victime: II. La réparation du dommage*, ed. Jacqueline Hoareau-Dodinau, Guillaume Métairie and Pascal Texier, Limoges 2009, 345–362.

Esders, Stefan, '"Eliten" und "Strafrecht" im frühen Mittelalter: Überlegungen zu den Bußen- und Wergeldkatalogen der *Leges barbarorum*', in: *Théorie et pratiques des élites au Haut Moyen Age. Conception, perception et réalisation sociale* (Collection Haut Moyen Age 13), ed. François Bougard, Hans-Werner Goetz and Régine Le Jan, Turnhout 2011, 261–282.

Esders, Stefan, 'Wergeld und soziale Netzwerke im Frankenreich', in: *Verwandtschaft, Name und soziale Ordnung (300–1000)*, ed. Steffen Patzold and Karl Ubl, Berlin et al. 2014, 141–159.

Geißler, Friedmar, Art. 'Brautwerbung', in: *RGA* 3, Berlin and New York 1978, 423–424.

Goebel, Julius, *Felony and Misdemeanor*, New York 1937.

Grimm, Jacob, *Deutsche Rechtsaltertümer*, Leipzig [4]1899.

Jarnut, Jörg and Jürgen Strohmann, *Die Merowingischen Monetarmünzen als Quelle zum Verständnis des 7. Jahrhunderts in Gallien*, Paderborn 2013.

Kaser, Max, *Das römische Privatrecht* 1, Munich [2]1971.

Klausberger, Philipp, 'Vom Tierdelikt zur Gefährdungshaftung: Überlegungen zur Haftungsstruktur bei der *actio de pauperie* und dem *edictum de feris*', in: *Teoria e Storia del Diritto Privato: rivista internationale on line* 4 (2011), 1–30.

Kluge, Friedrich and Seebold, Elmar, *Etymologisches Wörterbuch der deutschen Sprache*, Strasbourg [23]1999.

Kroeschell, Karl, 'Germanisches Recht als Forschungsproblem', in: *Festschrift für Hans Thieme zu seinem 80. Geburtstag*, ed. Karl Kroeschell, Sigmaringen 1986, 3–19.

Lade, Ulrike, *Flur und Feld: Volkssprachige Bezeichnungen in den frühmittelalterlichen Leges*, Muenster 1986.

Lenel, Otto, *Das Edictum perpetuum: Ein Versuch zu seiner Wiederherstellung*, Leipzig [3]1927, reprinted 1956.

Lenel, Otto, *Palingenesia iuris civili* 2, Leipzig 1889, reprinted 1960.

Levy, Ernst, *Weströmisches Vulgarrecht: Das Obligationenrecht*, Weimar 1956.

Meens, Rob, *Penance in Medieval Europe 600–1200*, Cambridge 2014.

Moeglin, Jean-Marie, 'Le "droit de vengeance" chez les historiens du droit au Moyen Âge (XIXe–XXe siècles)', in: *La vengeance 400–1200* (Collection de l'École française de Rome 357), ed. Dominique Barthélemy, François Bougard and Régine Le Jan, Rome 2006, 101–148.

Müller, Lothar, Art. 'pauperies', *Realencyclopädie der classischen Altertumswissenschaft*, Supplement 10, 521–529.

Nehlsen, Hermann, 'Der Grabfrevel in den germanischen Rechtsaufzeichnungen', in: *Zum Grabfrevel in vor- und frühgeschichtlicher Zeit*, ed. Herbert Jankuhn, Hermann Nehlsen and Helmuth Roth, Göttingen 1978, 3–19.

Nehlsen, Hermann, 'Reaktionsformen der Gesellschaft auf Verletzung und Gefährdung von Gemeinschaftsinteressen in Spätantike und frühem Mittelalter bei den germanischen Stämmen. Ein Beitrag zur Strafrechtsgeschichte', in: *Das Recht und seine historischen Grundlagen: Festschrift für Elmar Wadle zum 70. Geburtstag*, ed. Tiziana Chiusi, Thomas Gergen and Heike Jung, Berlin 2008, 759–781.

Schlosser, Hans and Willoweit, Dietmar, *Neue Wege strafrechtsgeschichtlicher Forschung* (Konflikt, Verbrechen und Sanktion in der Gesellschaft Alteuropas: Symposien und Synthesen 2), Cologne 1999.

Schröbler, Ingeborg, 'Langobardisch-deutsches Glossar', in: *Die Gesetze der Langobarden*, ed. Franz Beyerle, Weimar 1947, 501–502.

Schumann, Eva, Art. 'Kompositionensystem', in: *HRG* 2, Berlin ^{2}2012, col. 2003–2011.

Siems, Harald, 'La vie économique des Francs d'après la *lex salica*', in: *Clovis, histoire et mémoire*, ed. Michel Rouche, vol. 1, Paris 1997, 607–630.

Van der Rhee, Florus, *Die germanischen Wörter in den langobardischen Gesetzen*, Rotterdam 1970.

Vogel, Cyrille, 'Composition légale et commutations dans le système de la pénitence tarifée', *Revue de droit canonique* 8 (1958), 289–318; 9 (1959), 1–38, 341–359.

Weidemann, Margarete, *Das Testament des Bischofs Berthramn von Le Mans vom 27. März 616: Untersuchungen zu Besitz und Geschichte einer fränkischen Familie im 6. und 7. Jahrhundert*, Mainz 1986.

Weitzel, Jürgen (ed.), *Hoheitliches Strafen in der Spätantike und im frühen Mittelalter* (Konflikt, Verbrechen und Sanktion in der Gesellschaft Alteuropas: Symposien und Synthesen 7), Cologne et al. 2002.

Weitzel, Jürgen, 'Der Strafgedanke im frühen Mittelalter', in: *Der Strafgedanke in seiner historischen Entwicklung: Ringvorlesung zur Strafrechtsgeschichte und Strafrechtsphilosophie*, ed. Eric Hilgendorf and Jürgen Weitzel, Berlin 2007, 21–35.

Weitzel, Jürgen, 'Strafe und Strafverfahren in der Merowingerzeit', *ZRG GA* 111 (1994), 66–147.

Wilda, Wilhelm Eduard, *Das Strafrecht der Germanen*, Halle 1842.

Willoweit, Dietmar, *Die Entstehung des öffentlichen Strafrechts* (Konflikt, Verbrechen und Sanktion in der Gesellschaft Alteuropas: Symposien und Synthesen 1), Cologne et al. 1999.

Wittman, Roland, *Die Körperverletzung an Freien im klassischen römischen Recht*, Munich 1972.

CHAPTER 3

Monetary Fines, Penalties and Compensations in Late Antiquity

Ralph W. Mathisen

Late Roman imperial attempts to regulate civil and criminal activities created a whole taxonomy of punishments for criminal acts, some of which involved confiscating the material wealth of malefactors. There were *multationes* or *multae*, or fines that consisted either of a fixed amount of money, a piece of property, or so many times the value of a piece of property under adjudication. Or *exilium*, of which there were two forms, *deportatio*, which also included loss of civil rights and confiscation of property, and *relegatio*, which did not. Or 'proscription,' that is, *proscriptio* or *publicatio bonorum*, the confiscation of property. And finally, *damnatio capitis*, execution, which in some cases was accompanied by confiscation and could not be imposed by governors but only by the emperor.

A dizzying number of late Roman laws imposed fines of so many pounds of gold or silver upon high-ranking officials and their office staffs for a multitude of infractions.[1] Most are preserved in the Theodosian Code and the Code of Justinian, although a few survive elsewhere, such as an edict of Anastasius (491–518) inscribed in a Byzantine fort at Qasr al-Hallabat (Jordan) fining *praesides* 20 pounds of gold and their office staffs 30 pounds for failure to deal with legal cases in a timely manner.[2]

But there is not much evidence that these exorbitant fines, ranging from 20 to 100 pounds of gold, ever were enforced: a rare example of such a penalty supposedly being implemented was a joke, when Ammianus related that after

1 E.g., Klaus Rosen, 'Iudex Kollektivstrafe, Kontrolle und Effizienz in der spätantiken Provinzialverwaltung', *Ancient Society* 21 (1990), 273–292, here 288–292; Chantal Vogler, *Constance II et l'administration impériale*, Strasbourg 1979, 254–257; Christopher Kelly, *Ruling the Later Roman Empire*, Cambridge, Massachusetts 2004, 143–144, 209–210; Karl L. Noethlichs, *Beamtentum und Dienstvergehen: zur Staatsverwaltung in der Spätantike*, Wiesbaden 1981, 223–225; also Roger C. Blockley, 'Internal Self-Policing in the Late Roman Administration: Some Evidence from Ammianus Marcellinus', *Classica et Medievalia* 30 (1969), 403–419, here 403–405, 414–416.

2 Enno Littmann, David Magie and Duane R. Stuart (ed.), *Syria: Publications of the Princeton University Archaeological Expeditions to Syria, in 1904–5 and 1909*, Leiden 1921, Div. III, Sec. A, 24–42.

 | DOI:10.1163/9789004466128_004

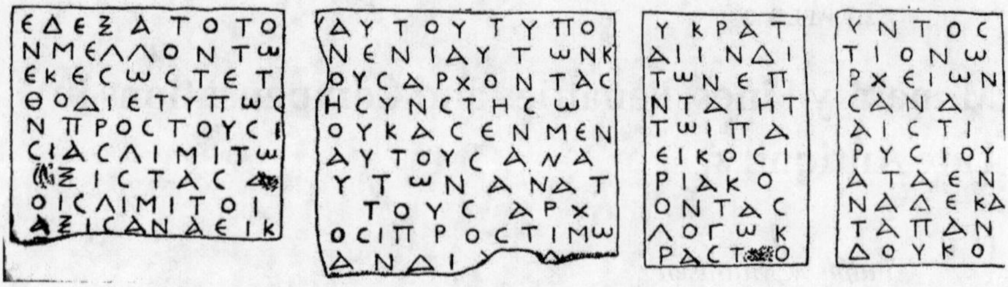

FIGURE 3.1 A section of an otherwise unknown law of Anastasius establishing fines for failing to deal with legal cases expeditiously
SOURCE: LITTMANN, MAGIE, STUART, *SYRIA*, 24–42

the emperor Julian mistakenly pronounced the words to free slaves during Mamertinus' assumption of the consulate on 1 January 362, he 'fined himself ten pounds of gold for usurping another's jurisdiction.'[3] The concern in this study, however, is to concentrate on fines and confiscations involving not public officials but private persons, a topic that has received exceptionally little attention in the scholarship.[4]

1 Private Persons and the State

In some cases, *privati* could be fined for interfering with the imperial administration. A constitution of 410 decreed that if a person attempted to transfer his tax payments from one territory to another, the office staff of the Praetorian Prefect was fined 100 pounds of gold and the guilty party 20 pounds of gold.[5] In

3 *Ammiani Marcellini Rerum gestarum libri qui supersunt* 22.7.2, ed. Wolfgang Seyfarth, Bibliotheca scriptorum Graecorum et Romanorum Teubneriana, Leipzig 1978 (cited as Amm.): *Dein Mamertino ludos edente circenses, manu mittendis ex more inductis per admissionum proximum, ipse lege agi dixerat, ut solebat, statimque admonitus iuris dictionem eo die ad alterum pertinere, ut errato obnoxium decem libris auri semet ipse multavit.*

4 Many lengthy discussions of Roman law fail to mention confiscations and fines; see Otto Karlowa, *Römische Rechtsgeschichte I., Staatsrecht und Rechtsquellen,* Leipzig 1885; Max Kaser, *Das altrömische ius,* Göttingen 1949, 53–63 on 'Ius in der Strafrechtspflege' concerns only the Republic and has nothing on exile or confiscation; Max Kaser, *Römische Rechtsgeschichte,* Göttingen 1950. And the 32 columns in *RE*, Manfred Fuhrmann, Art. 'Publicatio bonorum', *RE* 23 (1959) 2498–2516, includes only a single column on the late empire.

5 *Theodosiani libri XVI cum constitutionibus Sirmondianis et leges novellae ad Theodosianum pertinentes* 11.22.5 (410), ed. Theodor Mommsen and Paul M. Meyer, Berlin 1905 (cited as *CTh*): *Centum librarum auri multa ferietur, sed et singuli, qui nequaquam prohibitis temperabunt, viginti librarum auri dispendia sustinebunt.*

this case, moreover, we see a manifestation of a general policy of fining imperial officials much more severely than private persons.

Other laws forbade expansions of rural *patrocinium*, the end result of which were to defraud the fisc and impede the performance of required munera. An eastern ruling of 399 fined persons ranging from Masters of Soldiers down to *curiales* and 'anyone of another rank' 40 pounds of gold for each infraction, unless they immediately ceased; and double the established fine was inflicted on any who fled to *patrocinium* 'for the sake of defrauding the exchequer.'[6] A law of 396, moreover, fined anyone who lured a Roman soldier into private service 5 pounds of gold; a subsequent law of only two years later raised the ante to 20 pounds of gold, suggesting how unsuccessful this measure must have been.[7] In a law of the next year, those who had their cases heard in military as opposed to civil courts were sentenced to deportation; their lawyers were fined ten pounds of gold.[8] Other laws tried to deal with the problem of persons who illegally attempted to usurp rank and dignity. One of 383 fined those who usurped greater rank than they were due 20 pounds of gold, but when that ruling apparently did not succeed, a law of 397 raised the stakes by imposing the joint penalties of *publicatio bonorum* and deportation.[9]

A large number of laws attempted to enforce Roman pro-Christian agendas. A constitution of 392, for example, imposed a fine of 20 pounds of gold on anyone who carried out pagan sacrifices in a temple or a fanum on private land; in the latter case, the owner of the land suffered a similar penalty if he/she knew what was going on. In addition, this law also illustrates the policy of

6 *CTh* 11.24.4 (399), ed. Mommsen and Meyer: *Quadraginta librarum auri se sciat dispendium pro singulorum fundorum praebito patrocinio subiturum* [...] *qui clientelam susceperint rusticorum, sed eos quoque, qui fraudandorum tributorum causa ad patrocinia solita fraude confugerint, duplum definitae multae dispendium subituros*; also *CTh* 11.24.2 (370), ed. Mommsen and Meyer: *Viginti et quinque auri libras dare debeant et non quantum patroni suscipere consuerant, sed dimidium eius fiscus adsumat.*

7 *CTh* 7.1.15 (396), ed. Mommsen and Meyer: *Si quis posthac militem in privato obsequio repertus fuerit retinere, quinque libras auri multae nomine feriatur*; *CTh* 7.1.17 (398), ed. Mommsen and Meyer: *Si qui miles* [...] *repertus fuerit vel sibi vacans vel alieno obsequio contentus, nobis ilico nuntietur, ita ut conscii, qui talium praesentiam non praebuerint, viginti libras auri sciant esse se multandos.*

8 *CTh* 2.1.9 (397), ed. Mommsen and Meyer: *Si quis* [...] *ad militare iudicium crediderit deferendam, praeter poenas ante promulgatas intelligat* [...] *advocatum eius decem librarum auri condemnatione feriendum.*

9 *CTh* 6.22.7 (383), ed. Mommsen and Meyer: *Si quis neglexerit ordinem constitutum vel amplius in hisdem honorariis dignitatibus usurpandum impetrandumque crediderit* [...] *sciat* [...] *viginti quoque auri libris multandum*; CTh 9.26.1 (397), ed. Mommsen and Meyer: *Si quis ad illustrem palatii nostri ambierit dignitatem atque ad eos honores ascendere ambitione temptaverit* [...] *amissis bonis et fisco nostro protinus vindicatis deportationis multetur exilio.*

confiscating to the fisc only the property associated with the crime, in much the same way as personal property associated with drug related crimes in the U.S. and Canada likewise is confiscated.[10] And persons who used anti-pagan legislation as a cover for ransacking public buildings were punished with the rather light fine of only two pounds of gold — perhaps a slap on the wrist compared to the value of the building materials being looted.[11] Anti-Jewish legislation likewise imposed financial penalties. An eastern law of 423, for example, executed and confiscated the property of a Jew who circumcised a Christian.[12] This ruling is one of the very few such laws that is cited in a historical source, in this case Sozomen: 'The Jews were strictly forbidden to purchase a slave belonging to any other heresy than their own. If they transgressed this law, the slave was confiscated to the public; but if they administered to him the Jewish rite of circumcision, the penalties were death and total confiscation of property.'[13]

Anti-heretic legislation was even more extensive. An eastern law of 428 presented a list of violations that were punished by fines and a multitude of other penalties.[14] A person who became a heretical cleric and the person who per-

---

10 *CTh* 16.10.12 (392), ed. Mommsen and Meyer: *Si quis* [...] *vanas imagines* [...] *plena religionis iniuria honorare temptaverit, is utpote violatae religionis reus ea domo seu possessione multabitur, in qua eum gentilicia constiterit superstitione famulatum. namque omnia loca, quae turis constiterit vapore fumasse* [...] *fisco nostro adsocianda censemus. sin vero in templis fanisve publicis aut in aedibus agrisve alienis tale quispiam sacrificandi genus exercere temptaverit, si ignorante domino usurpata constiterit, viginti quinque libras auri multae nomine cogetur inferre.* For drug charges and asset forfeiture, see Leonard Williams Levy, *A License to Steal: The Forfeiture of Property*, Chapel Hill 1996.

11 *CTh* 16.10.15 (399), ed. Mommsen and Meyer: *Sicut sacrificia prohibemus, ita volumus publicorum operum ornamenta servari. si illicitis evectiones aut suo aut alieno nomine potuerint demonstrare, quas oblatas ad nos mitti decernimus. qui vero talibus cursum praebuerint, binas auri libras inferre cogantur.*

12 *CTh* 16.8.26 (423), ed. Mommsen and Meyer: *Iudaei et bonorum proscriptione et perpetuo exilio damnabuntur, si nostrae fidei hominem circumcidisse eos vel circumcidendum mandasse constiterit.*

13 Sozomenos, *Historia ecclesiastica* 3.9, ed. Günther C. Hansen, Fontes Christiani 73, Turnhout 2004.

14 *CTh* 16.5.65 (428), ed. Mommsen and Meyer: *Dein ut, si alios sibi adiungant clericos vel, ut ipsi aestimant, sacerdotes, decem librarum auri multa per singulos ab eo, qui fecerit et qui fieri passus sit vel, si paupertatem praetendant, de communi clericorum eiusdem superstitionis corpore vel etiam donariis ipsis extorta nostro inferatur aerario*[...] *cunctisque legibus*[...] *valituris* [...] *sive de privatis aedificiis, in quae domino permittente vel conivente convenerint, venerandae nobis catholicae vindicandis ecclesiae, sive de procuratore, qui hoc nesciente domino fecerit, decem librarum auri multam vel exilium, si sit ingenuus, subituro, metallum vero post verbera, si servilis condicionis sit*[...] *Nulli haereticorum danda licentia vel ingenuos vel servos proprios* [...] *ad suum rursus baptisma deducendi*[...] *quod qui fecerit*

mitted this to happen both were fined 10 pounds of gold; if they pled poverty, then the fine was imposed on the heretical clergy or church. Private buildings used for heretical purposes were confiscated to the orthodox church, and the person who had permitted this was fined 10 pounds of gold and exiled if free born or sent to the mines after receiving a good whipping if a slave. Someone who permitted heretical baptisms was sentenced to a fine of 10 pounds of gold, exile, and loss of civil rights. And a western law of 408 fined each of the *decemprimi* of a *civitas* the princely sum of 2 pounds of gold if they colluded in permitting a defrocked clergyman to refrain from re-assuming his curial duties.[15]

2 Private Matters

Still other laws involved purely private matters. These fines tended to be even smaller. A law of 386, for example, set a fine of a mere 6 ounces of gold (that is, 36 solidi) for anyone who made off with someone else's *colonus*.[16] Other laws dealt with the appropriation of someone else's land. In 386, in a simple case of illegal seizure the only penalty was the return of what had been seized, but in the case where trustees attempted to appropriate the property of their charges, something that threatened the very foundations of Roman law, the penalty was much more severe: eternal exile and *publicatio bonorum*.[17]

---

vel, cum sit ingenuus [...] *exilio ac decem librarum auri multa damnabitur, testamenti et donationis faciendae utrique deneganda licentia.*

15 *CTh* 16.2.39 (408), ed. Mommsen and Meyer: *Quemcumque clericum indignum officio suo episcopus iudicaverit et ab ecclesiae ministerio segregaverit* [...] *ut liber illi ultra ad ecclesiam recursus esse non possit, et pro hominum qualitate et quantitate patrimonii vel ordini suo vel collegio civitatis adiungatur* [...] *per singulos igitur binae librae auri inferendae aerario nostro a decemprimis curialibus exigantur, si aliquibus illicitam conniventiam et colludia foeda praestiterint, hominibusque improbissimis ab omnibus officiis militiae aditus obstruatur.* Cf. *CTh* 16.5.40 (407), ed. Mommsen and Meyer, regarding officials who delayed punishing heretics: *Rector provinciae, si haec crimina dissimulatione vel gratia delata distulerit aut convicta neglexerit, sciat se multa viginti librarum auri feriendum. defensores quoque et principales urbium singularum nec non et officia provincialia decem librarum auri poena constringet.*

16 *CTh* 5.17.2 (386), ed. Mommsen and Meyer: *Quisquis colonum iuris alieni aut sollicitatione susceperit aut occultatione celaverit, pro eo, qui privatus erit, sex auri uncias, pro eo, qui patrimonialis, libram auri cogatur inferre.*

17 *CTh* 4.22.2 (386), ed. Mommsen and Meyer: *Quisquis* [...] *possessorem quietum dominio suo huiusmodi terrore turbaverit, ea in perpetuum lite mulctetur quam praeoccupaverit violentia*[...] *si autem, habito plerumque colludio, curatores vel tutores minorum his rem debitam ea occasione pervadant* [...] *reddatur curatores autem vel tutores aeterna deportatione punitos bonorum quoque publicatio persequatur.*

FIGURE 3.2 A solidus issued in the name of the Caesar Crispus ca. 320 CE celebrates a victory over the Franks as 'the joy of the Romans'
SOURCE: HTTP://WWW.ROMANCOINS.INFO/VIC-HISTORICAL2.HTML

Other laws attempted to restrict the victimization of the disadvantaged. Some attempted to protect the poor from forced 'voluntary contributions' on special occasions. For example, a law of 364 attempted to protect the 'tenuiores' and 'pauperes' from enforced contributions of New Year's *sportulae*: provincial governors who allowed this to happen were fined 20 pounds of gold and their office staffs 40 pounds.[18] A similar law of 383 protected 'miserable persons' from forced contributions as the 'price of the joys' that resulted from imperial victories, the same 'joys' that were reflected on imperial victory coinage. Officials and their office staffs who did so in 'shameful collusion' were fined 30 pounds of gold.[19]

Even the rights of unfortunate prisoners were protected. A western law of 409 specified that every Sunday governors were to see to it that prisoners were queried regarding whether they had enough to eat and were escorted to the baths. Governors and their staffs who failed in this were fined 20 pounds of gold each, and the local curia was fined 3 pounds of gold. The bishop, moreover,

18 *CTh* 8.11.1 (364), ed. Mommsen and Meyer: *Quod quidem interdicti severitate fieri vetamus in posterum, ut rectores provinciarum vicenis auri libris, porro officia quadragenis constituamus esse multanda, si quicquam pauperes hac adscriptione praebuerint vel his extorqueri quicquam passi fuerint.*

19 *CTh* 8.11.4 (383), ed. Mommsen and Meyer: *Iudices statuimus esse sollicitos, ne turpi colludio quaeratur ex miseris pretium gaudiorum. quod si id sacrilega fuerit dissimulatione violatum, et accipientem pudoris fortunarumque manebit excidium et cogentem par poena multabit et officium triginta librarum auri vexatione quatiatur.*

was appointed to keep an eye on the governor.[20] And a law of 409 specified that persons taken captive by barbarians but subsequently returned were to have their full rights of *postliminium*, which entailed a restoration of their property and their civil rights. Plebeians who interfered with this regulation suffered deportation along with condemnation to the mines and a good whipping, whereas property owners suffered deportation and *publicatio bonorum*. Provincial governors and their staffs who neglected to enforce the regulation were fined 10 pounds of gold, and Christians were commanded to take care of the physical needs of the ex-captives.[21]

3 Legal Principles: Types and Levels of Punishment

The assessment of punishments was based on the social and economic status of the culprit. The allocation of punishments for the very same offense could involve the implicit distinction between *honestiores* and *humiliories*, or, in the case of monetary penalties, could simply be based on the person's ability to pay. For example, a law of 412 granted governors blanket authority to punish persons who took advantage of shipwrecked sailors and shipowners with fines, exile, and confiscation of property, 'according to their rank and status.'[22] As a general principle, *humiliores* and the poor were sent to the mines, whereas propertied persons suffered confiscation or a fine. In a law of 365, the punishment for harboring a deserter was condemnation *ad metallum* for those of 'plebeian and humbler status' and confiscation of half of the property of a

20 *CTh* 9.3.7 (409), ed. Mommsen and Meyer: *Iudices omnibus dominicis diebus productos reos e custodia carcerali videant et interrogent, ne his humanitas clausis* [...] *negetur. victualem substantiam non habentibus faciant ministrari* [...] *mulcta iudicibus viginti librarum auri et officiis eorum eiusdem ponderis constituta, ordinibus quoque trium librarum auri mulcta proposita, si saluberrime statuta contempserint. nec deerit antistitum christianae religionis cura laudabilis, quae ad observationem constituti iudicis hanc ingerat monitionem.*

21 *CTh* 5.7.2 (409), ed. Mommsen and Meyer: *Si quis itaque huic praecepto fuerit conatus obsistere actor, conductor procuratorque, dari se metallis cum poena deportationis non ambigat; si vero possessionis dominus, rem suam fisco noverit vindicandam seque deportandum. Et ut facilis exsecutio proveniat, Christianos proximorum locorum volumus huius rei sollicitudinem gerere*[...] *ita ut noverint rectores universi, decem libras auri a se et tantundem a suis apparitionibus exigendum.*

22 *CTh* 13.9.6 (412), ed. Mommsen and Meyer: *De submersis navibus decernimus, ut levato velo istae causae cognoscantur. et si quisquam de talibus negotiis aliquid accepisse detegitur, iudex, aput quem constiterit, his conquerentibus qui nudantur pro qualitatibus personarum multandi removendi proscribendi habeat potestatem.*

person 'of any superior rank and status.'[23] This must have had little effect, for in 380 another ruling confiscated the property where the deserter had hidden and sentenced the person who had concealed him to be burned alive.[24] And yet another law, of 383, was even more specific about the nature of the status differences in such cases. If a person harboring a deserter on their property 'was able to undergo corporeal punishment,' his property was preserved but he was given a good beating and sent to work in the mines, with the possibility of being sentenced to permanent *relegatio*. But if the malefactor was 'of the sort that he was exempted from corporeal punishment out of regard for his rank or status,' then he was required either to provide 10 army recruits or pay 50 pounds of gold. In addition, the person who had actually provided the hiding place was sentenced *to damnatio capitis*.[25]

There could be detailed levels of payment based on one's rank and position. In 405, those who attempted to move into residences owned by the *res privata* were fined 20 pounds of gold if they 'possessed any rank or wealth,' but were sent into exile if they 'were of more humble means.' Vicars who permitted this were fined 30 pounds of gold, governors were fined 20 and sacked, and curiales were threatened with some unspecified future condemnation.[26] And a western law of 412 provided a graduated scale of penalties for those who remained

23 *CTh* 7.18.1 (365), ed. Mommsen and Meyer: *Unusquisque, apud quem desertor fuerit deprehensus, si plebeiae et humilioris condicionis est, metalli se sciat supplicio puniendum, qui autem superioris cuiuscumque loci dignitatisve sit, media se bonorum parte cognoscat esse multandum.*

24 *CTh* 7.18.4 (380): *Si quis latebram praebuerit desertori, possessionis, in qua latuerit, amissione multatus etiam graviorem sententiam pertimescat. porro actorem flammis subiciendum esse non dubitet, qui in perniciem fortasse domini aut sceleris participatione confovit aut dissimulatione neglexit.*

25 *CTh* 7.18.8 (383), ed. Mommsen and Meyer: *Quisquis desertorem vel a se receptum vel in suo latitantem cognoscit* [...] *pro qualitate ordinis atque personae incurrat in legem. et si quidem potuerit corporali iniuriae subiacere, servata ex iure substantia et fustibus coerceatur vel metallo operi publico deputetur et nonnumquam se ulterius erigente censura exilio perpetuae relegationis plectatur. quod si eiusmodi fortasse fuerit, ut iniuria corporali intuitu generis aut honoris excipiatur* [...] *denos iuniores maxime idoneos militiae offerat aut quinquaginta pondo argenti restituat. Quod si procurator possessionis sive actor vel etiam colonus latebram desertori domino ignorante praestiterit, detectus in crimine capitali supplicio mancipetur.*

26 *CTh* 7.10.1 (405), ed. Mommsen and Meyer: *Nulli manendi intra palatia nostra in qualibet civitate vel mansione facultas pateat*[...] *Quod nisi omni instantia fuerit observatum, triginta libras a vicariis, XX a consularibus seu praesidibus totidemque ab eorum officiis multae nomine profligentur, ita ut ne curiales quidem a condemnatione se cognoscant inmunes futuros. Ii quoque, qui huiusmodi sibi mansionem prava temeritate praesumpserint, si vel dignitate aliqua vel fortunis nituntur, XX librarum auri condemnationi subiaceant: qui humilioris fortunae sunt, exilio tradantur.*

Donatists: 50 pounds of gold for *inlustres*, 40 for *spectabiles*, 30 for senators and for priests, 20 for *clarissimi*, and 5 for decurions, merchants, and plebeians, and so on down to *Circumcelliones*, who got off with only 10 pounds of silver.[27]

4 Specific Examples

So far, the discussion of confiscations only has involved legal theory, that is, what the government wanted to happen. We have yet to look at any actual examples of confiscations. Along with the multitudes of generic penalties assessed for potential misdeeds, under the heading 'Concerning the Property of Proscribed and Condemned Persons,'[28] the Theodosian Code cites a few marquee instances of confiscation of the property of particular individuals that provide examples of the problems the government encountered when trying to round up confiscated properties, such as private persons who appropriated confiscated property, as seen in the cases of Rufinus, Gildo, a certain Marcharidus, and Stilicho.

After the murder of the eastern Praetorian Prefect Rufinus in 395, for example, the government ordered his property to be left intact and not to be spontaneously seized by private persons. But rather than setting a specific penalty, the law merely threatened violators with 'a more weighty confiscation and the risk of losing all their property.'[29]

In the west, five constitutions relating to the confiscation in 398 of the property of the North African rebel Gildo exemplify well the kinds of problems that could arise. A law of 400 set a fine of five pounds of gold for anyone who entered an estate confiscated from Gildo or one of his *satellites* 'for the purpose of being quartered.'[30] This ruling, however, was insufficient. Nine years later another law stated,

27 *CTh* 16.5.52 (412), ed. Mommsen and Meyer: *Illustres singillatim poenae nomine fisco nostro auri pondo quinquaginta cogantur inferre, spectabiles auri pondo quadraginta, senatores auri pondo triginta, clarissimi auri pondo viginti, sacerdotales auri pondo triginta, principales auri pondo viginti, decuriones auri pondo quinque, negotiatores auri pondo quinque, plebei auri pondo quinque, circumcelliones argenti pondo decem.*

28 *CTh* 9.42, ed. Mommsen and Meyer: *De bonis proscriptorum seu damnatorum.*

29 *CTh* 9.42.14 (396), ed. Mommsen and Meyer: *Commonemus, ut ea, quae Rufinus quondam, cum viveret, quoquo pacto possedit, in eodem statu interim maneant nec quisquam sibi post eius obitum spontaneam vindicandi tribuat potestatem[...] hoc [...] praecipimus divulgari, quo cuncti sciant iacturam se perpessuros graviorem totiusque rei familiaris periculum, nisi [...] ab his, quae Rfinus vivus possederat, voluerint abstinere.*

30 *CTh* 7.8.7 (400), ed. Mommsen and Meyer: *Praedia ex Gildonis hostis publici et satellitum eius bonis sociata domui nostrae ne transeuntes hospitii gratia intrent, decernimus, ut sciant*

> Although we recently ordered that the estates of Gildo were to be free from quartering, with a fine of 5 pounds of gold, we now again command that if anyone acts contrary to this order, let the fine inflicted earlier be assessed.[31]

One might well suppose that the second law had just as much success as the first. On top of this, a constitution of 405 decreed that estates appropriated from the property of Gildo and the produce therefrom both were to be doubly restored.[32] And a ruling of 408 reiterated the early statement that the *satellites* of Gildo were to be remanded into custody and their property confiscated.[33]

Meanwhile, a ruling of 401 discusses one of the dodges used by persons about to be proscribed. A certain Marcharidus, probably one of the aforementioned *satellites* of Gildo, had transferred his property to other persons during the course of his trial, and the government ordered it to be returned, threating violators with *publicatio bonorum* and deportation.[34] And two laws of 408 dealt with the fallout from the murder of the western Master of Soldiers Stilicho: one ordered the return of property of his that had been stolen — without, however, even establishing a penalty for those who failed to do so — and another denied any claims from persons who had entrusted their own property to the 'public enemy.'[35]

An interesting twist on the management of monetary penalties is provided by the case of Chronopius, an otherwise unknown bishop who was deposed in

---

omnes a possessoribus nostris penitus abstinendum, quinque auri libras multae nomine inferre cogendo, quisquis praedium nostrum manendi causa importunus intraverit.

31 *CTh* 7.8.9 (409), ed. Mommsen and Meyer: *Licet proxime iusserimus quinque librarum auri condemnatione proposita praedia, quae ex Gildonis bonis ad nostrum aerarium delata sunt, ab hospitibus excusari, nunc etiam praecipimus*[...] *si quis igitur contra nostram fecerit iussionem, multa pridem ferietur inflicta.*

32 *CTh* 9.42.19 (405), ed. Mommsen and Meyer: *Possessiones, quae ex bonis Gildonis aut satellitum eius* [...] *nostro patrimonio adgregentur, ita ut ab his ex eo tempore, quo indebite retentarunt, praestationum simplum inferatur. qui si conventi intra Kalendas Octobres possessiones putaverint retinendas, sciant se ad dupli restitutionem coartandos et duplos fructus esse reddendos.*

33 *CTh* 9.40.19 (408), ed. Mommsen and Meyer: *Satellites Gildonis custodiis mancipentur et proscriptione damnentur.*

34 *CTh* 9.42.18 (401), ed. Mommsen and Meyer: *Marcharidus proscriptus plurima rerum penes diversos reliquit, sicut quaestio habita patefecit. ut quisque igitur aliquid ex eius facultatibus retinet* [...] *patrimonio suo fisco sociato poenam se deportationis noverit subiturum.*

35 *CTh* 9.42.21 (408), ed. Mommsen and Meyer: *Qui in facultates Stilichonis et actus videntur esse versati vel ex isdem facultatibus aliquid subtraxisse vel aliquid rapuisse, omnifariam reddant*; *CTh* 9.42.22 (408), ed. Mommsen and Meyer: *Qui suas opes praedoni publico* [...] *dederunt vel iure vel corpore* [...] *his omnem repetendi viam iubemus esse praeclusam.*

369 at a church council attended by 70 bishops. Chronopius then appealed the decision in an imperial court, something he was not permitted to do. He therefore was sentenced to pay a fine assessed in silver, which was turned over to the church so it could 'be distributed to those who are indigent.'[36] Curiously, the original law does not specify the amount of the fine, whereas the interpretation from the *Lex romana Visigothorum* of 506 CE sets the amount at 50 pounds. The compilers of the *interpretationes* certainly had done their homework, for the standard fine for this kind of offense was in fact 50 pounds of silver.[37]

The case of Chronopius is the only example from the law codes of these kinds of fines actually being assessed. It also is difficult to find references to fines in other textual sources.[38] One of the few comes from an undated early fifth-century African church council requesting that a law of Theodosius I that imposed a fine of 10 pounds of gold upon various offenses regarding heretics be enforced,[39] which might suggest that this was not being done. This would

---

36 *CTh* 11.36.20 (369), ed. Mommsen and Meyer: *Imppp. Valentianus, Valens et Gratianus* AAA. *ad Claudium pf. u. Quoniam Chronopius ex-antistite idem fuit in tuo, qui fuerat in septuaginta episcoporum ante iudicio, et eam sententiam provocatione suspendit, a qua non oportuit provocare, argentariam mulctam, quam huius modi facto sanctio generalis imponit, cogatur expendere. hoc autem non fisco nostro volumus accedere, sed his, qui indigent, fideliter erogari*[...] *interpretatio.* [...] *eum gravi mulctae, id est quinquaginta librarum argenti addictum fuisse dicit.* Given that the law is addressed to the Urban Prefect of Rome, one might suppose that Chronopius was Italian, and thus is omitted from the Italian volume of *PCBE*.

37 *CTh* 11.36.15 (4 February 364), ed. Mommsen and Meyer: *Ab executione vel a praeiudicio provocantes decrevimus non admitti, in tantum, ut contra definita facientes quinquaginta libras argenti condemnatione feriantur*; *CTh* 11.36.16 (8 October 364), ed. Mommsen and Meyer: *Interpositas appellationes a praeiudicio vel ab exsecutione damnantes et eum, qui ab istiusmodi titulis provocaverit, et officium, quod non renuntiarit, quinquagenas argenti libras fisco nostro iubemus inferre*; also *CTh* 11.36.25 (378) and 11.36.30 (385), ed. Mommsen and Meyer. The same fine was imposed on officials and office staffs that permitted such appeals, see *CTh* 11.30.48 (387) and 11.36.10 (354), ed. Mommsen and Meyer.

38 The language for penalties measured in pounds of gold in legislation is similar to that used by jurists, e.g., Scaevola, in Justinian, *Digesta* 34.4.30, ed. Theodor Mommsen, 2 vols., Berlin 1870 (cited as *Dig.*): *Viginti dari voluit his verbis: "hoc amplius do lego darique volo viginti auri libras"* [...] *ita viginti auri libras ei reddere* [...] *viginti libras auri transtulit et fidei eius commisit in haec verba: "viginti libras auri* [...] *eas dari volo".*

39 *Registri ecclesiae Carthaginensis* 93, ed. Charles Munier, CCSL 149, Turnhout 1974: *Simul etiam petendum est, ut illam legem quae a religiosae memoriae eorum patre Theodosio de auri libris decem in ordinatores vel ordinatos haereticos seu etiam in possessores, ubi eorum congregatio deprehenditur, promulgata est, ita deinceps confirmari praecipiant.*

TABLE 3.1 Examples of confiscations from Ammianus Marcellinus

Person	Place	Date	Penalty	Ref.
Quis	Gaul	353	'capite vel multatione bonorum aut insulari solitudine damnabatur'	14.5.3
Alii	Orientales provincii	353	'obductio capitum et bonorum ubique multatio'	14.7.20–1
Alii	Alexandria	353	'pars necati, alii puniti bonorum multatione actique laribus suis extorres'	14.11.4
Hymetius, Procos. Afr.	Africa	370	'eum bonorum parte multavit'	28.1.18
Alypius	The west	372	'post multationem bonorum exulare praeceptus'	29.1.44
Iuvenes aliique	The east	372	'indefensi bonis ablatis [...] promiscue iuvenes aliique [...] ad supplicia [...] ducebantur'	29.2.3

seem to be a reference to a law of 392 that mentions the 10 pound fine no less than four times.[40]

On the other hand, there are many reports of full-scale confiscation, usually involving cases of either *maiestas* or necromancy. Some are generic references to fines and confiscations.[41] But others, as found especially in the pages of

40 *CTh* 16.5.21 (392), ed. Mommsen and Meyer: *In haereticis erroribus quoscumque constiterit vel ordinasse clericos vel suscepisse officium clericorum, denis libris auri viritim multandos esse censemus* [...] *si ingenuus est, decem libras fisco nostro inferre praecipimus* [...] *praecavemus, ut, si villa dominica fuerit seu cuiuslibet publici iuris et conductor et procurator licentiam dederint colligendi, denis libris auri proposita condemnatione multentur. verum si quos talibus repertos obsecundare mysteriis ac sibi usurpare nomina clericorum iam nunc proditum fuerit, denas libras auri exigi singulos et inferre praecipimus.*

41 E.g., Lactantius, *De mortibus persecutorum* 8.4 4 (Diocletian), ed. Alfons Städele, Fontes Christiani 43, Turnhout 2003: *Et cum opus esset, non deerant locupletissimi senatores qui subornatis indiciis affectasse imperium dicerentur, ita ut effoderentur assidue lumina senatus. Cruentissimus fiscus male partis opibus affluebant*; Eusebius, *Ecclesiastical History* 8.14 10 (Maxentius), ed. Kirsopp Lake, 2 vols., Loeb Classical Library 153 and 265, Cambridge, Massachusetts 1926: *From this time on he distressed and harassed* [...] *all the provinces under his authority, by extreme exactions of gold and silver and goods, and most grievous prosecutions and various fines*; Eusebius, *De vita Constantini* 1.55 (Licinius), ed. Horst Schneider, Fontes Christiani 83, Turnhout 2007: 'But why should I mention how many innocent persons he punished with exile; how much property he confiscated; how many men of noble birth and estimable character he imprisoned'; *De vita Constantini* 3.1

Ammianus, refer to specific cases. In these cases, the confiscation often was accompanied by other forms of punishment ranging from exile to execution.

5 Confiscation Procedures

The actual means by which the fisc took control of confiscated property was rife with complications. A constitution of 369 provides a detailed account of the administrative procedures for doing so. First, a complete inventory was taken by the governor's office staff; it was to include the extent and nature of agricultural holdings, how they had been cultivated, how much was used for vines, olives, planted crops, grazing, and woods, what the 'curb appeal' of the property was, a description of the buildings, how many slaves were occupied in domestic or agricultural services and what their skills were, how many cottagers and *coloni* there were, how many oxen, flocks and herds there were, how much gold and silver, and so on.[42] One can imagine a standard form that was filled out by the imperial inventory takers. Moreover, much as in the modern day, in North America at least, confiscated property is officially marked and tagged. Indeed, a curious law of 393 forbade the *palatini* in charge of overseeing confiscations from including the names of either the emperors or the condemned person on the tags that were affixed to the confiscated items: palatine officials who ignored this prohibition were to be fined 20 pounds of gold.[43]

---

7 (rivals of Constantine), ed. Schneider: 'They committed countless murders, so that they might plunder or confiscate the wealth of their victims'; *Panegyricus Latini Pacati Drepani dictus Theodosio* 2.12 (the sins of Magnus Maximus), ed. Emil Baehrens, XII Panegyrici Latini, Leipzig 1874: *Quid perfunctorum honoribus summis virorum bona publicata, capita diminuta, vitam aere taxatam?*

42 *CTh* 9.42.7 (369), ed. Mommsen and Meyer: *Si qui intra provinciam pro qualitate delicti stilum proscriptionis incurrerit, per ordinarii officii sollicitudinem bonorum eius indago diligentissime celebretur, ne quid rei privatae commodis per gratiam atque colludium furto subducatur. et plena descriptio comprehendat, quod spatium et quod sit ruris ingenium, quid aut cultum sit aut colatur, quid in vineis olivis aratoriis pascuis silvis fuerit inventum, quae etiam gratia et quae amoenitas sit locorum, quis aedificiis ac possessionibus ornatus, quotve mancipia in praediis occupatis vel urbana vel rustica vel quarum artium generibus inbuta teneantur, quot sint casarii vel coloni, quot boum exercitiis terrarum atque vomeribus inservientium, quot pecorum et armentorum greges et in qua diversitate numerati sint, quantum auri et argenti, vestium ac monilium vel in specie vel in pondere et in quibus speciebus quidve in enthecis sit repertum.*

43 *CTh* 9.42.11 (393), ed. Mommsen and Meyer: *Si qui pro atrocitate commissi formam eiusmodi sustinebunt, ut bona eorum proscriptionis nomine vindicata fiscalibus sint socianda corporibus, commemorationem nostrorum nominum in his titulis nolumus fieri, qui eorum*

FIGURE 3.3 The Hódmezövásárhely-Szikáncs hoard contains 1439 solidi (almost exactly 20 pounds) of Theodosius II dated to the 430s, nearly all of the same types and with many die-links, indicating that the coins were put into circulation at nearly the same time. It is preserved in the Hungarian National Museum in Budapest. PHOTO: R. W. MATHISEN

At the same time, private persons and imperial officials alike saw an imperial confiscation as an opportunity to engage in some personal looting of their own, and there was great imperial concern about fraud and the misappropriation of the confiscated property. A western constitution of 362 condemned those who concealed the property of proscribed persons: the rich were punished by proscription themselves, and as for the poor, who 'through poverty had been plunged into filth and plebeian worthlessness,' the emperor Julian declared, 'let them cleanse their deserved debts with *damnatio capitis*.'[44]

It also appears that condemned real estate initially remained in the hands of the government for at least two years; that is, it was not immediately sold or auctioned off.[45] This provided a field day for opportunists who attempted

postibus adfigentur, vel his, quorum ius ac proprietas auferetur. officium etenim palatinum decem librarum auri multae dispendio vexabitur, si hoc deinceps crediderit neglegendum.

44 *CTh* 9.42.5 (362), ed. Mommsen and Meyer: *Quidam scelerate proscriptorum facultates occultant. hos praecipimus, si locupletes sint, proscriptione puniri, si per egestatem abiecti sunt in faecem vilitatemque plebeiam, damnatione capitali debita luere detrimenta.*

45 It is unclear what happened to the moveable property: gold and silver presumably were delivered to the fisc, and other items may well have been sold.

to get their own share of prime real-estate. A law of 380 made it clear that the property of those convicted of *maiestas* was to go to the fisc, and was not to be requested by private persons,[46] in the way that making property *vacantia* or *caduca* could get it back on the tax rolls. And this was to say nothing of additional problems associated with *delatores* laying claim to part of the confiscated property, something that had to go through channels all the way up.[47]

6 The Purpose of Fines and Confiscations: Coercion, Deterrence, Impoverishment

One now might turn to the ostensible purpose served by fines and confiscations. One obvious role was to serve as a punishment for crimes that already had been committed. In addition, the threat of confiscations and fines was meant to be coercive, and the levels of punishment could be increased as a means of enforcing proper behavior. A law of 414, for example, proposed to punish high-ranking persons with a fine of 20 pounds of silver for each time they took Donatist communion, and,

> if the same thing happens five times and they cannot be recalled from their error by financial penalties, then let the matter be referred to Our Clemency, so that we might judge about their entire property and status more harshly.[48]

The efficacy of such methods is suggested by the report of Socrates that in 365, the emperor Valens coerced bishop Eleusius of Cyzicus to subscribe to the Creed of Rimini with 'threats of banishment and confiscation of property.'[49]

---

46 *CTh* 10.10.15 (380), ed. Mommsen and Meyer: *Quisquis in crimine maiestatis deprehensus fuerit et punitus, bonaque eius, sicut plectendi consuetudo criminis habet, fiscus invaserit.*

47 *CTh* 10.10.7 (345), ed. Mommsen and Meyer: *Nulli palatino delatorios libellos de competentibus rei privatae nostrae rebus accipere liceat.*

48 *CTh* 16.5.54.3 (414), ed. Mommsen and Meyer: *Damna quoque patrimonii poenasque pecuniarias evidenter imponimus viris mulieribus* [...] *nisi ad observantiam catholicam mentem propositumque converterit, ducentas argenti libras cogetur exsolvere fisci nostri utilitatibus adgregandas. ac ne id solum putetur ad resecandam intentionem posse sufficere, quotienscumque ad communionem talem accessisse fuerit confutatus, totiens multam exigatur, et si quinquies eundem constiterit nec damnis ab errore revocari, tunc ad nostram clementiam referatur, ut de solida eius substantia ac de statu acerbius iudicemus.*

49 Socrates, *HE* 4.6: 'The emperor, having convened a council of Arian bishops, commanded Eleusius to give his assent to their faith. At first he refused to do so, but on being terrified

Punishments also were intended to have a deterrent effect: a law of 383 regarding the concealment of deserters and establishing fines of up to 50 pounds of gold, editorialized, 'His sad example also shall deter others of those with similar knowledge.'[50] Fines of this size represented a great deal of wealth. These were amounts that the government was used to working with. For example, the Hódmezövásárhely-Szikáncs hoard, found in southeastern Hungary, contains 1439 solidi of Theodosius II struck during the 430s. That amount is just 1 solidus short of exactly 20 pounds of gold. Although it has been suggested that this hoard represents 'tribute paid to the Huns,'[51] this looks more like a payment either to or from a particular person and intended for a particular purpose. But the use of fines as a deterrent seems to have been ineffectual, given that in several cases a prohibition against a certain kind of activity had to be reiterated, usually with an even more stringent punishment.

Another purpose of confiscation was to create poverty for the guilty party. A law of 380 that allowed children to inherit only one-sixth of the property of someone convicted of *maiestas*, commented, 'Truly, with respect to someone convicted of such an atrocious crime it is fitting that they be punished not only with deportation but also with poverty.'[52] Likewise, an anti-Donatist law of 405 punished those guilty of being rebaptized, 'So that, punished by the confiscation of all their property, they will incur the punishment of poverty, with which they will be perpetually afflicted.'[53] Ammianus dwells on the pitiful straits into which those who had their property confiscated fell. At Alexandria in 353, he says, 'Some persons [...] were put to death, others punished by the confiscation of their property (*bonorum multatione*) and driven from their homes into exile, where, having nothing left save tears and complaints, they lived on the

---

with threats of banishment and confiscation of property, he was intimidated and assented to the Arian belief.'

50 *CTh* 7.18.8.1 (383), ed. Mommsen and Meyer: *Ceteros quoque similis conscientiae exemplum triste deterreat illorum.*

51 Péter Somogyi, 'New Remarks on the Flow of Byzantine Coins', in: *The Other Europe in the Middle Ages: Avars, Bulgars, Khazars and Cumans*, ed. Florin Curta and Roman Kovalev, Leiden and Boston 2008, 83–150, at 131–132.

52 *CTh* 9.42.8 (380), ed. Mommsen and Meyer: *Ipsum vero in tam atroci facinore convictum non solum deportatione, sed egestate puniri conveniet.*

53 *CTh* 16.6.4 (405), ed. Mommsen and Meyer: *Quare hac lege sancimus, ut quisquis post haec fuerit rebaptizasse detectus, iudici qui provinciae praesidet offeratur, ut facultatum omnium publicatione multatus inopiae poenam, qua in perpetuum afficiatur, expendat*; repeated in the next entry, *CTh* 16.6.5 (405), ed. Mommsen and Meyer: *Si quis posthac fuerit rebaptizare detectus, iudici qui provinciae praesidet offeratur, ut facultatum omnium publicatione multatus inopiae poenam expendat.*

doles of charity.'[54] He lamented the disgrace of Alypius, Vicar of Britain in 358 and *Comes* in Jerusalem in 363, who was condemned to exile and confiscation of his property for practicing magic in 371/2 and as a consequence 'was turned about in the greatest squalor.'[55] Regarding another instance at the same time, he commented,

> Many innocent persons under the appearance of mercy were driven headlong into exile and their property was consigned to the treasury, while the condemned, worn out by the privations of fearful poverty, were reduced to beggary, for fear of which the wise old poet Theognis advises us actually to hurl ourselves into the sea.[56]

Such examples of the creation of poverty could have been expected to have their own deterrent effect on others.

In spite of the economic straits to which those who had some or all of their property confiscated were reduced, one still could say that 'it sure beat the alternative,' that is, execution. Seen in this light, confiscation of property could be seen as the equivalent of a slap on the wrist. Ammianus suggests, for example, that the father of Valentinian, the general Gratianus, escaped with confiscation of his property (*multatione bonorum*) after being convicted of having shown hospitality to Magnentius.[57] Likewise, a certain Bassianus, who had

54 Amm. 14.11.4, ed. Seyfarth: *Quorum pars necati, alii puniti bonorum multatione actique laribus suis extorres nullo sibi relicto praeter querelas et lacrimas, stipe conlaticia victitabant, et civili iustoque imperio ad voluntatem converso cruentam, claudebantur opulentae domus et clarae.*

55 Amm. 29.1.44, ed. Seyfarth: *Ecce autem Alypius quoque ex vicario Brittanniarum* [...] *in squalore maximo volutatus, ut veneficii reus citatus est* [...] *post multationem bonorum exulare praeceptus*; see 'Alypius 4', *The Prosopography of the Later Roman Empire* 1, ed. Arnold H. M. Jones, John R. Martindale and John Morris, 3 vols., Cambridge 1971–1992, 46–47 (cited as PLRE).

56 Amm. 29.1.21, ed. Seyfarth: *Inde factum est, ut clementiae specie penatibus multi protruderentur insontes, praecipites in exilium acti, quorum in aerario bona coacta et ipse ad quaestus proprios redigebat, ut damnati cibo precario victitarent, angustiis formidandae paupertatis adtriti, cuius metu vel in mare nos ire praecipites suadet Theognis poeta vetus et prudens.*

57 Amm. 30.7.3, ed. Seyfarth: *Multatione bonorum adflictus est a Constantio hoc nomine, quod civili flagrante discordia, hospitio dicebatur suscepisse Magnentium, per agrum suum ad proposita festinantem.*

TABLE 3.2 Fines from Coptic papyrological sources[a]

Reference	Date	Pounds AV	Ounces AV	Solidi
P.KRU 105	576–578	1/2	6	36
P.Mich.inv. 6898	632?	1/2	6	36
P.Vat.Copti Doresse 1	640/41?	~ 1/20	0.6	3 ½
P.KRU 75	7th c	1/2	6	36
P.KRU 65	650/700	5/12	5	30
P.CLT 1	698	1/3	4	24
P.CLT 4	702	1/12	1	6
P.CLT 2	703?	1/2	6	36
P.CLT 5	711	1	12	72
P.KRU 34	713	1/36	1/3	2
P.KRU 9	715	1/6	2	12
P.KRU 35	719	1/3	4	24
P.KRU 55	720	1	12	72

a Courtesy of Leslie S. B. MacCoull, personal communication; see also Leslie S. B. MacCoull, *Coptic Legal Documents: Law As Vernacular Text and Experience in Late Antique Egypt*, Turnhout 2009. The original amount of the fine is printed in bold.

consulted soothsayers to determine the sex of his unborn child, 'deprived of his rich patrimony, was snatched from death.'[58]

7 Fine Amounts

Fines in the law codes for imperial officials generally ranged from 20 to 100 pounds of gold, whereas those for *privati* generally were in the 2 to 10 pound range, or roughly 10 times smaller. Thus, it seems that when Julian fined himself 10 pounds of gold for usurping the consul's rights, he was letting himself off easily, and fining himself more as a *privatus* than an imperial magistrate. Fines cited in papyrological sources, either in pounds or ounces of gold or number of solidi, were even smaller.

58 Amm. 29.2.5, ed. Seyfarth: *ambitioso necessitudinum studio, quibus tegebatur, morte ereptus, patrimonio opimo exutus est.*

The smaller amounts for *privati* bring the fines more into the realm of reality and could suggest that some of these fines actually were enforced, even if the huge fines on officials were intended more to serve as deterrents.

8 Mitigating Factors

One also might observe that there always was the possibility of mitigating factors in the case of crimes punished by confiscations, ranging from acquittals to restorations. Ammianus suggests, however, that, at some times anyway, acquittals were rare, observing, 'Nor indeed does anyone remember easily that anyone, when accusations had even been whispered, was acquitted under Constantius.'[59] And when three senators were accused under Valentinian I, on doubtful evidence, of having knowledge of poisons, Ammianus claims that they were acquitted only because a close friend of theirs was a close friend of the judge.[60] In other regards, however, emperors could be more humane. In *relegatio*, a lighter form of exile, the condemned person was permitted to retain his property. And in cases involving the death penalty, except for *maiestas* or magic, imperial *humanitas* was manifested insofar as the property of executed persons remained in the family.[61]

Furthermore, convicted persons often had hopes of receiving pardon, and restitution of their confiscated property,[62] often not long after the original conviction.[63] As already noted, the government even imposed a two-year moratorium on the disposition of confiscated property; this was done

59 Amm. 14.5.9, ed. Seyfarth: *Nec enim quisquam facile meminit sub Constantio, ubi susurro tenus haec movebantur, quemquam absolutum.*

60 Amm. 28.1.27, ed. Seyfarth: *Super his etiam Tarracius Bassus, postea urbi praefectus et frater eius Camenius et Marcianus quidam et Eusaphius, omnes clarissimi, arcessiti in crimen, quod eiusdem conscii veneficii* [...] *documentis etiam tum ambiguis suffragante absoluti sunt Victorino* [...] *qui erat amicus Maximino iunctissimus.*

61 *CTh* 9.42.2 (356), ed. Mommsen and Meyer: *Si quem forte gladius ultor adflixerit aliave quaelibet vitam adimens poena consumpserit, usque ad tertium gradum generis copulationis eiusdem successio deferatur fisco penitus quiescente, ut accipiat hereditatem* [...] *alia sit condicio damnatorum ex crimine maiestatis aut magicae*; also *CTh* 9.42.4 (358), 9.42.6 (364), 9.42.10 (383), ed. Mommsen and Meyer.

62 *Dig.* 48.23.2, ed. Mommsen: *Si deportatus restitutus dignitatem quidem indulgentia principis reciperavit* [...] *cum ei facultas oblata esset a principe bona quoque sua reciperandi*; *Dig.* 48.23.3, ed. Mommsen: *Si bona cum dignitatis restitutione concessa reciperaverit.*

63 See Cassius Dio, *Roman History* 54.14.4–5, 77.3.3, 79.3.5, ed. Earnest Cary, vols. 6 and 9, Loeb Classical Library 83 and 177, London 1917–27; *Cornelii Taciti libri qui supersunt* 12.59, 13.11, 14.46–48 (Annales), 1.77, 2.86. (Historiae), ed. Kenneth Wellesley, 2 vols., Leipzig 1986–1989.

> either so that someone might recover their own property if, as is our inborn nature, we soften a harsh outcome and sad fate with imperial humanity, or so that one might at length make a request when he understands that he is petitioning for property of the fisc rather than of proscribed persons.[64]

For example, Olybrius, son of Anicia Juliana and Areobindus and Consul in 491, in 533 was recalled from an unattested exile and his property was restored by Justinian.[65] Restorations to favor could happen for any number of reasons. Sometimes a malefactor benefited from intercession by another senator, as when Memmius Vitrasius Orfitus signo Honorius, Prefect of Rome for the second time in 357–359, was convicted of peculation relating to deficiencies in the wine tax and exiled, but ca. 368 was recalled and had his property restored through the intercession of Vulcacius Rufinus.[66]

If one emperor was intransigent, one could bide one's time and wait for the next one. Fl. Taurus Seleucus Cyrus, a past Prefect of Constantinople, Praetorian Prefect, and Consul in 441, was dismissed by Theodosius II and had his property confiscated because he was too popular, and was made bishop of Cotyaeum in Phrygia in 443. But after the death of Theodosius he returned to secular life in Constantinople, and was pardoned and had his property restored by Marcian.[67] It even was possible to receive pardon posthumously, as was the case with Hypatius, Consul in 500 and Master of Soldiers, who was proclaimed emperor in 532 during the Nika rebellion, suffered execution, confiscation of property, and a burial in disgrace; subsequently, however, he was allowed an honorable burial and his property was restored.[68]

---

64 *CTh* 10.10.23 (401), ed. Mommsen and Meyer: *Ne quis proscriptorum bona vel eorum, qui publicam videntur excepisse sententiam, intra biennium aestimet postulanda. abstineant facultatibus intra id temporis expetendis, ut aut proprias quis recipiat, si, ut nobis ingenitum est, duriores casus et tristiorem fortunam imperatoria humanitate molliamus, aut tum demum postulet, cum iam fiscalem potius quam proscriptorum expetisse noscatur*; also *CTh* 10.10.29 (412), ed. Mommsen and Meyer.

65 *PLRE* 2, 795 s.v. 'Olybrius 3', ed. Jones, Martindale and Morris: see Johannes Malalas, *Chronographia* 478, ed. Hans Thurn, Corpus Fontium Historiae Byzantinae 35, Berlin 2000.

66 *PLRE* 1, 651–652, s.v. 'Honorius 3', ed. Jones, Martindale and Morris; *Q. Aurelii Symmachi quae supersunt*, 9.150 (Epistulae), 34 (Relationes), ed. Otto Seeck, MGH AA 6, 1, Berlin 1883; *Amm.* 27.3.2–3, ed. Seyfarth.

67 *PLRE* 2, 339, s.v. 'Cyrus 7', ed. Jones, Martindale and Morris.

68 *PLRE* 2, 580, s.v. 'Hypatius 6', ed. Jones, Martindale and Morris; Procopius, *De bello Persico* 1.24.19–31 and 57-58, ed. Jacob Haury, *Procopii Caesariensis Opera omnia*, vol. 1, Leipzig 1905.

Some senators went through repeated cycles of promotion, disgrace, confiscation, and restoration. In 532, for example, John the Cappadocian was sacked as Praetorian Prefect during the Nika riots, but was restored the next year. Then, after a failed plot against Belisarius in 540, John was sacked as Praetorian Prefect once again, ordained as a priest in Cyzicus, and had his property confiscated, although much of it later was restored. Then, after being involved in the murder of his bishop, his property again was confiscated and he was exiled to Antinoë in Egypt: Procopius notes, 'He was forced onto a ship, where the fullness of his degradation was manifested in being allowed just one cheap cloak and being forced to beg for food and money at each stop.'[69] One common factor in all these accounts is that everything was dependent on the will of the emperor, which emphasized the emperor's ability both to remove and restore the status, rank, honors, and property that were so dear to the hearts of senators and officials.

9 *Compensatio*

One now might turn to Roman *lex privata* and conclude with a few words on the concept of *compensatio* — compensation — in late Roman law. In general, *compensatio* was a means of reconciling differences between credits and debits; according to the mid third-century jurist Modestinus, '*compensatio* is a distribution of a debt and a credit between themselves.'[70] The second-century jurist Salvius Julianus added, 'Anyone can keep away his creditor, who also is his debtor and is seeking him, if he is prepared to make a compensation.'[71]

This topic receives very little attention, indeed virtually no attention at all, from late Roman legal scholars.[72] But perhaps that is no surprise, for references to *compensatio* in legal documents become more and more rare as one moves into Late Antiquity. In the *Digest*, for example, Roman jurisprudents of the third

69 *PLRE* 3, 627–635, s.v. 'Fl. Ioannes 11 the Cappadocian', ed. Jones, Martindale and Morris; Procopius, *De Bello Persico* 1.25.13–43, ed. Jacob Haury.

70 *Dig.* 16.2.1, ed. Mommsen. *Modestinus 6 pand. Compensatio est debiti et crediti inter se contributio.*

71 *Dig.* 16.2.2, ed. Mommsen: *Unusquisque creditorem suum eundemque debitorem petentem summovet, si paratus est compensare.*

72 E.g., the topic goes unmentioned in Jill Harries, *Law & Empire in Late Antiquity*, Cambridge 1999; John F. Matthews, *Laying Down the Law. A Study of the Theodosian Code*, Yale 2000; Fritz Schulz, *Principles of Roman Law*, Oxford 1936; and Bruce Frier, *A Casebook on the Roman Law of Delict*, Atlanta 1989. Hans Julius Wolff, *Roman Law. An Historical Introduction*, Norman 1951, 59, has a single mention of 'composition' referring to the Twelve Tables.

century and earlier refer to *compensatio* and its variants no less than 169 times. Thirty-four of the pre-Constantinian rescripts cited in the *Codex* Justinianus likewise mention issues relating to *compensatio*. But after Constantine, *compensatio* makes fewer and fewer appearances in statute law. In the Theodosian Code, only six constitutions mention *compensatio*, along with one of the Sirmondinian Constitutions, two of the Visigothic *interpretationes*, and two of the post-Theodosian novels. Some of these citations deal with public matters such as tax adjustments and private matters involving inheritances, property, and the repayment of debts. But others deal with compensation for people. For example, a law of 408 specified that persons who had provided sustenance for those taken captive by barbarians, and slave dealers who had purchased them, were to be provided *compensatio*.[73] There is nothing, however, relating to criminal law or even delicts, and no indication of any punitive use of *compensatio*. Even in the case of illegally appropriated land, the only penalty, as in a law of 386, was the return of what had been seized.[74] By the sixth century, the concept of *compensatio* was even further reduced. In the *Codex Justinianus*, there are only five mentions of *compensatio* for the entire period Constantine to Justinian; and judges were advised 'not to be inclined toward allowing compensations nor to permit them with a pliant spirit.'[75] All of which leads to the inescapable conclusion that the concept of composition for wrongs or injuries simply was not a part of the mainstream of Roman legal practice.

10 Wergild

So where does that leave one with regard to wergild? There was a long tradition in Roman law, going back to the Twelve Tables of 451 BCE, of assessing penalties for personal injuries in fixed sums of money, which were cited twice by jurists in the first half of the third century. Paul, in his *Iniuriae*, noted,

73 *Constitutiones Sirmondianae* 16 (the full version of *CTh* 5.7.2) (408), ed. Mommsen and Meyer: *Quibus si quicquam in usum recuperandarum virium vestium vel alimoniae dicatur impensum, humanitati sit praestitum,* [...] *cum forsitan alimoniae istius mercedes operarum reddiderit compensatio*[...] *Nec honestas emptoribus quinquennii tempus ad compensationem maioris forsitan pretii datum ingemiscat exiguum.*

74 *CTh* 4.22.2 (386), ed. Mommsen and Meyer.

75 *Codex Iustinianus* 4.31.14 (*hoc itaque iudices observent et non procliviores in admittendas compensationes existant nec molli animo eas suscipiant*), 4.34.11, 11.58.4, 11.66.7, 12.39.2, ed. Paul Krüger, Berlin 1877. And as for the word *compositio*, forms of it occur 27 times in the Digest, 19 times in the Theodosian Code, and 26 times in the Code of Justinian.

> This comes from a law of the Twelve Tables: "whoever does injury to another, there is an immediate penalty of 25 sesterces", which was a general law; there also were special cases, such as this: "If someone breaks the bone of a free man, the immediate penalty is 300 sesterces, if a slave, 150 sesterces".[76]

And Ulpian's early third-century 'Commentary on the Aedilician Edict,' cited in the *Digest*, compiled in the early 530s, recapitulated a terse edict forbidding dangerous animals from being kept near public thoroughfares:

> If anything should be done against these regulations and a free man should perish from this business, twenty solidi; if it is said that there was injury to a free men, let him be condemned to however much seems good and fair to the judge; of other properties, with respect to however much the damage was given and committed, double.

Here, the amount of the composition has been expressed by the sixth-century editors in gold *solidi*; there is no way to know what the original amount was.[77] The original edict cited could not have dated after the early second century CE, when the Aedilician and Praetorian Edicts were codified by Hadrian's jurist Salvius Julianus, and probably goes back to the Republican period.

As a result of typical Roman respect for *mos maiorum*, therefore, the concept of compositions for deaths and injuries survived in Roman legal tradition into the sixth century and every law student was familiar with them. But such compositions did not make their way into Roman statute law, nor is there any evidence that they actually were put into effect at any time during the Roman Republic or Empire. By Late Antiquity, the ancient tradition of fixed penalties thus had long since fallen into desuetude. Indeed, the late antique source that comes closest to looking like a catalogue of wergild compositions is not a legal source at all, but an early fifth-century comedy known as the *Querolus*. The author makes a multitude of legal jokes and more than likely had legal training.

---

76 *Collatio legum Mosaicarum et Romanarum* 2.5.5, ed. Theodor Mommsen, *Collectio librorum iuris anteiustiniani* 3, Berlin 1890: *Paulus Iniuriae. Legitima ex lege duodecim tabularum: "qui iniuriam alteri facit, quinque et viginti sestertiorum poenam subito," quae lex generalis fuit; fuerunt et speciales, velut illa: "si os fregit libero, CCC, si servo, CL poenam subito sestertiorum."*

77 *Dig.* 21.1.42, ed. Mommsen: *Ulpianus 2 ad ed. aedil. curul*[...] *si adversus ea factum erit et homo liber ex ea re perierit, solidi ducenti, si nocitum homini libero esse dicetur, quanti bonum aequum iudici videbitur, condemnetur, ceterarum rerum, quanti damnum datum factumve sit, dupli.*

One silliness comes when the author cooks up a fake 'Senatus consultum servilianum et parasiticum,'[78] the 'Porcian-Caninian-Furian-Fufian Law, from the consulate of Torquatus and Taurea,' which ostensibly prescribes the penalties to be assessed for injuries done to parasites: a quarter (*quadrans*) of a solidus for spitefulness, a third (*triens*) for conceit, but for both together, 'two-thirds (*bessis*) of a solidus is justly assessed.' Moreover, 1/12 (*uncia*) of a solidus was added 'in consideration of embarrassment,' three-fourths (*dodrans*) of a solidus was assessed for wounds, and 11/12 (*deunx*) for sprains and dislocations.[79] The problem with these penalties is that the *triens* was the only one of these sub-units of the solidus that actually existed. But the author's audience of legal cognoscenti would have been quite familiar with these fractions in late Roman legal literature and statute law in the context of the division of estates, including even references to the Twelve Tables,[80] and no doubt would have found

---

78 *Querolus (Aulularia). Le Grincheux (Comédie de la petite marmite)* 109, ed. Catherine Jacquemard-Le Saos, Collection des Universités de France, Paris 1994 (cited as *Quer.*): *QUER. Senatus consultum dico egomet servilianum et parasiticum. MAND. Ohe, visne interdictorum capita iam nunc eloquar ad legem Porciam, Caniniam, Furiam, Fufiam, consulibus Torquato et Taurea?*

79 *Quer.* 111–112, ed. Jacquemard-Le Saos: *Mercedem vulnerum victus accipiat parasitus* [...] *de livoribus in quadrantem solidi unius, de tumoribus in trientem poena transibit, quod si et tumor fuerit et livor solidi unius bessem iure optimo consequetur. Unam vero unciam aporiae, hoc est excoctionis, contemplationi concedimus. Placuit autem ut etiam de plagis et vulneribus infixis, summoto strepitu criminali, amicorum praestetur inspectio ita ut dodrantem solidi nec inspicientum gratia nec largientis excedat humanitas. In luxu autem et ossibus loco motis usque ad deuncem solidi iniuriarum commodum placuit extendi.*

80 E.g., *CTh* 9.42.8 (380), ed. Mommsen and Meyer: *Deportato si erunt liberi nepotesve sui seu emancipati, nepotes quoque ex filia, semissem tantum bonorum fiscus usurpet, semissis ipsi ac liberis hac distributione servetur, ut sextantem ipse ad fortunam ab extrema inopia vindicandam suae habeat potestatis, trientem liberi nepotesve*[...] *Quod si deportatus sine liberis vel nepotibus patrem habebit ac matrem vel etiam utrumque, non semissis a fisco, sed bessis patrimonii vindicetur, triens residuus in duos sextantes redactus inter parentes ac deportatum aequaliter dividatur, ita ut unciam mater, si ius liberorum habuerit, usurpet; sin fecunditatis privilegium non habebit, patri unciam iam habenti mater semunciam ex uncia sua cedat*; *CTh* 9.42.9.1–3 (380), ed. Mommsen and Meyer: *Quod si supplicio huius modi adflictus comprehensorum graduum liberos non habebit, tum capite secundo pater ac mater in trientem dumtaxat vocetur, besse ad aerarium publicum transferendo, atque ita, si matri ius fuerit liberorum, partes inter utrumque parentem sextantibus impleantur, sin deerit, quadrantem pater, unciam mater accipiat. quod si interfectus patrem tantum reliquerit, nihilo setius vindicatione trientis utatur, item si matrem, dummodo ea ius habeat liberorum. sin autem sola supererit mater, papiae tamen legis privilegiis destituta neque trino partu fecunditati publicae gratiosa, sextante contenta sit fisco dextantem usurpante*[...]. *Iungimus tamen capite tertio avo aviaeque fratrem perempti ac sororem, ita ut in capita dividi quadrantem isdem existentibus sanciamus. ac si cui perempto cum fratre ac sorore manserit consanguinitatis agnatio, sit duodecim tabulis locus ac ius civile praevaleat.*

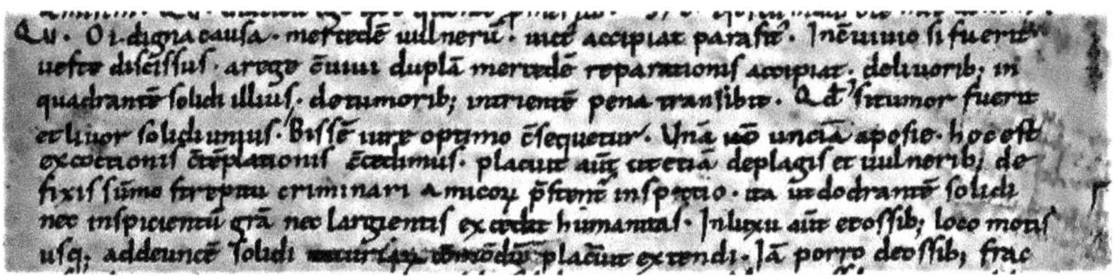

FIGURE 3.4 The section of the early fifth-century comedy the *Querolus* that discusses the penalties, in solidi, to be paid for wounds to a parasite
SOURCE: VAT.PAL.LAT. 1615, FOL.9R

their use here quite humorous. Indeed, this entire passage was meant as a joke, not to reflect the real world. It would have lost its humorous value if it reflected legal realities. It thus would be a mistake to see this passage as a late Roman example of the implementation of wergilds.

11 Conclusion

The imposition of fines and confiscations of property served several purposes in the late Roman administrative world. For one thing, it provided a money-making opportunity for a government that was always short of funds. When one was caught in the snares of the law, being wealthy could serve as a safety net, for the ability to pay off the government could save one from something much worse, execution. There is no evidence, moreover, for fines ever being paid to private persons. But this does not mean that private persons did not profit. A confiscation could provide a windfall profit for the unscrupulous, who concealed condemned property, illegally appropriated it, or attempted to have it illegally assigned to them. An imperial confiscation therefore was rather analogous to a shipwreck, with everyone in the neighborhood — ranging from imperial officials to the lowest ranking *humiliores* — rushing to share in the pickings.

There are few examples, moreover, of fines actually being assessed — only one example of silver and none of gold — although there are plenty of examples of property confiscation. The size of the fines, and the lack of evidence of their imposition suggests another purpose for them. The government was quite clear that huge fines, which would result in poverty for the guilty party, were meant to serve a deterrent role, something that should come as no surprise in a state where the government lacked the means to enforce the thousands of laws that it issued. If laws were going to take effect, they would have to be self-enforcing. Establishing huge monetary fines, not to mention the death penalty, was one of the few means that the government had to coerce good behavior and to provide deterrents to bad behavior.

Bibliography

Primary Sources

Ammiani Marcellini Rerum gestarum libri qui supersunt, ed. Wolfgang Seyfarth, Bibliotheca scriptorum Graecorum et Romanorum Teubneriana, Leipzig 1978.

Cassius Dio, *Roman History*, ed. Earnest Cary, vols. 6 and 9, Loeb Classical Library 83 and 177, London 1917–27.

Codex Iustinianus, ed. Paul Krüger, Berlin 1877.

Collatio legum Mosaicarum et Romanarum, ed. Theodor Mommsen, Collectio librorum iuris anteiustiniani 3, Berlin 1890, 107–198.

Cornelii Taciti libri qui supersunt, ed. Kenneth Wellesley, 2 vols., Leipzig 1986–1989.

Eusebius, *De vita Constantini. Über das Leben Konstantins*, ed. Horst Schneider, Fontes Christiani 83, Turnhout 2007.

Eusebius, *Ecclesiastical History*, ed. Kirsopp Lake, 2 vols., Loeb Classical Library 153 and 265, Cambridge, Massachusetts 1926.

Johannes Malalas, *Chronographia*, ed. Hans Thurn, Corpus Fontium Historiae Byzantinae 35, Berlin 2000.

Justinian, *Digesta*, ed. Theodor Mommsen, 2 vols., Berlin 1870.

Lactantius, *De mortibus persecutorum. Die Todesarten der Verfolger*, ed. Alfons Städele, Fontes Christiani 43, Turnhout 2003.

Panegyricus Latini Pacati Drepani dictus Theodosio, ed. Emil Baehrens, *XII Panegyrici Latini*, Leipzig 1874, 271–314.

Procopii Caesariensis Opera omnia, ed. Jacob Haury, vol. 1, Leipzig 1905.

Q. Aurelii Symmachi quae supersunt, ed. Otto Seeck, MGH AA 6, 1, Berlin 1883.

Querolus (*Aulularia*). *Le Grincheux* (*Comédie de la petite marmite*), ed. Catherine Jacquemard-Le Saos, Collection des Universités de France, Paris 1994.

Registri ecclesiae Carthaginensis, ed. Charles Munier, Corpus Christianorum Series Latina 149, Turnhout 1974, 173–247.

Sozomenos, *Historia ecclesiastica. Kirchengeschichte*, ed. Günther C. Hansen, Fontes Christiani 73, Turnhout 2004.

Theodosiani libri XVI cum constitutionibus Sirmondianis et leges novellae ad Theodosianum pertinentes, ed. Theodor Mommsen and Paul M. Meyer, Berlin 1905.

The Prosopography of the Later Roman Empire (*PLRE*), ed. Arnold H. M. Jones, John R. Martindale and John Morris, 3 vols., Cambridge 1971–1992.

Secondary Works

Blockley, Roger C., 'Internal Self-Policing in the Late Roman Administration: Some Evidence from Ammianus Marcellinus', *Classica et Medievalia* 30 (1969), 403–419.

Frier, Bruce, *A Casebook on the Roman Law of Delict*, Atlanta 1989.

Fuhrmann, Manfred, Art. 'Publicatio bonorum', *RE* 23 (1959), 2498–2516.

Harries, Jill, *Law & Empire in Late Antiquity*, Cambridge 1999.

Karlowa, Otto, *Römische Rechtsgeschichte I., Staatsrecht und Rechtsquellen*, Leipzig 1885.

Kaser, Max, *Das altrömische ius*, Göttingen 1949.

Kaser, Max, *Römische Rechtsgeschichte*, Göttingen 1950.

Kelly, Christopher, *Ruling the Later Roman Empire*, Cambridge, Massachusetts 2004.

Levy, Leonard W., *A License to Steal: The Forfeiture of Property*, Chapel Hill 1996.

Littmann, Enno, Magie, David and Stuart, Duane R. (ed.), *Syria: Publications of the Princeton University Archaeological Expeditions to Syria, in 1904–5 and 1909*, Leiden, 1921, Div. III, Sec. A, 24–42.

MacCoull, Leslie S. B., *Coptic Legal Documents: Law As Vernacular Text and Experience in Late Antique Egypt*, Turnhout 2009.

Matthews, John F., *Laying Down the Law. A Study of the Theodosian Code*, Yale 2000.

Noethlichs, Karl L., *Beamtentum und Dienstvergehen: zur Staatsverwaltung in der Spätantike*, Wiesbaden 1981.

Rosen, Klaus, 'Iudex, Kollektivstrafe, Kontrolle und Effizienz in der spätantiken Provinzialverwaltung', *Ancient Society* 21 (1990), 273–92.

Schulz, Fritz, *Principles of Roman Law*, Oxford 1936.

Somogyi, Péter, 'New Remarks on the Flow of Byzantine Coins', in: *The Other Europe in the Middle Ages: Avars, Bulgars, Khazars and Cumans*, ed. Florin Curta and Roman Kovalev, Leiden and Boston 2008, 83–150.

Vogler, Chantal, *Constance II et l'administration impériale*, Strasbourg 1979.

Wolff, Hans J., *Roman Law. An Historical Introduction*, Norman 1951.

CHAPTER 4

Wergeld: The Germanic Terminology of *Compositio* and Its Implementation in the Early Middle Ages

Wolfgang Haubrichs

Abbreviations: Alem. = Alemannic; Burg. = Burgundian; EGerm. = East Germanic; Frk. = Frankish; Germ. = Germanic; Goth. = Gothic; IE = Indo-European; It. = Italian; Lat. = Latin; Lgb. = Langobardic; MDutch = Middle Dutch; MHG = Middle High German; MLat = Middle Latin; NHG = New High German; ODutch = Old Dutch; OE = Old English; OF = Old Frisian; OHG = Old High German; ON = Old Norse; OS = Old Saxon; PN = personal name; Rom. = Romance; WGerm. = West Germanic.

1 Introduction[1]

Let us begin with a legal definition of the term that gave the lexical field of *compositio* its name: 'In the medieval sources of law, *compositio* stands for a ritualized extrajudicial or in-trial agreement (where necessary involving the participation of a mediator) between the perpetrators and victims, with the goal of reconciling the dispute provoked by the injustice, in which the victims forgo vengeance and feud (*faida*) in exchange for the perpetrators compensating the injustice with a sum of money (penance, wergeld)' (E. Schumann).[2]

1 Translated by Melanie Huchler and William Blakemore Lyon, translation revised by Courtnay Konshuh.

2 Eva Schumann, Art. 'Kompositionensystem', in: *HRG* 2, Berlin ²2012, col. 2003–2011; cf. Wolfgang Schild, Art. 'Wergeld', in: *HRG* 5, Berlin 1998, col. 1268–1271; Ruth Schmidt-Wiegand, 'Fränkische und frankolateinische Bezeichnungen für soziale Schichten und Gruppen in der Lex Salica', in: *Stammesrecht und Volkssprache. Ausgewählte Aufsätze zu den Leges barbarorum. Festgabe für Ruth Schmidt-Wiegand zum 1.1. 1991*, ed. Dagmar Hüpper and Clausdieter Schott, Weinheim 1991, 355–391, here 357–359 (cited as Schmidt-Wiegand, 'Bezeichnungen'); Ruth Schmidt-Wiegand, Art. 'Wergeld', in: *RGA* 33, Berlin and New York 2006, 457–463 (cited as Schmidt-Wiegand, 'Wergeld'); Philippe Depreux, 'Wergeld, composition et rachat dans les capitulaires des rois Francs', in: *La victime, 2: La réparation du dommage*, ed. Jacqueline Hoareau, Guillaume Métairie, and Pascal Texier, Limoges 2009, 345–362; Stefan Esders, '"Eliten" und "Strafrecht" im frühen Mittelalter. Überlegungen zu den Bußen- und Wergeldkatalogen der Leges Barbarorum', in: *Théorie et pratiques des élites au Haut Moyen*

 | DOI:10.1163/9789004466128_005

Vernacular terms in this lexical field should be treated with the aim of exploring the semantic aspects of the words more accurately. Admittedly, historians and legal historians should not expect too much information about the later development of meanings of terms that belong to the content complex of *compositio*. Those consistently stem from the context in Latin. Only occasionally can the early written vernacular languages Gothic, Old English, Old Saxon, Old High German etc. help.

The difficulty in parsing these terms is partly due to the fact that most of the original vernacular legal terms in the *leges* had already developed into Latin-Romance loanwords, linguistically given Latin endings and assimilated to Romance phonetic development such as *weregild-us, bann-us* or *fred-us, -a* < Germ. **frithu-*. A few exceptions can be found in Frankish vocabulary *in Mallobergo* ('in the legal assembly'),[3] un-declined forms in Langobardic legislation, and for the words in the *Lex Alamannorum* or slightly later *Lex Baiuwariorum* which are referenced as *quod Alamanni* (sc. *Baiuvarii*) *dicunt*.[4]

Thus, the philologist can essentially offer an assertion about the early and initial meanings of the terms, and this on the basis of an etymological analysis, which can never be as semantically accurate as an additional context-oriented semantic analysis would be.

The analysis comprises three parts: the core terms of *compositio,* terms that metonymically switched their meaning, and institutions that implement the payments that are claimed in the procedure of *compositio.*

Age. Conception, perception et réalisation sociale (Collection Haut Moyen Age 13), ed. François Bougard, Hans-Werner Goetz and Régine Le Jan, Turnhout 2011, 261–282 (cited as Esders, 'Eliten').

3 Ruth Schmidt-Wiegand, Art. 'Malbergische Glossen' und 'Mallus', in: *RGA* 19, Berlin and New York 2001, 184–186 and 191–192; Daniela Fruscione, Art. 'Malbergische Glossen', in: *HRG* 3, Berlin [2]2016, col. 1210–1216.

4 Cf. Wolfgang Haubrichs, 'Quod Alamanni dicunt. Volkssprachige Wörter in der Lex Alamannorum', in: *Recht und Kultur im frühmittelalterlichen Alemannien. Rechtsgeschichte, Archäologie und Geschichte des 7. und 8. Jahrhunderts* (RGA Ergänzungsbände 102), ed. Sebastian Brather, Berlin and Boston 2017, 169–209; Vincenz Schwab, *Volkssprachige Wörter in Pactus und Lex Alamannorum*, Bamberg 2017; Heinrich Tiefenbach, 'Quod Paiuvarii dicunt. Das altbairische Wortmaterial der Lex Baiovariorum', in: *Die bairische Sprache. Studien zu ihrer Geographie, Grammatik, Lexik und Pragmatik. Festschrift Ludwig Zehetner*, ed. Albrecht Greule, Rupert Hochholzer and Alfred Wildfeuer, Regensburg 2004, 263–290.

2 Catalogue of Evidence

2.1 *Compositio and Wergeld*

(1) Compound *Wer-geld,* 'remuneration for a man (human)', OHG *werigelt, wer-ageld,* Lgb. *wergild, virgild-, wiregeld-*, MLat. *wer(e)gildus,* OF *werjeld,* OE *wer(e) gild,* MLG *weregelt*; but MLG Dutch ON *man-gelt,*[5] as a compound < Germ. **wira-* 'man, human' (cf. also Lat. *vir,* air. *fer*), from which Goth. *wair,* ON *verr,* OE *wer,* OS *wer* 'man', OS *folk-wer* 'fellow countryman' (both only in the Biblical epic 'Heliand'), OS *liud-wer* 'fellow countryman, tribesman', OHG *wer* (lastly isolated as a gloss in Sang. 913 for Lat. *vir* in a group glossary that also preserves archaic words)[6] + Germ. **geld-a-* 'retaliation, remuneration.'[7]

The first pieces of evidence are in the ca. 596 *Decretio Childeberti* II. 2,3; 2,4; 3,3:[8] ... *suum uuere(gi)ldum conponat; ... suo uuergildo omnino conponat*; a. 643 ER (Edictus Rothari) 9; 11 (and more often in the Langobardic laws): ... *wergild suo conponat, .. ille qui homicida est, conponat ipsum mortuum sicut adpraetiatus fuerit, id est wergild.*;[9] 7th c. Lex Ribuaria 40 (36), 11 ... *Si quis were-geldum solvere coeperit ...*;[10] late-7th c. Formulae Marculfi I,18: *Si quis fortasse eum* (an antrustio) *interficere presumpserit, noverit se wiregeldo suo soledos 600 esse culpabilem ...*;[11] furthermore Lex Al. 28,1 (*wirigildum*),[12] Lex Baiw. 8,1 (*cum*

5 Cf. Heino Speer (ed.), *Deutsches Rechtswörterbuch* 9 (1992/96), 132–133; Jan F. Niermeyer and Cor van de Kieft, *Mediae Latinitatis Lexicon Minus*, 2nd ed., rev. by Jan W. J. Burgers, Leiden 2002, 1471–1472 (cited as Niermeyer and van de Kieft, *Mediae Latinitatis Lexicon*).

6 Friedrich Kluge and Elmar Seebold, Art. 'Welt' and 'Wergeld', in: *Etymologisches Wörterbuch der deutschen Sprache*, Berlin and Boston [25]2011, 981–982 and 983 (cited as Kluge and Seebold, *Etymologisches Wörterbuch*); Vladimir Orel, *A Handbook of Germanic Etymology,* Leiden and Boston 2003, 463 (cited as Orel, *Handbook*). Cf. Note 1.

7 Kluge and Seebold, Art. 'Geld', in: *Etymologisches Wörterbuch*, 343; Albert L. Lloyd, Rosemarie Lühr and Otto Springer, *Etymologisches Wörterbuch des Althochdeutschen* (*EWA*) 4, Göttingen 2009, 152–155 (cited as *EWA*).

8 *Decretio Childeberti* 5–6 and 10, ed. Alfred Boretius, MGH Capitularia regum Francorum 1, Hanover 1883, 15–17, here 16 and 17.

9 *Edictus Rothari*, ed. Friedrich Bluhme, MGH LL 4, Hanover 1868, 3–90, here 14: [...] *conponat ipsum mortuum sicut adpraetiatus fuerit, id est wergild.* Cf. Florus van der Rhee, *Die germanischen Wörter in den langobardischen Gesetzen*, Rotterdam 1970, 138–140 (cited as van der Rhee, *Die germanischen Wörter*).

10 *Lex Ribuaria*, ed. Franz Beyerle and Rudolf Buchner, MGH LL nationum Germanicarum 3, 2, Hanover 1954, 94. Cf. Esders, 'Eliten', 267; Lukas Bothe in this volume.

11 *Marculfi Formulae*, ed. Karl Zeumer, MGH Formulae Merowingici et Karolini aevi, Hanover 1886, 32–112, here 55.

12 *Leges Alamannorum*, ed. Karl Lehmann, MGH LL nationum Germanicarum 5, 1, Hanover [2]1966, 87.

werageldo),[13] Lex Sax. Lex Cham., Lex Fris. and in Carolingian capitularies; moreover in 8th-century deeds from St. Gallen and Fulda.

(2) Short form OE *wer*, MLat. (England, *leges*) *wera* 'wergeld': ... *solvat eum wera sua ...; ... si quis occisi weram exigat ... ; ... wera sua gildet* (*cognatio*) *eum ...*;[14] short form Lgb. *uir* also in Liutprand 130 a. 753 (var.).[15] For such abbreviations compare NHG *Dirndl* for *Dirndl-kleid* (a Bavarian traditional costume).

There are further compounds in early medieval legal language, which are comparable (in some cases only in a limited way) to the formation *wer-geld:*

(3) Numeral compounds with **gelda-*: a. 517 *Lex Burg.* 63: *tri-gildus* 'triple remuneration'; 8, 9, 12, 19, 38, 45, 76: *novi-gildus* 'ninefold remuneration' (*gild-* may show e > i as EGerm. phonetic development; however the Lat. elements may have meant these words were no longer perceived as Burg.);[16] clearly vernacular formations are *ER* 229 and more often Lgb. *Acto-gild,actu-gild, acti-gild* 'eightfold consideration' with Romance sound substitution [-ct-] for Germ. [-ht-] < Germ. **ahtau-* 'eight';[17] *Lex Baiw. niun-geldo* 'ninefold money' < Germ. **newun* 'nine'.[18]

Other compounds with **gelda-* are:

(4) *Laune-gild*: a. 643 ER 175, 184, 8th c. *Liutprand* 73, *Aistulf* 12 Lgb. *launi-, laune-gild*;[19] in documents from the 8th century also Lgb. *laun-child, laune-child* etc.; short-form *launo* a. 762 or. (Ceneda, now Vittorio Veneto) 'legal return-gift

13 *Lex Baiwariorum*, ed. Ernst von Schwind, MGH LL nationum Germanicarum 5, 2, Hanover 1926, 353.

14 Niermeyer and van de Kieft, *Mediae Latinitatis Lexicon*, 1471. Cf. for *wergeld* in Anglo-Saxon law: Patrick Wormald, Art. 'Wergeld. II. Englisches Recht', in: *LexMA* 8, Munich and Zurich 1997, col. 2201–2202.

15 *Leges Liutprandi regis*, ed. Bluhme, MGH LL 4, 163. Cf. van der Rhee, *Die germanischen Wörter*, 138; Schmidt-Wiegand, 'Bezeichnungen', 377.

16 *Leges Burgundionum*, ed. Ludwig Rudolf von Salis, MGH LL nationum Germanicarum 2, 1, Hanover 1892, 94 l. 20 (var.), 49 l. 13, 50 l. 10, 51 ll. 10–11, 59 l. 2, 70 l. 20, 76 l. 6 and 101 l. 1. Cf. Wolfgang Haubrichs, 'Burgundische und intergentile Rechtswörter des "Liber constitutionum" (a. 517) im Kontext der Burgundenforschung', *Sprachwissenschaft* 40 (2015), 127–146, here 141 (cited as Haubrichs, 'Rechtswörter').

17 *Edictus Rothari*, ed. Bluhme, MGH LL 4, 57; van der Rhee, *Die germanischen Wörter*, 18–20.

18 *Lex Baiwariorum*, ed. v. Schwind, MGH LL nat. Germ. 5, 2, 270 l. 8, 306 l. 3 and 366 l. 4.

19 *Edictus Rothari*, ed. Bluhme, MGH LL 4, 41 ll. 1–2, 44 l. 3, 137 l. 3 and 200 l. 15. Cf. van der Rhee, *Die germanischen Wörter*, 96–98.

for a donation';[20] OS *lôn-geld* 'remuneration',[21] OHG *lôn-gelt* 'service in return, gift in return'[22] to Germ. **launa-* 'wage'.[23] This word is formally comparable to *Wer-geld*, but does not belong to the lexical field of *compositio* in a strict sense. Because of its spread in Langobardic, Old High German, and Old Saxon, it is probably an inherited word from the Elbe Germanic proto-language.

(5) *Wider-gild*: In many later manuscripts of Langobardic law and corresponding law glossaries 'wergeld' is replaced by Lgb. *uuidri-gild, uuidri-child, guidri-gilt* etc. 'payback, repayment, retaliation, retribution, revenge'[24] to Germ. **withra-*, **widra-* 'against'.[25] It could derive from an Old Langobardic interpretation of *compositio*, in which Lat. *con-* was depicted by a corresponding Germ. prefix, after the first element of *wergild, wiregeld* had become incomprehensible in Old Langobardic.

2.2 *Metonymic-Elliptic Terms*

(6) *Leod(i), Leodis, Leuda* etc. as monetary terms of service: *Pactus legis Salicae* 35,8 (var.) and more often *leodis, leudis*, but also l*eodi* 'wergeld, manbote'[26] (but also multiple times *leodardi* see below no. 7); besides numerous compounds, which show that *leod* etc. was already a common term in the time of the '*Lex Salica*': e.g. constantly *in mallobergo* ('at the place of trial, in Frankish legal language') *Pactus legis Salicae* 41,2ff. 41,7 *matte-leodi* 'great wergild' (also *Lex*

20 *Codice diplomatico Longobardo*, ed. Luigi Schiaparelli, 2, Rome 1933, no. 168, 124 l. 5. Cf. Maria Vòllono, 'Methodik und Probleme bei der Erforschung des Langobardischen am Beispiel einiger juristischer Fachbegriffe: "mundoald", "launegild", "sculdhais"', in: *Die Langobarden. Herrschaft und Identität* (Forschungen zur Geschichte des Mittelalters 9), ed. Walter Pohl and Peter Erhart, Vienna 2005, 477–502, here 491–496 (cited as Vòllono, 'Methodik und Probleme').

21 Heinrich Tiefenbach, *Altsächsisches Handwörterbuch — A concise Old Saxon Dictionary*, Berlin and New York 2010, 249.

22 Rudolf Schützeichel, *Althochdeutsches Wörterbuch*, Tübingen ^{6}2006, 219 (cited as Schützeichel, *Althochdeutsches Wörterbuch*); Rudolf Schützeichel, *Althochdeutscher und altsächsischer Glossenwortschatz* 6, Tübingen 2004, 150 (cited as Schützeichel, *Glossenwortschatz*); *EWA* 5, Göttingen 2014, 1435.

23 Kluge and Seebold, Art. 'Lohn', in: *Etymologisches Wörterbuch*, 584; *EWA* 5, Göttingen 2014, 1431–1434.

24 Van der Rhee, *Die germanischen Wörter*, 138–140; Niermeyer and van de Kieft, *Mediae Latinitatis Lexicon*, 1472.

25 Kluge and Seebold, Art. 'wider', in: *Etymologisches Wörterbuch*, 986.

26 *Pactus legis Salicae*, ed. Karl August Eckhardt, MGH LL nationum Germanicarum 4,1, Hanover 1962, 131. Cf. Niermeyer and van de Kieft, *Mediae Latinitatis Lexicon*, 783; Schmidt-Wiegand, 'Bezeichnungen', 376–377; Ruth Schmidt-Wiegand, Art. 'Leod, leodes, leudes, leodi ... ', in: *HRG* 3, Berlin 1978, col. 1845–1848 (cited as Schmidt-Wiegand, 'Leod').

Sal. 69,2: *mallobergo mathdaleo ...*)[27] referring to *ingenui*, in the first element to Germ. **mahti-* 'power, force' (here with Rom. loss of the [h]):[28] cf. Lat. *potentes*; Pactus 41,15 perhaps **smala-leodi* (text has corrupt (*h*)*ismala* with Rom. anteposition of vowels before [sm-]) 'money for a girl'[29] referring to a *puella ingenua*, to Germ. **smala-* 'narrow, small, low' (cf. in hunting-jargon *Schmaltier* 'doe');[30] 35,1 *theo-leodi, theo-leod-inia* 'money for a serf'[31] with reference to killing of a *servus* (cf. **theo-texaga* 'theft of a serf') < Germ. **thewa-*, Runic *thewaz*, Goth. *thius* 'servant', OHG *thiu, diu* 'handmaid';[32] 41,9f. *uuala-leodi* 'money for a man of Roman origin':[33] *Si vero Romanus homo, ..., occisus fuerit ... qui eum occidere probatur, mallobergo uualaleodi sunt, ...*, to Germ. **wala*(*h*)*a-* 'Romance'.[34] Declined forms: *Pactus* 53,6: *Ista redemptio de manu redemenda usque ad leudem* (acc.) *sic permanet*; also 53,7 *leodem* (acc.);[35] *Lex Sal.* emendata (K), tit. 41, 13:[36] *leodis suae* (gen.); *Lex Sal.* 69,6:[37] *Si Romanus homo, conviva regi, occisus fuerit, mallobergo leoti* (simplex) ...; 69,3:[38] *Si vero eum de allis aut de ramis super cooperuit aut eum incenderit, mallobergo modileodi* < **mordi-leodi* to WGerm. **mortha-*, OHG OS *mord*, OF OE *morth* 'murder'.[39] Lemma *leudis, leodis* also in *Lex Cham.*, *Lex Thur.*, *Lex Fris.*, *leuda* 'manbote' in *Lex Baiw.*

27 *Pactus legis Salicae*, ed. Eckhardt, MGH LL nat. Germ. 4, 1, 156–157; *Lex Salica*, ed. Karl August Eckhardt, MGH LL nationum Germanicarum 4, 2, Hanover 1969, 114.

28 Kluge and Seebold, Art. 'Macht', in: *Etymologisches Wörterbuch*, 590; *EWA* 6, Göttingen 2017, 54–55.

29 *Pactus legis Salicae*, ed. Eckhardt, MGH LL nat. Germ. 4, 1, 160.

30 Kluge and Seebold, Art. 'schmal', in: *Etymologisches Wörterbuch*, 814.

31 *Pactus legis Salicae*, ed. Eckhardt, MGH LL nat. Germ. 4, 1, 128–129.

32 Kluge and Seebold, Art. 'dienen' and 'Dirne', in: *Etymologisches Wörterbuch*, 199 and 204; *EWA* 2, Göttingen 1988, 662–665, 681–684.

33 *Pactus legis Salicae*, ed. Eckhardt, MGH LL nat. Germ. 4, 1, 157. Cf. Ulrich Stutz, 'Das Wergeld des Romanus nach den fränkischen Volksrechten', in: Ulrich Stutz, *'Römerwergeld' und 'Herrenfall'*, Berlin 1934, 4–48; Heinrich Dannenbauer, 'Die Rechtsstellung der Gallorömer im fränkischen Reich', in: Heinrich Dannenbauer, *Grundlagen der mittelalterlichen Welt. Skizzen und Studien*, Stuttgart 1958, 94–120; Schmidt-Wiegand, 'Bezeichnungen', 383–384.

34 Kluge and Seebold, Art. 'welsch', in: *Etymologisches Wörterbuch*, 981. Cf. Walter Pohl, Ingrid Hartl and Wolfgang Haubrichs (ed.), *Walchen, Romani und Latini. Variationen einer nachrömischen Gruppenbezeichnung zwischen Britannien und dem Balkan* (Forschungen zur Geschichte des Mittelalters 21), Vienna 2017.

35 *Pactus legis Salicae*, ed. Eckhardt, MGH LL nat. Germ. 4, 1, 202–203.

36 *Pactus legis Salicae*, ed. Eckhardt, MGH LL nat. Germ. 4, 1, 161.

37 *Lex Salica*, ed. Eckhardt, MGH LL nat. Germ. 4, 2, 116.

38 *Lex Salica*, ed. Eckhardt, MGH LL nat. Germ. 4, 2, 114.

39 Kluge and Seebold, Art. 'Mord', in: *Etymologisches Wörterbuch*, 634; *EWA* 6, Göttingen 2017, 552–557.

(IX, 3);[40] in Anglo-Saxon law, the long form (compound) *léod-geld* can be found alongside the short form *léod*.[41]

One explanation could be that the forms *leodis, leodi, leoda* (with varying Latinisation) in the meaning 'manbote, Manngeld' are derived from the appellative **leudi-, *leuda-,* which exists in the *leges* but also in Merovingian chronicles as 'member of the *gens,* free man, warrior', OE *léoda* 'noble, inhabitant of a landscape', OS *liud*(*i*), OHG *liut*(*i*) 'man, plural: people, folk'[42] which are thought to have originated via metonymic ellipse (cf. below).

A second explanation: In addition, a consonantic n-derivation < Early Frk. **leodîn* offers itself for Frk. *leodi* according to Ruth Schmidt-Wiegand. That would be in line with the fem. gender inflection of Lex Sal. 31,2; 32; 33,1 with fem. ja-suffix *leod-în-ia* 'women money, remuneration for a free woman'.[43]

(7) Aside from *leod*(*i*) there is also the compound *leod-ardi*: *Pactus legis Salicae* 34, 3 and often several variations *leodardi, leudardi, ledardi* (with Rom. sound substitution [e] < Germ. [eu]; cf. PN *Ted-bert* < *Theud-bert*) 'man-fine, specifically for the small fine of only 15 solidi'; *Lex Sal.* 69,1: *Si quis ingenuos Francum aut barbarum, qui Salica lege vivit, occiserit, mallobergo leodardi* ...[44]

According to Ruth Schmidt-Wiegand *leod-ardi* developed from Early Frk. **leod-wardi*: 'violation of a man' to a noun, derived from Germ. **wardjanan,* Goth. *fra-wardjan* 'damage, destroy', OE *wirdan* 'to injure, to hurt, to annoy', OS *a-werdian* 'damage, destroy', OHG *fir-werten* id.; cf. OE *aef-werdelsa* 'damage, detriment, loss', OHG *wertisala* 'damage'. This is apparently still visible in OF

40 *Lex Baiwariorum*, ed. v. Schwind, MGH LL nat. Germ. 5, 2, 369 l. 6: [...] *cum XII sacramentalibus iuret de leuda sua.* Perhaps here we have better to understand *leuda* as the *gens* or the clan to which the defendant belongs.

41 Niermeyer and van de Kieft, *Mediae Latinitatis Lexicon*, 783. Cf. Gabriele von Olberg-Haverkate, Art. 'Leod, leudes', in: *HRG* 3, Berlin [2]2016, col. 843 (cited as von Olberg-Haverkate, 'Leod, leudes').

42 Kluge and Seebold, Art. 'Leute', in: *Etymologisches Wörterbuch*, 574; Wolfgang Haubrichs, '"Leudes", "fara", "faramanni" und "farones": Zur Semantik der Bezeichnungen für einige am Konsenshandeln beteiligte Gruppen', in: *Recht und Konsens im frühen Mittelalter* (Vorträge und Forschungen 82), ed. Verena Epp and Christoph H.F. Meyer Ostfildern 2017, 235–263, here 236–247.

43 *Lex Salica*, ed. Eckhardt, MGH LL nat. Germ. 4, 2, 70, 72. Cf. Schmidt-Wiegand, 'Bezeichnungen', 376–377; Schmidt-Wiegand, 'Leod', 1845; Schmidt-Wiegand, 'Wergeld', 458; von Olberg-Haverkate, 'Leod, leudes', 842–846.

44 *Pactus legis Salicae*, ed. Eckhardt, MGH LL nat. Germ. 4, 1, 284 (Glossar); *Lex Salica*, ed. Eckhardt, MGH LL nat. Germ. 4, 2, 114; auch in: *Lex Salica: 100-Titel-Text*, ed. Karl August Eckhardt, Weimar 1953, 276 (Glossar).

liod-werdene 'violation of a man'.[45] During Romanization one would certainly not expect a complete loss of w, but rather a Rom. vocalization with [-oa-, -ua-], like for example with PN Rom. *Leodoaldus* < *Leod-walda-, Leoduinus* < *Leod-wini-*. The hypothesis should be discussed again and in detail, together with the new etymological reconstruction by Elmar Seebold (see note 45).

In any case, we find here a metonymic switch of meaning from 'injury' as an element of an offense to the fine that has to be paid for it.

(8) *Bannus*: The older meaning of MLat. *bannus* and vernacular OHG OS *ban,* OF *ban*(*n*), OE *ge-ban*(*n*) is 'a solemnly notified order deriving from public authority, commanding or prohibiting a definite action under pain of a fixed fine' (J.F. Niermeyer).[46] Loanwords — like Old French *ban* 'public promulgation' — and vernacular equivalents (cf. also ON *bann* 'prohibition') are derived from (West) Germ. **banna-* masc. 'summon, order, ban', abstracted from the verb Germ. *banna-n* 'to mobilize, to demand', with the more frequent in Germ. nasal infix to IE **bhâ-* 'to speak solemnly', including Greek *phêmi* 'I say, claim, order' and (with Italic phonetic development) Lat. *fâri* 'to speak solemnly', *fâs* 'divine right'.[47] The preservation of this basic meaning in the Germanic legal terminology is remarkable and indicates old formation.

In legal history Heinrich Brunner argues the same point, and indeed he suggests an additional alternative explanation: 'Others derive the sense of the banner from the emblem (Goth. *bandwa* "sign", MLat. loan word *bandum* "warflag, German also *Banner* < French *bannière*"), which was proclaimed during the peace of assemblies by raising a flag, hanging a shield or raising

45 Cf. Schmidt-Wiegand, 'Bezeichnungen', 376, Anm. 6; Schmidt-Wiegand, 'Leod', 1845; Gabriele von Olberg, *Die Bezeichnungen für soziale Stände, Schichten und Gruppen in den Leges Barbarorum,* München 1991, 65 and 73; Dieter Hägermann, Art. 'Leudes', in: *LexMA* 5, Munich and Zurich 1991, col. 1919; Elmar Seebold, 'Malbergisch "Leodardi" und die altfriesischen Gesetze. Untersuchungen zu den Malbergischen Glossen I', *Beiträge zur Geschichte der deutschen Sprache und Literatur* 129 (2007), 8–17 (reconstructing germ. **laewa-dwardî*(*n*)- 'damaging, violation by abandon'). Cf. Siegmund Feist, *Vergleichendes Wörterbuch der gotischen Sprache,* Leiden 1939, 166 (cited as Feist, *Vergleichendes Wörterbuch*); Orel, *Handbook,* 448.

46 Niermeyer and van de Kieft, *Mediae Latinitatis Lexicon,* 109–112.

47 Kluge and Seebold, Art. 'Bann', in: *Etymologisches Wörterbuch,* 89; *EWA* 1, Göttingen 1988, 453–456; Orel, *Handbook,* 36. Cf. Jörg Müller-Volbehr, Art. 'Bann', in: *RGA* 2, Berlin and New York 1976, 34–40; Robert Scheyhing, Art. 'Bann', in: *LexMA* 1, Munich and Zurich 1980, 1414–1415; Katrin Kastl, Art. 'Bann, weltlicher', in: *HRG* 1, Berlin ^{2}2008, col. 432–436 (cited as Kastl, 'Bann').

a sword'[48] — according to Schröder and von Künßberg (1922),[49] Kaufmann (1971) and Kastl (2004).[50] This opinion is linguistically untenable.

Early evidence for the metonymically derived meaning 'fines for an offence against the public authority' are: 6th c. Gregory of Tours (V,26):[51] *Chilpericus rex de pauperibus et junioribus eclesiae vel basilicae bannos jussit exigi, pro eo quod in exercitu non ambulasset* (fee for refraining from military service); apparently not further documented until the 8th c.; then *Lex Saxonum*, c. 23:[52] *bannum solvat*; *Capit. Haristallense* a. 779, c. 19:[53] *Tantos vices bannos solvat quanta mancipia vendidit* ... Numerous similar formulations appear from the 8th c. onwards in the *leges*, deeds, capitularies. Its usage as a 'fine' seems to be an originally West Frankish coinage.

(9) *Fredus, freda*: The MLat. loan word (with Vulgar Latin lowering of the syllable from Germ. [i] > [e])[54] originally belongs to Germ. **frithu-*, OHG OS *fridu* 'peace', a tu-abstract word to IE **pri-* 'close, familiar, dear': '*Friede* thus must be roughly the "being together" in the sense of "treating each other as within the clan"' (E. Seebold).[55] It can be seen as a contrast to Germ. **faih-ida* 'feud, enmity', MLat. *faida* (cf. below).[56]

The metonymically derived meaning of a 'fine that is to be paid to the central authority, in addition to compensation to a damaged party; originally as remuneration to the central authority for the re-establishment of the peace' (J. F. Niermeyer)[57] is documented early: a. 555/58 *Decretum Chlotharii* I, c. 16:[58] *Fretus iudici, in cuius provincia est latro, reservetur*; a. 511/558 *Pactus Childeberti*

48 Heinrich Brunner, *Deutsche Rechtsgeschichte* vol. 2, Leipzig 1892, 34–41.

49 Richard Schröder and Eberhard Frh. v. Künßberg, *Lehrbuch der deutschen Rechtsgeschichte*, Berlin and Leipzig [6]1922, 121–125.

50 Ekkehard Kaufmann, Art. 'Bann', in: *HRG* 1, Berlin 1971, col. 308–311; Kastl, 'Bann', 433.

51 Gregory of Tours, *Decem Libri Historiarum*, ed. Bruno Krusch and Wilhelm Levison, MGH SS rerum Merovingicarum 1, 1, Hanover 1951, 233.

52 *Lex Saxonum*, ed. Karl Frh. von Richthofen and Karl Friedrich Frh. von Richthofen, MGH LL 5, Hanover 1875/1879, 61.

53 *Capitulare Haristallense*, ed. Boretius, MGH Capit. 1, 51.

54 Niermeyer and van de Kieft, *Mediae Latinitatis Lexicon*, 593–594.

55 Kluge and Seebold, 'Friede', in: *Etymologisches Wörterbuch*, 318; *EWA* 3, Göttingen 2007, 559–562.

56 Cf. note 67.

57 Niermeyer and van de Kieft, *Mediae Latinitatis Lexicon*, 593–594. Cf. Heinrich Brunner, *Deutsche Rechtsgeschichte* vol. 1, Leipzig [2]1906, 333–334; Heinrich Brunner and Claudius von Schwerin, *Deutsche Rechtsgeschichte* vol. 2, Leipzig [2]1928, 806–809; Schmidt-Wiegand, 'Bezeichnungen', 355; Ekkehard Kaufmann, Art. 'Fredus', in: *HRG* 1, Berlin 1971, col. 1275, 1292; Eva Schumann, Art. 'Fredus', in: *HRG* 1, Berlin [2]2008, col. 1713–1714.

58 *Pactus Childeberti et Chlotharii*, ed. Boretius, MGH Capit. 1, Hanover 1883, 7.

et Chlotharii, c. 12:[59] ... *iuxta modum culpae inter fredo et faido conpensetur ...;* end of 6th c. Gregory of Tours, *Miracula S. Martini* IV, c. 26:[60] *Conpositionem fisco debitam quam illi fretum vocant* (here clearly considered as part of *compositio*); *Pactus legis Sal.* 13,6; 24,7; 50,3; 53,2,4,6,8; furthermore 35,9 to the *homicidia servorum* the clause:[61] *Inter fredo et faido sunt 1800 denarii ...;* 88:[62] with reference to *servi accusati* the clause: ... *inter fredo et faido conpensabitur ...* (with an alliterative verse formula as above in the pactus between Childebert and Chlothar and in a deed a. 694 see below); *Lex Sal.* 34; 86,3; 89,2–4; furthermore 14,5:[63] Si *vero puella in verbo regis fuerit, qui traetur, fredus exinde ... cogatur exsolvere ...;* according to 86,3 the peacekeeping *grafio* received a third of the whole wergeld:[64] *duas partes cuius causa est, tertia parte grafio frito ad se recolligat, si tamen fritus iam ante de ipsa causa non fuit solutus* (with preservation of Germ.[i]); also early documentary evidence from 7th c.: MGH DD Merov. No. 49 (a. 635 F. 7th/8th c.) Rebais:[65] *Sub omni emunitate hoc monasterium sibimet omnes fredos concessos debeat possidere vel quicquid exinde fiscus poterat sperare*; no. 99 (a. 662/75) Speyer:[66] *Nullus iudex publicus in curtis ecclesiae suae freda nec sthopha* (duty) *nec herebanno recipere nec requirere non praesumat*; no. 141 (a. 694) Valenciennes:[67] *Ei fuit iudecatum, ut in exfaido et fredo sol. 15 pro ac causa fidem facere debirit.* Furthermore *fredus* is to be found in the *Formulae Marculfi*, in the *Lex Al.*, *Lex Baiw.*, *Lex Rib. Lex Thur.*, *Lex Sax.*, *Lex Fris.* and in Carolingian capitularies.

(10) *Faidus, faida*: The *faida* 'private war, feud' is derived linguistically from WGerm. **faih-ithô* fem., OHG *gi-fêhida*, OE *faehd(u)*, OF *faithe*, abstraction from adjective WGerm. **faiha-*, OE *fâh*, OF *fâch*, OHG *gi-fêh*, MDutch *ge-vee*

59 *Pactus Childeberti et Chlotharii*, ed. Boretius, MGH Capit. 1, Hanover 1883, 6. One may note the alliteration *fredus* vs. *faida*.

60 Gregory of Tours, *Liber de virtutibus sancti Martini episcopi*, ed. Bruno Krusch, MGH SS rerum Merovingicarum 1, 2, Hanover 1885, 134–211, here 206.

61 *Pactus legis Salicae*, ed. Eckhardt, MGH LL nat. Germ. 4, 1, 60, 92, 195, 201–203, 132.

62 *Pactus legis Salicae*, ed. Eckhardt, MGH LL nat. Germ. 4, 1, 252.

63 *Lex Salica*, ed. Eckhardt, MGH LL nat. Germ. 4, 2, 72, 151, 154, 156, 52.

64 *Lex Salica*, ed. Eckhardt, MGH LL nat. Germ. 4, 2, 148–150.

65 *Die Urkunden der Merowinger*, ed. Theo Kölzer, vol. 1, Hanover 2001, 128 (falsification of an authentic document, cited as *Urkunden der Merowinger*, ed. Kölzer).

66 *Urkunden der Merowinger*, ed. Kölzer, 254.

67 *Urkunden der Merowinger*, ed. Kölzer, 356.

'hostile, outlawed'.[68] This corresponds with a. 643 *ER* 45 Lgb.... *faida, hoc est inimicitia*.[69]

The metonymically developed meaning 'amount of money with which one can ransom oneself from a retributive action' appears early in Frankish contexts in the alliterative verse formula *inter fredo et faido* (cf. no. 9); it therefore is related to the practice of peace-building and peace-keeping. In the Langobardic region, it seems to be more clearly defined as a ransom amount. Cf. a. 643 *ER* 188 Penalty for the robbery of a girl which could provoke a feud:[70] *Si puella libera aut vedua sine volontatem parentum ad maritum ambolaverit, libero tamen, tunc maritus qui eam accepit uxorem, conponat anagrip* (sexual assault) *sol. 20 et propter faida alius 20*; furthermore *ER* 387 and more often: ... *faida non requiratur* ...[71]

Certainly, a non-linguist would wonder why in addition to the meanings *leodi* 'Leudes, warriors, people', *fredus* < **frithu* 'peace, order' and *bannus* 'ban, command' the same words or phonetic units also always have the additional meaning of 'what one must pay for the sake of the killed persons, for the sake of the violated force of the ban, or for the sake of restoring the peace'.

This shift of meaning is initially hard to understand. However, such a shift in meaning is a normal process in the languages of the world (not only in the legal language), subsumed under the rhetorical device *metonymy*. Examples from today's everyday language include when you say 'I have to pay a ticket', that is actually 'I have to pay the amount fixed via a ticket as a fine for a violation of the road traffic regulation'. Thus this shift of meaning has an effect of abbreviation, an elliptic impact. It can also often be a matter of 'pars pro toto'; for example if you say 'Today I bought the new Walser'. Anyone who hears that of course knows that it does not mean one has bought the German writer Martin Walser (like for example a professional football player) but rather his book.

2.3 *Terms for Enforcement Officers*

(11) *Büttel*: OS *budil* 'collectarius, tax collector', OHG *butil* 'court usher, barker, emissarius, lictor, praeco', MDutch *bodel, buedel, beudel* 'court bailiff', OE *bydel* 'carrier' < WGerm. **budila* 'summoner envoy', agent noun to Germ. **beuda-* 'to

68 Kluge and Seebold, Art. 'Fehde', in: *Etymologisches Wörterbuch*, 284; *EWA* 3, Göttingen 2007, 105–106; *EWA* 4, Göttingen 2009, 247–248. Cf. Eva Schumann, Art. 'Faida', in: *HRG* 1, Berlin ^{2}2008, col. 1478–1479.

69 *Edictus Rothari*, ed. Bluhme, MGH LL 4, 20. Cf. van der Rhee, *Die germanischen Wörter*, 47.

70 *Edictus Rothari*, ed. Bluhme, MGH LL 4, 45. Cf. van der Rhee, *Die germanischen Wörter*, 46–48; Niermeyer and van de Kieft, *Mediae Latinitatis Lexicon*, 531–532.

71 *Edictus Rothari*, ed. Bluhme, MGH LL 4, 90.

command' (apophony — zero grade) with suffix *-ila*.[72] In OHG and OS the word appears only in glosses, not in the *leges*.

(12) *Schultheiß*: OS *skuld-hêtio*, OE *scyld-haeta*, OF *skelt-â*(*ta*), ODutch *skolt-hêti*, latinized *scultetus*, MDutch *scout-hete*, OHG *sculd-heizo* (with sound shift of [t]> [ts, z, s]) Lgb. (esp. *ER* 15, but also in Langobardic deeds and Italian capitularies) *sculd-hais, sculd-ais* (with Rom. h-loss), *sculd-ahis* (with Diphthong-Hiatus-Marker <h>), with further Romanization and Rom. phonetic substitution [a] for Germ. [ai] : *sculdassio, sculdassius*, all as designation of an office holder with functions in administration, executive and court (chair of jury)[73] < WGerm. **skuldi-hait*(*j*)*ôn* masc., compound from Germ. **skuldi-* 'guilt' + **haita-n* 'to be called, order', that probably had the initial meaning 'the person who sets the debt (payment) or who fixes the duties' (E. Seebold).[74]

Besides extensive documentary evidence in the Langobardic-Italian region the word also occurs early in the Alemannic (St. Gallen a. 771/74, Raetisches Reichsurbar, 9th c., 1st half)[75] and Bavarian areas (Freising a. 809: *sculthetus*),[76] that is, in the three closely related 'Elbe Germanic' languages, but not in the Frankish or other *leges*. In OHG literary sources the legal word appears in the Alem. Notker from St. Gallen (11th c.), in Otfrid of Weissenburg (863/71) and in the Fulda Tatian (around 840).[77] In the early medieval sources, the word glosses or translates Lat. *tribunus, pretor, centurio, exactor populi, quaestor, postulator, vicarius,* as well as *villicus* 'municipal administrator'.[78] In the so called *Capitula Remedii* from Churrätien (c. 3) the *scultaizius* is a clerk ranking below *camararius, senescalcus* and *iudex publicus* and is equated with a *capitanius ministerialis* in the *compositio*. In Italy Paulus Diaconus (HL VI,24) tells an adventurous story for the second half of the 7th century about Slavic 'robbers'

72 Kluge and Seebold, Art. 'bieten', in: *Etymologisches Wörterbuch*, 121–122; *EWA* 2, Göttingen 1998, 90–93; Orel, *Handbook*, 43.

73 *Edictus Rothari*, ed. Bluhme, MGH LL 4, 15: *gastaldius regis aut sculdahis*. Cf. van der Rhee, *Die germanischen Wörter*, 115–119; Vòllono, 'Methodik und Probleme', 496–502.

74 Kluge and Seebold, Art. 'Schultheiß', in: *Etymologisches Wörterbuch*, 829.

75 *Chartularium Sangallense* (*700–840*), ed. Peter Erhard, vol. 1, St. Gallen 2013, no. 66 (*Boazo sculdatione* in Seen bei Winterthur, CH); *Bündner Urkundenbuch*, ed. Elisabeth Meyer-Marthaler and Franz Perret, vol. 1, Chur 1955, 380.

76 *Die Traditionen des Hochstifts Freising*, ed. Theodor Bitterauf, vol. 1, Munich 1905, no. 288.

77 Schützeichel, *Althochdeutsches Wörterbuch*, 314; Johann Kelle, *Otfrids von Weissenburg Evangelienbuch* 3, *Glossar der Sprache Otfrids*, Regensburg 1881, 539.

78 Niermeyer and van de Kieft, *Mediae Latinitatis Lexicon*, 1237; Schützeichel, *Glossenwortschatz* 8, 406.

in Friuli:[79] *Subsecutus est hos rector loci illius, quem sculdahis lingua propria* (of the Langobards) *dicunt, vir nobilis animoque et viribus potens* ... This *sculdahis* had the functions of a *rector*, stood in competition with the duke of Friuli, and fulfilled prominent military functions during the attack on a mountain fortress. Certainly, the Langobardic *sculdahiis* belonged 'to a class of intermediate office holders', here equivalent to a 'nobleman', but were they really classed 'below the *arimanni*, the free born Langobards who were committed to military service' (as claimed by R. Schmidt-Wiegand)?[80]

According to the evidence, the designation comes from two core geographic focal areas, the North Sea Germanic languages, Anglo-Saxon, Saxon, and Frisian, and the languages of the above-mentioned Elbe Germanic grouping. From there the word spread to the Frankish linguistic landscapes.

An older, formally analogous term can be seen in Goth. *dulga-haitja* 'creditor' to Goth. *dulgs* 'guilt, fine' (S. Feist, R. Schmidt-Wiegand); originally 'one who mandates or determines a debt'.[81]

(13) *Witi-scalcus*: cf. MHG *wîzenaere, -er* 'bailiff, penal servant, *tortor*'.[82]

The unique term of *witi-scalcus* is to be found in the Burgundian *Liber constitutionum* (a. 517) once in dat. plural *witiscalcis* (manuscript groups AB, var. *widi-, vti-* B, *witti-* A, *victi-, vici-* B), and once in acc. plural *witiscalcos* (AB, var. *witti-* A, *bitti-, sviti-, svitu-* B). It appears in the title 76 under the headline *De wittiscalcis*, in a manuscript with the addition *et qui eis violenter fecerunt* ('On bailiffs and those who attack them violently') and is considered with its own amendment in the year 513 (von Salis, *Lex Burg*. 1892, tit. 76):[83]

---

79 Paulus Diaconus, *Historia Langobardorum*, ed. Georg Waitz, MGH SS rerum Germanicarum in usum scholarum separatim editi 48, Hanover 1878, 222–223.

80 Adalbert Erler and Marian Neidert, Art. 'Schultheiß, Schulze', in: *HRG* 4, Berlin 1990, col. 1519–1521; Ruth Schmidt-Wiegand, Art. 'Schultheiß', in: *RGA* 27, Berlin and New York 2004, 370–371 (cited as Schmidt-Wiegand, 'Schultheiß').

81 Feist, *Vergleichendes Wörterbuch*, 128–129; Schmidt-Wiegand, 'Schultheiß', 370.

82 Matthias Lexer, *Mittelhochdeutsches Handwörterbuch* 3, Leipzig 1878, 959–960.

83 *Leges Burgundionum*, ed. v. Salis, MGH LL nat. Germ. 2, 1, 101–102. — 'On Royal Servants. 1. The complaint is made by our counts that some of our people have become so presumptuous that they have struck down our servants who execute our judgments and collect fines at our command, and have not hesitated to seize by force the pledges given by the order of the counts. Because of such acts we decree in the present law that if anyone hereafter strikes down our servants or removes pledges insolently, and these facts are established upon investigation by order of a judge, he shall be held liable to a triple satisfaction, that is, he who did violence will be compelled to pay three solidi for a blow for which a single solidus would be paid ordinarily. 2. And also those things which were removed by violence shall be returned with a thrice ninefold payment; with the further provision that such presumptuous persons must pay the fine owed to us. 3. Also women will likewise be held to the payment of the fine if they treat our servants with contempt. 4. Now we

LXXVI. De wittiscalcis [et qui eis violenter fecerunt: add. B7]

(1) Comitum nostrorum querela processit, quod aliqui in populo nostro eiusmodi praesumptionibus abutantur, ut pueros nostros, qui iudicia exsequuntur, quibusque multam iubemus exigere, et caede conlidant et sublata iussu comitum pignera non dubitent violenter auferre.

Qua de re praesenti lege decernimus: ut quicumque post haec pueros nostros ceciderit et insolenter abstulerit, quod ex ordinatione iudicis docebitur fuisse praesumptum, tripla satisfactione teneatur obnoxius, hoc est: ut per singulos ictus, pro quibus singuli solidi ab his inferuntur, ternos solidos is, qui percusserit, cogatur exsolvere.

(2) Ea etiam, quae fuerunt violenter erepta, tripla novigildi solutione reddantur, ita ut multam nobis debitam praesumptores solvant.

(3) Mulieres quoque, si wittiscalcos nostros contempserint, ad solutionem multae similiter tenebuntur.

(4) Nam statutam districtionis formam volumus ita custodiri, ut pueri nostri, periculi sui memores, providere curabunt, ut non amplius in quibuscumque causis, quam fuerint ordinati, praesumant. Nam ut iniurias eorum iussimus vindicari, ita in se distringendum esse non dubitent, nisi omni diligentia quae sunt praecepta servaverint.

Datum V. kalendas Iulias, Probo viro clarissime consule.

The Burgundian law of 513 above, like many Burgundian epitaphs, is dated according to Roman consuls. Provoked complaints by the royal *comites,* it apparently aims to protect the *wittiscalci* from assaults and hostilities by the *populus noster* of the king by imposing higher penalties. The following are specifically treated as encroachments: physical resistance (beating) and insolence, bold refusal of judicially ordered claims, and also defamation by female persons. Very clearly the *wittiscalci* are marked as *pueri regis*, royal servants and even enforcement officers, *qui iudicia exsequuntur*, who must execute court judgements.

This notion is confirmed by etymological analysis: the root word is clearly and unambiguously identifiable as Germ. **skalka-* 'slave, serf, servant' (cf.

wish this stated form of punishment to be observed then, that our servants, mindful of their danger, will take care not to exceed their orders presumptuously in any case whatsoever. We have ordered that injuries committed by them be avenged, so that they may have no doubt that punishment will ensue unless they observe with all diligence those orders which have been given them. Given on the 27th of June (513), in the consulship of Probus, *vir clarissimus.*' (*The Burgundian Code. Book of Constitutions or Law of Gundobad. Additional Enactments.* Translated by Katherine Fischer-Drew, Philadelphia 1949, 73). See Haubrichs, 'Rechtswörter', 142–143.

Goth. *skalks*, ON *skalkr*, OHG scalc, OS OF *skalk*, OE *scealc*; cf. It. *scalco* 'steward' and the early loan words for court officials as *seni-scalcus* 'old serf, head servant', *mara(h)-scalcus* 'groom, supervisor of the royal stable').[84] In another East Germanic language that is closely related to Burgundian, the Wulfila-Gothic *skalks* translates Greek *doúlos* 'servant, serf'.[85] The Gothic historian Jordanes (before 552), possibly regarding 453, mentions (XLIII, 228) that the Visigothic King Thorismod was murdered *ab[a]scalc suo* ('by his servant').[86] The name-type *Gudi-scalc* etc. 'God's servant' is especially well documented in the East Germanic region as well.[87]

But what is contained in the first element, in the determiner of the compound? The variants of both classes of manuscripts of Burgundian law (AB) show forms with <d> (*widi-*), <t> (*witi-*) and double t (*witti-*, *bitti-*). In the Romance linguistic environment, these variants are traceable to a single <t>, thus *Wîti-*, but not reverse <t> to <tt>. Therefore the sound [t] must be estimated for the initial form. The forms with double t (also present in numerous names with *Wit[t]i-*) are explained by the fact that following the late antique Romance degemination of double consonants in spoken Latin, double spellings were perceived as equivalent to single consonant marks. The spellings with <d> can be explained by the Gallo-Romance sonorization of the tenuis consonants, voiceless mute sounds, here [t] > [d], between vowels.

The element *Wîti-* appears very early especially in East Germanic personal names: several times *Wîti-mir, Wîti-gis, Wîti-rîk, Wîti-wulf*, and also later with Romance sound substitution [gu] for Germ. [w] *Guidi-scalcus*.[88] The lexeme belongs to Germ. **wîtan-* 'to punish, to avenge' with long [î]; there are no variants with the Romance lowering from short [i] to [e]. The element can be observed, for example, in Goth. *fra-weitan* 'to procure the right, to avenge', OE OS *wîtan*, OHG *wîzan* 'to accuse, to punish'.[89] Additionally, the derived Germ. noun **wîtjan*, OE OF *wîte*, OS *wîti*, and OHG *wîzi*, means 'punishment', and ON *wîti* 'monetary penalty'. The *wîti-scalcus* should therefore be translated with

84 Kluge and Seebold, Art. 'Schalk', in: *Etymologisches Wörterbuch*, 793; Manlio Cortelazzo and Paolo Zolli, *Dizionario Etimologico della Lingua Italiana (DELI)*, Bologna ²1999, 1452 (scalco).

85 Feist, *Vergleichendes Wörterbuch*, 428.

86 Jordanes, *Iordanis Romana et Getica*, ed. Theodor Mommsen, MGH AA 5, 1, Berlin 1882, 116, ll. 11–14.

87 Hermann Reichert, *Lexikon der altgermanischen Namen* 1, Vienna 1987, 391 (cited as Reichert, *Lexikon*).

88 Reichert, *Lexikon* 1, 789–793. Cf. for the East Germanic name-system Wolfgang Haubrichs, 'Personennamen sprachlich ostgermanischer Provenienz', *Studia Anthroponymica Scandinavica* 32 (2014), 5–35.

89 Orel, *Handbook*, 468; Feist, *Vergleichendes Wörterbuch*, 167; Kluge and Seebold, Art. 'verweisen', in: *Etymologisches Wörterbuch*, 958.

'penal servant' or 'enforcement servant' (or in the special context 'official in charge of collecting the amercements' J. F. Niermeyer).[90] This corresponds well with the content of the amendment from 513 — and take note of the use of the word Lat. *vindicari* 'to punish, to avenge, to repay' (§ 4) in the law. The semantics correspond with the title *De apparitoribus* ('On the enforcement officers') in the parallel paragraph in the *Lex Romana* (tit. 30), which was intended for the Roman-Romance population of the Burgundian Kingdom.[91]

3 Conclusion

Finally the individual legal words of the lexical field of *compositio* and their chronological classification must be discussed in terms of historical linguistics.

The central term *wer-geld* < Germ. **wira-gelda-* (no. 1), with the clear etymological identifiable meaning 'remuneration for a man (person)', was undoubtedly a West Germanic word, likely widespread through early contacts among the individual *gentes*. It is attested in Old English, Old Frisian, Langobardic, Old High German and in Frankish Merovingian legal texts. It first appears around 596 in the legislation of Childebert II, three times in the formula *suum weregildum conponere*, then with the same formula a. 643 in the Langobardic *Edictus Rothari*. It appears in the eighth century *leges* of the Alamanni, Bavarians, Saxons and Chamavian Franks and in the *Lex Ribuaria*, though surprisingly not in the core *lex* of the Franks. The determinant of the compound is a very archaic designation for 'man, person', which possibly died out in most continental vernacular languages in the Carolingian period. Its disappearance probably resulted from the fact that the north developed a new synonymous word when the first element had become incomprehensible, namely *man-gelt*. This word spread from the Low German and Dutch regions into Old Norse. Another replacement word developed with *wider-gild* 'repayment' (no. 5) in Langobardic, which is evidenced in late manuscripts and legal glossaries. This replacement of course occurred before the death of this vernacular language in the late-eighth century.

The short form *wer(a)* (Nr. 2) appears in England and, in the form *wir*, in the Langobardic legislation of king Liutprand (712–744). This could point to a West-Germanic basis for the form, but is more likely an independent development among the Anglo-Saxons and Langobards.

Some numeric compounds with the root word **gelda-* (Nr. 3) are formally comparable with *Wer-geld* and emphasise the amount of money to be paid.

90 Niermeyer and van de Kieft, *Mediae Latinitatis Lexicon*, 1477.

91 Haubrichs, 'Rechtswörter', 143.

There are hybrid compound words with a Latin first element used by the Burgundians; this indicates their relatively quick acculturation. The romanized Langobardic *acto-gild* 'eightfold remuneration' and the Bavarian *niungeldo* 'ninefold remuneration' certainly developed independently from the Burgundian coinages.

The metonymic-elliptic designations for such fines must be very old; they developed through a shift of the affected group or the subject to the payment itself. That *leodi, leuda* and 'manbote, Manngeld' (no. 6) can be understood as synonyms of *Wer-geld* probably derives from a metonymic shift of *leodi-* 'people, men' as the object of *compositio*. The legal term appears in this meaning in the *Pactus legis Salicae*, and additionally in the further versions of the *Lex Salica*, from whence it spreads to the *leges* of the Bavarians, Thuringians, Chamavian Franks, and Frisians. Since the same meaning is also held among the Anglo-Saxons, one could assume a West Germanic foundation, unless it is a case of secondary diffusion. In contrast, *leodardi* < **leod-wardi* (no. 7) which originally meant 'personal injury to a man' and owes its new meaning to a metonymic shift from the crime to the atonement for the reparation itself, is only Frankish.

Concerning *bannus*, the meaning shifted from 'command of an act by the public authority' to the fine and reparation which was due in the event of an infringement. This legal term is not evidenced in metonymic meaning in the early Frankish laws; however, it appears in this sense by the end of the sixth century as a Latin loan word in Gregory of Tours, where a fine claim is attributed to the Neustrian king Chilperich (561–584). As a Frankish legal term, *bannus* must be old, even though the exact form cannot be found in the other older *leges*.

It is very different with *fredus, freda* 'fine payment to the public authority as compensation for the restoration of peace' (no. 9), in which the metonymic shift occurs from the object of atonement to the payment of the fine. In Gregory of Tours, the *quam illi* (sc. the Franks) *fretum vocant*, is defined significantly as *compositio fisco debita*, as a reparation to pay to the treasury. The legal term already appears several times in the *Pactus*, then in the later versions of the *Lex Salica*, and in the circle of Chlodwig's son Chlothar I (511–561). Occurring as it does in the alliterative verse formula *inter fredo et faido* suggests this Frankish coinage is quite old, where the contrast of the infringement (West Germ. **faihithô* 'hostility' (no. 10)) and the restoration of justice (Germ. **frithu-* 'peace, order') are bound together. In other Germanic languages *fredus, freda* does not seem to occur in this sense.

In the case of the early identifiable vernacular designations for enforcement officers, the situation is regionally and factually very differentiated. The 'bailiff', OS *budil*, OHG *butil* (no. 11), originally with the meaning 'messenger', does not occur in the *leges* at all and only has the meaning of 'tax collector, lictor' in Old Saxon and Old High German glosses. This must be a particular regional development.

In contrast the designation of *sculd-heizo* 'state officer, village mayor' (no. 12) is widespread and may be regarded as being generally West Germanic. It is certainly old. Only the etymology provides insight into the fact that an initial meaning was probably an 'official who fixes the debt or obligation'. But it seems that in the entire scope of application, the semantic development to a lower or intermediate level office holder took place early. In Old High German the word is glossed or translated at least (e.g. Lat. *tribunus, praetor, centurio*, however also *villicus* 'local chief'). In the Elbe Germanic languages, especially in Langobardic, already by the second half of the seventh century it is an office of regional importance which a *vir nobilis* can exercise. Only in the Langobardic *Edictus Rothari* and later in Italian capitularies does this function appear in laws, but not in any of the other *leges*.

The unique Burgundian compound word *witi-scalc-us* < **wîti-skalk-* 'penal servant' (no. 13) is a genuine vernacular coinage. It can only be an old Burgundian legal term that designated a royal enforcement officer who was in charge of the implementation of judicially fixed judgements and punishments.

The above examination of vernacular legal terms in the lexical field of *compositio* should have demonstrated both how differentiated this vocabulary is, but also that the vernacular terminology in this field is mostly not derived from Latin, but presupposes older legal language, even if this is often *gens-* or area-specific.

Bibliography

Primary Sources

Bündner Urkundenbuch, ed. Elisabeth Meyer-Marthaler and Franz Perret, vol. 1, Chur 1955.

Capitularia regum Francorum 1, ed. Alfred Boretius, MGH Capitularia regum Francorum 1, Hanover, 1883.

Chartularium Sangallense (700–840), ed. Peter Erhard, vol. 1, St. Gallen 2013.

Codice diplomatico Longobardo, ed. Luigi Schiaparelli, vol. 2, Rome 1933.

Die Traditionen des Hochstifts Freising, ed. Theodor Bitterauf, vol. 1, Munich 1905–1909.

Die Urkunden der Merowinger, ed. Theo Kölzer, vol. 1, Hanover 2001.

Edictus Langobardorum, ed. Friedrich Bluhme, MGH LL 4, Hanover 1868, 1–225.

Gregory of Tours, *Liber de virtutibus sancti Martini episcopi*, ed. Bruno Krusch, MGH SS rerum Merovingicarum 1, 2, Hanover 1885, 134–211.

Gregory of Tours, *Decem Libri Historiarum*, ed. Bruno Krusch and Wilhelm Levison, MGH SS rerum Merovingicarum 1, 1, Hanover 1951.

Jordanes, *Iordanis Romana et Getica*, ed. Theodor Mommsen, MGH AA 5, 1, Berlin 1882.

Leges Alamannorum, ed. Karl Lehmann, MGH LL nationum Germanicarum 5, 1, Hanover ²1966.

Leges Burgundionum, ed. Ludwig Rudolf von Salis, MGH LL nationum Germanicarum, 2, 1, Hanover 1892.

Leges Saxonum, ed. Karl Freiherr von Richthofen and Karl Friedrich Freiherr von Richthofen, MGH LL 5, Hanover 1875–1879, 1–102.

Lex Baiwariorum, ed. Ernst von Schwind, MGH LL nationum Germanicarum 5, 2, Hanover 1926.

Lex Ribuaria, ed. Franz Beyerle and Rudolf Buchner, MGH LL nationum Germanicarum 3, 2, Hanover, 1954.

Lex Salica, ed. Karl August Eckhardt, MGH LL nationum Germanicarum 4, 2, Hanover 1969.

Lex Salica: 100-Titel-Text, ed. Karl August Eckhardt, Weimar 1953.

Marculfi Formulae, ed. Karl Zeumer, MGH Formulae Merovingici et Karolini aevi, Hanover 1886, 32–112.

Pactus legis Salicae, ed. Karl August Eckhardt, MGH LL nationum Germanicarum 4, 1, Hanover, 1962.

Paulus Diaconus, *Pauli Historia Langobardorum*, ed. Georg Waitz, MGH SS rerum Germanicarum in usum scholarum separatim editi 48, Hanover 1878.

The Burgundian Code. Book of Constitutions or Law of Gundobad. Additional Enactments. Translated by Katherine Fischer Drew, Philadelphia 1949.

Secondary Works

Brunner, Heinrich, *Deutsche Rechtsgeschichte* vol. 1, Leipzig ²1906.

Brunner, Heinrich, *Deutsche Rechtsgeschichte* vol. 2, Leipzig 1892.

Brunner, Heinrich and C. von Schwerin, *Deutsche Rechtsgeschichte* vol. 2, Leipzig ²1928.

Cortelazzo, Manlio and Zolli, Paolo, *Dizionario Etimologico della Lingua Italiana* (*DELI*), Bologna ²1999.

Dannenbauer, Heinrich, 'Die Rechtsstellung der Gallorömer im fränkischen Reich (1941)', in: Heinrich Dannenbauer, *Grundlagen der mittelalterlichen Welt. Skizzen und Studien*, Stuttgart 1958, 94–120.

Depreux, Philippe, 'Wergeld, composition et rachat dans les capitulaires des rois Francs', in: *La victime, 2: La réparation du dommage*, ed. Jacqueline Hoareau-Dodinau, Guillaume Métairie and Pascal Texier, Limoges 2009, 345–362.

Erler, Adalbert and Neidert, Marian, Art. 'Schultheiß, Schulze', in: *HRG* 4, Berlin 1990, col. 1519–1521.

Esders, Stefan, '"Eliten" und "Strafrecht" im frühen Mittelalter. Überlegungen zu den Bussen- und Wergeldkatalogen der Leges Barbarorum', in: *Théorie et pratiques des élites au Haut Moyen Age. Conception, perception et réalisation sociale* (Collection Haut Moyen Age 13), ed. François Bougard, Hans-Werner Goetz and Régine Le Jan, Turnhout 2011, 261–282.

Feist, Siegmund, *Vergleichendes Wörterbuch der gotischen Sprache*, Leiden 1939.

Fruscione, Daniela, Art. 'Malbergische Glossen', in: HRG 3, Berlin ²2016, col. 1210–1216.

Hägermann, Dieter, Art. 'Leudes', *LexMA* 5, Munich and Zurich 1991, 1919.

Haubrichs, Wolfgang, 'Personennamen sprachlich ostgermanischer Provenienz', *Studia Anthroponymica Scandinavica* 32 (2014), 5–35.

Haubrichs, Wolfgang, 'Burgundische und intergentile Rechtswörter des "Liber constitutionum" (a. 517) im Kontext der Burgundenforschung', *Sprachwissenschaft* 40 (2015), 127–146.

Haubrichs, Wolfgang, '*Leudes, fara, faramanni* und *farones*: Zur Semantik der Bezeichnungen für einige am Konsenshandeln beteiligte Gruppen', in: *Recht und Konsens im frühen Mittelalter* (Vorträge und Forschungen 82), ed. Verena Epp and Christoph H. F. Meyer, Ostfildern 2017, 235–263.

Haubrichs, Wolfgang, '*Quod Alamanni dicunt*. Volkssprachige Wörter in der *Lex Alamannorum*', in: *Recht und Kultur im frühmittelalterlichen Alemannien* (RGA-Ergänzungsbände 102), ed. Sebastian Brather, Berlin and Boston 2017, 169–209.

Kastl, Katrin, Art. 'Bann, weltlicher', in: HRG 1, Berlin ²2008, col. 432–436.

Kaufmann, Ekkehard, Art. 'Bann', in: HRG 1, Berlin 1971, col 308–311.

Kaufmann, Ekkehard, Art. 'Fredus', in: HRG 1, Berlin 1971, col. 1275.

Kelle, Johann, *Otfrids von Weissenburg Evangelienbuch 3: Glossar der Sprache Otfrids*, Regensburg 1881.

Kluge, Friedrich and Seebold, Elmar, *Etymologisches Wörterbuch der deutschen Sprache* Berlin and Boston ²⁵2011.

Lexer, Matthias, *Mittelhochdeutsches Handwörterbuch* 3, Leipzig 1878.

Lloyd, Albert L., Lühr, Rosemarie and Springer, Otto, *Etymologisches Wörterbuch des Althochdeutschen (EWA)*, vols. 1–6, Göttingen 1988–2017.

J. Müller-Vobehr, Art. 'Bann', in: RGA 2, Berlin 1976, 34–40.

Niermeyer, Jan F. and Cor van de Kieft, *Mediae Latinitatis Lexicon Minus*, 2nd edition, revised by Jan W. J. Burgers, Leiden 2002.

Orel, Vladimir, *A Handbook of Germanic Etymology*, Leiden and Boston 2003.

Pohl, Walter, Hartl, Ingrid and Haubrichs, Wolfgang (ed.), *Walchen, Romani und Latini. Variationen einer nachrömischen Gruppenbezeichnung zwischen Britannien und dem Balkan* (Forschungen zur Geschichte des Mittelalters 21), Vienna 2017.

Reichert, Hermann, *Lexikon der altgermanischen Namen* 1, Vienna 1987.

Scheyhing, Robert, Art. 'Bann', in: *LexMA* 1, Munich and Zurich 1980, 1414–1415.

Schild, Wolfgang, Art. 'Wergeld', in: HRG 5, Berlin 1998, col. 1268–1271.

Schmidt-Wiegand, Ruth, Art. 'Leod, leodes, leudes, leodi …', in: HRG 3, Berlin 1978, col. 1845–1848.

Schmidt-Wiegand, Ruth, 'Fränkische und frankolateinische Bezeichnungen für soziale Schichten und Gruppen in der Lex Salica', in: Ruth Schmidt-Wiegand, *Stammesrecht und Volkssprache*, Weinheim 1991, 355–391.

Schmidt-Wiegand, Ruth, Art. 'Malbergische Glossen', in: RGA 19, Berlin 2001, 184–186.

Schmidt-Wiegand, Ruth, Art. 'Mallus', in: RGA 19, Berlin 2001, 191–192.

Schmidt-Wiegand, Ruth, Art. 'Schultheiß', in: RGA 27, Berlin 2004, 370–371.

Schmidt-Wiegand, Ruth, Art. 'Wergeld', in: RGA 33, Berlin 2006, 457–463.

Schröder, Richard and Frh. von Künßberg, Eberhard, *Lehrbuch der deutschen Rechtsgeschichte*, Berlin and Leipzig ^{6}1922.

Schumann, Eva, Art. 'Fredus', in: HRG 1, Berlin ^{2}2008, col. 1713–1714.

Schumann, Eva, Art. 'Kompositionensystem', in: HRG 2, Berlin ^{2}2012, col. 2003–2011.

Schützeichel, Rudolf, *Althochdeutsches Wörterbuch*, Tübingen ^{6}2006.

Schützeichel, Rudolf, *Althochdeutscher und altsächsischer Glossenwortschatz*, Tübingen 2004.

Schwab, Vincenz, *Volkssprachige Wörter in Pactus und Lex Alamannorum*, Bamberg 2017.

Seebold, Elmar, 'Malbergisch *Leodardi* und die altfriesischen Gesetze. Untersuchungen zu den Malbergischen Glossen I', *Beiträge zur Geschichte der deutschen Sprache und Literatur* 129 (2007), 8–17.

Speer, Heino (ed.), *Deutsches Rechtswörterbuch* 9, Stuttgart 1992.

Stutz, Ulrich, 'Das Wergeld des Romanus nach den fränkischen Volksrechten', in: Ulrich Stutz, *'Römerwergeld' und 'Herrenfall'*, Berlin 1934, 4–48.

Tiefenbach, Heinrich, '*Quod Paiuvarii dicunt* — Das altbairische Wortmaterial der Lex Baiovariorum', in: *Die bairische Sprache. Studien zu ihrer Geographie, Grammatik, Lexik und Pragmatik. Festschrift Ludwig Zehetner*, ed. Albrecht Greule, Rupert Hochholzer and Alfred Wildfeuer, Regensburg 2004, 263–290.

Tiefenbach, Heinrich, *Altsächsisches Handwörterbuch — A concise Old Saxon Dictionary*, Berlin and New York 2010.

van der Rhee, Florus, *Die germanischen Wörter in den langobardischen Gesetzen*, Rotterdam 1970.

Vòllono, Maria, 'Methodik und Probleme bei der Erforschung des Langobardischen am Beispiel einiger juristischer Fachbegriffe: *mundoald, launegild, sculdhais*', in: *Die Langobarden. Herrschaft und Identität* (Forschungen zur Geschichte des Mittealters 9), ed. Walter Pohl and Peter Erhart, Vienna 2005, 477–502.

von Olberg, Gabriele, *Die Bezeichnungen für soziale Stände, Schichten und Gruppen in den Leges Barbarorum*, Munich 1991.

von Olberg-Haverkate, Gabriele, Art. 'Leod, leudes', in: HRG 3, Berlin ^{2}2016, col. 842–846.

Wormald, Patrick, Art. 'Wergeld', in: *LexMA* 8, Munich 1997, 2201–2202.

CHAPTER 5

Wergild, Mund and *Manbot* in Early Anglo-Saxon Law

Lisi Oliver†

Anglo-Saxon society was organized according to a *wergild* system, which placed a monetary value on people according to ranks, with categories ranging from king to freeman. Although *wer*, the first element of the compound, refers to a man (cognate with Latin *vir*, from which we get the words 'virile' and 'virility'), *wergild* was also assigned to women and children at the rank of freeman or above.[1]

We tend to think of *wergild* as a payment made for bodily injury, and certainly this was encompassed in the concept. Our earliest laws, those of Æthelberht of Kent, contain 38 clauses in the personal injury tariff schedule, regulating payment by a perpetrator to a victim for injuries ordered from pulling the hair on the top of the head to tearing off the little toenail. Alfred the Great's *Domboc* lists 36 clauses similarly addressing personal injury, many of which are based on Æthelberht's rulings (although considerably emended) and others of which seem to be drawn from a tradition common to the Anglo-Saxon and Frisian territories (but not used in Æthelberht).[2] Indeed, personal injury schedules of varying rank and composition are common to all the laws in early Germanic territories; the restitution demanded is often referred to as *wergild*. But this definition ignores the far greater sense of what *wergild* meant for a person living in a *wergild*-organized society.

Legal applications of *wergild* can be schematically indicated in three categories:

---

1 The present chapter, supplied by her family and published with their permission, was in what appeared to be a finished state when Lisi Oliver passed away suddenly on June 7, 2015. Stefan Jurasinski has added citations, most of which were incomplete, and made other minor changes where necessary. Translations are Oliver's unless otherwise indicated.

2 On the commonalities between Alfredian and Frisian practice, see Lisi Oliver, 'Genital Mutilation in Medieval Germanic Law', in: *Capital and Corporal Punishment in Anglo-Saxon England*, ed. Jay Paul Gates and Nicole Marafioti, Woodbridge 2014, 48–73 (cited as Oliver, 'Genital Mutilation'); Lisi Oliver, 'Who Wrote Alfred's Laws?', in: *Textus Roffensis: Law, Language, and Libraries in Early Medieval England*, ed. Bruce O'Brien and Barbara Bombi, Turnhout 2015, 231–256.

 | DOI:10.1163/9789004466128_006

Internal   Incoming ⬅   Outgoing ➡

The first represents a position of stasis: *wergild* as assigned by birth (or eventually gained by a rise or fall in status). The second represents the occasions on which a person receives (sometimes only a percentage of) his *wergild* from another for damages caused (as, for example, personal injury).[3] The third comprises instances in which a person must pay (sometimes only a percentage of) his own *wergild* for an offense he has committed. The following discussion examines the range of these applications of *wergild* in the legislation of Kent and Wessex. The paper will then address instances in which a person forfeits the right to *wergild*, procedures for payment of *wergild*, and examples of *wergild* outside royal legislation.

The laws to be considered and approximate dates of composition are:

Kent:		*Wessex*:	
Æthelberht	c. 600		
Hloþhere and Eadric	c. 680		
Wihtred	695	Ine	c. 690
		Alfred	c. 890

All other texts discussed fall within these chronological boundaries.

Internal

1 Determination according to Rank

A person's *wergild* was legally set at birth according to rank. The first Anglo-Saxon laws, those of Æthelberht, establish in §24 the 'medium person-price' of 100 shillings.[4] The next laws, those of Hloþhere and Eadric, echo the fact that restitution for killing a freeman 'should be compensated for with a hundred shillings' (§2) and add that 'a man of noble birth ... should be compensated

3 See Oliver, 'Genital Mutilation'.

4 *The Laws of Æthelberht* 24, ed. and trans. Lisi Oliver, *The Beginnings of English Law*, Toronto 2002, 66–67 (cited as Oliver, *Beginnings*). Note that the numeration of chapters in this edition differs from that of the classical edition *Die Gesetze der Angelsachsen* by Felix Liebermann (see footnote 8).

for with three hundred shillings' (§1).[5] Thus a nobleman's *wergild* (at least in Hloþhere and Eadric) is three times that of a freeman; the *wergild* for the king is never addressed.

The West Saxon laws of Ine (§71 [L70]) set 200 shillings as a freeman's *wergild*.[6] They also establish two different ranks of noblemen not differentiated in the laws of Kent. We find rulings on those whose *wer* is 600 shillings, but also those having a *wergild* of 1200 shillings. The former matches the 3:1 ratio of nobleman to freeman in Kent; the latter adds a rank of nobleman with double their *wergild*.

Alfred §4.1 is the first to mention the king's *wergild*, albeit in the context of how great an oath must be sworn to exculpate a person charged with treason. Although the specific amount is never mentioned in these laws, the *Anglo-Saxon Chronicle* for the year 694 states that 'This year the people of Kent settled (*geþingodan*) with Ine, and gave him 30,000 [sceattas?], because they had burned his brother Mul.'[7] The settlement with Ine was more likely legal reparation than friendship. *Mircna Laga* §2 gives the same figure for a king's *wergild*: *Đonne bið cynges anfeald wergild syx þegna wer be Myrcna laga, þæt is* XXX *þusend sceatta 7 þæt bið ealles cxx punda* 'Then the king's single *wergild* is the *wer* of six thanes according to the law of the Mercians, that is 30 thousand *sceattas*'.[8] If the Wessex shilling contained 5 pence, then the king's *wergild* was 6000 shillings, or the worth of five thanes (in contradistinction to Mercia).

Ine §23 states that *Wealh gafolgelda* CXX *scill, his sunu* C, *ðeowne* LX, *somhwelcne fiftegum* 'A Welsh tax-payer 120 shillings, his son 100, a slave 60, some fifty.' Although the clause is unclear as to whether the 120 or 100 shillings represent *wergild* (as the 60 and 50 surely do not), §32 both clarifies this issue and appears to contradict §23:

> *Gif Wiliscmon hæbbe hide londes, his wer bið* CXX *scill; gif he þonne healfes hæbbe,* LXXX *scill; gif he nænig hæbbe,* LX *scillinga.*
>
> If a Welshman has a hide of land, his *wer* is 120 shillings; if he, however, has half, 80 shillings; if he has none, 60 shillings.

5 *The Laws of Hloþhere and Eadric*, 1–2, ed. and trans. Lisi Oliver, *Beginnings*, 126–127.

6 The laws of Ine and Alfred are cited according to chapters assigned in Stefan Jurasinski and Lisi Oliver, The Laws of Alfred: The Domboc and the Making of Anglo-Saxon Law, Cambridge 2021. Where our numeration differs from Liebermann's, his are given in square brackets.

7 See *Two Saxon Chronicles Parallel*, ed. John Earle and Charles Plummer, vol. 1, Oxford 1892, repr. 1972, 40–41.

8 *Die Gesetze der Angelsachsen*, ed. Felix Liebermann, vol. 1, Halle 1903, 462–463.

Some previous scholars have assumed these two clauses must have been added to the body of the laws at different times.[9] Indeed, it is odd that they are separated in the text by eight unrelated paragraphs. They are not, however, irreconcilable. A Welshman with a hide of land (who thus pays taxes) has a *wergild* of 120 shillings (60% of an English freeman); his son will have a lesser *wergild* of 100 (50% of an English freeman's son). If the Welshman has only a half hide of land, his *wer* will be 80, and that of his son presumably concomitantly lowered. A Welshman with no land is approximately the same as the Kentish *esne* ('a hireling of servile status'): he must work the land of another.[10] The reference to the two worths of slaves as 60 and 50 may well represent the difference between a freeman bound to the land and an actual slave.[11]

Finally, Ine §33 states that: 'A Welsh horseman in the king's service who can act as his courier: his *wergild* is 200 shillings.' By dint of his position his *wergild* is raised to that of an English freeman.

The laws of Æthelberht require that (damage to) an *esne* be compensated with the 'worth' without specifying a value. Æthelberht §16 and §21 set three different values for the female slaves of the king and a freeman respectively (discussed in next section).[12] Many barbarian laws recompense the value of a slave according to the work he or she is expected to perform.[13] Indeed, the laws of Wessex set themselves apart by giving the Welsh slave a fixed worth regardless of service.

If a person's standing changed over the course of his life, it was possible to either gain or lose *wergild* status. The *esne* and the slave were excluded from the system: damage to their 'worth' was payable to the owner.[14] But a slave could be manumitted. Æthelberht §27 lists three ranks of *læt*, which likely represent

9 See, for example, Patrick Wormald, *The Making of English Law: King Alfred to the Twelfth Century*, vol. 1, Oxford 1999, 105.

10 For discussion of the position of *esne*, see David Pelteret, *Slavery in Early Mediaeval England*, Woodbridge 1995, 271–274 (cited as Pelteret, *Slavery*).

11 The difference between the *esne* and the slave was clearer in seventh-century Kent than it would be later; see Pelteret, *Slavery*, 271–274.

12 *Æthelberht* 16 and 21, ed. and trans. Oliver, 64–67.

13 See the remarks in Katherine Fischer Drew, ed. and trans., *The Laws of the Salian Franks*, Philadelphia 1991, 47.

14 But the status of even slaves seems to have been rising in this period. Although *Ine* 57.1 [L54.1] allows a slave to be given as part of a wergild payment, *Alfred* 21 [L18.1] requires that a woman betrothed by contract who sleeps with another man must pay the guarantor of the marriage 60 shillings, 'and that must be in livestock, and no [slave]person can be given for that.' Pelteret (*Slavery*, 84–85) proposes that this clause 'provides the first evidence in the laws of slaves as more than mere chattels … [The fact that the woman could pay in cattle but not slaves] implies that slaves were regarded by some members of society as property just like cattle, but the very promulgation of this provision suggests that this

the family of a freedman growing into freeman's status in the fourth generation: their *wergilds* range from 40 through 60 to 80 shillings as they approach full freedom.[15]

Wihtred §7 establishes a procedure for immediate manumission at the altar.[16] Following the manumission, 'the freedomgiver owns his [the freedman's] inheritance and *wergild* and protection of the kin.' I have addressed the significance of this phrase before. The phrase 'owns his inheritance' probably means one or both of two things. First, the previous owner is responsible for protecting the claims to inheritance, *wergild*, and protection of the new freeman, who may well not have any free kinsmen to help guarantee these rights. Second, should the newly freed man die without naming his beneficiaries, his inheritance reverts to the previous owner. If he has been killed, the *wergild* would also be paid to that owner.[17]

As a former slave can advance into *wergild* status, so a freeman entering penal servitude would likely lose his *wergild* during the period of his slavery. Penal servitude is required in the early laws for working on a Sunday and theft under certain circumstances; later laws add this penalty for incest and 'as an alternative for a condemned man who had reached sanctuary'.[18] If this servitude is lifelong, it almost surely was accompanied by a lifelong loss of *wergild* status; the master would be compensated for any injury to the slave according to his worth. A person could also be enslaved for a period of time to work off an otherwise unpayable debt. We have no evidence discussing what would happen to a man thus temporarily enslaved if he should be attacked, but the supposition that restitution similarly is paid to the temporary master seems reasonable.

Finally, Alfred §10 [L9] requires that 'If a woman bearing a child is slain when the child is in her, let [the slayer] pay full recompense for the woman, and compensate for the child by half the *wergild* [appropriate to] the father's kin.'[19] Thus the *wergild* structure extends into the pre-natal period.

---

view of them was becoming unacceptable.' Nonetheless, they still did not participate in the wergild system.

15 *Æthelberht* 27, ed. and trans. Oliver, 68–69. See the discussion in Lisi Oliver, 'Who was Æthelberht's *læt*?', in: *Confrontation in Late Antiquity*, ed. Linda Jones Hall, Cambridge 2003, 153–166.

16 *The Laws of Wihtred* 7, ed. and trans. Lisi Oliver, *Beginnings*, 156–157. The procedure appears to contain an oral formula of great archaism: see Lisi Oliver, 'Towards Freeing a Slave in Germanic Law', in: *Mír Curad: Studies in Honor of Calvert Watkins*, ed. Jay Jasanoff, H. Craig Melchert and Lisi Oliver, Innsbruck 1998, 549–560.

17 Oliver, *Beginnings*, 170.

18 List and citation taken from Pelteret, *Slavery*, 328–330.

19 *Pactus legis Salicae* 41.19, ed. Karl August Eckhardt, MGH LL nationum Germanicarum 4, 1, Hanover 1962, 161 and *Lex Ribuaria* 40 (36).10, ed. Franz Beyerle and Rudolf Buchner,

Table 5.1 lays out the comparisons discussed in this first section.

TABLE 5.1 *Wergild* and Worth in Kent and Wessex [Kentish shilling value in square brackets]

	Kent	Wessex
6000		King
1200		high nobleman
600 [300]	*Eorl*	English nobleman
		Welshman with six hides
200 [100]	freeman	freeman
		king's Welsh horseman
160 [80]	top rank freedman	
120 [60]	2nd rank freedman	Welshman with 1 hide
100		his son
80 [40]	lowest rank freedman	Welshman with ½ hide
60		?bound Welsh labourer
50		Welsh slave

Incoming

2 Own Wergild Received by Offended Party

The most commonly recognized payment of *wergild* is what is given by a person who kills another: the killer compensates the victim's family with the slain person's full *wergild*. Personal injury tariffs set the percentage of *wergild* to be paid to an injured man depending on what part of his body was damaged and the severity of the injury: a hand or eye struck off would yield 50% in

MGH LL nationum Germanicarum 3, 2, Hanover 1954, 94, similarly require half a *wergild* (100 solidi) for the killing of a fetus or a child before he has a name. *Lex Ribuaria* stipulates that killing both mother and unborn/newly-born child, however, draws a fine of 700 solidi (ibid.). *Pactus legis Salicae* 65e, ed. Eckhardt, MGH LL nat. Germ., 4, 1, 235, contradicts the earlier clause in requiring a payment of 600 *solidi* for killing a fetus if it can be determined that the fetus was male. On the background of these and other provisions, see Marianne Elsakkers, 'Genre Hopping: Aristotelian Criteria for Abortion in Germania', in: *Germanic Texts and Latin Models: Medieval Reconstructions*, ed. Karin E. Olson, Antonina Harbus, and Tette Hofstra, Leuven 2001, 73–92.

Æthelberht and roughly 33% in Alfred; a rib broken 3% in Æthelberht and 5% in Alfred; a front tooth knocked out 6% in Æthelberht and 4% in Alfred; etc.

Closely linked to *wergild* are payments for violation according to rank: indeed, these could be seen as included in the *wergild* configuration as their assessment is directly linked to the *wergild* valuation. The two most prominent of these are violation of *mund* (roughly 'protection')[20] and *manbot* (the price paid to a lord for killing someone under his *mund*).

In Æthelberht, breach of the king's *mund* is at issue when harm is done to anyone in an assembly called by the king (§8);[21] someone kills a person in the king's dwelling (§11);[22] and general 'violation of the king's protection' (§14): it is reckoned at 50 shillings.[23] (Wihtred §2 will later set the identical *mund* for the church.)[24] Although the term *manbot* is never actually attested in Kentish law, Daniela Fruscione has convincingly argued that it is represented in Æthelberht §12 by the term *drihtinbeag* 'lord-payment' (literally 'lord-ring'), which is 50 shillings paid to the king for the killing of a freeman.[25] Thus the *mund* and the *manbot* are equal. Hloþhere and Eadric §9.1 demonstrates the close connection between these two concepts: if a person draws a weapon where men are drinking and blood is shed, he must pay the king fifty shillings: this could represent either *mund* (if only injury results) or *manbot* (if someone is killed). Æthelberht §13 requires the payment of *meduman leodgelde* 'an ordinary person-price' for killing the king's smith or herald/guide (*laadrincmann*).[26] This clause then doubles the *manbot* payment to the king for the slaying of a man in his service.[27] (Recall that Ine's Welsh horseman had his *wergild* increased due to his position in the king's service.)

20 The 'king's protection' is the right to peace for members of the king's household, retinue, and guests. Injury or damage done to any of these constitutes a violation of protection. The same 'protection' holds but at a different level for every head of a household, and to a lesser degree to every free person.

21 *Æthelberht* 8, ed. and trans. Oliver, 62–63.

22 *Æthelberht* 11, ibid. As discussed later, §12 provides that a *manbot* of 50 shillings should be paid to the king for *any* freeman slain; this clause must thus represent an additional payment if this slaying occurs in the king's dwelling.

23 *Æthelberht* 14, ed. and trans. Oliver, 64–65.

24 *Wihtred* 2, ed. and trans. Oliver, 152–153.

25 See Daniela Fruscione, '*Drihtinbeag* and the Question of the Beginnings of Punishment', in: *Textus Roffensis: Law, Language, and Libraries in Early Medieval England*, ed. Bruce O'Brien and Barbara Bombi, Turnhout 2015, 157–174.

26 *Æthelberht* 13, ed. and trans. Oliver, 64–65. There may actually be three servants of the king addressed in this law; the difficulty lies in the ambiguity of word division. See Oliver, *Beginnings*, 65.

27 See discussion in Oliver, *Beginnings*, 87–88.

Æthelberht §18 sets a nobleman's *mund* at 12 shillings (assessed for killing someone in his dwelling); a freeman's *mund* is half that at 6 shillings (set in §20 and reiterated in §22 for the first person to break into his dwelling).[28] Interestingly, the *wergild* ratio of nobleman to freeman established in Hloþhere and Eadric §§1 and 2 is 3:1 (also true for Wessex) as opposed to the 2:1 ratio of the *munds* set in Æthelberht.

The only other figures whose *mund* is mentioned are widows. The *mund* of the highest rank of noble woman is 50 shillings; the next is 20, the third 12 and the fourth 6.[29] A fair supposition is that the *mund* of noble widows was secured by the king (with the concomitant opportunity to arrange another marriage if appropriate). The *mund* of the highest rank of widow was equal to the king's own. The third rank was thus probably under the *eorl*'s protection, as the 12 shillings equals his *mund*, and the same for the 6 shillings of the lowest ranking widow and the *ceorl*'s *mund*. This ranking raises an intriguing possibility. As discussed above, the later laws of Wessex define two ranks of noblemen. Although these are never overtly mentioned in Kentish law, it seems possible that the bifurcation in *mund* for the two highest classes of widow represents precisely that distinction in early Kent.

Returning to the question of *manbot* in early Kent, it has already been postulated that this concept is expressed by the *drihtinbeag* of Æthelberht §12. Another clause that may refer to *manbot* is the case of a person killing the *ceorl*'s 'loaf-eater' or dependent (§26), an offense assessed at 6 shillings, equal to the ceorl's *mund*.[30] If the loaf-eater is a slave or *esne*, then this would equal the payment for violating a *ceorl*'s top-ranked female slave. This interpretation seems unlikely, however, given the fact that — as previously mentioned — the lowest ranking freedman has a *wer* of forty shillings: it seems out of proportion that a slave would have a value of only six. If, then, the loaf-eater is a free dependent, the killing would need to be recompensed according to the slain person's *wer* paid to his kin, and the 6 shillings would represent the payment to the ceorl for *manbot*.

The first two clauses of Hloþhere and Eadric address the necessary recompense if a person's *esne* kills an *eorl* or a *ceorl*. In the case of the slaying of a *ceorl*, the owner is required to 'give up that killer and also a man-worth thereto'.[31] Although this could refer to the value of the *esne*, the phraseology

28 *Æthelberht* 18, 20 and 22, ed. and trans. Oliver, 66–67.

29 *Æthelberht* 74, ed. and trans. Oliver, 76–77.

30 *Æthelberht* 26, ed. and trans. Oliver, 68–69: *Gif man ceorlæs hlafætan ofslæhð, VI scillingum gebete* — 'If a person kills a freeman's loaf-eater, let him pay with 6 shillings'.

31 See footnote 5. Oliver (*Beginnings*, 127) translates the clause *se agend þone banan agefe 7 oþer manwyrð þær to* as 'the owner should give up that killer and add another man-worth

makes that interpretation far from certain. This 'worth' could also refer to the *manbot* due for slaying a *ceorl*; the *manbot* is then tripled for an *eorl* in the same ratio as the *wergild*.

Unlike the Welsh slaves in Wessex (whose value of fifty shillings would also represent a payment incoming to the owner), the laws of Æthelberht — as is more typical for Continental barbarian laws — rank slaves according to their jobs. Lying with the king's maiden of highest rank (presumably his cup-bearer if we follow the model for *eorl*s and *ceorl*s) is assessed a fine of fifty shillings; the 'grinding slave' (responsible for the preparation of food) twenty-five, and the third rank twelve. Note that the violation of the highest order of female slave is equal to the full amount of the king's *mund*. Lying with a freeman's cupbearer is assessed at six shillings (similarly equal to his *mund*), with lower ranks valued at fifty *sceattas* (two and a half shillings) and thirty *sceattas* (one and a half shillings) respectively. Lying with an *eorl*'s cupbearer must be compensated for with twelve shillings — again the value of his *mund*. Although the two lower ranks are not specified for the *eorl*, it is a safe assumption that their worth would follow the same ratio (approximately six shillings and three and a half shillings). Although the payment for violation of slaves is probably best interpreted as restitution for damage to property, at least in the case of the top-ranked slave such an offense still represents a breach of the owner's *mund*.

Table 5.2 presents the values for *mund*, *manbot* and slaves in Æthelberht's Kent.

As discussed above, the ratio in Æthelberht of 2:1 for noble to freeman does not match that of 3:1 in Hloþhere and Eadric. The latter ratio, however, does match those between the lower rank of noble and the freeman in West Saxon law. If this indeed represents a real change in valuation, later Kentish laws would provide the relative proportions shown in Table 5.3.[32]

Against this hypothesis is Wihtred §4 (discussed below), which appears to set a *gesiþcund* man's *wer* at two-hundred shillings. The Hloþhere and Eadric ruling may simply be an anomaly.

The final consideration before leaving Kent is that women both have and can be paid *wergild*. Following the personal injury schedule in Æthelberht §73 explicitly states that compensation for a maiden is the same as for a free

in addition'. The problem here is that I seem to have translated *oþer* twice, both as 'another' and as 'in addition', thus obscuring what I now believe to be the correct interpretation of *manwyrð*.

32 Attempting to set up a system with two-tiered rank of noble based on the widow's *mund* probably muddies the waters inaccurately. The *mund* for king — noble 1 — noble 2 — *ceorl* would be 50 — 18 — 12 — 6, while the *mund* for the widows is 50 — 20 — 12 — 6. The numbers do not align.

TABLE 5.2 *Mund, manbot* and the worth of slaves in Æthelberht's laws

Value	*Owner*	*Assessment*	*Other parallels*
100 shillings		*manbot*	
	king	for man in service	
50 shillings		*mund*	*mund* of highest widow
		manbot	violation of top-rank female slave
25 shillings			violation of mid-rank female slave
20 shillings			*mund* of 2nd noble widow
12 shillings	king		violation of lowest-rank female slave
	eorl	*mund*	violation of top-rank female slave
			mund of 3rd rank of widow
6 shillings		*mund*	*mund* of 4th rank of widow
	ceorl	*?manbot*	violation of top-rank female slave
			killing 'loaf-eater'
2 ½ shillings			violation of mid-rank female slave
1 ½ shillings			violation of lowest-rank female slave

TABLE 5.3 *Wergild, mund* and *manbot* in later Kent (An hypothesis)

?	king's *wergild*	50 shillings	king's *mund* and *manbot*
300 shillings	*eorl*'s *wergild*	18 shillings	*eorl*'s *mund* and *manbot*
100 shillings	ceorl's *mund* and *manbot*	6 shillings	*ceorl*'s *mund* and *manbot*

man.[33] §31 is less clear: 'If a freeman lies with a free man's wife, let him buy [him/her] off [with] his/her wergild and obtain another wife [for the husband] [with] his own money and bring her to the other man at home.'[34] Old English *wif* is neuter, and thus the possessive pronoun his could refer to either the husband or the wife. In the case of consensual intercourse, I would favour the former (in which case the *wergild* is paid to the husband); in the case of rape, I would favour the latter (in which case the *wergild* is paid to the woman). I actually think rape may be implied here but it is nowhere made explicit: the clause remains ambiguous, grammatically and otherwise. Finally, in the case

33 *Æthelberht* 73, ed. and trans. Oliver, 76–77.

34 *Æthelberht* 31, ed. and trans. Oliver, 68–69.

of violation of a widow's *mund* discussed above, the actual payment probably would go to the widow herself.

Alfred claims in the prologue to his secular laws to have drawn on both the laws of his ancestor Ine and of Æthelberht, the first English king to receive baptism. The extent to which the concepts of *mund* and *manbot* laid down in the Kentish laws, which preceded Alfred's by a good two-and-a-half centuries, underlie Alfred's laws as well, is unclear. None of the stipulations discussed above is contradicted; the laws of Wessex perhaps build on what was common tradition.

Indeed, Ine §40 [L39] requires someone fighting in a *ceorl*'s house to recompense him with six shillings. This is a clear violation of the ceorl's *mund*, but we might expect the assessment to be doubled to twelve shillings in the same way that the *wergild* of a *ceorl* in Wessex is twice that of Kent. The effect is that the actual value of the *ceorl*'s *mund* has decreased by half. However, the ratios of *mund* to *wergild* remain internally the same in West-Saxon law: the *mund* is tripled for a six-hundred man (and the law specifically remarks that this is three times the compensation of a *ceorl*) and doubled again for a twelve-hundred man. Alfred §3 adds to this the breach of security for higher ranks: five pounds of greater pennies for the king; three for the archbishop; and two for an ealdorman or bishop. However, Alfred §41 [L40] sets different assessments according to rank for breaking and entering and §12 [L10] different again for sleeping with a man's wife. Table 5.4 tabulates the comparisons for these violations individually.

TABLE 5.4 Comparison of violations of *mund* in Kent and Wessex [Kentish shillings in square brackets]

	Kent	**Wessex**			
		Ine	Alfred		
	Lying with female slave	Fighting	Breach of security	Breaking and entering	Lying with a man's wife
King	100 [50]		5 lbs shillings	120	
Archbishop			3 lbs shillings	90	
bishop/ ealdorman			2 lbs shillings	60	
1200 man		36		30	120
Eorl	24 [12]				
600 man		18		15	100
Ceorl	12 [6]	6		5	40

Several interesting points arise from this comparison:

- The *mund* for breaking into the king's fortified dwelling was assessed only slightly higher in Wessex than the Kentish king's *mund*; the difference is negligible. However, following the ratio of fines for breaking and entering, breaching the king's security, i.e. violating his *mund*, might be in the realm of 150 shillings, thus considerably higher. (Alfred §5 also requires paying the king's *mund* for dragging an offender out of sanctuary, which must have served as a considerable deterrent.)
- The Kentish eorl had a *mund* mid-way between that of the 1200- and 600-*wer* West Saxon; again, this bifurcation indicates that the essential value of a noble's *mund* compared to his *wergild* remained unchanged.
- The *mund* of the freeman was at least twice in Kent what it later was in Wessex.
- The violation of a man's wife, although tied to his *wergild*, constituted a category calculated apart from *mund*. Interestingly, the percentage of the *wergild* assessed decreased as the rank of the offended husband increased. A ceorl received 20% of his *wergild*, a 600-man 16 2/3%, and a 120-man 10%. Perhaps this reflected the better financial capability of a high-ranking man to obtain a new wife.

To sum up the discussion on the differences in *mund* between Kent and Wessex, it appears as if the parameters were stretching in the later laws. The king's *mund* became higher and the ceorl's *mund* lower.

Another interesting discrepancy between the two territories is that, while in Kent *mund* and *manbot* were assessed equally, in Ine §71 [L70] the price owed a householder for killing one of his dependants is considerably higher than his *mund*, as demonstrated by Table 5.5.

TABLE 5.5 *Mund* and *manbot* in Wessex

	Ine	*Alfred*		
	manbot	fighting	breaking and entering	violating wife
1200-man	120	36	30	120
600-man	80	18	15	100
Ceorl	30	6	5	40

The West-Saxon system then establishes two different sub-systems of restitution according to *wergild*. The first involves a simple breach of *mund* (fighting or breaking and entering) and the second an extended definition of *manbot*, where a householder receives payment for damage to a member of his household. While these two were financially parallel in Kent, West Saxon law considerably raises the payment to the head of house for killing his dependant or raping his wife. No such parallel increase is seen in the personal injury tariffs. The motivation, thus, must lie rather in a heightened sense of the responsibility of a householder for those under his protection.

Two final considerations in the rulings on *manbot* follow. First, Ine §34 requires that a man who has taken part in a raid on which a man is slain compensate with 50 shillings, the price to rise according to the man's *wer*. This is presumably a type of *manbot* paid to the king; although the amount seems very low, the compilation of the payments from all present on the raid would have led to a much greater payment. Second, Ine §78 [L76] requires *manbot* to be paid to a godfather or godson in addition to that paid to the secular lord. Relationships developed by the still nascent English church are supported by the force of the king's laws.

3 Payments to the King

Throughout the laws of Anglo-Saxon England, various fines unrelated to the *wergild* structure are paid to the king for a range of delicts. Furthermore, as discussed earlier, the king himself is often due *mund* or *manbot* for the breach of public security — as public security was the responsibility of the king — or for the killing of a man under his rule. This section discusses other instances in which *wergild* payment would go to the king.

Ine §22 [L23–23.1] states that if a foreigner is killed, the king gets two parts of the *wer*, the third going to the son[s] or kinsmen. If he is without kinsmen, half goes to the king and half to the nobleman [under whose protection he has been residing]. The second stipulation is echoed for any man who dies without kin in Alfred §32.2 [L28]. The king stands as paterfamilias to all lacking a family.

Much the same ruling underlies Afred §9.3 [L8.3]: if the child of a nun abducted from a cloister is killed, the mother's portion of the *wergild* (1/3) is given to the king; the father's portion (2/3) to the father's kin. The child in a sense has no mother, since the abducted nun has lost her right to be compensated for the death of her child. (Although it seems unfair from a 21st century perspective that the kin of the abductor receive restitution.)

Finally a person who slays the king's godson must pay two *wergilds*, one to the kin and one to the king.

Outgoing

4 Own Wergild Paid by Offending Party

This next section addresses instances in which a person who commits an offense is charged his own *wergild* or *mund* as fine. This practice is hinted at in the laws of Kent, but is not made explicit until Ine. Æthelberht §23 requires a man who provides weapons to another where strife occurs to pay six shillings if no harm occurs, and (presumably another) six if highway robbery is done.[35] This figure equals the ceorl's *mund*. The next subclause requires him to pay a fine of twenty shillings if the man to whom he loaned the weapon kills someone, and this figure does not immediately seem to accord anywhere with the Kentish *wergild* structure. However, two of Wihtred's laws require that a man pay with *healsfang*.[36] The first of these is for a freeman who works on the Sabbath (§8), the second for a man who gives his household meat in a fast (§11).[37] Attenborough indicates that 'the Old Norse *halsfang* ('embrace') suggests the possibility that this payment denoted the re-establishment of peace between the families involved in the vendetta,' and, following Schmid, links it to the 20-shilling payment made by the killer's kin at the grave of a slain man in Æthelberht §24.1.[38] If this hypothesis is correct, then Æthelberht §23 would require payment of mund for providing weapons for a robbery and of *healsfang* if someone is killed in the process. Typically Wihtred requires *healsfang* for violating church law, neatly combining the pagan fine structure with the Christian delicts.

Assessing his own full *wergild* as a fine against the perpetrator first appears in Anglo-Saxon England in the laws of Ine.[39] Ine §11 states that 'If someone sells over the sea his own countryman, slave or free, even though he is guilty

35 *Æthelberht* 23, ed. and trans. Oliver, 66–67.

36 See discussion in Oliver, *Beginnings*, 170–173.

37 *Wihtred* 8 and 11, ed. and trans. Oliver, 156–159.

38 *Æthelberht* 24.1, ed. and trans. Oliver, 66–67.

39 This assessment also appears elsewhere in barbarian laws: for example, *Lex Frisionum* 17.5, ed. Karl August Eckhardt and Albrecht Eckhardt, MGH Fontes iuris Germanici antiqui in usum scholarum separatim editi 12, Hanover 1982, 62, and the Lombard laws of Liutprand 91.7, ed. Friedrich Bluhme and Alfred Boretius, MGH LL (in Folio) 4, Hanover

[of an offense], let him compensate by payment of his [own] *wer*.' (The clause is grammatically ambiguous as to whether the *wer* is that of the sold person or the seller. Since a slave has no *wergild* the interpretation must fall to the latter.) Ine §12 (echoed by Wihtred §21)[40] allows a thief to redeem his life by payment of his *wergild*, and the near-identical Ine §20 and Wihtred §23[41] allow a stranger going off the road who does not blow a horn to announce his presence to redeem himself from being put to death by payment of his *wergild*. Further Ine §14.2 [L15] allows a man accused of taking part in a raid by a troop of thieves to 'redeem himself with his *wergild* or clear himself by [an oath equal to] his *wergild*.' All of these clauses requiring payment of one's own *wergild* for an offense are directly connected to theft.

Ine §37 [L36] similarly concerns theft: 'He who catches a thief, or to whom [a thief] is entrusted as a prisoner, and then lets him go or conceals the theft, let him compensate by the *wer* of the thief.' Here, however, the fine is based on the *wergild* of the thief, not the (second) offender. Interestingly, Ine §30 does just the opposite: a person accused of harbouring a fugitive must either clear himself with an oath equal to his own *wer* or compensate with his *wer*. Both these clauses concern aiding (and perhaps abetting), so the difference in whose *wer* must be paid as fine seems inconsistent. Alfred §8 [L7.1] requires a fugitive fleeing the charge of having fought in the king's hall to pay his own *wergild* on top of recompense for whatever damage he has caused: he apparently has no associate to shelter him. Alfred §4 reverses Ine's ruling on harbouring a fugitive, at least in the case of a person who has been banished for plotting against the king: the one who offers him shelter is liable for 'his life and all he owns'.

Both Ine and Wihtred include one clause based on the *wergild* structure without necessarily requiring full payment of *wergild*. Chronologically first, Ine §54 [L51] requires of a 'nobly-born man who owns property' who neglects his *fyrd* duty 120 shillings, and of one who does not own property, 60 shillings; a man of *ceorl*-rank is fined 30 shillings. In the case of the noblemen, the fine is 10% of their *wer*, in the case of the *ceorl*, a relatively higher 15%. This might have been intended as a greater deterrent for a *ceorl* to neglect *fyrd* duty to tend to his own lands; a noble would have someone else to do this work for him. Ine's Wessex was often plagued by warfare as he strove to push the boundaries of the kingdom to the north and west, and this concern is evident in this clause. Wihtred, conversely, concentrated on shoring up the recently

1868, 144–145. (Thanks to Danielle Fruscione for these comparisons). See also Harald Siems' contribution in this volume, p. [12].

40 *Wihtred* 21, ed. and trans. Oliver, 162–163.

41 *Wihtred* 23, ibid.

established English church, to which purpose a great number of his rulings were dedicated. If a *gesiþ*-born man (the term is borrowed from Ine) takes up a non-Christian marital union, he must pay a hundred-shilling fine, while a freeman must pay fifty.[42] Here the fine for a nobleman (33 1/3%) is higher than that for a freeman (25%); perhaps Wihtred expected his closest associates to both adhere to his own example and also set one for those of lower status.

Alfred's laws are the first to require judicial mutilation. A thief who steals from the church must have his hand struck off (§7 [L6]); a person who engages in public slander must have his tongue cut out (§33 [L32]). Nowhere else in the early laws is Pooh-Bah's exhortation in *The Mikado* to 'let the punishment fit the crime' more apt! However, the law-breaker is also given the option to redeem the offending limb.

The other offense Alfred regulates requiring payment of a proportion of the *wergild* concerns a contractually betrothed woman who fornicates with someone other than her intended husband (§21 [L18.1–3]). A noble woman whose *wer* is 1200 shillings must compensate the guarantor to the marriage with 120 shillings (10% *wergild*); a noble woman whose *wer* is 600 with 100 shillings (16 2/3%) and a ceorl-rank woman with 60 shillings (33 1/3%). The lower the ranking, the higher the percentage of the *wergild*. This might reflect the fact that the higher a woman's rank, the more valuable she was as a marriage commodity, and thus the closer watch her kin kept on her. Whether or not this supposition has any validity, this clause demonstrates that — as determined earlier for the laws of Æthelberht — a woman had her own *wergild*. And, as Alfred indicates, this could be assessed against her for her own transgressions.

5 Forfeiting the Right to Wergild

Beginning again in the laws of Ine, a person can forfeit his right to *wergild*. For Ine in Wessex (and echoed in the slightly later laws of Wihtred in Kent), the most prominent reason involves being killed in the act of theft. Ine §12 (echoed in Wihtred §21[43]) allows a thief to avoid being put to death by redeeming himself by payment of his *wergild*; Ine §20.1 [L21] (with a similar if not identical ruling in Wihtred §20[44]) stipulates that the kin of a person caught in the act of theft cannot claim his *wergild*. This is reiterated in Ine §35 in which if a man swears on oath that he killed a thief in the act of fleeing, then 'the kin of

42 *Wihtred* 4, ed. and trans. Oliver, 154–155.

43 *Wihtred* 21, ed. and trans. Oliver, 162–163.

44 *Wihtred* 20, ed. and trans. Oliver, 160–161.

the dead men must swear him an oath not to engage in hostilities against him.' These paragraphs parallel (and are sometimes even part of) the clauses ruling that a thief must pay his own *wergild*. The connection is clear: theft is a capital offense from which the thief may only redeem himself by payment of his wer. The kin of a thief slain in the act has no claim on his *wer*, as it would have been forfeit had he lived.

Ine §27 also includes the stipulation that a person 'who conceives a child out of wedlock and hides it, does not have its *wer* at its death, but [it goes to] his lord and the king.' This ruling sheds an interesting light on kinship requirements under the laws of Ine. Had the father acknowledged the offspring of his extra-marital liaison, the child would presumably have been incorporated into the *wergild* structure of the kin. But since he has concealed the child's birth, it becomes what would later be called a ward of the lord and/or king, with the *wergild* structure devolving to that guardian.

The laws of Alfred remove a man's right to *wergild* compensation for offenses against public peace. Very early in Alfred's laws, §2 [L1.2] addresses a person who has either committed treason against his lord or given unlawful assistance (presumably to treasonous action). He must then 'humbly give his weapons and his possessions to his *freond*-group to hold, and let him be in the prison on an estate of the king for forty nights, and there do atonement according to what the bishop prescribes.' But if he resists and is killed while being forced to the prison, his kin cannot claim his *wergild*.

Alfred §44.2 [L.42.4] is somewhat more difficult to interpret. This involves a man found in his house by an enemy with a legal grudge against him. If he is willing to give up his weapons, then he must be held in his house for 30 nights while his friend-group (kin and close associates) is notified. But if the complainant attacks him anyway, 'let [the attacker] pay such *wer* as due for wounding [he has caused], and a fine, and he has forfeited his kin-compensation.' The payment of the *wer* to the beleaguered man is clear, as is the additional fine. The textual problem here is in the interpretation of the term *mægbot* 'kin-compensation'. Oliver and Jurasinski in their edition of Alfred's *domboc* concur with Liebermann's interpretation of this term roughly as '*wergild* paid to the kin'. The clause then rules that whatever percentage of *wergild* the original offender might owe the kin-group for damages to his victim is nullified by the subsequent illegal attack. The attacker does not forfeit his *own wergild*, but that which would have been owed to him and his kin for damage to his kinsman due to his illegal counterattack.

Turning this discussion in reverse, Alfred §45 [L42.5–7] defines circumstances in which a person need not pay *wergild* for his actions. These exemptions are:

- If a man fights on behalf of his lord, or the lord at the side of his dependant(s).
- If a man fights on behalf of his born kin wrongfully attacked (except against his lord)
- If a man 'finds another with his lawful wife, behind doors or under a single blanket or with his lawfully born daughter, or with his born sister, or with his mother who was given as lawful wife to his father.'

6 Wergild Outside the Laws

Curiously, for a system so well recognized in the legal texts, we find very little discussion of *wergild* outside the laws themselves. The first instantiations are in the will of the reeve Abba (S1482, 833x39) and of the *ealdorman* Alfred (S1508, 871x99). Among other directives, Abba requests that whoever should succeed to his land (at the time of writing the will, he was childless) take to St. Peter's *min wærgeld twa ðusenda*. The charter donations are located in Kent (and Harmer even postulates that St Peter's in this instance could refer to a church in Kent). If we accordingly assume here that the 'two thousand' designate pennies, then Abba's *wærgeld* would be consistent with the 100 shillings of a Kentish *ceorl*. Alfred — whom Harmer postulates to have been Earl of Surrey, although he also owned lands in Kent — asks his wife Wærborh (!) to take to Saint Peter's (this time almost surely in Rome) *min twa wergeld* 'my two *wergilds*' as a donation, if she is able to make the journey. Harmer assumes that the two *wergild*s imply that the standard *wergild* of an *eorl* was twice that of a *ceorl*. I am not convinced, however, that Harmer is correct here. Hloþhere and Eadric §1 implies that a Kentish *eorl's* wergild is 300 Kentish shillings — that is, three times the *wergild* of a Kentish *ceorl*; Alfred §10 enumerates fines paid for men whose *wergild* is 1200 shillings, 600 shillings, and *ceorl*s (whose normal *wergild* was 200 West Saxon shillings). In both cases, the legal texts support a *wergild* for Alfred of three times the *ceorl*s on his estates. More likely the ealdorman is requesting the contribution of two *wergilds*. It strikes me that when making a donation for the preservation of your immortal soul, twice your *wergild* is a pretty cheap bargain, no matter what the actual *wergild* is.

The only prose work we have that actually incorporates *wergild* into a narrative is — perhaps counterintuitively — a saint's life. St Eormenburg (or Domne Eue), was a 7th-century daughter of King Eadbald of Kent.[45] Her brothers were

45 London, British Library, MS. Stowe 944: ed. Walter de Gray Birch, *Liber Vitae: Register and Martyrology of New Minster and Hyde Abbey, Winchester*, London 1892, 84–85; Cambridge, Corpus Christi College, MS. 201: ed. Felix Liebermann, *Die Heiligen Englands*, Hanover 1889, 3.

fostered with her uncle, King Ecgberht of Kent; they were murdered by the king's reeve, perhaps at his behest.[46]

Whatever the truth, Ecgberht offered to pay Eormenburg *wergild* for her slain brothers (*hyre broðra wergildes*): as much land as her pet hind could run around in a single lap. This indefatigable courier managed to encompass eighty *sulungs*.

> *And he* [se cyning] *wæs swiðe afyrht, & he þa be þam wiste þæt he hæfde Gode abolgen, & he þa het heora swustor Domne Euan him to gefeccean þæt heo heora* **wergyld** *onfon mihte. And heo þa swa dyde, þæt is þonne* LXXX *sulunga landes, þæt hi þæt mynster on arærdon þam sawlum to gebedrædenne þe hit heora* **wergyld** *wæs.*
>
> And he [the king] was very much afraid, and he then by that knew that he had enraged God, and he then commanded that their [the dead *æthelings*'] sister Domne Eue be brought to him, so that she could receive their *wergild*. And so she did — that is the eighty *sulungs* of land — so that she could erect the minster there, to speak the offices of prayer for their souls whose *wergild* it was.

On the land offered as *wergild* for her slain brothers, Eormenburg founded the double house of Minster-on-Thanet. The problem is that this narrative contradicts almost everything the law tells us about *wergild*. In the laws the sum is fixed according to rank. In this story, however, Ecgberht sets what must be a completely random amount of restitution. He had mistakenly assumed that the value of the land the hind could encircle would not equal the value of the *æthelings*' *wergild*, but the God-assisted deer made the value of compensation considerably higher, hence Ecgberht's (well-justified) fear.

Bibliography

Primary Sources

Die Gesetze der Angelsachsen, ed. Felix Liebermann, 3 vols. Halle 1903–1916.

Die Heiligen Englands, ed. Felix Liebermann, Hanover 1889.

Lex Frisionum, ed. Karl-August Eckhardt and Albrecht Eckhardt., MGH Fontes iuris Germanici antiqui in usum scholarum separatim editi 12, Hanover 1982.

46 The two extant manuscript versions differ as to the assignment of blame: London, BL, Ms. Stowe 944 — which I have cited here — is considerably more accusatory than C.C.C.C. 201.

Leges Langobardorum, ed. Friedrich Bluhme and Alfred Boretius, MGH LL (in Folio) 4, Hanover 1868.

Lex Ribuaria, ed. Franz Beyerle and Rudolf Buchner, MGH LL nationum Germanicarum 3, 2, Hanover 1954.

Liber Vitae: Register and Martyrology of New Minster and Hyde Abbey, Winchester, ed. Walter de Gray Birch, London 1892.

Pactus legis Salicae, ed. Karl-August Eckhardt, MGH LL nationum Germanicarum 4, 1, Hanover 1962.

The Laws of Æthelberht, ed. and trans. Lisi Oliver, *The Beginnings of English Law*, Toronto 2002, 52–116.

The Laws of Alfred: The Domboc and the Making of Anglo-Saxon Law, ed. and trans. Stefan Jurasinski and Lisi Oliver, Cambridge 2021.

The Laws of Hlophere & Eadric, ed. and trans. Lisi Oliver, *The Beginnings of English Law*, Toronto 2002, 117–146.

The Laws of the Salian Franks, ed. and trans. Katherine Fischer Drew, Philadelphia 1991.

The Laws of Wihtred, ed. and trans. Lisi Oliver, *The Beginnings of English Law*, Toronto 2002, 147–180.

Two Saxon Chronicles Parallel, ed. John Earle and Charles Plummer, 2 vols., Oxford 1892, repr. 1972.

Secondary Works

Elsakkers, Marianne, 'Genre Hopping: Aristotelian Criteria for Abortion in Germania', in: *Germanic Texts and Latin Models: Medieval Reconstructions*, ed. Karin E. Olson, Antonina Harbus, and Tette Hofstra, Leuven 2001, 73–92.

Fruscione, Daniela, '*Drihtinbeag* and the Question of the Beginnings of Punishment', in: *Textus Roffensis: Law, Language, and Libraries in Early Medieval England*, ed. Bruce O'Brien and Barbara Bombi, Turnhout 2015, 157–174.

Oliver, Lisi, 'Genital Mutilation in Medieval Germanic Law', in: *Capital and Corporal Punishment in Anglo-Saxon England*, ed. Jay Paul Gates and Nicole Marafioti, Woodbridge 2014, 48–73.

Oliver, Lisi, 'Towards Freeing a Slave in Germanic Law', in: *Mír Curad: Studies in Honor of Calvert Watkins*, ed. Jay Jasanoff, H. Craig Melchert and Lisi Oliver, Innsbruck 1998, 549–560.

Oliver, Lisi, 'Who was Æthelberht's *læt*?', in: *Confrontation in Late Antiquity*, Linda Jones Hall, Cambridge 2003, 153–166.

Oliver, Lisi, 'Who Wrote Alfred's Laws?', in: *Textus Roffensis: Law, Language, and Libraries in Early Medieval England*, ed. Bruce O'Brien and Barbara Bombi, Turnhout 2015, 231–256.

Pelteret, David, *Slavery in Early Mediaeval England*, Woodbridge 1995.

Wormald, Patrick, *The Making of English Law: King Alfred to the Twelfth Century*, vol. 1, Oxford 1999.

CHAPTER 6

Compensation, Honour and Idealism in the Laws of Æthelberht

Tom Lambert

1 Introduction

At some point around the year 600, in the wake of his conversion to Christianity, King Æthelberht of Kent ordered the creation of a written law code.[1] The Old English text survives in something close to its original form in a twelfth-century manuscript, providing a potentially invaluable window onto law and culture in an otherwise deeply obscure period.[2] In spite of this promise it has proven a difficult historical source. Partly this is because of its contents. Though quite long by the standards of Anglo-Saxon law it is extremely terse, little more than a list of offences associated with sums of money with almost no discussion of the legal processes that led to those payments. Perhaps more fundamentally, though, it is because of uncertainty about the way the laws it contains relate to real-life behaviour. Few historians were ever naïve enough to take the text as an objective description of Kentish legal practice, but scepticism about its capacity to cast light on late sixth-century social realities has been fuelled in recent decades by the increased emphasis placed on early medieval laws' ideological significance. Patrick Wormald's argument that in

1 On dating: Carole Hough, 'Legal and Documentary Writings', reprinted in and cited from: Carole Hough, *'An Ald Recht': Essays on Anglo-Saxon Law*, Newcastle upon Tyne 2014, 2–6 (cited as Hough, 'Writings').

2 For the text see Lisi Oliver, *The Beginnings of English Law*, Toronto 2002, 59–81 (cited as Oliver, *Beginnings*), which supersedes Felix Liebermann, *Die Gesetze der Angelsachsen* 1, Halle 1903, 3–8. (However, note that Liebermann's enumeration of the clauses in this and other Anglo-Saxon law texts has been retained for citation purposes here, as it is that on which all editions and translations prior to Oliver's are based.) A compelling linguistic case for understanding the text that survives as something close to Æthelberht's original is made in Carole Hough, 'The Earliest English Texts? The Language of the Kentish Laws Reconsidered', in: *Textus Roffensis: Law, Language, and Libraries in Early Medieval England*, ed. Bruce O'Brien and Barbara Bombi, Turnhout 2015, 137–156 (cited as Hough, 'Texts'); cf. Patrizia Lendinara, 'The Kentish Laws', in: *The Anglo-Saxons from the Migration Period to the Eighth Century: An Ethnographic Perspective*, ed. John Hines, Woodbridge/Suffolk 1997, 211–230 (cited as Lendinara, 'Kentish Laws'). On the manuscript itself, see Bruce O'Brien, '*Textus Roffensis*: An Introduction', in: *Textus Roffensis: Law, Language, and Libraries in Early Medieval England*, ed. Bruce O'Brien and Barbara Bombi, Turnhout 2015, 1–16.

 | DOI:10.1163/9789004466128_007

northern Europe written law was produced not so it could be consulted in practice but as part of a broader effort to project an image of Romano-Christian kingship has, quite rightly, met with little dissent for Kent in this period, and this has obvious implications for our use of Æthelberht's text as a source for legal behaviour.[3] Given the distinct possibility it was never used for practical legal purposes, it would plainly be wrong to interpret it as though it had 'legal force' in the sense modern laws do — the sort of practical legal 'reality' conferred on written rules by a network of courts which formulate their judgements in accordance with them and have access to the coercive power necessary to enforce their will. However, while this model for the relationship between written law and real-life behaviour is now generally understood to be anachronistic for our period, it has not been replaced with a clear alternative,[4] and the uncertainty limits the text's analytical usefulness.[5]

3 Patrick Wormald, *The First Code of English Law*, Canterbury 2005, 17: 'In "following the examples of the Romans", therefore, the king of Kent was entering the civilized world where Christian kings lived up to imperial and biblical standards, not to mention their neighbours', by making written laws, however otherwise irrelevantly.' For the general case, see Patrick Wormald, 'Lex Scripta and Verbum Regis: Legislation and Germanic Kingship from Euric to Cnut', reprinted in and cited from: Patrick Wormald, *Legal Culture in the Early Medieval West: Law as Text, Image and Experience*, London 1999, 1–43; Patrick Wormald, 'Kings and Kingship', in: *The New Cambridge Medieval History. Volume I: c. 500–c. 700*, ed. Paul Fouracre, Cambridge 2005, 571–604. Directly on Æthelberht's code: Patrick Wormald, *The Making of English Law: King Alfred to the Twelfth Century. Volume 1: Legislation and its Limits*, Oxford 1999, 93–101 (cited as Wormald, *Making*); id., 'Inter Cetera Bona Genti Suae: Law-Making and Peace-Keeping in the Earliest English Kingdoms', reprinted in and cited from: Patrick Wormald, *Legal Culture in the Early Medieval West: Law as Text, Image and Experience*, London 1999, 179–186, 196–198 (cited as Wormald, 'Law-Making'). For acceptance see Oliver, *Beginnings*, 14–20; Hough, 'Writings', 3–4, 12; cf. Thomas M. Charles-Edwards, 'Law in the Western Kingdoms between the Fifth and Seventh Centuries', in: *The Cambridge Ancient History Volume 14: Late Antiquity: Empire and Successors, AD 425–600*, ed. Averil Cameron, Bryan Ward-Perkins and Michael Whitby, Cambridge 2001, 264–266 (cited as Charles-Edwards, 'Law').

4 Charles-Edwards, 'Law', 265–266 comes closest in his discussion of the intimate conceptual link between 'decrees' and 'judgements' in contemporary terminology — 'A *dom* is, therefore, as much a decree promulgated by a king as a judgement which a judge, *dema*, might judge, *deman*' (265) — and in arguing that royal legislation was fundamentally oral: 'writing law down, if it happened at all, was an entirely secondary matter' (266). (*Written* law is thus essentially irrelevant to legal practice but can still provide useful information about a potentially effective oral legislative process.) However, it is not clear that Æthelberht's code can safely be regarded as royal legislation on the same model as later texts that declare themselves to be *domas*: see Wormald, *Making*, 94–95, Nicholas Brooks, 'The Laws of King Æthelberht of Kent: Preservation, Content, and Composition', in: *Textus Roffensis: Law, Language, and Libraries in Early Medieval England*, ed. Bruce O'Brien and Barbara Bombi, Turnhout 2015, 110 (cited as Brooks, 'Æthelberht'). A full discussion is provided in Tom Lambert, *Law and Order in Anglo-Saxon England*, Oxford 2017, chapter 2.

5 Indeed, a prominent, anthropologically influenced strand in the historiography of early medieval law holds that normative texts are inherently so divorced from the realities of legal

The crux of the problem is that without a working model for how the laws fitted into their social and legal environment we cannot fully understand their significance. The risk is that our attempts to reconstruct their meaning or to explain their composition are skewed towards less uncertain contexts. With sufficient scholarly industry it is possible to situate the text within its macro-political, religious and intellectual environment — the world of kings and elite churchmen that, for its own reasons, created and preserved legal manuscripts — because we have quite a lot of information about that world and the way written legal texts fit into it. This is useful, but it only gives us part of the picture. The fundamental problem is that the rules within the text have very little to do with this environment, and the context they presuppose — a world of legal practice characterised by injury, insult and compensation, probably a world with no place for written documents, certainly one without archives — is less directly accessible.

We should not mistake this relative inaccessibility for unimportance. Not only did this context inform the composition of the laws — it was evidently at the forefront of the mind of whoever originally formulated the rules within our text — it must have shaped how contemporary audiences understood them. It is, we should remember, likely that virtually all adults in Æthelberht's Kent had a working understanding of their local legal environment: not just the freemen who are the text's main focus but kings and nobles, and surely all but the most cloistered of clergymen. Their understanding of this environment must have shaped their views of formalised laws, the significance they attributed to them,

---

practice as to make any attempt to analyse laws for this purpose futile. For a clear statement of this position, see Chris Wickham, *Framing the Early Middle Ages: Europe and the Mediterranean, 400–800*, Oxford 2005, 830; for its anthropological roots, see the juxtaposition of 'rule-centred' and 'processual' approaches in Simon Roberts, 'The Study of Disputes: Anthropological Perspectives', in: *Disputes and Settlements: Law and Human Relations in the West*, ed. John Bossy, Cambridge 1983, 3–4; for critical historiographical overviews: Alice Rio, 'Introduction', in: *Law, Custom, and Justice in Late Antiquity and the Early Middle Ages: Proceedings of the 2008 Byzantine Colloquium*, ed. Alice Rio, London 2011, 1–22 (cited as Rio, 'Introduction'); Warren C. Brown and Piotr Górecki, 'What Conflict Means: The Making of Medieval Conflict Studies in the United States, 1970–2000', in: *Conflict in Medieval Europe: Changing Perspectives on Society and Culture*, ed. Warren C. Brown and Piotr Górecki, Aldershot/Hampshire 2003, 1–35. For recent reappraisals of this rather limiting view of laws, see Alice Taylor, 'Lex Scripta and the Problem of Enforcement: Anglo-Saxon, Scottish and Welsh Law Compared', in: *Legalism: Justice and Community*, ed. Judith Scheele and Fernanda Pirie, Oxford 2014, 47–75; Matthew Innes, 'Charlemagne, Justice and Written Law', in: *Law, Custom, and Justice in Late Antiquity and the Early Middle Ages: Proceedings of the 2008 Byzantine Colloquium*, ed. Alice Rio, London 2011, 155–203; Peter Heather, 'Law and Society in the Burgundian Kingdom', in: ibid., 115–153; and, from an anthropological perspective, Paul Dresch, 'Legalism, Anthropology and History: A View from the Part of Anthropology', in: *Legalism: Anthropology and History*, ed. Paul Dresch and Hannah Skoda, Oxford 2012, 9–15.

regardless of whether they were aware of the written text commissioned by Æthelberht. Even those who knew about Æthelberht's act of codification and had the necessary frame of reference to comprehend its Roman and Christian connotations (quite possibly a small minority) must also have understood the laws' significance in terms of contemporary legal culture. It follows that if we are to understand what the laws meant to contemporaries, we need a working model for real-life legal practice. It is only in that context that we will be able to appreciate the ideals the laws represent, the aspirations for good order they reflect and the personal qualities and conduct they promote. The ideological significance of the laws themselves in Kentish society needs, in short, to be distinguished from the ideological significance of written legislation for Kentish kings and literate churchmen.

This article attempts to do this, and thus to provide a more balanced assessment of the contemporary significance of Æthelberht's laws. It begins with the text itself. Although it accepts Wormald's core argument — the Romano-Christian connotations of royal law-giving were almost certainly what prompted Æthelberht to order the production of a written law code — it emphasises the limits of its explanatory power. The crucial point is one to which Wormald himself was clearly open: it is likely that Æthelberht's text essentially reproduces a pre-existing memorised set of laws.[6] If this is accepted, Wormald's arguments about Romano-Christian ideology may explain these earlier laws' *transcription* but they do not and cannot explain their original *composition*. An alternative context must thus be sought if we are to understand the original significance of the laws as a text, rather than the significance of committing that text to the medium of writing. There is no reason to think that the laws' primary meaning to contemporary Kentish audiences — should the earlier memorised set of laws have been recited in an assembly, for example, or even had Æthelberht ordered his manuscript read aloud — would have been anything to do with Æthelberht's Romanness or Christianity.

It is thus clear that there are questions to be answered here. What did the laws themselves (as opposed to Æthelberht's act of codification) mean? Could they have had an ideological significance within their social and legal context? The obscurity of this context is problematic, but only to a certain extent. It is true that we lack contemporary Kentish evidence for legal practice, but there is no shortage of comparative historical and ethnographic examples of societies with broadly similar legal traditions. Legal environments characterised by injury, insult and compensation are not obscure to us, and there is nothing to stop us exploring their dynamics in general terms and thinking through the

6 Wormald, *Making*, 95–96.

significance such a memorised text of laws might have held within them. The second half of the article attempts to do this and to suggest some conclusions. Specifically, it argues that in their original social and legal context the laws were a powerful statement of a native ideal of good order, and of a socially responsible model of masculinity — a formal articulation of a particular set of ideals which could, because of its acknowledged authority, usefully be called upon by mediators trying to bring about compensation settlements. In their unwritten form the laws thus had considerable ideological significance in pre-Christian Kent, and it perhaps follows that Æthelberht's act of codification should be understood, in part, as an attempt to co-opt their power: the king associating his rule with prestigious and well-established Kentish ideals of social order at the same time as aligning himself, in the way Wormald suggested, with the Romano-Christian model of kingship to which his Frankish in-laws subscribed.

It is worth noting that this interpretation could readily be applied to other early medieval European law texts. The historiographical tendency to situate law texts in their macro-political and intellectual environment, and to neglect that of real-life legal practice because of doubt about written law's place in it, is a more general one.[7] Moreover, the core of the solution proposed here — the construction of a working model for the relationship between formal law and legal practice based on comparative material — could just as readily be applied in other early medieval contexts (few of which are quite so obscure as Æthelberht's Kent). Indeed, what follows could be read as a general argument for the ideological significance of compensation tariffs in feuding cultures, taking its cue from modern anthropological and early medieval literary scholarship. The reason for taking Kent as the focus is pragmatic. Attempting to show that this argument holds good for compensation tariffs across early medieval Europe would take much more space than is available here, and require a much deeper understanding of the continental texts and their context than I possess. As the discussion that follows should make clear, interpreting even one early medieval law text — and a relatively straightforward one at that — is far from simple. While I suspect there may be some merit in the idea that the reading offered here applied more widely, in this article my aim is limited: to establish as firmly as possible that it makes sense of the evidence derived from at least this one early medieval context.

7 Rio, 'Introduction', 1–5.

2 Texts and Contexts

Several features of this Kentish example make it a good, relatively straightforward case study. Æthelberht's laws are, of course, unlike their continental European parallels for being written in Old English rather than Latin, and this should be understood as symptomatic of the broader atypicality of Britain's experience in the fifth and sixth centuries. Evidence for the period is scarce indeed, and much is debated, but it is widely accepted that the economic, social and political turmoil that accompanied the end of Roman rule in Britain was much more severe than elsewhere in Europe and, especially in those regions which came under the rule of pagan Anglo-Saxon kings, was accompanied by a near-total break with Roman culture.[8] This lack of meaningful continuity with Roman Britain makes the interpretation of Æthelberht's laws simpler than that of comparable continental texts, because problematic uncertainties about the weight to give to Roman law's continuing influence simply do not arise. However, Æthelberht's laws' key virtue for present purposes is probably a side-effect of this unusually de-Romanised context: they show few signs of having been shaped by the elite intellectual culture responsible for their preservation. This makes the inadequacy of readings which explain the text solely as an artefact of this intellectual culture much more readily apparent, thus highlighting the need for an analysis that adopts a different perspective.

To be specific, the text makes no reference to Æthelberht, Kent or Rome, and references to Christianity are confined to its brief, syntactically distinct opening set of clauses, which do little more than define the status of various ranks of churchmen. These features should not be taken to undermine Wormald's arguments about the ideological significance of early medieval legal codifications. Æthelberht almost certainly was prompted to have laws committed to writing (using the Roman rather than the runic alphabet) by the desire to make a statement that he had joined the club of powerful Christian kings who, across Europe, ruled as heirs of the Roman emperors. He and his

8 The seminal statement of this view is A. Simon Esmonde Cleary, *The Ending of Roman Britain*, London 1989. For its widespread acceptance in modern textbook overviews, see Chris Wickham, *The Inheritance of Rome: A History of Europe from 400 to 1000*, London 2009, 150–155; Robin Fleming, *Britain after Rome: The Fall and Rise*, London 2010, chs. 1–2; Bryan Ward-Perkins, *The Fall of Rome and the End of Civilization*, Oxford 2005, 117–120 and ch. 7. (A slight exception is Nicholas J. Higham and Martin J. Ryan, *The Anglo-Saxon World*, New Haven 2013, 51.) For a heavyweight reassessment that nuances Esmonde Cleary's picture in important ways, see Thomas M. Charles-Edwards, *Wales and the Britons, 350–1064*, Oxford 2013, chs. 1–6. More radical interpretations include Kenneth R. Dark, *Civitas to Kingdom: British Political Continuity 300–800*, Leicester 1994; Guy Halsall, *Worlds of Arthur: Facts and Fictions of the Dark Ages*, Oxford 2013, esp. 270–281.

kingdom's elite may also have understood the text as an assertion of Kentish identity and autonomy: the men of Kent were a distinct people with their own laws, and were henceforth to be recognised as such by their European (and perhaps particularly their Frankish) peers.[9] The absence of any hint of these ideological agendas within the text strongly suggests that it was not *composed* with them in mind, but it is still entirely plausible that they explain its being publicly *written down*. This would make sense if — as much of the modern literature accepts — the writing-down process prompted by Æthelberht did not involve the composition of a new text but the relatively superficial emendation of an existing one, perhaps only through the addition of the initial handful of clauses on the Church.

What, then, was this pre-existing text of laws, slightly modified and committed to writing at Æthelberht's behest, which appears to have been unmarked by any hint of a Romano-Christian ideology of kingship? Several possibilities have been suggested in the literature (including runic and Latin originals), but the most plausible theory is that its earlier existence was in a memorised form: certain Kentish people invested effort in learning the laws by rote and passed on their knowledge orally.[10] The most forceful and detailed case for this interpretation is that of the text's most recent editor, the late and very sadly missed Lisi Oliver. She suggested that the text may contain 'traces of an elevated prose style, using the poetic device of alliteration as an aid to memory', and argued that its notably orderly structure (strikingly different from the more chaotic codes produced in later, more literate centuries) is most plausibly understood as an 'architectural mnemonic' inherited from a period of oral transmission.[11] The most far-reaching aspect of Oliver's case, however, lies in her analysis of

9 Patrick Wormald, 'The *Leges Barbarorum*: Law and Ethnicity in the Post-Roman West', in: *Regna and Gentes: The Relationship Between Late Antique and Early Medieval Peoples and Kingdoms in the Transformation of the Roman World*, ed. Hans-Werner Goetz, Jörg Jarnut and Walter Pohl, Leiden 2003, 21–53; Charles-Edwards, 'Law', 262–263; Lisi Oliver, *The Body Legal in Barbarian Law*, Toronto 2014, 11–14. Cf. Roger Collins, 'Law and Ethnic Identity in the Fifth and Sixth Centuries', in: *Medieval Europeans: Studies in Ethnic Identity and National Perspectives in Medieval Europe*, ed. Alfred P. Smyth, Basingstoke 1998, 1–23.

10 Runic original: Brooks, 'Æthelberht', 111–112, 125–130. Latin original: Lendinara, 'Kentish Laws'. The idea that the laws had been circulated orally before being committed to writing is widely accepted. In addition to Oliver's case, discussed below, see Wormald, 'Law-Making', 184; Charles-Edwards, 'Law', 270–271. Note that 'oral transmission' is in some ways an ambiguous concept: it could refer to the rote-learning of a more-or-less fixed text or the memorisation of legal customs that were not articulated in a set form of words. It is not entirely clear which of these Wormald preferred; Charles-Edwards's arguments suggest the former.

11 Oliver, *Beginnings*, 34–41 (quotations at 37 and 41).

syntax, from which she concluded that some parts of the code are likely to be older than others. Specifically, she identified an archaic 'dative of quantity' in the sections of the text concerned with personal injury and offences against freemen. This is a usage familiar in other West Germanic languages but unattested in the Old English corpus outside early Kentish law. Oliver argued that we should infer that these sections were first formulated at an earlier point than the rest of the code, fossilising a syntactical construction that later fell out of use.[12]

Oliver's argument thus implies the existence of at least three stages in the evolution of the text we know as Æthelberht's laws: the earliest oral version, marked by the use of the dative of quantity, which covered offences against freemen and personal injury; a more elaborate oral version which included the material on kings, nobles, women and the unfree, which was current at the time of Æthelberht's conversion; and the written version, which added the initial clauses on the Church.[13] Much of the evidence underlying this interpretation is necessarily circumstantial, and therefore suggestive rather than conclusive. Individually, each of the considerations cited are susceptible to alternative explanations but in each case it seems to me that Oliver's reading is eminently plausible, and cumulatively I find them convincing. For present purposes, though, the specifics of her argument — for instance the issue of chronological layering — are immaterial; it is the basic thrust of her case that is essential. It matters for what follows that Æthelberht's code was based on a pre-existing Kentish text which was subject to only minor emendation when committed to Roman script.[14]

The crucial issue here is the intertextual environment in which our text was composed. The validity of this article's core arguments is much more readily apparent if it is accepted that the laws (except for the initial set of clauses on the Church) were composed in pre-conversion Kent, drawing on a range of earlier texts (such as that represented by Oliver's earliest chronological layer) that probably only existed in a memorised form. In this reading the intertextual influences shaping the laws are taken to have been oral rather than written (and thus, sadly, largely irrecoverable), to have been Kentish rather than European, and to have been practical and legal rather than political and intellectual. Fundamentally, the text was framed by native Kentish authors with a native Kentish agenda, familiar with native Kentish socio-legal practice and

12 Oliver, *Beginnings*, 32–34, 41–51.

13 Oliver, *Beginnings*, 51.

14 The argument here is thus also consistent with the suggestion of a runic original in Brooks, 'Æthelberht'.

drawing on pre-existing (almost certainly oral and memorised) native Kentish texts. The literate ecclesiastical intellectuals responsible for the text's transcription, emendation and subsequent manuscript transmission were not its authors in any significant sense. The intertextual environment within which these churchmen operated gave written laws a significance without which our text probably would not have survived to the present. This environment shaped decisions about which texts to write down, copy and keep, but it did not significantly influence the laws our text contains.

The alternative interpretation, which would render the validity of the arguments put forward here less immediately apparent, is that the laws were composed (as opposed to merely being written down and slightly amended) in the wake of Æthelberht's conversion, modelled on and borrowing from written continental exemplars.[15] If this were so, we would have to view the laws as a product of a broader European intertextual environment associated with the literate intellectual culture of elite churchmen. The validity of an interpretation which prioritised a native Kentish intertextual environment, associated with practical legal culture, would then be open to question. Arguments for this environment's relevance would have to be constructed on the basis of the text's contents, and the problematic possibility that some or all of its clauses result from a skilled author's attempts to imitate exemplars found in manuscripts brought from the continent would need continuously to be taken into account. Æthelberht's code is a helpfully clear-cut case study because this scenario is so evidently unlikely. An ecclesiastical author attempting to increase Æthelberht's prestige by composing a text in imitation of a continental model would surely have written in Latin, he would surely have mentioned the king and his kingdom by name, and he would scarcely have forgotten to include the Church except as an afterthought. It is, in short, quite readily apparent that understanding the Romano-Christian ideology of kingship which prompted Æthelberht's decision to have the laws written down does not help us to

15 Stefan Jurasinski, 'The Continental Origins of Æthelberht's Code', *Philological Quarterly* 80 (2001), 1–15, argues essentially this case, concluding that stylistic and syntactical similarities between Æthelberht's text's Old English and the Latin of continental laws show that the code was dependent on 'one or several examples of lost Merovingian legislation' (12). However, in the absence of demonstrable dependence on an extant text this conclusion is little more than a suggestion; it is not obvious that similarities of syntax — or indeed of structure and content — need imply direct borrowing rather than merely the linguistic and legal similarities of the cultures concerned. Lendinara, 'Kentish Laws' would have similar implications. However, her linguistic arguments are comprehensively refuted in Hough, 'Texts'.

understand why the pre-existing text on which they were based was composed, or what it meant. To address these issues, we need to situate the text in another context entirely.

We can begin to do this by considering the laws' subject matter. Our text is essentially a compensation tariff. It defines the compensation appropriate to various forms of affront. These affronts can be divided into three basic categories, which can overlap. First, there are offences against the person, which are most obvious in the long tariff of personal injuries in the middle of the code.[16] Second, there are offences against property, including theft from people of various ranks and probably also damage to property in the form of unfree dependants; for example it is stated that striking off the eye or foot of an *esne* necessitates compensation equivalent to his full value, which is clearly due not to the *esne* but to his master.[17] Third, there are offences against protection. These do not harm the victim directly nor need they involve a reduction in the value of his property, and as such they are perhaps best understood as a form of insult. Thus, lying with 'the king's maiden' (*cyninges mægdenman*) or the 'cupbearer' (*birele*) of either a nobleman or a freeman requires compensation equivalent to the relevant protector's *mundbyrd* ('protection value'), as does killing his household dependant, or killing anyone at all within his home.[18] It is worth noting that wergild itself fits best in this category. The recipients of the payment (a slain man's family) have not been harmed personally, nor has their property been taken or damaged, but they were the primary protectors of their kinsman and his killing thus represents a serious affront.

Importantly, it seems clear that the text aims for comprehensive coverage of rules defining affronts and the compensation they require. This is apparent from its orderly structure. It begins at the top of society with affronts against the king and proceeds downwards through affronts against nobles to affronts against freemen; it then deals with personal injuries, beginning with the head and working down to the foot, before the concluding sections that deal with affronts relating to women and two categories of unfree dependant (the *esne* and the *þeow*).[19] The text does sometimes depart from its core task of defining affronts and their appropriate compensations — there is a discussion of marital property, for instance[20] — but these digressions are infrequent and brief. There is no mistaking the text's thematic unity; it is so wholly devoted

16 *Æthelberht* 32–71.1 (Liebermann: 32–72.1), ed. and trans. Lisi Oliver, *The Beginnings of English Law*, Toronto 2002, 70–77.

17 *Æthelberht* 80 (Liebermann: 87), ed. and trans. Oliver, 80–81.

18 *Æthelberht* 11, 14, 16, 18–21, 26 (Liebermann: 5, 8, 10, 13–16, 25), ed. and trans. Oliver, 62–69.

19 Oliver, *Beginnings*, 36–37.

20 *Æthelberht* 76–76.5 (Liebermann: 77–81), ed. and trans. Oliver, 78–79.

to one specific species of rule that when other types of rule make an appearance they clearly do so as incidental extras. It is a compensation tariff. One way of explaining this would be as a generic convention derived from manuscript exemplars circulating within a broader European intellectual culture. Æthelberht's code would then be a compensation tariff simply because it had come to be expected that foundational law codes be compensation tariffs.[21] Fortunately this is unlikely. As has just been argued, there is no reason to think that the laws written down at Æthelberht's behest were originally composed within a European intertextual environment dominated by literate ecclesiastical intellectuals. The fact that this text is a compensation tariff must in some way reflect native Kentish legal culture. This basic insight can be pursued fruitfully.

We must, of course, assume that other types of rule beside those defining affronts and compensations existed in late sixth-century Kent: rules about inheritance and rights over land, rules governing the operation of legal procedures such as those relating to collective oath-taking and suretyship, perhaps even rules about the punishment of forms of wrongdoing judged threatening to communities as a whole rather than (or as well as) affronts against specific individuals. The fact that our text focuses so clearly on one type of legal rule is highly significant. It implies that this type of rule was accorded particular prestige in Kentish society. It seems that when Kentish men took the trouble to memorise and recite law, they focused their efforts almost exclusively on the

21 This explanation is suggested in Wormald, *Making*, 101: 'it became appropriate to write down Kentish law on certain matters, because these were matters on which eminent Frankish legislators had pronounced.' It is worth pointing out that this idea, taken to its logical conclusion and rolled out across early medieval Europe, would reduce early medieval law's characteristic focus on compensation to something close to coincidence: a feature that exists simply because it was inherited from some early manuscript exemplar, which thus need not imply compensation had any particularly prominent place in contemporary legal culture. I resist this logic here partly for the reasons just given — if Æthelberht's text was a slightly modified version of an oral precursor it simply does not make sense — but also because of the existence of comparative examples with no connection to early medieval Europe, in which compensation is a similarly dominant concern of formalised law. For two such extra-European examples, see Fernanda Pirie, 'Rules, Proverbs, and Persuasion: Legalism and Rhetoric in Tibet', in: *Legalism: Rules and Categories*, ed. Paul Dresch and Judith Scheele, Oxford 2015, 109–115; Paul Dresch, *The Rules of Barat: Tribal Documents from Yemen*, Sanaa 2006. To make this argument forcefully one would of course need many more examples, but it seems probable that the phenomenon of law texts produced by feuding cultures focusing on compensation for affronts extends well beyond early medieval Europe. If this is so it cannot adequately be explained as an idiosyncrasy produced by the circulation of legal manuscripts in early medieval intellectual culture.

precise definition of affronts and the compensations appropriate to them. This raises questions. What was so special about this type of law? Why was it judged so important?

To answer these questions, we need to consider the dynamics of legal practice associated with affront and compensation. The laws themselves offer us very little here. Their purpose was evidently to provide authoritative information on how much compensation should ultimately be paid in any given situation, not to discuss the practicalities of bringing the parties involved to agreement. They do, however, allow us to make some important inferences about contemporary legal culture. Most broadly, this was a feuding culture. This is the obvious conclusion to draw from the discussion of wergild and indeed the focus on compensation generally. The laws never state explicitly that compensations were intended as peaceful resolutions to conflicts which otherwise had the potential to erupt into violence (a remarkable and thus potentially significant fact in itself), but they cannot plausibly be read in any other way.[22] Equally crucial is a point so closely related that it need not be regarded as separate: this was a legal order that recognised offences to honour. This is apparent in the specification of compensations for offences that neither harmed nor affected the property of the person being compensated, and also in the disproportionately high compensations given to offences with symbolic significance: denying a man's masculinity by castrating him (compensation three times that for killing him);[23] denying his freedom by binding him (compensation equivalent to serious wounds: a broken jaw, a chopped-off thumb, an impaled abdomen);[24] and inflicting wounds which would serve as visible marks of shame (front teeth valued more highly than those further back; bruises that show outside the clothing worth fifty percent more than those which do not).[25]

This is not much to go on, and of course we lack any other sources bearing on the practicalities of compensation settlements in a contemporary Kentish context. This problem with source material does not mean we should despair and give up, however; nor should it be understood to give free licence for our imaginations to run riot. There is no reason to suspect that the difficulties of achieving successful compensation settlements in late sixth-century Kent differed markedly from the difficulties encountered in other societies which tried

---

22 This is not controversial; see Wormald, *Making*, 96. In the text itself, this conclusion is most heavily implied in *Æthelberht* 24.2 (Liebermann: 23), ed. and trans. Oliver, 66–67.

23 *Æthelberht* 64 (Liebermann: 64), ed. and trans. Oliver, 74–75. On the interpretation of this clause, see Lambert, *Law and Order*, 22 n. 32.

24 *Æthelberht* 25, 47, 53, 61.1 (Liebermann: 24, 50, 54, 62.1), ed. and trans. Oliver, 66–67, 70–75.

25 *Æthelberht* 48–48.3, 61.3–61.4 (Liebermann: 51, 59–60), ed. and trans. Oliver, 70–73. See Oliver, *Beginnings*, 100–101.

to resolve potentially violent conflicts through compensation settlements — societies that are sometimes labelled 'honour cultures'.[26] The range of comparative examples we might draw on to help us imagine our way into this aspect of early Kentish legal practice is vast, and we ought to make use of them. The ones chosen here are drawn principally from sixth- and seventh-century Francia, medieval Iceland as portrayed in the sagas, and modern anthropologists' accounts of Yemen and Tibet. I make no special claim for these examples; I have chosen them primarily because they happen to be familiar to me.[27] They do, however, have the benefit of diversity: there is no reason to think that any similarities result from close connections between them, or from shared religious or ethnic heritage. The broad observations about the dynamics of compensation settlements that follow could, I think, be applied just as readily to any of these medieval European and modern extra-European contexts, and this gives me some confidence that what I am describing are generic challenges associated with compensation in feuding cultures that are highly likely to have applied in late sixth-century Kent as well. Readers will have to judge for themselves how convincing they find this.

3 The Dynamics of Compensation Settlements

What, then, were the key practical challenges involved in bringing about compensation settlements? The crucial point here is that the parties to any such settlement are likely to be highly sensitive to its implications for their personal honour. This applies most obviously to the affronted party. Whatever the nature of the original offence — whether it involves interference with his property, harm to his person, a breach of his protection, or some combination of the three — in social terms its meaning is the same: it is an affront. The man whose toe has been cut off, whose female slave has been raped, whose horse has been stolen, or whose brother has been killed, will be understood by his peers to have been insulted, and the way he responds to that insult will be judged by them. That is, his reputation among his peers — his honour — is at stake and this will inform his decision-making. He will be aware that his behaviour is under scrutiny and that a failure to conduct himself properly could have

26 For example, in William Ian Miller, *Eye for an Eye*, Cambridge 2006, 17–23 (cited as Miller, *Eye*).

27 My familiarity with Yemen and Tibet arises from conversations with my former Oxford colleagues, Paul Dresch and Fernanda Pirie, my considerable debt to whom should be obvious from what follows. The workshop paper that became Pirie, 'Rules, Proverbs, and Persuasion' was particularly influential on the argument presented here.

significant negative effects on his social standing. My use of the term 'honour' here is no more technical than this: it refers to a person's reputation in their community, a fundamentally social matter.[28] My emphasis on men, moreover, is no accident. In feuding societies men are invariably the main public actors, their conduct judged in gendered terms. Proper conduct in a man should be understood as properly *masculine* conduct. Thus, in Gregory of Tours's narrative of a late sixth-century Frankish feud, one of the participants is said to have been prompted to kill his opponent by the thought, 'if I don't avenge my relatives [...] they will say that I am weak as a woman, for I no longer have the right to be called a man!'[29]

Properly masculine conduct in response to an affront could involve exhibiting a suitable emotional reaction, a level of anger appropriate to the severity of the affront. Thus, Fernanda Pirie reports nomadic tribesmen in Eastern Tibet explaining that they 'have' to get angry if a family member is killed, or in the event of a major theft of livestock.[30] To be taken seriously in a society that accepts the legitimacy of violent feuding, however, angry displays need to be regarded as credible threats, not comical outpourings of impotent rage or insincere posturing. That is, a large part of their point is to signal that the angered party is genuinely intent on taking violent action and is only prevented from doing so by practical considerations: the absence of an appropriate target, for example, or an unwillingness to offend a respected figure by attacking someone in breach of his protection. So, in Pirie's Tibet, anger may be 'more a performative than an emotional term', but it remains deadly serious. Although the victims of a theft 'may be restrained from initiating a fight, if they happen to meet a member of the thief's family, they would "have" to get angry and fight him'.[31] The crux of the matter is that affronts require not just words but action. A man's honour, his reputation, his social standing will suffer if his peers judge that he has failed to respond adequately to an insult he has suffered.

---

28 For a succinct explication, see Thomas M. Charles-Edwards, 'Honour and Status in some Irish and Welsh Prose Tales', *Ériu* 29 (1978), 123–124.

29 Gregory of Tours, *Decem Libri Historiarum* 9.19, ed. Bruno Krusch and Wilhelm Levison, MGH SS rerum Merovingicarum 1, 1, Hanover 1951, 433; *History of the Franks*. Translated by Lewis Thorpe, Harmondsworth/ Middlesex 1974, 501 (cited as *History of the Franks*. Translated by Thorpe).

30 Fernanda Pirie, *Feuding, Mediation and the Negotiation of Authority among the Nomads of Eastern Tibet* (Max Planck Institute for Social Anthropology Working Papers 72), Halle 2005, 13 (cited as Pirie, *Feuding*). A comparable point is made in William Ian Miller, *Bloodtaking and Peacemaking: Feud, Law, and Society in Saga Iceland*, Chicago and London 1990, 61–68 (cited as Miller, *Bloodtaking*).

31 Pirie, *Feuding*, 13.

So what constitutes an adequate response? One option is direct retaliation. The affronted party could seek to harm or dishonour the original offenders, thus demonstrating to everyone that his wrath is to be feared, the consequences of offending him severe. The key benefit of this approach is that the message thus sent is relatively unambiguous. If a man takes an eye for an eye, a life for a life, a horse for a horse, few can argue that he has failed to avenge the original insult adequately.[32] The obvious problem is that in practice the ideal of parity is difficult to achieve. Indeed, the risk of escalation is obvious, given the unlikelihood of the targets of vengeance acquiescing in their treatment, and the distinct possibility of those taking direct action doing so in a spirit of self-righteous rage rather than cold calculation. Such an escalation would be dangerous for the avenger, of course, and the prospect of further reciprocal violence must have provided a clear disincentive to this course of action. It is probably safe to assume, however, that Kentish men (or at least free Kentish men) aspired to a model of masculinity in which personal bravery was a core value: a truly masculine man would not allow fear of reprisals to restrain him from taking action. In such an environment, any public recognition that the risk of meeting a violent death was a significant factor in one's decision-making could be interpreted as an admission of cowardice. One 'has' to get angry. For those determined to live up to this masculine ideal — angry men unwilling to allow fear to affect their conduct — direct action will appear a rational choice. Indeed, if the dangers of escalation are excluded from consideration, a disproportionate response is logically superior to one that merely re-establishes parity. It makes the message the affronted party's vengeful actions are intended to convey even more emphatic: the consequences of offending him are greatly to be feared.

For wider communities, of course, this is problematic. Left unchecked, men who invested in this model of masculinity could create long-lasting and polarising conflicts between neighbours, punctuated by ever more egregious acts of violence.[33] Whatever the feelings of the parties to a conflict, their neighbours had a strong interest in settlements that prevented violent escalation. A key ingredient in such settlements was compensation. The basic logic underlying compensation in this context is that it represents an acceptable alternative course of action for an affronted party. As with direct action, a compensation settlement can be understood as the affronted party inflicting a significant loss on his opponents. In theory it achieves the same goal — a public demonstration that the consequences of offending him are severe — without the need

32 Miller, *Eye*, provides a much more detailed discussion of these themes.

33 For perceptive discussion of literary treatments of this theme, see Peter S. Baker, *Honour, Exchange and Violence in Beowulf*, Cambridge 2013, 72–76. Also, Miller, *Eye*, 8.

for further violence and the associated risk of escalation. From a community perspective it is the optimal solution. For the affronted party in particular, however, it is more problematic. The potential critique of his actions is obvious enough: the man who accepts compensation rather than take vengeance could well be exhibiting a deplorable combination of cowardice and greed. He could be accused, as the medieval Icelandic expression has it, of 'carrying his kin in his purse', or to leap to late twentieth-century Yemen, of prioritising his 'lunch' over his 'good name'.[34] In the example from Gregory of Tours given above, the man assessing his own conduct in explicitly gendered terms had been provoked by a spectacularly ill-judged remark that cast doubt on the propriety of his earlier acceptance of a compensation settlement:

> Dear brother, you ought to be grateful to me for having killed off your relations. There is plenty of gold and silver in your house now that I have recompensed you what I did to them. If it weren't for the fact that the compensation which I've paid has restored your finances, you would still today be poor and destitute.[35]

The irony of compensation settlements is that what look from one perspective to be their key attractions — the acquisition of material goods, the avoidance of physical danger — make them morally hazardous for men of honour. Accepting compensation may provide safety and wealth, but to allow the fear of danger or the desire for riches to act as motivation for the acceptance of compensation would be contemptible.

What, then, would be an acceptable reason for an honourable man to enter into compensation negotiations? The late seventh-century Frankish *Formulary of Marculf* contains a template for a document (quite possibly derived from an earlier exemplar) recording a compensation settlement for homicide, which provides a clue:

> To [my] lord brother A, B. Since, at the instigation of the devil, you were seen to kill our brother C, which you should not have done, you could have been in danger of [losing your] life because of this; but through the intervention of priests and great men, whose names are added below, we were seen to restore the harmony of peace in this matter, so that you

34 Miller, *Eye*, 26–27 (also noting a comparable Kabyle phrase); Paul Dresch, *Tribes, Government, and History in Yemen*, Oxford 1989, 49 (cited as Dresch, *Tribes*).

35 Gregory of Tours, *Decem Libri Historiarum* 9.19, ed. Krusch and Levison, MGH SS rer. Merov. 1, 1, 433; *History of the Franks*. Translated by Thorpe, 501.

> were to give me n. solidi in compensation for this, which you were seen to deliver by your pledge, and we were seen to relinquish this claim against you by the rod.[36]

The recipient of the compensation thus emphasises the seriousness of the original offence and the resultant threat to the killer's life, and cites the intervention of 'priests and great men' (whose identities matter enough for their names to be appended) to explain his decision to accept compensation. This could be interpreted in a number of ways, but in the light of the other comparative examples discussed here I would read it as follows. The appropriately angry affronted party had been so intent on taking the killer's life that it took the personal intervention of highly respected figures to persuade him to change course; the entreaties of lesser men could not have swayed him, such was his determination. (The status of the men named in the documents could thus be interpreted as an index of the affronted party's masculine qualities.) In the event, however, he has magnanimously subordinated his personal inclinations to the greater good, recognising the pressing social need 'to restore the harmony of peace'.

In honour cultures the proper motivation for the acceptance of compensation is not fear or greed, it is the willingness to recognise that the wider community's need for peace and harmony is more important than an individual's or group's desire for vengeance. When the degree of offence is high, as in a homicide case, the expectation is that the affronted party will be correspondingly angry and reluctant to accept this logic, willing to do so only when the case is pressed by men of high standing and great authority. This is commonplace in comparative examples. Pirie describes senior nobles and Buddhist monks playing an essential role in persuading angry nomads to accept compensation settlements in early twenty-first-century Tibet.[37] In late twentieth-century Yemen, Paul Dresch reports that the involvement of such third parties was 'almost mandatory', and that at its most forceful it involved sacrificing their own property (specifically, slaughtering bulls) as a demonstration of their investment in their peace-making task.[38] Gregory of Tours likewise reports proffering ecclesiastical money in a similar context (though at first without

---

36 *Marculfi Formulae* 2.18, ed. Karl Zeumer, MGH Formulae Merowingici et Karolini aevi, Hanover 1886, 88–89; *The Formularies of Angers and Marculf. Two Merovingian Legal Handbooks*. Translated with an Introduction and Notes by Alice Rio [Translated Texts for Historians 46], Liverpool 2008, 204.

37 Pirie, *Feuding*, 14–20.

38 Dresch, *Tribes*, 53, 68–69.

success), which perhaps had a similar significance.[39] Rather more laconically, one tenth-century Anglo-Saxon law's account of idealised compensation procedure opens with the simple statement that 'wise men' (*witan*, a word with strong connotations of high status) should settle feuds.[40] In the world of saga Iceland, third-party peacemakers were characterised, as 'men of goodwill' (*góðjarnir menn*) which, as William Ian Miller observes, 'describes the idealized intervenor as a person interested in the general good, a partisan of everyone rather than a disinterested neutral'.[41] Such figures required a certain status to be effective: 'In cases held at local Things [assemblies] it was possible, for example in a dispute pitting two of the district chieftains against each other, for there to be no one present who was capable of pressuring the sides towards reconciliation.'[42]

At least in serious cases, then, sixth-century Kentish communities probably expected affronted parties to require persuasion even to begin compensation negotiations, but the need for persuasion did not end there. The really hard work may often have been the agreement of a specific sum. The dynamics of such negotiations are worth thinking through. In any such case the offending party is likely to be reluctant to pay too much. Economic considerations are part of this, of course, but it may not have been a good idea to acknowledge this publicly as it could be understood as a dishonourable admission of poverty or a sign of miserliness offensively out of place in such sensitive discussions. The compensation-paying party's proper concern is that if they pay more than is reasonable they emerge from the process dishonoured, their reputation harmed by the perception that they had been intimidated by their opponents and capitulated to their demands for an excessive sum. Economics may have factored in compensation recipients' thinking too — the desire to extract as much as possible — but to admit to this would be to admit to materialistic motivations, calling the honourableness of the earlier decision to accept compensation into question. Affronted parties were not supposed to care about compensation for its financial value but for what it symbolised. They needed to extract, and be seen to extract, an amount that corresponded to the affront they had suffered; to be bullied into accepting less would be shameful.

Importantly, the primacy of honour in such negotiations should not be understood as a mere matter of form, a socially acceptable facade for negotiations

---

39 Gregory of Tours, *Decem Libri Historiarum* 7.47, ed. Krusch and Levison, MGH SS rer. Merov. 1, 1, 367–368.

40 II *Edmund* 7, ed. and trans. Liebermann, vol. 1, 188–189.

41 Miller, *Bloodtaking*, 264.

42 Miller, *Bloodtaking*, 265.

that were really about securing the optimal financial outcome given the balance of naked power between the parties involved. Ideas about honour are significant not just externally — as a social framework for collective assessment of individuals' conduct — but also internally, as the ethical framework within which individuals understood their own actions and assessed their own moral worth. This internalisation is most obvious in ethnographic examples which show men valuing symbolic gestures over financial gain. Thus in Yemen Dresch reports that after — but *only* after — the performance of a range of gestures of apology (the symbolic removal of a head-cloth, the offering of slaughter-beasts or rifles), affronted parties commonly relinquished all or part of their right to compensation.[43] Dresch's summary of the course of negotiations in a case of accidental homicide in a road accident illustrates the process well:

> A delegation from Banī Maṭar [the killer's tribe] arrived three days later, bringing with them a bull, two rams, and YR 2,000 worth of *qāt*. In the course of the first day the blood-money demanded was halved 'on account of receiving the bull' [...], and on the second day YR 8,000 was dropped 'to honour those present', intermediaries [...] who had gathered from elsewhere. A further YR 8,000 was deducted the next day 'to honour Āl 'Ammār' [the victim's tribe]: in other words to honour the victim's own fellow tribesmen, who by now were pressing his immediate kin to settle. The sum finally demanded and agreed to was thus YR 16,000 or a quarter of that first demanded. This was eminently reasonable, since the killing was plainly an accident, but it would be wrong to see Āl 'Ammār's initial bellicose stance as bluster or a negotiating ploy. Were one a tribesman, it would be dangerous to do so. Had the protocols not been forthcoming promptly, the Maṭarīs would have seemed intransigent, insult would have been added to injury, and, accident or not, blood might well have led to blood.[44]

The key point here is that, fundamentally, it is the *affront* that is at issue in compensation negotiations; the display of disrespect implicit in the original offence can thus matter more than any material harm inflicted. Honourable men might be able generously to forgive material harm — particularly if pressed to do so by eminent figures for the sake of social harmony — but their reputations will suffer if they allow a display of disrespect to stand.

---

43 Dresch, *Tribes*, 49–51.

44 Dresch, *Tribes*, 53.

Symbolic gestures that apologised for the harm done and publicly denied the existence of any disrespect could therefore be more important than the transfer of wealth. So, in Tibet, Pirie describes a compensation negotiation that was deadlocked because some men had been not just been killed but killed within their own encampment — a display of disrespect: 'the case was settled by the intervention of a senior *lama*, who ordered a small, but symbolic, extra payment by way of apology.'[45] This, I suspect, is what underlies the provision in Æthelberht's laws that if a killer flees into exile his family are liable for only half the compensation that would otherwise have been owed. By dissociating themselves from the killer himself, they dissociate themselves from the insult implicit in his actions.[46] As Rob Meens has argued, the self-abasement involved in penitential rituals could perform this function in early medieval Europe, allowing the penitent publicly to dissociate himself from his earlier actions — and thus to deny the continuing existence of any disrespect implicit in those actions — through a display of remorse that, as a pious religious act, need not ultimately have a detrimental impact on the his social standing.[47] This is not to say that the transfer of wealth was unimportant in such contexts. The prospect of incurring ruinous material losses, in particular, must have been a powerful motivation driving the payers of compensation to appease their opponents in more affordable ways. Nonetheless, it is important to note that in the public discourse of compensation negotiations the transfer of wealth was probably significant for its symbolic rather than its economic value.

4 The Significance of Æthelberht's Laws

How, then, should we imagine the Kentish compensation tariff known to us as the laws of Æthelberht fitting into the processes by which compensation settlements were agreed? And how might this context help us understand our text? If we accept that Æthelberht's written law code was a slightly amended transcription of an earlier memorised text, it follows that there were people in late sixth-century Kent who learnt the text by rote and were able to recite it. This investment of effort suggests that the text had a degree of prestige (as does the fact that it was the first and quite probably the only text from

45 Pirie, *Feuding*, 15.

46 *Æthelberht* 24.2 (Liebermann: 23), ed. and trans. Oliver, 66–67.

47 Rob Meens, 'Penance, Shame and Honour in the Middle Ages', in: *Shame Between Punishment and Penance. The Social Uses of Shame in the Middle Ages and Modern Times* (Micrologus Library 54), ed. Bénédicte Sère and Jörg Wettlaufer, Florence 2013, 89–102.

pre-Christian times that was committed to writing), so I think we can safely assume that its existence was a matter of common knowledge. That is, most Kentish adults would have known that a text of laws existed in the memories of certain knowledgeable individuals. (In a Frankish context these people had a title: *rachinburgii*.)[48] We might speculate that they occasionally heard the laws recited in assemblies, as in medieval Iceland a third of the laws were recited by the law-speaker at the annual Althing, but this is not essential for the interpretation proposed here. What matters is that even if the contents of this memorised compensation tariff were not widely known, the existence of authoritative knowledge on the subject of compensation was a well-known social fact. This state of affairs would allow the text to be called upon in the context of compensation settlements. A high-status intermediary might appeal to the laws in one of two ways: either as the source of a monetary valuation (as part of an effort to persuade the parties to agree on a specific sum), or as a symbol of broader social ideals (perhaps as part of a bid to persuade a party to enter negotiations in the first place, or to make magnanimous concessions).[49] If the laws' existence was common knowledge and their authority generally accepted, such appeals could be effective rhetorical strategies: the validity of the monetary valuations the laws contained and the broader social ideals they represented were already established as common ground, and with enough persuasion from a sufficiently august source all but the most intransigent could probably be induced to negotiate on that basis.

The most straightforward of these two possible uses for the laws is the technical one: as a source of authoritative monetary valuations for affronts. It would be naïve to imagine that compensation tariffs rendered negotiation superfluous. Accepting that a generic right arm was worth a certain amount does not preclude disagreement about the value of the specific right arm under discussion, given all the potentially relevant particulars of the case (for example, the esteem in which the arm's erstwhile owner was held, whether he was right-handed)[50] and we must leave room for all sorts of adjustments in the

---

48 See Charles-Edwards, 'Law', 267–269.

49 Fernanda Pirie, 'From Tribal Tibet: The Significance of the Legal Form', in: *Law and Anthropology* (Current Legal Issues 12), ed. Michael Freeman and David Napier, Oxford 2009, 154–155, for an analogous argument: that in Tibet before the Chinese occupation law codes featuring compensation tariffs may have been invoked in the 'lengthy and sententious speeches' made by mediators to persuade reluctant tribal leaders to 'swallow their pride' and accept compensation settlements.

50 Lisi Oliver, 'Protecting the Body in Early Medieval Law', in: *Peace and Protection in the Middle Ages*, ed. Tom Lambert and David Rollason, Toronto 2009, 60–77, works through some potential complicating factors in detail.

light of symbolic gestures such as those discussed above. But for all this variability, the existence of an agreed framework for the calculation of compensations could still have a significant effect. Dresch, at any rate, reports that in Yemen in the 1970s and 1980s tribesmen generally accepted the standard rate of compensation for homicide set for the Islamic law courts by the Ministry of Justice: 'Negotiations begin with this shared understanding, whether admitted to or not, and most settlements are not widely removed from the rules' prescriptions.'[51] In late sixth-century Kent, then, we might imagine that general awareness of an authoritative compensation tariff meant that opposing parties accepted the validity of a single, precise set of valuations for affronts and, through appeals to that compensation tariff, could be persuaded to negotiate within that framework. The significance of this should not be underestimated. Without such a framework it is easy to imagine compensation negotiations running into serious difficulties before they even got started, there being an unbridgeable gap between the two parties' starting assumptions.

The second possible use for the laws — as a symbol of broader social ideals — is less obvious. This is because the ideals in question are implicit rather than explicit, and our appreciation of their significance depends on our appreciation of the difficulties of bringing about compensation settlements. We have no reason to assume that getting Kentish men to agree to compensation settlements was easy. It is likely that, just like men in the various other honour cultures touched upon here, they could be highly sensitive to the possibility that the acceptance of material wealth in preference to potentially dangerous violent action could look cowardly or self-interested. Just like men in other honour cultures, in cases where the original affront had been serious they were probably only willing to consider the possibility after the intervention of prominent third-parties and the application of considerable persuasive pressure. The laws, it seems to me, make sense not just as technical resources employed by these figures in the construction of an acceptable settlement, but as weapons in their broader ideological arsenal.

Let us take first the laws' most striking feature: their lengthy and repetitive stipulation of monetary valuations for affronts. This is significant. The *only* response to an affront the laws envision — again and again — is compensation. Vengeance is not even acknowledged as a possibility, let alone as a more honourable alternative. Indeed, the laws present compensation not just as the only course of action, but as a course of action which has been mapped out in intricate detail — presumably by the wise men of previous generations from whom the laws were passed down — so that the proper compensation

51 Dresch, *Tribes*, 48.

for virtually every conceivable eventuality can be calculated. This, I suspect, is the primary significance of valuation in monetary terms. The precision it offers creates the reassuring impression of a high level of accuracy, contributing to the laws' all-important authority in much the same way as their length and apparent comprehensiveness. Listening to their being recited would have been very dull indeed but we should not mistake the presence of rebarbative detail in these laws for the absence of a powerful ideological message. These laws were an assertion both that the proper response to an affront was to negotiate a compensation settlement, and that Kentish society had access to knowledge that allowed these settlements to be calibrated precisely to the circumstances of any given case. Properly applied, this knowledge could ensure that both parties to such settlements emerged with their honour intact, their conduct irreproachable because they had neither accepted too little compensation nor paid too much. The laws were thus a source of optimism.

Indeed, if we consider sixth-century Kent as it would have been had everyone behaved in the way the laws set out, we get an almost utopian vision of an ideal society — a society in which all free men maintain their honour in perfect equilibrium.[52] Stomachs may be impaled, eyes gouged out and slaves raped, but proper compensation settlements would allow all free men to live together in a state of mutual respect and peaceful goodwill. Socially divisive escalations caused by the irresponsible pursuit of violent vengeance simply do not exist in this world. Within this model of an ideal society of free males is a model of an ideal free man. He is strong and determined, in that he is willing and able do what is necessary to maintain his honour, insisting on being compensated in full for any affront. However, he is also level-headed and reasonable: his strength and determination are used to exact the compensation required to maintain his honour, and no more. He does not rush precipitately to avenge wrongs done to him, nor does he take advantage of his strength to dishonour his opponents by extorting more from them than is just. And he is careful not to impose obligations on others. He accepts full responsibility for all his own actions, personally paying compensation when it is right to do so (verbs of payment in the laws are always in the singular: it is 'he', the offender, who is envisaged as paying, not 'they'), and he certainly does not rush into reckless actions which will compel his family to use their wealth to bail him out. (One law specifically states that killers are to pay compensation with *their*

52 This is to follow the lead of Donald R. Jr. Davis, 'Rules, Culture, and Imagination in Sanskrit Jurisprudence', in: *Legalism: Rules and Categories*, ed. Paul Dresch and Judith Scheele, Oxford 2015, 29–52.

own resources.)[53] A proper man, the laws imply, is not just strong and determined, he understands the socially disruptive power of his own actions and exercises restraint because of his commitment to the ideal of a community of free men who respect one another's honour. The laws can thus be read as promoting a particular construction of masculinity, one distinctly tinged by social responsibility. Implicit in them is a message about how the free men who make up Kentish society ought to act to bring that society closer to its ideal form.

The laws, then, can be considered as an expression of contemporary ideals of social order. High-status intermediaries trying to persuade intransigent feuding parties to negotiate a compensation settlement had need of such ideals. Their role was to persuade angry men to subordinate their desire for blood to the wider community's need for a restoration of peaceful relations; they needed to assert that compensation was not only morally acceptable but the right course of action, that the maintenance of honour and properly masculine behaviour *were* compatible with socially responsible decisions which avoided violent escalation. I would suggest that the laws — probably primarily in their memorised form — were one resource they could draw upon in such processes of persuasion. This is not to say that the laws necessarily had a central role to play; there was doubtless a range of different rhetorical strategies that could be attempted in these circumstances, many of which need not have involved law at all. Nonetheless, the laws were clearly composed with the context of compensation negotiations in mind, and the considerable effort that seems to have been invested in their memorisation suggests that they had a real importance, so it is reasonable to suppose that they sometimes entered the discourse of compensation settlements. And when they did their meaning need not have been purely technical; they could have been invoked as a source of authority for the social ideals implied within them. They could have rammed home the point that a peaceful settlement was the proper course of action. This was not just something a noted intermediary was urging as a practical expedient, it was what the laws — which were accepted by the entire Kentish people — demanded and declared to be *right*. Their ideological significance as a symbol could, in other words, have had considerable importance in a practical context.

This is speculative, of course. There are no means by which we could confirm whether the laws were invoked in this symbolic way in the context of compensation negotiations, but in a sense that is immaterial. In truth we know little about any context in which the laws were invoked. If Oliver's arguments

53 *Æthelberht* 30 (Liebermann: 30), ed. and trans. Oliver, 68–69.

are correct, we know that they were learnt by rote and passed on orally, but we can only guess at the contexts in which they were recited. Nonetheless, the significance attributed to them by this culture — the effort invested in their memorisation and their subsequent memorialisation in writing — strongly suggests that they were symbolically important.

Understanding these existing laws' symbolism can help us appreciate what Æthelberht's act of codification might have signified in a contemporary Kentish context. There is, of course, no reason to suppose that the memorised text which formed the basis of the king's code would itself have been understood as an expression of a Romano-Christian ideology of kingship. (Indeed, even in its amended, Christianised form there is barely a hint of such an ideology in the text.) These laws' symbolic importance is much more likely to have lain in their articulation of the established social and legal ideals of the Kentish people. This reading makes sense of the text's contents, with its emphasis on precision (and thus implicitly on honourable balance) and more generally on the rightness of compensation; and, unless my comparative examples have led me badly astray, it fits the text's original social and legal context well. Æthelberht, then, in addition to emulating his Frankish neighbours' efforts to rule as Roman emperors, may well have been doing something more: attempting to associate himself with existing Kentish ideals of proper legal behaviour and good order, trying to take advantage of some of the prestige that was already attached to the laws he ordered to be written down. Indeed, to the Kentishmen who witnessed this royal act of codification, or heard about it, this may well have been its primary significance.

Bibliography

Primary Sources

Die Gesetze der Angelsachsen, ed. and trans. Felix Liebermann, 3 vols., Halle 1903–1916.

Formulae Merowingici et Karolini Aevi, ed. Karl Zeumer, MGH LL 5, Hanover 1886.

Gregory of Tours, *Decem Libri Historiarum*, ed. Bruno Krusch and Wilhelm Levison, MGH SS rerum Merovingicarum 1, 1, Hanover 1951.

Gregory of Tours, *History of the Franks*. Translated by Lewis Thorpe, Harmondsworth/ Middlesex 1974.

The Formularies of Angers and Marculf. Two Merovingian Legal Handbooks. Translated by Alice Rio (Translated Texts for Historians 46), Liverpool 2008.

The Laws of Æthelberht, ed. and trans. Lisi Oliver, *The Beginnings of English Law*, Toronto 2002, 52–116.

Secondary Works

Baker, Peter S., *Honour, Exchange and Violence in Beowulf*, Cambridge 2013.

Brooks, Nicholas, 'The Laws of King Æthelberht of Kent: Preservation, Content, and Composition', in: *Textus Roffensis: Law, Language, and Libraries in Early Medieval England*, ed. Bruce O'Brien and Barbara Bombi, Turnhout 2015, 105–136.

Brown, Warren C., and Górecki, Piotr, 'What Conflict Means: The Making of Medieval Conflict Studies in the United States, 1970–2000', in: *Conflict in Medieval Europe: Changing Perspectives on Society and Culture*, ed. Warren C. Brown and Piotr Górecki, Aldershot/Hampshire 2003, 1–35.

Charles-Edwards, Thomas M., 'Honour and Status in some Irish and Welsh Prose Tales', *Ériu* 29 (1978), 123–141.

Charles-Edwards, Thomas M., 'Law in the Western Kingdoms between the Fifth and Seventh Centuries', in: *The Cambridge Ancient History Volume 14: Late Antiquity: Empire and Successors, AD 425–600*, ed. Averil Cameron, Bryan Ward-Perkins and Michael Whitby, Cambridge 2001, 260–287.

Charles-Edwards, Thomas M., *Wales and the Britons, 350–1064*, Oxford 2013.

Collins, Roger, 'Law and Ethnic Identity in the Fifth and Sixth Centuries', in: *Medieval Europeans: Studies in Ethnic Identity and National Perspectives in Medieval Europe*, ed. Alfred P. Smyth, Basingstoke 1998, 1–23.

Dark, Kenneth R., *Civitas to Kingdom: British Political Continuity 300–800*, Leicester 1994.

Davis, Donald R. Jr., 'Rules, Culture, and Imagination in Sanskrit Jurisprudence', in: *Legalism: Rules and Categories*, ed. Paul Dresch and Judith Scheele, Oxford 2015, 29–52.

Dresch, Paul, *Tribes, Government, and History in Yemen*, Oxford 1989.

Dresch, Paul, *The Rules of Barat: Tribal Documents from Yemen*, Sanaa 2006.

Dresch, Paul, 'Legalism, Anthropology and History: A View from the Part of Anthropology', in: *Legalism: Anthropology and History*, ed. Paul Dresch and Hannah Skoda, Oxford 2012, 1–37.

Esmonde Cleary, A. Simon, *The Ending of Roman Britain*, London 1989.

Fleming, Robin, *Britain After Rome: The Fall and Rise*, London 2010.

Halsall, Guy, *Worlds of Arthur: Facts and Fictions of the Dark Ages*, Oxford 2013.

Heather, Peter, 'Law and Society in the Burgundian Kingdom', in: *Law, Custom, and Justice in Late Antiquity and the Early Middle Ages: Proceedings of the 2008 Byzantine Colloquium*, ed. Alice Rio, London 2011, 115–153.

Higham, Nicholas. J. and Ryan, Martin J., *The Anglo-Saxon World*, New Haven 2013, 41–56.

Hough, Carole, 'Legal and Documentary Writings', reprinted in and cited from: Carole Hough, *'An Ald Recht': Essays on Anglo-Saxon Law*, Newcastle upon Tyne 2014, 2–24.

Hough, Carole, 'The Earliest English Texts? The Language of the Kentish Laws Reconsidered', in: *Textus Roffensis: Law, Language, and Libraries in Early Medieval England*, ed. Bruce O'Brien and Barbara Bombi, Turnhout 2015, 137–156.

Innes, Matthew, 'Charlemagne, Justice and Written Law', in: *Law, Custom, and Justice in Late Antiquity and the Early Middle Ages: Proceedings of the 2008 Byzantine Colloquium*, ed. Alice Rio, London 2011, 155–203.

Jurasinski, Stefan, 'The Continental Origins of Æthelberht's Code', *Philological Quarterly* 80 (2001), 1–15.

Lambert, Tom, *Law and Order in Anglo-Saxon England*, Oxford 2017.

Lendinara, Patrizia, 'The Kentish Laws', in: *The Anglo-Saxons from the Migration Period to the Eighth Century: An Ethnographic Perspective*, ed. John Hines, Woodbridge/Suffolk 1997, 211–230.

Meens, Rob, 'Penance, Shame and Honour in the Middle Ages', in: *Shame Between Punishment and Penance. The Social Uses of Shame in the Middle Ages and Modern Times* (Micrologus Library 54), ed. Bénédicte Sère and Jörg Wettlaufer, Florence 2013, 89–102.

Miller, William Ian, *Bloodtaking and Peacemaking: Feud, Law, and Society in Saga Iceland*, Chicago and London 1990.

Miller, William Ian, *Eye for an Eye*, Cambridge 2006.

O'Brien, Bruce, '*Textus Roffensis*: An Introduction', in: *Textus Roffensis: Law, Language, and Libraries in Early Medieval England*, ed. Bruce O'Brien and Barbara Bombi, Turnhout 2015, 1–16.

Oliver, Lisi, *The Beginnings of English Law*, Toronto 2002.

Oliver, Lisi, 'Protecting the Body in Early Medieval Law', in: *Peace and Protection in the Middle Ages*, ed. Tom Lambert and David Rollason, Toronto 2009, 60–77.

Oliver, Lisi, *The Body Legal in Barbarian Law*, Toronto 2011.

Pirie, Fernanda, *Feuding, Mediation and the Negotiation of Authority among the Nomads of Eastern Tibet* (Max Planck Institute for Social Anthropology Working Papers 72), Halle 2005.

Pirie, Fernanda, 'From Tribal Tibet: The Significance of the Legal Form', in: *Law and Anthropology* (Current Legal Issues 12), ed. Michael Freeman and David Napier, Oxford 2009, 143–163.

Pirie, Fernanda, 'Rules, Proverbs, and Persuasion: Legalism and Rhetoric in Tibet', in: *Legalism: Rules and Categories*, ed. Paul Dresch and Judith Scheele, Oxford 2015, 105–128.

Rio, Alice, 'Introduction', in: *Law, Custom, and Justice in Late Antiquity and the Early Middle Ages: Proceedings of the 2008 Byzantine Colloquium*, ed. Alice Rio, London 2011, 1–22.

Roberts, Simon, 'The Study of Disputes: Anthropological Perspectives', in: *Disputes and Settlements: Law and Human Relations in the West*, ed. John Bossy, Cambridge 1983, 1–24.

Taylor, Alice, 'Lex Scripta and the Problem of Enforcement: Anglo-Saxon, Scottish and Welsh Law Compared', in: *Legalism: Justice and Community*, ed. Judith Scheele and Fernanda Pirie, Oxford 2014, 47–75.

Ward-Perkins, Bryan, *The Fall of Rome and the End of Civilization*, Oxford 2005.

Wickham, Chris, *Framing the Early Middle Ages: Europe and the Mediterranean, 400–800*, Oxford 2005.

Wickham, Chris, *The Inheritance of Rome: A History of Europe from 400 to 1000*, London 2009.

Wormald, Patrick, 'Lex Scripta and Verbum Regis: Legislation and Germanic Kingship from Euric to Cnut', reprinted in and cited from: Patrick Wormald, *Legal Culture in the Early Medieval West: Law as Text, Image and Experience*, London 1999, 1–43.

Wormald, Patrick, 'Inter Cetera Bona Genti Suae: Law-Making and Peace-Keeping in the Earliest English Kingdoms', reprinted in and cited from: Patrick Wormald, *Legal Culture in the Early Medieval West: Law as Text, Image and Experience*, London 1999, 179–199.

Wormald, Patrick, *The Making of English Law: King Alfred to the Twelfth Century. Volume 1: Legislation and its Limits*, Oxford 1999.

Wormald, Patrick, 'The *Leges Barbarorum*: Law and Ethnicity in the Post-Roman West', in: *Regna and Gentes: The Relationship Between Late Antique and Early Medieval Peoples and Kingdoms in the Transformation of the Roman World*, ed. Hans-Werner Goetz, Jörg Jarnut and Walter Pohl, Leiden 2003, 21–53.

Wormald, Patrick, 'Kings and Kingship', in: *The New Cambridge Medieval History. Volume I: c. 500–c. 700*, ed. Paul Fouracre, Cambridge 2005, 571–604.

Wormald, Patrick, *The First Code of English Law*, Canterbury 2005.

CHAPTER 7

Wergild and Honour: Using the Case of Frisia to Build a Model

Han Nijdam

This contribution uses a model of embodied honour which was built on the basis of an analysis of the medieval Frisian compensation tariffs to better understand the relationship between wergild and honour.

1 An Anthropological Approach to Wergild

Blood money or wergild has been a brilliant invention to stop endless feuding and retaliation. The essence of compensating a killing or an injury by paying money or other valuables is that it buys off revenge. Its oldest attestation is to be encountered in the laws of the Mesopotamian king Hammurabi, c. 1750 BC. Anthropologist Christopher Boehm describes it as 'a very prominent peace-making mechanism that has been invented over and over again, all over the world'.[1]

If wergild is attested in a certain society, this simultaneously typifies that society:

> the payment of blood money becomes diagnostic of a type of egalitarian political society that rather strictly limits centralised authority, and in which honour is of high importance culturally.[2]

It is easy to see how a feuding society has a limited centralised government: a king would benefit from issuing laws which made accepting compensation possible or even obligatory, since it would diminish the amount of violence among their citizens. This is exactly what we see in societies with a centralised

1 Christopher Boehm, 'The Natural History of Blood Revenge', in: *Feud in Medieval and Early Modern Europe*, ed. J. Büchert Netterstrøm and Bjørn Poulsen, Aarhus 2007, 189–203; 201 (cited as Boehm, 'The Natural History of Blood Revenge').

2 Boehm, 'The Natural History of Blood Revenge', 203.

 | DOI:10.1163/9789004466128_008

government: inhibiting violence and narrowing down liability for a killing to the perpetrator, thus separating the individual from the larger kin group.

Even when the institution of wergild was present in a given culture, this did not mean accepting wergild came easy. Because the drive to take revenge is so strong, people had to be persuaded to accept compensation rather than take revenge. Taking revenge was often seen as the more honourable option and it took some effort — usually from arbitrators — to see accepting compensation as equally honourable. William Miller describes this situation nicely for medieval Iceland, where two mentalities rivalled each other for primacy:

> The culture had contempt for the man too eager to give up on vengeance and too willing to settle for compensation at the same time that it honored men of peace and admitted infinite negotiability: 'everything is compensable'.[3]

In medieval Iceland people showing an overeagerness to sell out were seen as 'carrying their kin in their purse'.[4] And even from a modern perspective, we can relate to this. It feels like the perpetrator was able to simply buy the life of your kinsman. It feels cheap. People do not want a life to become commodified, but on the other hand, wergild has huge benefits, such as preventing a bloodfeud or establishing peace again afterwards.

The wergild phenomenon consists of a specific combination of human universals from the sphere of conflict and law. These universals have been identified by Donald Brown and later listed up by Steven Pinker in an appendix to his work *The Blank Slate*:[5]

- conflict;
- conflict, consultation to deal with;
- conflict, means of dealing with;
- conflict, mediation of;
- fairness (equity), concept of;
- kin groups
- law (rights and obligations);
- law (rules of membership);
- reciprocity, negative;

3 William Ian Miller, *Bloodtaking and Peacemaking. Feud, Law, and Society in Saga Iceland*, Chicago/London 1990, 189–190 (cited as Miller, *Bloodtaking and Peacemaking*).

4 Miller, *Bloodtaking and Peacemaking*, 190.

5 Donald E. Brown, *Human Universals*, New York 1991; Steven Pinker, *The Blank Slate. The Modern Denial of Human Nature*, London etc. 2002, 435–439.

– reciprocity, positive;
– redress of wrongs;
– shame;
– violence, some forms of proscribed.

I will shortly describe these in the form of four clusters:

1.1 *Violence and Revenge*

The starting point of an analysis of wergild based on human universals is negative reciprocity: revenge. Psychologist Nico Frijda analysed revenge as part of his study of human emotions.[6] At first glance, revenge seems counterproductive. It can consume one for years on end, some people sacrifice their lives in order to take revenge and revenge often leads to a level of violence that surpasses the original act. Yet, Frijda also discovered a productive side to revenge. He suggested the following benefits: (1) determent; (2) restoration of a loss or lack of power; (3) restoration of pride and escape from shame; (4) healing from pain; (5) bringing the scales of suffering (justice) into balance.

In other words, a wronged person is first brought into a state of powerlessness, shame and hurt. Taking revenge discourages one's wrongdoer from attacking again, which (1) restores one's sense of power; (2) provides a sense of winning the upper hand; (3) restores one's pride, eliminating feelings of shame at being defeated; (4) eases the emotional pain; and lastly, (5) makes the two parties equal. To these a sixth gain can perhaps tentatively be added: (6) revenge provides a life goal. The drive to take revenge can keep a person going for years.

1.2 *Kinship*

Kinship ties create mutual responsibilities and obligations. In the context of violence and revenge, close kin members are obliged to help their relatives in cases of revenge. Anthropologist Christopher Boehm comments on the near-universality of taking revenge for a homicide by the next of kin: 'The taking of blood revenge may not be universal to all human cultures, but in the recent natural history of our species it has been very widespread indeed'.[7]

In the case of medieval Frisia, these obligations were linked to the rights to inheritances and the rights to receive a share of the wergild. This means that revenge taking by kin groups was given a legal foundation.

---

6 Nico H. Frijda, *The Laws of Emotion*, New York and London 2013 (cited as Frijda, *The Laws of Emotion*).

7 Boehm, 'The Natural History of Blood Revenge', 189.

1.3 *Feud*

Helgi Þorláksson, using the insights on feuding in medieval Iceland by William Miller, succinctly sums up what a feud is:

> Feud involves two hostile groups, each with collective liability. They are of mixed origin, not necessarily of kinship. Violence is controlled and casualties are limited. A notion of 'my turn/your turn' rhythm governs the process, and people keep score of wounds and deaths. The participants believe that affronts to honour are the driving force behind hostilities. Feud is governed by norms that limit the class of possible expiators and the appropriateness of response. There are culturally acceptable means for making temporary or permanent settlements of hostility.[8]

From an evolutionary point of view, the phenomenon of feud arises out of a combination of revenge and kinship. If the gains of individual revenge that Frijda discovered are transferred to a human kin group, it is easy to see how taking revenge as a group yields profits from an evolutionary-biological point of view. Furthermore, one of the rules of feuding applied in all cultures which display the phenomenon is that when retaliating for a killing between kin groups, another member than the original killer can be targeted. In this way, the kin group turns into a kind of super-individual, made up of all its members. This is called 'social substitutability'.[9]

1.4 *Reconciliation and Peace*

In the end, serious conflicts cannot continue in any society without destabilising it. Therefore, reconciliation is desired when the first mutual killings have been made. Some cultures obviously are better at this than others. It requires institutions such as laws, arbitrators, wise men, and rituals to perform the peacemaking. Reconciliation is, however, a universal trait among humans and primates.[10]

---

8 Helgi Þorláksson, 'Feud and Feuding in the Early and High Middle Ages', in: *Feud in Medieval and Early Modern Europe*, ed. J. Büchert Netterstrøm and Bjørn Poulsen, Aarhus 2007, 69–94; 71.

9 Boehm, 'The Natural History of Blood Revenge', 199.

10 Frans de Waal, *Primate Reconciliation. A review of Peacemaking Among Primates*, Cambridge 1989.

2 Medieval Frisia

Medieval Frisia forms a very interesting case to study the wergild phenomenon, since it provides richer source material than have survived from the early middle ages, while at the same time the wergild system and feuding system were completely intact. This makes it possible to study wergild and honour (on which more below) in more detail and hence to draw up an explanatory model for the relationship between wergild and honour.

Over the last ten years or so, our understanding of medieval Frisia has increased to the extent that it is now possible to sketch a chronology of its history, social structure, landscape and laws. It is now clear that c. 400 AD Germanic speaking people from Saxony and Denmark arrived in a landscape that had previously been occupied by the Frisians described in the Roman sources of the first centuries AD. These new inhabitants were related to the people from Scandinavia, especially Denmark, as well as to the Angles and Saxons who moved on to England and inhabited the British Isles. Within a relatively short timespan, these New Frisians adopted the old name of the region and its inhabitants and developed a (material) culture that was clearly related to the neighbouring cultures across the North Sea but also displayed a distinct signature. Examples of this are the bracteates or pendants of gold foil from the 5th century, which are closely related to those found in Denmark, but which show a few indigenous Frisian types.[11] Later, during the 6th and 7th century, the links with Anglo-Saxon England became more pronounced. Examples are a partly shared runic alphabet and the minting of small silver coins known as *sceattas*. Furthermore, Frisian has long since been recognised as the language closest related to English.[12]

By the 8th century the Frisians occupied an extensive coastal zone along the North Sea, stretching from the Sincfal, a small river between Flanders (Belgium) and Zealand (Netherlands) all the way to the river Weser in Germany. In the course of that century the Frisians were conquered by the Carolingians. In the *Lex Frisionum*, written c. 785 and attesting of the incorporation of the Frisians into the Carolingian empire, three areas are distinguished, each with their own variant of Frisian legal customs: a central region between the rivers Vlie (now known as IJsselmeer) and Lauwers (the present day province of Fryslân in the

11 Johan A. W. Nicolay, *The Splendour of Power: Early Medieval Kingship and the Use of Gold and Silver in the Southern North Sea Area (5th to 7th Century AD)*, Groningen 2014.

12 John Hines, 'The Anglo-Frisian Question', in: *Frisians and their North Sea Neighbours. From the Fifth Century to the Viking Age*, ed. John Hines and Nelleke IJssennagger, Woodbridge 2017, 25–42.

Netherlands), a western region between Sincfal and Vlie (the present day provinces of Zealand, North Holland and South Holland in the Netherlands), and an eastern region between Lauwers and Weser (the present day provinces of Groningen in the Netherlands and Ostfriesland in Germany).[13]

Shortly after the Carolingians had incorporated Frisia into their realm they were already forced to loosen their grip due to the Viking raids that started to plague the European coasts from 810 onwards. Eventually, Danish pressure on the Frisian coasts forced the Carolingian kings Louis the Pious (778–840) and his successor Lothar (795–885) to give parts of Frisia in fief to Danish warlords in 826, 840, and in 850.[14] It has also become increasingly clear that the Frisians were not only passive victims of Viking raids, but that they continued to trade with the Scandinavians at the same time and also occasionally joined forces with the Vikings to go on raids together elsewhere along the North Sea coast. Furthermore, in their younger law texts, the Frisians refer to the fact that they owe their freedom (on which more below) to the fact that they defended the coast for the Carolingians against the Vikings.[15]

By 950 the Viking threat had abated to such an extent that the bishops of Utrecht and Münster (the two bishoprics under which the Frisian lands fell) independently started a restauration campaign. During this period, i.e. the second half of the 10th century, a grid of equally spaced baptismal churches and clearly demarcated parishes was established at high speed.[16] This was the closest grip the Carolingians could get on the Frisians, since the Carolingian and Ottonian counts that were appointed during this period lived abroad and only exerted their power from a distance.[17]

It is now becoming clear that the roots of the so-called Frisian Freedom must be sought in this period. From the 11th century onward the regions between the

13 *Lex Frisionum*, ed. Karl August Eckhardt and Albrecht Eckhardt, MGH Fontes iuris Germanici antiqui in usum scholarum separatim editi 12, Hanover 1982; Harald Siems, *Studien zur Lex Frisionum*, Ebelsbach 1980; Dirk Jan Henstra, *Fon Jelde. Opstellen van D. J. Henstra over middeleeuws Frisia*, Groningen 2010, 47–70.

14 Nelleke IJssennagger, 'Between Frankish and Viking: Frisia and Frisians in the Viking Age', *Viking and Medieval Scandinavia* 9 (2013), 69–98.

15 Nelleke IJssennagger, *Central because Liminal. Frisia in a Viking Age North Sea World*, Groningen 2017.

16 Gilles de Langen and Johannes A. Mol, 'Church Foundation and Parish Formation in Frisia in the Tenth and Eleventh Centuries: A Planned Development?', *The Medieval Low Countries* 4 (2017), 1–55.

17 Dirk Jan Henstra, *Friese graafschappen tussen Zwin en Wezer. Een overzicht van de grafelijkheid in middeleeuws Frisia (ca. 700–1200)*, Assen 2012.

rivers Vlie and Weser developed into autonomous districts.[18] The oldest Old Frisian vernacular law texts were probably written down in this same period.[19]

The Frisian Freedom meant that a number of developments that occurred elsewhere in Europe did not get a foothold in Frisia. One of the most important aspects was that the development of counts and earls into suzerains did not take place. This meant that there was no firm central government. The Frisian elite ruled themselves, choosing judges-administrators from their midst for the period of one year at the local and regional court meetings (OFris. *thing*), after which someone else was chosen to hold the office.[20]

The people eligible for the office of judge-administrator called themselves Free Frisians. They reflected the old estates of the *liberi* and of the *nobiles*. The estates had not disappeared in medieval Frisia but became almost invisible in the medieval Frisian sources, pointing at a small social distance between these estates. In the later middle ages, when we have slightly more source material at our disposal, the lower nobility and the higher echelons of the freeholders can be observed to intermarry. Nevertheless, the separate wergilds for freemen and nobles can still be found, albeit sparsely, in the Frisian law texts.[21]

As a consequence, medieval Frisia was what William Miller described as an economy of honour (more on this below) for medieval Iceland, with which Frisia had much in common (the Icelandic Free State lasted from 930 to 1262). It was a society in which feuds where an accepted means to end conflicts. In this respect, medieval Frisia remained 'early medieval' until 1498, when a central government was created.

---

18 Western Frisia, between the rivers Sincfal and Vlie, did not partake in the Frisian Freedom. It came to fall under the indigenous counts of Holland, who managed to develop into territorial lords from the 11th century onwards.

19 Han Nijdam, 'The Body Legal in Frisian Law. Bridging the Gap Between the *Lex Frisionum* and the Old Frisian Compensation tariffs', in: *Languages of the Law in Early Medieval England. Essays in Memory of Lisi Oliver*, ed. Andrew Rabin and Stefan Jurasinski, Leuven, Paris and Bristol 2019, 101–126; 105–107 (cited as Nijdam, 'The Body Legal in Frisian Law'); Jan Hallebeek, *Layci erant coiudices. Over de rol van leken in de Westerlauwerse seendprocedure. Rede in verkorte vorm uitgesproken bij het afscheid als hoogleraar Europese rechtsgeschiedenis aan de Vrije Universiteit te Amsterdam op 26 april 2019*, Amsterdam 2019, 9–10.

20 Oebele Vries, '*Frisonica Libertas*. Frisian Freedom as an Instance of Medieval Liberty', *Journal of Medieval History* (2015), 1–20.

21 Paul Noomen, 'Eigenerfd of edel? Naar aanleiding van de af komst van de Aytta's', *It Beaken* 74 (2012), 257–301.

3 Frisian Compensation Tariffs

The genre of compensation tariffs or injury lists, found in all early medieval *Leges Barbarorum*, continued to flourish throughout the entire period of the Frisian Freedom as these texts were used to prevent or end feuds. These law texts are of course based on wergild: if a lost life costs one wergild, then injuries can be interpreted as fractions of a wergild. The loss of principal limbs (eyes, hands and feet) for instance are often valued at a half wergild each.[22]

The tariffs take up a considerable portion of the corpus of Old Frisian law texts that has been handed down in a relatively small but significant collection of manuscripts. That should not come as a surprise, since the injury lists in the *Lex Frisionum* are already much longer than those in the other *Leges Barbarorum*. The tariffs are without a doubt the oldest texts in the corpus Old Frisian law texts. The Frisian Freedom caused the indigenous legal tradition to develop on its own. It was only during the late 14th and 15th centuries that it was influenced by learned (i.e. Roman and Canon) law.

The Frisian compensation tariffs show some peculiarities which make them comparable to the law Kentish king Æthelberht had put down in writing c. 600 AD. These commonalities also show that we are dealing with a very old legal tradition that most likely dates back to the time of the first new Frisians.[23] A comparison between the tariffs in the *Lex Frisionum* and the Old Frisian tariffs (handed down in manuscripts dating from c. 1300–c. 1500) confirmed that both are testimonies of the same legal tradition, which organically developed between the 8th and the 12th century (i.e. the date of the oldest texts).[24]

One of the developments from the tariffs in the *Lex Frisionum* to the Old Frisian tariffs is an increase in paragraphs dealing with other injuries than those to the physical body up to a portion of c. 25% (see table 7.1 for an overview).

22 Lisi Oliver, *The Body Legal in Barbarian Law*, Toronto, Buffalo and London, 2011; Patrick Wormald, 'The *Leges Barbarorum*: Law and Ethnicity in the Post-Roman West', in: *Regna and Gentes. The Relationship between Late Antique and Early Medieval Peoples and Kingdoms in the Transformation of the Roman World* (The Transformation of the Roman World 13), ed. Hans-Werner Goetz, Jörg Jarnut and Walter Pohl, Leiden and Boston 2003, 21–53.

23 Han Nijdam, 'A Comparison of the Injury Tariffs in the Early Kentish and the Frisian Law Codes', in: *Frisians and their North Sea Neighbours. From the Fifth Century to the Viking Age*, ed. John Hines and Nelleke IJssennagger, Woodbridge 2017, 223–242. For the Kentish laws see Lisi Oliver, *The Beginnings of English Law*, Toronto 2002.

24 Nijdam, 'The Body Legal in Frisian Law'.

TABLE 7.1 Overview of the content of the Old Frisian compensation tariffs

1) Physical injuries to the human body
2) Damaging a person
a) Pulling, singeing or cutting someone's hair or beard
b) Throwing someone into the water
c) Fettering someone or taking him hostage
d) Robbing
e) Threatening, waylaying
f) Chasing someone
g) Hitting someone in a humiliating way
h) Hitting someone so that he falls to the ground
i) Hitting someone unconscious
j) Pouring liquid over someone, spitting, urinating, throwing mud or dirt
k) Tearing up someone's clothes, tearing away headdress, making someone look naked
l) Verbal injury
m) Assaulting or raping a woman
3) Other damages
a) Stealing soil, crops or confiscating plots of land
b) Illegal entry into a house, laying siege on a house
c) Torturing, robbing or illegally riding livestock

The division made in the *Lex Frisionum* between a central, eastern and western region was also reflected in the regional tariff traditions. Since the western part became the county of Holland, there are no Old Frisian law texts from this region. The central and eastern regions have yielded regional tariff traditions.

Because of the Frisian Freedom the compensation tariffs remained in use throughout the middle ages. This can be seen not only by the fact that the texts kept evolving, but also by references in other legal texts and in 15th-century charters attesting of compensation being paid according to what the tariffs prescribe.[25]

25 Han Nijdam, *Lichaam, eer en recht in middeleeuws Friesland. Een studie naar de Oudfriese boeteregisters*, Hilversum 2008, 74; 126–127 (cited as Nijdam *Lichaam, eer en recht*).

4 Embodied Honour and Wergild: A Model

One of the big questions of the wergild phenomenon seems to be: how can a human life be expressed in terms of valuables? Earlier I quoted Christopher Boehm, who said that wergild is typically found in 'egalitarian political societ[ies]' that place a high value on honour. That implies that honour and wergild are strongly linked to each other. Thus we need to explain what honour is and how it works and then bring honour and wergild together to see whether we can explain the one in terms of the other.

Honour is an amalgam. It is the sum of a number of things, both cultural and universal. In order to explain how honour works and what it is, it has to be broken down into its various constituents. Below, I will do this first, then show how the data from the Frisian compensation tariffs and the analysis of medieval Frisia led me to the concentric model of embodied honour, how I think this model can explain how wergild functioned and finally discuss how the model could be applied to other cultures.

4.1 *Honour as Respect*

Honour has been recognized widely as an important phenomenon in cultures all over the globe.[26] Viewed from this perspective, through its lack of an explicit culture of honour modern Western culture forms the exception to the rule. One could say that honour has gone underground in the West.[27] A classic and often cited definition of honour is by Julian Pitt-Rivers:

---

26 The literature on honour is quite extensive. I will only offer a short overview of relevant literature here: Johanna Bond, 'Honour as familial value', in: *'Honour' Killing and Violence. Theory, Policy and Practice*, ed. Aisha Gill, Carolyn Strange, Karl Roberts, New York 2014, 89–107; James Bowman, *Honor. A History*, New York 2006 (cited as Bowman, *Honor*); Dagmar Burkhart, *Eine Geschichte der Ehre*, Darmstadt 2006 (cited as Burkhart, *Eine Geschichte der Ehre*); Martin Dinges, 'Ehre als Thema der historischen Anthropologie. Bemerkungen zur Wissenschaftsgeschichte und zur Konzeptualisierung', in: *Verletzte Ehre. Ehrkonflikte in Gesellschaften des Mittelalters und der Frühen Neuzeit*, ed. Klaus Schreiner and Gerd Schwerhoff, Cologne etc. 1995, 29–62; Arnved Nedkvitne, *Ære, Lov og Religion I Norge gjennom tusen år*, Oslo 2011 (cited as Nedkvitne, *Ære, Lov og Religion*); Julian Pitt-Rivers, 'Honour and Social Status', in: *Honour and Shame. The Values of Mediterranean Society*, ed. John George Peristiany, Chicago 1966, 19–77; Karl Roberts, 'Towards a Psychologically Oriented Motivational Model of Honour-Based Violence', in: *'Honour' Killing and Violence. Theory, Policy and Practice*, ed. Aisha Gill, Carolyn Strange, Karl Roberts, New York 2014, 69–88; Todd K. Shackleford, 'An Evolutionary Psychological Perspective on Cultures of Honor', *Evolutionary Psychology* 3 (2005), 381–391; Frank Henderson Stewart, *Honor*, Chicago 1994 (cited as Stewart, *Honor*).

27 Bowman, *Honor*.

> Honour is the value of a person in his own eyes, but also in the eyes of his society. It is his estimation of his own worth, his claim to pride, but it is also the acknowledgement of that claim, his excellence recognised by society, his right to pride.

This definition holds a number of elements that need to be spun out. But first, it is important to add Frank Henderson Stewart's concise definition of honour: 'a right to respect' in the sense that the bearer of honour can claim the right to be respected by others.[28]

Let us start with 'respect' or as Pitt-Rivers says 'excellence recognised by society'. Both the Romanic word *honor* and the Germanic word *aizō- (OFris. *ere*, OEng. *ar*, ModGm *Ehre*, ModDu *eer*) mean 'respect, awe'. Three observations. First, respect is given by others, pointing to the peer group or honour group of which a person of honour is part. Second, respect contains the notion of violence that can be exerted by the person of honour to exact the respect he is entitled to. Third, since violence is very much a male dominated activity, honour is first and foremost a thing of men: men are the bearers of honour cultures, men exert violence, honour as a phenomenon seems to be built primarily for men. Female honour is foremost related to chastity and shame.[29]

If we now recollect Frijda's observations on the emotion of revenge, we can see how honour is already implied, or at least lurking around the corner. He came to the conclusion that taking revenge is a way of escaping shame and restoring one's self-respect and pride. Shame and honour are each other's opposites, as I have tried to show elsewhere.[30] Frijda further observed that people with large egos are more prone to taking revenge or using violence than timid people.[31] This is also perfectly concomitant with what we know about honour: people with more honour need to defend it more. Frijda's observation can also be read as a confirmation of the link between honour, respect and violence. In any case, we can link one aspect of honour to deepseated human emotions and to males' proneness to violence.

28 Stewart, *Honor*, 21–29.

29 For female honour see a.o.: Burkhart, *Eine Geschichte der Ehre*, 200–205; Nedkvitne, *Ære, Lov og Religion*, 51–87.

30 Han Nijdam, 'Honour and Shame Embodied. The Case of Medieval Frisia', in: *Shame between Punishment and Penance. The Social Usages of Shame in the Middle Ages and Early Modern Times* (Micrologus Library 54), ed. Bénédicte Sère and Jörg Wettlaufer, Florence 2013, 65–88. Also: William Ian Miller, *Humiliation. And Other Essays on Honor, Social Discomfort, and Violence*, Ithaca and London 1993; William Ian Miller, *The Anatomy of Disgust*, Cambridge etc. 1997.

31 Frijda, *The Laws of Emotion*, 306.

Returning to the peer group, this also contains a number of elements. First, it implies inequality in society: some men have honour, some have not, some have it, but less than others. With a culture of honour comes a code of honour: a set of rules to behave by. Also, the code of honour prescribes with whom one can or cannot engage in competition for honour. If someone is below your own status, you don't fight him, or in the words of James Stanley, 10th Earl of Derby: 'Undertake no suit against a poor man [...] for then you make him your equal'.[32]

4.2 *Honour as Embodied Space*

As an introduction to the relationship between honour and space it is necessary to discuss the Frisian case a little further. Old Frisian *ere* 'honour' was an umbrella term for a number of other concepts: *mund* and *were*, both 'guardianship, protection' and *riucht*, which meant both 'law' and 'privilege, right, entitlement'. A Free Frisian was entitled to attend the *thing* or court meeting, where political and legal matters were decided. His *riucht*, however, meant more than that: it was synonymous to his social status. If he had 'lost his rights' (OFris. *riucht forwirka / forliasa*), it meant he could no longer function as a man of honour in society: he could not attend the *thing*, testify or bring a case to court.

Old Frisian *mund* is cognate to Old English *mund*; 'protection' is the core meaning of both. The etymology of the word is 'hand' (cf. Latin *manus*). Since William Miller made use of the Kentish laws for his book *Eye for an Eye*, he also encountered the Anglo-Saxon concept of *mund*:

> I like to think that *mund* is still present with us in the idea of a sacrosanct personal space upon which intrusions give rise sometimes to legal offenses, as in rape or assault, but mostly, among us, to social offenses and moral demands. The moral body does not really stop abruptly at the skin; there is an ever-weakening force field that extends out from it that establishes a space we claim by moral rights as our own. Think of the body proper as a point surrounded by a gray zone of shifting but reasonably predictable shape. In some cases the zone is very small, not even including all our skin, as in particularly crowded presses as we try to get into the stadium for a game. In other cases, the zone can expand to include our office, even our whole house or yard. Our *mund* asserts itself in that domain; in one sense it *is* that domain. It is the space in which we justly

32 Miller, *Bloodtaking and Peacemaking*, 314.

> feel that others must reckon with our demands for certain treatment or stand in a relation of formal offense toward us.[33]

This 'force field' starts at the body and all the elements belonging to it are seen as extensions of the body:

> It means the hand becomes the image of possession and protection of what is possesses. It thus symbolically controls children and hands them over in fosterage and marriage. And the *mund* is that space to which my hand so conceived extends, the space in which I claim a right or an interest in all that happens. The *mund* is more than just my turf; it makes no very clear distinction between my space, my things, my self, and my honor.[34]

Here cognitive science comes to our aid. I think the elements belonging to one's honour are somehow absorbed into what is known as the body schema. As Michael Arbib notes: 'When we use a screwdriver, our body ends at the end of the screwdriver, not at the end of the hand; when we drive a car, our body ends at the rear bumper, not at our buttocks'.[35] As has been showed by various researchers, the body schema is extremely flexible. This is a prerequisite for tool use. In the case of honour, this absorption of external elements into the body schema seems to work somewhat different, but the elements are seen as part of the self, even of the body, because damaging them really seems to hurt.[36]

Here we are reminded of the rubber hand experiment, where a subject's real hand is covered, and a rubber hand is placed right next to it. Through simultaneously stroking and touching the real and the rubber hand, the subject begins to feel as if the rubber hand is their own hand. Suddenly the rubber hand is hit with a hammer. This creates a shock and short sensation of pain in the subject. It has been noted that this phenomenon hasn't been fully studied.[37] It does point to a malleability of perception of the body and its part. I strongly suspect that the explanation for the fact that honour can be perceived as a kind

33 William Ian Miller, *Eye for an Eye*, Cambridge 2006, 135 (cited as Miller, *Eye for an Eye*).

34 Miller, *Eye for an Eye*, 137.

35 Michael Arbib, *In Search of the Person. Philosophical Explorations in Cognitive Science*, Armherst 1985, 75–76; Edward Slingerland, *What science offers the humanities. Integrating Body and Culture*, Cambridge 2008, 209–210.

36 See Shaun Gallagher, *How the Body Shapes the Mind*, Oxford 2005, esp. 24 on the distinction between body schema and body image.

37 Christophe Lopez, Pär Halje, Olaf Blanke, 'Body ownership and embodiment: Vestibular and multisensory mechanisms', *Neurophysiologie Clinique/Clinical Neurophysiology*, 38 /3 (2008), 149–161.

of sphere which emanates from the body and that honour at the same time causes people to perceive objects or relations outside themselves as belonging so intricately to them that damaging these cause such a hurt that it needs to be revenged is related to this cognitive phenomenon.

4.3 *Honour as Capital*

As already mentioned earlier, William Miller typifies medieval Iceland as an economy of honour.[38] This means a society in which honour was the highest priced commodity and almost everything people did evolved around gaining honour or at least not losing it. Honour thus meant everything to people living in economies of honour, as we can see from this adage from the Frisian nobleman Jancko Douwama (c. 1482–1533).

> Goedt voerloeren, wenich voerloeren
> Het lijff voerloeren, voele voerloeren
> Dan ere voerloeren, al voerloeren
>
> If possessions are lost, little is lost
> If the body is lost, much is lost
> If honour is lost, everything is lost[39]

Honour was thus perceived as a form of capital: you could have it, you could lose it and you could have more or less of it. Honour can thus also be seen as symbolic and social capital in the Bourdieuan sense of the word.[40]

This means honour was something that was quantifiable: it could be measured. Also, since it possessed commodity-like features it could be transformed into other commodities or valuables. One commodity can be expressed in terms of another one.

It is at this point that we should stop to consider what the term wergild actually meant. The original meaning of the Germanic word *gelda- was 'compensation, remuneration'.[41] Later, German *Geld* (Dutch *geld*, Frisian *jild*) came to mean 'money'. And only later still money developed into something detached, alienating, with which anything can be bought and anything has a price.[42] This

38 Miller, *Bloodtaking and Peacemaking*, 29–34.

39 *Jancko Douwama's geschriften*, ed. Hessel Brandenburgh, Leeuwarden 1830, 195.

40 Pierre Bourdieu, *Outline of a Theory of Practice*, Cambridge 1977; Dagmar Burkhart, *Ehre. Das symbolische Kapital*, Munich 2002.

41 See the article by Wolfgang Haubrichs in this volume.

42 Karl-Heinz Brodbeck, *Die Herrschaft des Geldes. Geschichte und Systematik*, Darmstadt 2012; David Graeber, *Debt. The First 5,000 Years*, New York 2011; Keith Hart, 'Notes towards

of course is where scholars such as Simmel have wrestled with since more than a century: what happens the moment we start involving money in valuating a human life?[43]

4.4 *A Model of Embodied Honour*

The three aspects of honour addressed above — respect, space, capital — allowed me to analyse the Frisian compensation tariffs as expressions of compensating for lost honour of a Free Frisian and led me to drawing up a model of medieval Frisian personhood or embodied honour (see figure 7.1). All elements in the model can be conceived of as constituents or building blocks of medieval Frisian personhood or honour. A Free Frisian had the *mund* 'protection, liability' over all these elements. Damaging these elements would mean damaging the personhood or honour of the Free Frisian. Reversely, the elements in the model could be used as compensation: they were accepted as repairing or replacing what had been damaged or lost from the totality of the embodied honour of a Free Frisian. It is because of the combination of aspects of honour, especially as a form of capital in combination with the notion of an extension of the body of the person of honour that wergild could conceptually be accepted as a replacement for revenge.

The three circles in the model denote the relative distance from the physical body of a Free Frisian. In the Frisian material two things can be observed. Apart from the physical body there seemed to be two categories or subsets of elements and relations within the *mund* of a Free Frisian. The first category consisted of those elements for which a body metaphor could be found in the Old Frisian law texts.[44] These elements seemed to be especially close to the Free Frisian: his house, his land, and his first degree relatives. The body metaphor for these relatives is 'the six hands' (mother, father, son, daughter, brother and sister). These elements were associated with the payment of gold. The second category consisted of his wife, his servants, his livestock, and the means of payment textile and silver. For these elements no body metaphors were found.

The two categories that can be discerned in the Frisian sources seem to reflect something similar to what anthropologists Jonathan Parry and Maurice

an anthropology of money', *Kritikos. An International and Interdisciplinary Journal of Postmodern Cultural Sound, Text and Image* 2 (June 2005) (https://intertheory.org/hart.htm); Georg Simmel, *The Philosophy of Money*, London 1978.

43 See the introduction to this volume by Stefan Esders. Contextualising Simmel and his ideas: David Graeber, *Toward an Anthropological Theory of Value. The False Coin of Our Own Dreams*, New York 2001 (cited as Graeber, *Toward an Anthropological Theory of Value*).

44 Nijdam, *Lichaam, eer en recht*, 238–249.

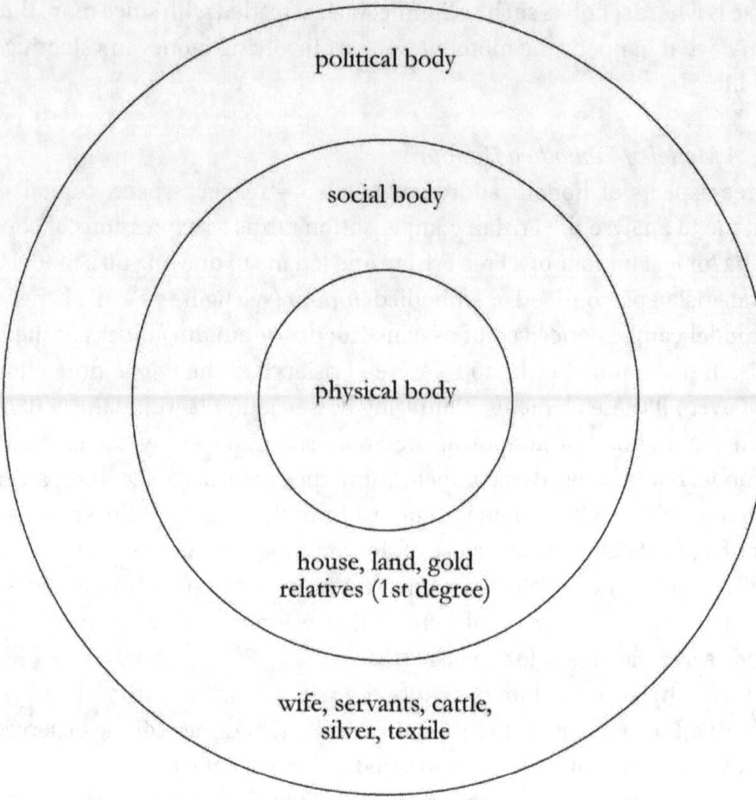

FIGURE 7.1 Model of embodied honour for medieval Frisia

Bloch described for pre-modern societies. They identified two spheres of exchange. On the one hand, there is 'a cycle of short-term exchange which is the legitimate domain of individual activity'. On the other, there is 'a cycle of long-term exchanges concerned with the reproduction of the social and cosmic order'.[45] In this second sphere we also find what Annette Weiner has called inalienable possessions: things that are not for sale. Even if you obtain them, they still are not yours entirely.[46]

The first circle of the model of embodied honour (the 'social body') certainly reflects the stable and durable elements of a Free Frisian; his land and

45 Jonathan Parry and Maurice Bloch, 'Introduction', in: *Money and the Morality of Exchange*, ed. Jonathan Parry and Maurice Bloch, Cambridge etc. 1989, 1–32; most recently discussed in: Graeber, *Toward an Anthropological Theory of Value*, 18–20; 41–45.

46 Anette B. Weiner, *Inalienable Possessions. The Paradox of Keeping-While-Giving*, Berkeley etc. 1992.

house, upon which his livelihood and a large part of his status depended. A few remarks can be found in the Old Frisian sources that point at the ranking of certain means of payment:

> Dine byt ende dine brand aeg ma mit gold to betten want hi mei nimmermeer to haegh bet wirda; deerom schil ma hine al mit goud beta.[47]
>
> Wounds caused by biting or burning are to be compensated with gold, because the victim will never be restored to his former health; for that reason it is to be compensated with gold.

And this citation on land and gold:

> Hwersa mar gold ieftha ferene clathar vrliust anda enre kase, and thi redieua thet rede, sa biswere hi sin eyn; thet gold ielde ma mith golde ieftha mith londe and tha ferena clathar mith pennigum.[48]
>
> If someone loses gold or dyed clothes in a fight and the judge confirms this in court, the victim must assess the worth of his lost possession; and the gold must be compensated with gold or with land and the dyed clothes with pennies.

Or, finally, this one: *Lif and lemethe skel ma mith londe bisetta* 'In cases of wergild and compensation for a paralysis, land must be offered as surety'.[49] From these scarce explicit remarks in the Frisian law texts we can see that gold and land were in the same category, and that they were used as payment for grave damages.

The second circle (the 'political body') reflects the more 'transitory' elements under the *mund* of a Free Frisian. But 'transitory' of course is not the best of descriptions for the relationship a Free Frisian had with his wife. The best way to describe the elements in this category is perhaps by holding on to the observation of the lack of a body metaphor for these elements and conclude that they were perceived as less intimate to the core identity of a Free Frisian. For a wife, this has a certain logic to it. A man's wife did not share his

47 *Bireknade Bota* D XIV, 229; Han Nijdam,'The Old West Frisian Composition Tariff *Bireknade Bota* (Part 2)', *Us Wurk* 50 (2001), 54.

48 *Brokmerbrief* 38, ed. Wybren Jan Buma and Wilhelm Ebel, *Das Brokmer Recht*, Göttingen 1965, 42.

49 *Brokmerbrief* 216, ed. Buma and Ebel, 114.

DNA in the way his first degree relatives did. Moreover, in Frisian inheritance law, the property of the wife could remain independent of her husband's. And only after she had given him a living child did she earn the right to inherit from him.[50]

5 Conclusion: Wergild, Honour, Money

The four means of payment mentioned in the model of embodied honour can also be found in a small gem of a Frisian law text, which describes in detail how an envoy of the person who has committed homicide is sent to the relatives of the victim, offering apologies and supplicating them to accept the wergild the killer is offering.[51] In one of the paragraphs, the means of payment of wergild are summed up:

> Deerefter haet ma mi biada ti betane mitta fiouwer geldim: mitta raeda golde, mitta hwita selvere, mitta grena eerwe ende mitta onscepena wede.
>
> Also, I was ordered to offer you compensation by means of the four types of *geld*: with red gold, white silver, green land and rough textile.

So here we find a confirmation that conceptually the wergild in Frisia consisted of these four means of payment.

The Old Frisian text on the offering of wergild also points to an important aspect of the wergild phenomenon that has only been addressed succinctly earlier: that wergild had to be offered and that it took effort to make the heirs of the homicide victim accept wergild rather than take revenge. The text describes in detail how the envoy assures the heirs that had the tables been turned, the family of the killer would surely have accepted the wergild. Moreover, the killer will come to the heirs barefoot, dressed in penitential garment and place his sword on his own neck, offering the handle of the sword to the heirs.[52]

We can now come to a conclusion. Honour and wergild complement each other. In my opinion wergild can only be explained as a way to compensate for loss of honour because of the way honour is composed of the three aspects

---

50 Nijdam, *Lichaam, eer en recht*, 312–313.

51 Nijdam, *Lichaam, eer en recht*, 133–134.

52 This is a variant of the ritual known as *deditio*. See Gerd Althoff, 'The Variability of Rituals in the Middle Ages', in: *Medieval Concepts of the Past. Ritual, Memory, Historiography*, ed. Gerd Althoff, Johannes Fried and Patrick J. Geary, Cambridge 2002, 71–88; 75, and the article by Rob Meens in this volume.

discussed earlier (respect, space / embodiment, capital). It is because honour is an extension or function of body and mind, that it is perceived by humans to contain the elements belonging to it as if they are part of the body itself. To this is added the fact that honour is simultaneously perceived as a form of capital. These notions together explain how wergild could compensate loss of honour. Because honour was composed of a number of elements, combined with the social aspects surrounding the accepting and payment of wergild, it made a human life resilient to becoming commodified. Revenge was always an option and this guaranteed that the right price was paid for a life.[53]

Today, the value of a human life can only be expressed in fiat money. There is no model of honour regulating either the payment or making sure the value is being kept in check. This becomes all the more peculiar when we realise that fiat money is based on nothing more than trust: there is no longer an amount of gold to back it up, as is honour. Could it perhaps be that in a world in which honour has mostly lost its meaning, money will follow suit and lose its worth too?

Bibliography

Primary Sources

Das Brokmer Recht, ed. Wybren Jan Buma and Wilhelm Ebel, Göttingen 1965.

Das Fivelgoer Recht, Wybren Jan Buma and Wilhelm Ebel, Göttingen 1971.

Jancko Douwama's geschriften, ed. Hessel Brandenburgh, Leeuwarden 1830.

Lex Frisionum, ed. Karl August Eckhardt and Albrecht Eckhardt, MGH Fontes iuris Germanici antiqui in usum scholarum separatim editi 12, Hanover 1982.

Secondary Works

Althoff, Gerd, 'The Variability of Rituals in the Middle Ages', in: *Medieval Concepts of the Past. Ritual, Memory, Historiography*, ed. Gerd Althoff, Johannes Fried and Patrick J. Geary, Cambridge 2002, 71–88.

Arbib, Michael, *In Search of the Person. Philosophical Explorations in Cognitive Science*, Armherst 1985.

Boehm, Christopher, 'The Natural History of Blood Revenge', in: *Feud in Medieval and Early Modern Europe*, ed. J. Büchert Netterstrøm and Bjørn Poulsen, Aarhus 2007, 189–203.

53 Also: Miller, *Eye for an eye*, 48–54.

Bond, Johanna, 'Honour as familial value', in: *'Honour' Killing and Violence. Theory, Policy and Practice*, ed. Aisha Gill, Carolyn Strange, Karl Roberts, New York 2014, 89–107.

Bourdieu, Pierre, *Outline of a Theory of Practice*, Cambridge 1977.

Bowman, James, *Honor. A History*, New York 2006.

Brodbeck, Karl-Heinz, *Die Herrschaft des Geldes. Geschichte und Systematik*, Darmstadt 2012.

Brown, Donald E., *Human Universals*, New York 1991.

Burkhart, Dagmar, *Ehre. Das symbolische Kapital*, Munich 2002.

Burkhart, Dagmar, *Eine Geschichte der Ehre*, Darmstadt 2006.

Dinges, Martin, 'Ehre als Thema der historischen Anthropologie. Bemerkungen zur Wissenschaftsgeschichte und zur Konzeptualisierung', in: *Verletzte Ehre. Ehrkonflikte in Gesellschaften des Mittelalters und der Frühen Neuzeit*, ed. Klaus Schreiner and Gerd Schwerhoff, Cologne etc. 1995, 29–62.

Frijda, Nico H., *The Laws of Emotion*, New York and London 2013.

Gallagher, Shaun, *How the Body Shapes the Mind*, Oxford 2005.

Graeber, David, *Debt. The First 5,000 Years*, New York 2011.

Graeber, David, *Toward an Anthropological Theory of Value. The False Coin of Our Own Dreams*, New York 2001.

Hallebeek, Jan, *Layci erant coiudices. Over de rol van leken in de Westerlauwerse seendprocedure. Rede in verkorte vorm uitgesproken bij het afscheid als hoogleraar Europese rechtsgeschiedenis aan de Vrije Universiteit te Amsterdam op 26 april 2019*, Amsterdam 2019.

Hart, Keith, 'Notes towards an anthropology of money', *Kritikos. An International and Interdisciplinary Journal of Postmodern Cultural Sound, Text and Image* 2 (June 2005) (https://intertheory.org/hart.htm).

Henstra, Dirk Jan, *The Evolution of the Money Standard in Medieval Frisia. A Treatise on the History of the Systems of Money of Account in the Former Frisia (c. 600–c. 1500)*, Groningen 2000.

Henstra, Dirk Jan, *Fon Jelde. Opstellen van D. J. Henstra over middeleeuws Frisia*, Groningen 2010.

Henstra, Dirk Jan, *Friese graafschappen tussen Zwin en Wezer. Een overzicht van de grafelijkheid in middeleeuws Frisia (ca. 700–1200)*, Assen 2012.

Hines, John, 'The Anglo-Frisian Question', in: *Frisians and their North Sea Neighbours. From the Fifth Century to the Viking Age*, ed. John Hines and Nelleke IJssennagger, Woodbridge 2017, 25–42.

IJssennagger, Nelleke, 'Between Frankish and Viking: Frisia and Frisians in the Viking Age', *Viking and Medieval Scandinavia* 9 (2013), 69–98.

IJssennagger, Nelleke, *Central because Liminal. Frisia in a Viking Age North Sea World*, Groningen 2017.

Johnston, Thomas Stanley Baker, 'Old Frisian Law and the Frisian Freedom Ideology: Text and Manuscript Composition as a Marketing Device', in: *Approaches to Old Frisian Philology*, ed. Rolf Hendrik Bremmer, Thomas Stanley Baker Johnston and Oebele Vries, Amsterdam, Atlanta and Groningen 1998, 179–214.

Langen, Gilles de, and Johannes A. Mol, 'Church Foundation and Parish Formation in Frisia in the Tenth and Eleventh Centuries: A Planned Development?', *The Medieval Low Countries* 4 (2017), 1–55.

Lopez, Christophe, Pär Halje, Olaf Blanke, 'Body ownership and embodiment: Vestibular and multisensory mechanisms', *Neurophysiologie Clinique/Clinical Neurophysiology*, 38 /3 (2008), 149–161.

Miller, William Ian, *Bloodtaking and Peacemaking. Feud, Law, and Society in Saga Iceland*, Chicago and London 1990.

Miller, William Ian, *Humiliation. And Other Essays on Honor, Social Discomfort, and Violence*, Ithaca and London 1993.

Miller, William Ian, *The Anatomy of Disgust*, Cambridge etc. 1997.

Miller, William Ian, *Eye for an Eye*, Cambridge 2006.

Nedkvitne, Arnved, *Ære, Lov og Religion I Norge gjennom tusen år*, Oslo 2011.

Nicolay, Johan A. W., *The Splendour of Power: Early Medieval Kingship and the Use of Gold and Silver in the Southern North Sea Area (5th to 7th Century AD)*, Groningen 2014.

Nijdam, Han, 'The Old West Frisian Composition Tariff *Bireknade Bota* (Part 2)', *Us Wurk* 50, 2001, 27–64.

Nijdam, Han, *Lichaam, eer en recht in middeleeuws Friesland. Een studie naar de Oudfriese boeteregisters*, Hilversum 2008.

Nijdam, Han, 'Honour and Shame Embodied. The Case of Medieval Frisia', in: *Shame between Punishment and Penance. The Social Usages of Shame in the Middle Ages and Early Modern Times* (Micrologus Library 54), ed. Bénédicte Sère and Jörg Wettlaufer, Florence 2013, 65–88.

Nijdam, Han, 'Compensating Body and Honor: The Old Frisian Compensation Tariffs', in: *Medicine and Law in the Middle Ages* (Medieval Law and its Practice 17), ed. Wendy Jo Turner and Sara M. Butler, Leiden and Boston 2014, 25–57.

Nijdam, Han, 'Indigenous Or Universal? A Comparative Perspective On Medieval (Frisian) Compensation Law', in: *How Nordic are the Nordic Laws? Ten years after. Proceedings of the Tenth Carlsberg Conference on Medieval Legal History 2013*, ed. Per Andersen et al., Copenhagen 2014, 161–181.

Nijdam, Han, 'A Comparison of the Injury Tariffs in the Early Kentish and the Frisian Law Codes', in: *Frisians and their North Sea Neighbours. From the Fifth Century to the Viking Age*, ed. John Hines and Nelleke IJssennagger, Woodbridge 2017, 223–242.

Nijdam, Han, 'The Body Legal in Frisian Law. Bridging the Gap Between the *Lex Frisionum* and the Old Frisian Compensation tariffs', in: *Languages of the Law in*

Early Medieval England. Essays in Memory of Lisi Oliver, ed. Andrew Rabin and Stefan Jurasinski, Leuven, Paris and Bristol 2019, 101–126.

Noomen, Paul, 'Eigenerfd of edel? Naar aanleiding van de af komst van de Aytta's', *It Beaken* 74 (2012), 257–301.

Oliver, Lisi, *The Beginnings of English Law*, Toronto 2002.

Oliver, Lisi, *The Body Legal in Barbarian Law*, Toronto, Buffalo and London 2011.

Parry, Jonathan, and Maurice Bloch, 'Introduction', in: *Money and the Morality of Exchange*, ed. Jonathan Parry and Maurice Bloch, Cambridge etc. 1989, 1–32.

Pinker, Steven, *The Blank Slate. The Modern Denial of Human Nature*, London etc. 2002.

Pitt-Rivers, Julian, 'Honour and Social Status', in: *Honour and Shame. The Values of Mediterranean Society*, ed. John George Peristiany, Chicago 1966, 19–77.

Roberts, Karl, 'Towards a Psychologically Oriented Motivational Model of Honour-Based Violence', in: *'Honour' Killing and Violence. Theory, Policy and Practice*, ed. Aisha Gill, Carolyn Strange, Karl Roberts, New York 2014, 69–88.

Shackleford, Todd K., 'An Evolutionary Psychological Perspective on Cultures of Honor', *Evolutionary Psychology* 3 (2005), 381–391.

Siems, Harald, *Studien zur Lex Frisionum*, Ebelsbach 1980.

Simmel, Georg, *The Philosophy of Money*, London 1978.

Slingerland, Edward, *What science offers the humanities. Integrating Body and Culture*, Cambridge 2008.

Stewart, Frank Henderson, *Honor*, Chicago 1994.

Vries, Oebele, '*Frisonica Libertas*. Frisian Freedom as an Instance of Medieval Liberty', *Journal of Medieval History* (2015), 1–20.

Waal, Frans de, *Primate Reconciliation. A review of Peacemaking Among Primates*, Cambridge 1989.

Weiner, Anette B., *Inalienable Possessions. The Paradox of Keeping-While-Giving*, Berkeley etc. 1992.

Wormald, Patrick, 'The *Leges Barbarorum*: Law and Ethnicity in the Post-Roman West', in: *Regna and Gentes. The Relationship between Late Antique and Early Medieval Peoples and Kingdoms in the Transformation of the Roman World* (The Transformation of the Roman World 13), ed. Hans-Werner Goetz, Jörg Jarnut and Walter Pohl, Leiden and Boston 2003, 21–53.

Þorláksson, Helgi, 'Feud and Feuding in the Early and High Middle Ages', in: *Feud in Medieval and Early Modern Europe*, ed. J. Büchert Netterström and B. Poulsen, Aarhus 2007, 69–94.

CHAPTER 8

Triplice Weregeldum: Social and Functional Status in the *Lex Ribuaria*

Lukas Bothe

1 Wergild and Status

The notorious wergild tariffs of the early medieval *leges* suggest that wergild generally depended on the killed person's individual status. Thus, the *leges* have been studied for what they allegedly reveal about social stratification in the post-Roman kingdoms.[1] Since early medieval societies were anything but egalitarian, wergilds differed substantially. The *Lex Ribuaria* for instance, dating from the early seventh century and pertaining to the Austrasian subkingdom of Sigibert III,[2] lists a wide range of wergilds. Topping the list is the 900 *solidi* wergild charged for a killed bishop,[3] with only 36 *solidi* for a killed slave at the bottom of the list.[4] If a Ripuarian freeman died a violent death somewhere around early medieval Cologne, i.e. in the *terra Ribuaria*, his relatives would have had a fair idea of *how much* to expect, as his wergild was fixed

1 Cf. most notably Gabriele von Olberg, *Die Bezeichnungen für soziale Stände, Schichten und Gruppen in den Leges Barbarorum*, Berlin 1991.

2 *Chronicle of Fredegar* 4.75, ed. Bruno Krusch, MGH SS rerum Merovingicarum 3, Hanover 1888, 158–159.

3 *Lex Ribuaria* 40.9 (*De diversis interfectionibus*), ed. Franz Beyerle and Rudolf Buchner, MGH LL nationum Germanicarum 3, 2, 94: [9] *Si quis episcopum interfecerit, ter tricentenus solid. multetur.* — 'If anyone kills a bishop, let him be fined thrice 300 solidi' (*Laws of the Salian and Ripuarian Franks*. Translated with an Introduction by Theodore John Rivers, New York 1986, 185 [cited as *LSRF*. Translated by Rivers]).

4 *Lex Ribuaria* 8 (*De homicidiis servorum*), ed. Beyerle and Buchner, MGH LL nat. Germ. 3, 2, 77: *Si quis servum interfecerit, 36 solid. culpabilis iudicetur, aut cum sex iuret quod hoc non fecisset.* — 'If anyone kills a slave, let him be held liable for thirty-six solidi, or let him swear with six [oathtakers] that he did not do it' (*LSRF*. Translated by Rivers, 174). — It has been argued that the 36 *solidi* constituted damages rather than wergild, because slaves counted as things rather than persons in the tradition of Roman law; cf. Heinrich Brunner, *Deutsche Rechtsgeschichte* vol. 1, Leipzig [2]1906, 140–141 and 369–370; for the ensuing controversy about the wergild of slaves, see: Arnold Ehrhardt, 'Rechtsvergleichende Studien zum antiken Sklavenrecht I, Wergeld und Schadensersatz', *ZRG RA* 68 (1951), 93–94, as well as Hermann Nehlsen, *Sklavenrecht zwischen Antike und Mittelalter: germanisches und römisches Recht in den germanischen Rechtsaufzeichnungen*, Frankfurt 1972, 268–270.

 | DOI:10.1163/9789004466128_009

at 200 *solidi*.[5] A Ripuarian freewoman's wergild could amount to 600 *solidi* and a freedman's wergild to only 100 *solidi*.[6] It thus seems as if the 200 *solidi* due for Ripuarian freemen were the standard wergild and the basic unit from which all other wergilds derived by partition or multiplication.[7] The hard-and-fast rule of the tariff is that higher status called for higher wergilds. In this way, wergilds were a means to visualise status differences among the living beyond death, similar to the furnishing of tombs with grave goods. However, there is more to the practice of wergild payment than the symbolic capital of a dead man's reputation.

Georg Simmel dedicated some pages of his 'Philosophy of Money' to the evolution of monetary fines from the equivalent of personal values explicitly encapsulated in the idea of wergild.[8] In a speculative pre-historic and pre-legal state of affairs, he theorises, wergilds would have been subject to constant bargaining. Since the possibility of bargaining for wergild unlocked the potential for new conflicts instead of their resolution, some sort of authority eventually fixed wergilds. To Simmel, the fixation of wergilds by royal or religious authorities represents the crucial psychological step that transformed the originally subjective-utilitarian evaluation of human life into the purely objective conception that a person of a certain status inevitably had a certain value. The anthropological process described by Simmel is reciprocal. Because wergilds were fixed along the lines of social status, this resulted in a certain solidification of status groups. Simmel's ideas are thought provoking; this article

5 *Lex Ribuaria* 7 (*De homicidio*), ed. Beyerle and Buchner, MGH LL nat. Germ. 3, 2, Hanover 1954, 77: *Si quis hominem ingenuum Ribvarium interfecerit, 200 solid. culpabilis iudicetur; aut si negaverit cum 12 iuret.* — 'If a man kills a free Ripuarian, let him be held liable for 200 solidi. Or if he denies it, let him swear with twelve [oathtakers]' (*LSRF*. Translated by Rivers, 173).

6 *Lex Ribuaria* 12.1 (*De homicidiis mulierum*), ed. Beyerle and Buchner, MGH LL nat. Germ. 3, 2, 78: [1] *Si quis feminam Ribvariam interfecerit, postquam parere coeperit usque ad quadregesimum annum, sexcentos solid. culpabilis iudicetur* [...] — 'If anyone kills a Ripuarian woman, from the time that she begins to have children until age forty, let him be held liable for 600 solidi [...]' (*LSRF*. Translated by Rivers, 175); for freedmen see 64.2 (61.2) (*De libertis secundum legem Romanum*), ibid. 117: [...] *Et qui eum interfecerit, centum solidos multetur.* — '[...] And let him who kills him be fined 100 solidi' (*LSRF*. Translated by Rivers, 200).

7 Heinrich Brunner, 'Duodecimalsystem und Decimalsystem in den Busszahlen der fränkischen Volksrechte', *Sitzungsberichte der Preussischen Akademie der Wissenschaften* 2 (1889), 1039–1043; Ruth Schmidt-Wiegand, 'Rechtsvorstellungen bei den Franken und Alemannen vor 500', in: *Die Franken und die Alemannen bis zur 'Schlacht bei Zülpich' (496/497)*, ed. Dieter Geuenich, Berlin 1998, 545–557; for a systematic overview of injury tariffs see: Lisi Oliver, *The Body Legal in Barbarian Law*, Toronto 2011.

8 Georg Simmel, *Philosophie des Geldes*, ed. David P. Frisby and Klaus Christian Köhnke (Georg Simmel Gesamtausgabe 6), Frankfurt/Main 1989, 482–504 passim, esp. 485–488 and 493–496 (cited as Simmel, *Philosophie des Geldes*).

therefore seeks to analyze the relation of status and wergild in the *Lex Ribuaria* with special emphasis on the characteristic triplication of wergild in this text. It will focus on the various parameters that defined legal status and hence the wergild tariff of the *Lex Ribuaria* (2), on social mobility and stability as its constraints (3), and on the seizure of the wergild scheme by royal authority (4). Finally, this article posits that the triplication of wergild in the *Lex Ribuaria* marked a subtle transition of wergild from a primarily compensatory to a punitive measure (5).

2 Parameters of Legal Status

There are a number of criteria that influence the categories of legal status in Frankish law, and in that respect the *Lex Ribuaria* does not vary significantly from the *Lex Salica*. On the one hand, there are markers of ascribed status such as gender, age, as well as the degree of individual freedom and ethnic affiliation, although the latter two were changeable; there are also markers of achieved status, i.e. function or office. The first group of markers are straight forward, as any person would be male or female, young or old, either free or unfree. As a rule of thumb, Ripuarian status categories applied to men and women alike, hence *ingenuus Ribuarius* and *femina Ribuaria, homo regius vel ecclesiasticus* and *femina regia vel ecclesiastica, servus* and *ancilla*. Nonetheless, women were usually represented by their fathers, husbands or other guardians (*mundeburdium*).[9] When it comes to actual wergilds, however, all women in childbearing age were valued thrice higher.[10] By using childbearing as a

9 *Lex Ribuaria* 39 (35) (*De eo qui uxorem alienam tulerit*), ed. Beyerle and Buchner, MGH LL nat. Germ. 3, 2, 91–92: [1] *Si quis uxorem alienam tulerit vivo marito, ducenos solidos multetur.* [...] [3] *Si quis ingenuam puellam vel mulierem qui in verbo regis vel ecclesiastica est, accipere vel seducer sine parentum voluntatem de mundepurdae abstulerit, bis 30 solid. culpabilis iudicetur.* — '[1] If anyone abducts another's wife in the lifetime of the husband, let him be fined 200 solidi. [...] [3] If anyone abducts without her parents' consent a freeborn girl who is under guardianship [*mundepurdae*] or if a woman is taken or led away who is under the king's or a church's protection, let him be held liable for twice thirty solidi' (*LSRF*. Translated by Rivers, 185).

10 *Lex Ribuaria* 12.1 (*De homicidiis mulierum*), ed. Beyerle and Buchner, MGH LL nat. Germ. 3, 2, 78: [1] *Si quis feminam Ribvariam interfecerit, postquam parere coeperit usque ad quadregesimum annum, sexcentos solid. culpabilis iudicetur. Aut si negaverit cum 70 duobus iuret;* — 'If anyone kills a Ripuarian woman, from the time that she begins to have children until age forty, let him be held liable for 600 solidi. Or, if he denies it, let him swear with seventy-two [oathtakers]' (*LSRF*. Translated by Rivers, 175). *Lex Ribuaria* 14 (*De muliere ecclesiastica*), ibid. 79: *Si quis feminam regiam aut ecclesiasticam parientem interfecerit, 300 solidi culpabilis iudicetur aut cum 36 iuret.* — 'If any one kills a king's woman or a

wergild-defining factor, the *Lex Ribuaria* ignores marital status in favour of a functional criterion, namely the ability to create offspring. In the *Lex Salica* women were excluded from land inheritance,[11] perhaps because military obligations were connected to a specific type of landholdings (*terra Salica*).[12] The *Lex Ribuaria* reiterates that principle in its rule on ancestral land (*hereditate aviatica*),[13] but, like the Merovingian capitularies[14] and formularies,[15] this specification suggests that women were not generally excluded from land inheritance, while they claimed equally in movables anyway.[16] It may be a reflection of this development that the *Lex Ribuaria* refers to free women as *feminae Ribuariae*, thereby expanding Ripuarian identity beyond the group of freemen. Regarding age, long-haired boys under twelve years of age were especially valued in the *Lex Salica*, probably as prospective warriors.[17] Ripuarian

churchwoman who is capable of having children, let him be held liable for 300 solidi, or let him swear with thirty-six [oathtakers]' (*LSRF*. Translated by Rivers, 175–176).

11 *Pactus legis Salicae* 59.5 (A), ed. Karl-August Eckhardt, MGH LL nationum Germanicarum 4, 1, Hanover 1962, 222: [5] *De terra vero nulla in muliere hereditas non pertinebit, sed ad uirilem secum qui fratres fuerint tota terra pertenunt* [...] — 'But of land belonging to the Salian Franks [*terra Salica*], no portion shall be inherited by a woman, but the entire land shall belong to the male sex, [and only those] who are brothers [...]' (*LSRF*. Translated by Rivers, 106–107).

12 Thomas Anderson, 'Roman military colonies in Gaul, Salian ethnogenesis and the forgotten meaning of Pactus legis Salicae 59.5', *Early Medieval Europe* 4 (1995), 129–144.

13 *Lex Ribuaria* 57.4 (56.4) (*De alodibus*), ed. Beyerle and Buchner, MGH LL nat. Germ. 3, 2, 105: [4] *Sed dum virilis sexus exteterit, femina in hereditate aviatica non succedat.* — '[4] But while a man lives, a woman may not succeed to the ancestral landed inheritance [*hereditas aviatica*]' (*LSRF*. Translated by Rivers, 192).

14 *Chilperici Edictum* 561–584, c. 3, ed. Alfred Boretius, MGH Capitularia regum Francorum 1, Hanover 1883, No. 4, 8.

15 *Marculfi Formulae* 2.12, ed. Karl Zeumer, MGH Formulae Merovingici et Karolini aevi, Hanover 1886, 8; cf. Alice Rio, *Legal Practice and the Written Word in the Early Middle Ages, Frankish Formulae c. 500–1000*, Cambridge 2009, 206–207 (cited as Rio, *Legal Practice*).

16 Cf. Alexander C. Murray, *Germanic Kinship Structure. Studies in Law and Society in Antiquity and the Early Middle Ages*, Toronto 1983, 201–215 contra Heinrich Brunner, 'Kritische Bemerkungen zur Geschichte des germanischen Weibererbrechts', *ZRG GA* 21 (1900), 1–19, esp. 16–17. — On women and property, see: Janet Nelson, 'The wary widow', in: *Property and Power in Early Medieval Europe*, ed. Wendy Davies and Paul Fouracre, Cambridge 1995, 82–113.

17 *Pactus legis Salicae* 24 *De homicidiis paruolorum ⟨et mulierum⟩*, ed. Eckhardt, MGH LL nat. Germ. 4, 1, 90: [1] *Si quis puerum ⟨ingenuum⟩ infra XII annos usque ad duodecimum plenum occiderit, cui fuerit adprobatum, mallobergo leode sunt, XXIVM denarios qui faciunt solidos DC culpabilis iudicetur* ... [4] *Si quis puerum crinitum occiderit ⟨cui fuerit adprobatum⟩, mallobergo leode sunt, XXIVM denarios qui faciunt solidos DC culpabilis iudicetur.* — '[1] If any one kills a boy who is free-born and under twelve years of age, but who has not yet completed his twelfth year, and it can be proven that he did this, let him be held liable for 24,000 denarii, which make 600 solidi ...[4] But if anyone kills a boy who has long hair,

age specifications include woman's fertility and the decree that children do not have to answer in court before the age of 15, thereby extending legal childhood by three more years.[18] Finally, the most important factor remains the degree of personal freedom. The wergild of semi-free king's and church men, and of Roman freedmen was only 100 *solidi*,[19] and thus only half a freeman's wergild. One could therefore say that freeborn Ripuarian men and women represent the legal standard with their basic 200 *solidi* wergild, from which all other types of status were derived.

Ethnic affiliation is equally decisive, yet it appears to have been a situational construct.[20] While the *Lex Salica* followed a dual structure, dividing Romans from Franks and other barbarians living under Salic law, the *Lex Ribuaria* distinguishes between Ripuarians and other Franks as the constitutive people of the kingdom, at the same time it promotes the integration of other *gentes* in its legal framework by establishing the principle of legal personality:

> Lex Ribuaria 35.3–4 (31) [Concerning a freeman brought before the court]
> [3] This we also command, that within the Ripuarian county, Franks, Burgundians, Alamans or whatever nation one dwells in, when

---

and it can be proven that he did this, let him be held liable for 24,000 denarii, which make 600 solidi' (*LSRF*. Translated by Rivers, 65).

18 *Lex Ribuaria* 84 (81) (*Ut parvulus non respondeat ante 15 annos*), ed. Beyerle and Buchner, MGH LL nat. Germ. 3, 2, 130: *Si quis homo Ribvarius defunctus fuerit vel interfectus, et filium relinquerit, usque quinto decimo anno pleno nec causa prosequatur nec in iudicium interpellatus responso reddat; post autem annorum aut ipse respondeat aut defensorem eligat. Similiter et filia;* — 'If a Ripuarian man dies or is killed and he leaves a son, let [his son] neither prosecute a complaint nor, being called into court, respond until his fifteenth year. However, after [he is] fifteen, let him either respond or choose a defender [that is, a champion who would engage in trial by combat for him]. And let a daughter do likewise' (*LSRF*. Translated by Rivers, 210).

19 *Lex Ribuaria* 9 (*De homicidiis hominum regis*), ed. Beyerle and Buchner, MGH LL nat. Germ. 3, 2, 77: *Si quis regium hominem interfecerit, 100 solid. culpabilis iudicetur aut cum 12 iuret;* — 'If anyone kills a king's man, let him be held liable for 100 solidi, or let him swear with twelve [oath-takers] that he did not do it' (*LSRF*. Translated by Rivers, 174); 10 (*De homicidiis hominum ecclesiasticus*), ibid. 77: *Si quis hominem ecclesiasticum interfecerit, 100 solid. culpabilis iudicetur aut cum 12 iuret;* — 'If anyone kills a churchman, let him be held liable for 100 solidi, or let him swear with twelve [oathtakers]' (*LSRF*. Translated by Rivers, 174); 64.2 (61.2) (*De libertis secundum legem Romanum*), ibid. 117: [...] *Et qui eum interfecerit, centum solidos multetur.* — '[...] And let him who kills him be fined 100 solidi' (*LSRF*. Translated by Rivers, 200).

20 Patrick Geary, 'Ethnic identity as a situational construct', *Mitteilungen der Anthropologischen Gesellschaft in Wien* 113 (1983), 15–26. According to *Lex Ribuaria* 64 (61), slaves could acquire Roman and later Ripuarian status through successive acts of manumission.

interrogated in court, shall answer according to the laws of their birthplace, not to the Ripuarian law.

[4] If condemned, let him sustain the loss according to his own law, not according to Ripuarian law.[21]

When accused, migrants and foreigners had recourse to their own laws and customs. When injured on the other hand, Franks, Burgundians, Romans, Alamans and Bavarians had their own wergilds assigned to them and those were not on a par with a Ripuarian's wergild.[22] One may agonise over the purpose of the different wergilds, but the most important aspect is that the compilers of the *Lex Ribuaria* had a vision for the integration of people coming to *Ribuaria* from other parts of the Merovingian kingdoms, because they were dealing with an extremely heterogeneous society in Austrasia in the first place. The choice of *gentes* named in the respective titles is no coincidence either. 'Franks' probably refers to Neustrians, Burgundians are self-explanatory, while Alamans and Bavarians of course refer to the inhabitants of the two frontier duchies under jurisdiction of the Austrasian *Teilreich*. Frisians and Saxons appear to be later additions, while the Thuringians' noteworthy absence from the list gave rise to all sorts of speculations regarding the dating and application of the *lex*.[23] Whether *alienus Romanus* refers to Aquitanians or descendants of other

21 *Lex Ribuaria* 35.3–4 (31.3–4) (*De homine ingenuo repraesentando*), ed. Beyerle and Buchner, MGH LL nat. Germ. 3, 2, 87: [3] *Hoc autem constituimus, ut infra pago Ribvario tam Franci, Burgundiones, Alamanni seu de quacumque natione commoratus fuerit, in iudicio interpellatus sicut lex loci contenit, ubi natus fuerit, sic respondeat.* [4] *Quod si damnatus fuerit, secundum legem propriam, non secundum Ribvariam damnum sustineat*; (*LSRF*. Translated by Rivers, 182).

22 *Lex Ribuaria* 40 (36) (*De diversis interfectionibus*), ed. Beyerle and Buchner, MGH LL nat. Germ. 3, 2, 92: [1] *Si quis Ribvarius advenam Francum interfecerit, ducentos solidos culpabilis iudicetur.* [2] *Si quis Ribvarius advenam Burgundionem interfecerit, bis octaginta solid. multetur.* [3] *Si quis Ribvarius advenam Romanum interfecerit, bis quinquagenos solid. multetur.* [4] *Si quis Ribvarius advenam Alamannum seu Fresionem vel Bogium, Saxonem intempserit, bis octogenos solid. culpabilis iudicetur.* — '[1] If a Ripuarian kills a Frankish foreigner, let him be held liable for 200 solidi. [2] If a Ripuarian kills a Burgundian foreigner, let him be held liable for twice eighty solidi.[3] If a Ripuarian kills a Roman foreigner, let him be held liable for twice fifty solidi. [4] If a Ripuarian kills an Alaman, Frisian, Bavarian or Saxon foreigner, let him be held liable for twice eighty solidi' (*LSRF*. Translated by Rivers, 185).

23 Cf. Hubert Mordek, 'Die Hedenen als politische Kraft im austrasischen Frankenreich', in: *Karl Martell in seiner Zeit*, ed. Jörg Jarnut, Ulrich Nonn and Michael Richter, Sigmaringen 1994, 345–366, esp. 360 fn. 86.

Roman provincials remains an open question, but most probably, it referred to people living under Roman law anywhere in the Frankish kingdoms.[24]

The final criterion seems to be independent from the other categories, as it is more concerned with what people *do* rather than who they *are*. Function or office in royal and ecclesiastical service increased a person's legal status substantially.[25] The wergild of the *iudex fiscalis* who was called count (*comes*) was thrice 200 *solidi* according to Ripuarian law, while the wergild of a freedman who had risen to that office was 300 *solidi*.[26] A man could thus occupy a rather high position in the wergild scheme despite his inferior social background. More importantly, these functional wergilds had significant implications for the payment of wergild itself. The 200 *solidi* due for a killed Ripuarian would go largely to his heirs and family, with a share of one third reserved for the *fiscus* as peace money (*fredus*).[27] Refusing to pay would have meant that hostilities continued in most of these cases, but if the debtor were in a position of strength vis-à-vis the victim's party, it could perhaps afford him an opportunity to negotiate a better deal. Refusing to pay compensation for a killed *iudex fiscalis,* however, would mean entering hostilities with the king! These considerations show that the distinction between social and functional status actually mattered.

One could even argue that the exploitation of the wergild system, which is implicit in the special protection for office holders, led to a gradual transformation of the originally compensatory wergild system into a more proper penal regime. This notion is also evoked in Simmel's passage on the evolution of the

---

24 Cf. Lukas Bothe, 'From Subordination to Integration: Romans in Frankish Law', in: *Transformations of Romanness. Early Medieval Regions and Identities*, ed. Walter Pohl, Clemens Gantner, Cinzia Grifoni and Marianne Pollheimer-Mohaupt, Berlin 2018, 345–369.

25 E.g. as royal count in *Pactus legis Salicae* 54 *De grafione occiso*, ed. Eckhardt, MGH LL nat. Germ. 4, 1, 203–204: [1] *Si quis grafionem occiderit, XXIVM denarius qui faciunt solidos DC culpabilis iudicetur.* — 'If anyone kills a *grafio*, let him be held liable for 24,000 denarii, which make 600 solidi' (*LSRF*. Translated by Rivers, 101).

26 *Lex Ribuaria* 54 (*De eo qui grafione occiderit*), ed. Beyerle and Buchner, MGH LL nat. Germ. 3, 2, 103: [1] *Si quis iudicem fiscalem, quem comitem vocant, interfecerit, ter ducenos solidos multetur.* [2] *Quod si regius puer vel ex tabulario ad eum gradum ascenderit, sexis quinqagenos solidos multetur.* — '[2] If anyone kills a judge that has fiscal duties, who is called count, let him be fined thrice 200 solidi. [2] If [the person killed is] a servant of the king or a freedman who has risen to that position, let him be fined six times fifty solidi' (*LSRF*. Translated by Rivers, 191).

27 *Pactus legis Salicae* 50.3, (ed. Eckhardt, MGH LL nat. Germ. 4, 1, 192–195) suggests *fredus* payment resulted from involvement of the count but the exemptions from *fredus* payment in *Lex Ribuaria* 48.1 (46.1) and 73.1 (70.1), ed. Beyerle and Buchner, MGH LL nat. Germ. 3, 2, 99 and 124 suggest it depended mainly on intent; cf. also *Lex Ribuaria* 91.2 (89), ibid. 134.

monetary fine ('Geldstrafe') from the originally purely utilitarian wergild.[28] Simmel argues that the aim of every punishment can only derive either from society's need for protection or from the obligation to compensate the aggrieved party for their loss. In the notorious wergild and injury tariffs, the primary aim is indemnity of the injured party. Only after king and church begin to care for the atonement of wrongs[29] can we speak of punishment, because the aim of the fine is now to hurt the individual perpetrator. These are preventive measures, which reveal a different regulatory intention. The protection of royal and ecclesiastical office holders by royal authority is the beginning of punishment proper. Before developing that thought in more detail, I will consider social mobility and the possibility of multiple status.

3 Social Mobility vs. Social Stability

The relation between wergild and status is obviously more complicated than simple correlation. Contrary to its etymology, status is seldom absolute. There is abundant evidence for upward and downward social mobility in the legal sources originating from the Merovingian kingdoms. Take for instance the various collections of *formulae*. In the *Formulary of Marculf*, which, like the *Lex Ribuaria*, dates to the seventh century, we find acts of manumission as well as acts of self-sale.[30] *Formulae* might have a higher claim to practical relevance than *leges*, but similar issues feature prominently in the *lex* as well. Self-enslavement comes into play only relatively late through Charlemagne's *leges* reform,[31] but upward social mobility through manumission and the definition of social boundaries are a common theme in Frankish law. The *Lex*

28 Simmel, *Philosophie des Geldes*, 494–96 passim.

29 On penance and ecclesiastical conflict mediation, see Rob Meens' contribution to this volume, 212–239.

30 *Marculfi Formulae* 2.28 and 2.23–24, ed. Zeumer, MGH Formulae Merovingici et Karolini aevi, 93, 95–96; cf. Alice Rio, 'Freedom and unfreedom in early medieval Francia: The evidence of the *formulae*', *Past & Present* 193 (2006), 7–40, esp. 27–34; cf. also Alice Rio, 'Self-sale and voluntary entry into unfreedom, 300–1100', *Journal of Social History* 23 (2012), 661–685.

31 *Capitulare legi Ribuariae additum* a. 803, ed. Alfred Boretius, MGH Capitularia regum Francorum 1, Hanover 1883, No. 41, 117: [3] *XII cap. Homo ingenuus qui multa qualibet solvere non potuerit et fideiussores non habuerit, liceat ei semetipsum in wadium ei cui debitor est mittere usque dum multa quam debuit persolvat.* — '[3] Concerning the 12th chapter. A free-born man who cannot pay off any fine and cannot find oath-helpers either, may have permission to pledge himself to him whose debtor he is, until the debt he owes is settled' (trans. L.B).

Ribuaria provided for four different forms of manumission, each resulting in a different legal status. First among them was manumission by penny throw in front of the king (*denaratio*) which turned a freedman into a freeman equal in status to other Ripuarians.[32] The king declared and guaranteed for that person's freedom. He threatened a fine of 200 *solidi* to him who wrongfully manumitted a person as well as to anyone who tried to recall a manumitted person to slavery. The king also held a claim to the wergild and inheritance, should the manumitted person die without heirs.

Apparently second best was manumission to Roman citizenship that turned a former slave into a Roman citizen.[33] Such a freedman or freedwoman enjoyed freedom of movement, lived under Roman law, had a 100 *solidi* wergild and was eligible for further manumission by *denaratio*, if desired by his or her *dominus*. Despite the substantial improvement in personal status, the Roman citizen remained under the patronage of his former owner. Thirdly, there was a manumission to an obscure rent-paying status (*tributarius*) with a 36 *solidi* wergild.[34] Since the *Lex Ribuaria* already provides 36 *solidi* as compensation for a killed slave, manumission to rent-paying status seems only a very minor improvement. As Beyerle highlights, the three original manumission practices leading to Ripuarian freedom, Roman citizen status, and rent-paying status reveal a clear hierarchy between them, which shows that these subsequent titles on manumission were preserved in their original order, if not without insertions.[35]

One such insertion deals with a fourth type of manumission that was almost certainly drafted in the aftermath of Chlothar II's Paris council of 614 and concerns *manumissio in ecclesia*. This kind of manumission turned a former slave into a church villein called a *tabularius*. It is particularly interesting because it created an equilibrium of social mobility and stability through ecclesiastical patronage that was at the heart of *manumissio in ecclesia*:

> *Lex Ribuaria* 61 (58) [Concerning church freedmen]
> [1] This we also command so that any free Ripuarian [or church freedman] of whatever sort [who] wishes to free his own slave for the salvation

32 *Lex Ribuaria* 60 (58) (*De libertis a domino ante regem dimissis*), ed. Beyerle and Buchner, MGH LL nat. Germ. 3, 2, 107/8 passim.

33 *Lex Ribuaria* 64 (61) (*De libertis secundum legem Romanam*), ed. Beyerle and Buchner, MGH LL nat. Germ. 3, 2, 117 passim.

34 *Lex Ribuaria* 65 (62) (*De homine qui servum tributarium facit*), ed. Beyerle and Buchner, MGH LL nat. Germ. 3, 2, 117; cf. Guy Halsall, *Settlement and Social Organization: The Merovingian Region of Metz*, Cambridge 1995, 441–442, 55.

35 *Lex Ribuaria*, Sachkommentar 60, ed. Beyerle and Buchner, MGH LL nat. Germ. 3, 2, 159.

> of his soul or for his price in accordance with Roman law shall hand him over with charters in a church in the presence of priests and deacons, or [let him hand over] the slave into the hand of the bishop before all the clergy and the laity. And let the bishop command the archdeacon to compose charters for him in accordance with Roman law under which the church lives. And let one and all descendants of him remain free and be under the church's protection, and let the entire income of [their social] position remain with the church. And let no one presume to manumit [a man who became] a church freedman [or the slave of a church freedman] by penny-throw before the king. If he does [this], let him be held liable for 200 *solidi*. Nevertheless, let the church freedman and his descendants remain freedmen, and let the entire income of [their social] position remain with the church. And let them hold court nowhere else than at the church where they were freed.[36]

The law regulates the procedure according to which a free Ripuarian could manumit his slave in church according to Roman law by which the church lived. Apparently, the procedure built on the existing Roman practice of manumission 'before the consul', and transformed this well-known public ritual into an ecclesiastical one designed to increase the amount of ecclesiastical dependents and to secure their status.[37] The performative act of ecclesiastical manumission is characterised by three central elements: publicity, authority and literacy. To manumit a slave, the owner presented him or her to the bishop with charters (*tabulae*[38]), which prove his right of dominion over the slave, in front of all the clergy and the laity. The bishop thus oversees the act of manumission

36 *Lex Ribuaria* 61 (58) (*De tabulariis*), ed. Beyerle and Buchner, MGH LL nat. Germ. 3, 2, 108–110: [1] *Hoc etiam iubemus, ut qualiscumque francus Ribvarius [seu tabularius] servum suum pro animae suae remedium seu pro pretium secundum legem Romanam liberare voluerit, ut eum in ecclesia coram presbyteris et diaconibus seu cuncto clero et plebe in manu episcopi servo cum tabulas tradat, et epicopus archidiacono iubeat, ut ei tabulas secundum legem Romanum, quam ecclesia vivit, conscribere faciat; et tam ipse quam et omnis procreatio eius liberi permaneant et sub tuitione ecclesiae consistant vel omnem reditum status eorum ecclesiae reddant. Et nullus tabularium [aut servum tabularii] denariare ante regem praesumat. Quod si fecerit, ducentos solidos culpabilis iudicetur et nihilominus ipse tabularius et procreatio eius tabularii persistant, et omnis reditus status eorum ad ecclesiam reddant; et non aliubi quam ad ecclesiam, ubi relaxati sunt, mallum teneant* [square brackets denote possible interpolations]; (*LSRF*. Translated by Rivers, 195).

37 Stefan Esders, *Die Formierung der Zensualität. Zur kirchlichen Transformation des spätrömischen Patronatswesens im frühen Mittelalter*, Ostfildern 2010, 32–36; 50–60 (cited as Esders, *Zensualität*).

38 Cf. Bernhard Bischoff, *Latin Palaeography: Antiquity and the Middle Ages*, trans. Dáibhí ó Cróinín and David Ganz, Cambridge 1990, 34.

and commands the archdeacon to compose the charters of manumission arising from this.

Correct procedure and authoritative approval turned a slave into a nominally free person, but the charter really defined his or her new status in relation to the place of manumission. Hence, the *tabularius* or *tabularia* and their descendants would remain free and under the same church's protection (*sub tuitione ecclesiae*), while any subsequent manumission to proper Ripuarian freedom by penny throw (*denaratio*) was prohibited. This caveat must be understood as a safeguard against the alienation of church property.[39] Quite significantly, the same mechanism that claimed to emancipate slaves for religious motives barred the manumitted from further social advancement for patronage reasons. Since they lacked a family or a household of their own, manumitted slaves were usually dependent on their former masters or a chosen patron. The change brought about by this law was that the manumitted were no longer free to choose their patron but belonged to the church in which their manumission had taken place.[40] *Tabularii* came under the church's protection for good, they held court only at the church and paid their dues only to the church where they were freed. No other person should dare to usurp patronage over *tabularii*, and even though the church gladly incorporated alien slaves as *tabularii*, it accepted manumissions of its own slaves only if a substitute was provided.[41] Moreover, a number of regulatory statutes attached to the same title flesh out the 'principle of the worse hand' (Grundsatz der ärgeren Hand),[42] claiming that children originating from marriages between persons of unequal status acquired the lower status. Forestalling autonomous emancipation through marriage, these provisions sought to maintain social stability as much as they preserved the vested rights of slave owners.

It is difficult to assess how binding all these rules were in practice, but the formulary collections allow some conclusions. *Formulae Salicae Merkelianae*

---

39 Beyerle suggests that the 200 *solidi* fine for him who dared to manumit a *tabularius* by *denaratio* is possibly Roman *poena dupli* [for theft]; cf. *Lex Ribuaria*, Sachkommentar 61, ed. Beyerle and Buchner, MGH LL nat. Germ. 3, 2, 160–161.

40 Esders, *Zensualität*, 50–60.

41 *Lex Ribuaria* 61.3, ed. Beyerle and Buchner, MGH LL nat. Germ. 3, 2, 110: [3] *Nemo servum ecclesiasticum absque vicarium libertum facere presumat.* — '[3] Let no one presume to make a church slave a freedman without [providing] a substitute' (*LSRF*. Translated by Rivers, 195).

42 Wulf-Eckart Voss, 'Der Grundsatz der ärgeren Hand bei Sklaven, Kolonen und Hörigen', in: *Römisches Recht in der europäischen Tradition*, ed. Okko Behrends, Malte Deisselhorst and Wulf-Eckart Voss, Ebelbach 1985, 117–184, esp. 169–172 fn 248 and 254.

No. 14 seems to resemble the procedure established in *Lex Ribuaria* 61.[43] A master set his *servus* free for pious reasons and transferred him to the *patrocinium* of a church, which was to protect the manumitted slave from any attempts of his former master or his heirs to recall him into slavery. The freedman was obliged to render a small tribute of one candle to the church on the festive days of its patron saint. Formulary II.29 from the *Marculf* collection, on the other hand, gives evidence that the marriage rules were not always mandatory, and that children of such marriages could indeed remain free as long as the unfree parent's master agreed.[44] This is not necessarily a 'customisation' of written law by legal practice, as Alice Rio suspects.[45] The formulary in question would hardly have survived had it not preserved such an exceptional case, in which an unfree man had abducted a freewoman. Abduction of women as a unilateral perversion of courting was a serious problem in the early middle ages addressed in the *leges* in some detail.[46] However, we cannot exclude the possibility that any unequal or unpopular marriages were deliberately condemned as abductions by the spouse's family who were of higher status because they would not accept any lower status in-laws. The case recorded in *Marculf* II.29 was exceptional precisely because all parties involved gave their consent to the marriage despite written law's uncompromising approach.

Overall, the *Lex Ribuaria* is quite clear on social mobility. Social advancement was possible and even encouraged if it followed the mechanisms provided and respected the property rights of slave owners and patrons of freed persons. Obviously, some people managed to 'marry up' against the odds, but what the bulk of these provisions really suggests is that legislators cared a great deal about the maintenance of status differences and the stability of social order while the people at the lower echelons of society did not pay much attention

43 Cf. *Formulae Salicae Merkeliane* 14, ed. Zeumer, MGH Formulae Merovingici et Karolini aevi, Hanover 1886, 246.

44 *Marculfi Formulae* 2.29, ed. Zeumer, MGH Formulae Merovingici et Karolini aevi, 93–94.

45 Rio, *Legal Practice*, 207.

46 Cf. for example *Lex Ribuaria* 39 (35) (*De eo qui uxorem alienam tulerit*), ed. Beyerle and Buchner, MGH LL nat. Germ. 3, 2, 91: [1] *Si quis uxorem alienam tulerit vivo marito, ducenos soldi multetur.* [2] *Si quis cum ingenuam puelllam moechatus fuerit, quinquaginta solid. culpabilis iudicetur* [3] *Si quis ingenuam puellam vel mulierem qui in verbo regis vel ecclesiastica est, accipere vel seducer sine parentum voluntatem de mundepurdae abstulerit, bis 30 solid. culpabilis iduicetur.* — '[1] If anyone abducts another's wife in the lifetime of the husband, let him be fined 200 solidi. [2] If anyone engages in sex with a free-born girl, let him be held liable for fifty solidi. [3] If anyone abducts without her parents' consent a freeborn girl who is under guardianship [*mundepurdae*] or if a woman is taken or led away who is under the king's or a church's protection, let him be held liable for twice thirty solidi' (*LSRF*. Translated by Rivers, 185).

to the nuances of status definition. People married locally and usually within their social peer group; there was no need to prohibit unequal marriages from a class standpoint. After all, it seems as if the differences in living conditions were much smaller than is suggested by the legal framework.[47] The motives for those provisions are thus protection of property and dominion rights over the unfree and dependent population rather than fear of social levelling through unequal marriages. By adopting such a bottom-up perspective, we learn that status and wergild were neither definite nor absolute. Social advancement of individuals could come through various ways, most prominently through manumission, by marrying up, and by the acquisition of official functions in royal or ecclesiastical service.

Some passages from the *Lex Ribuaria* provide evidence for single persons enjoying various status depending on the reference system. For example, title 54 (53), concerning him who kills a count, makes provisions for a royal servant [*puer regis*] or church freedman [*tabularius*] as occupants of the judicial office that is equated with the comital office.

> *Lex Ribuaria* 54 (53) [Of him who kills a count]
> 1. If anyone kills a judge who has fiscal duties, who is called a count, let him be fined thrice 200 *solidi*.
> 2. If [he] is a servant of the king or a church freedman who has risen to this status, let him be fined six times fifty *solidi*.[48]

Both provisions reinforce the imperative that everyone holding royal office enjoyed higher legal protection. As mentioned above, their enhanced standing can be called functional status, because the judge's threefold wergild results directly from his function as a royal agent. More importantly, however, the second provision of the law also shows that the enhanced functional status of judges and counts did not level their inherent social status. While freeborn judges had thrice a freeman's wergild, judges recruited among the king's servants (*pueri*) or the church freedmen had thrice a freedman's wergild. Apparently, it was considered important to leave the original wergild recognisable. The distinction of social and functional status encountered in this

47 At least that is suggested by Alice Rio, '"Half-free" categories in the early middle ages: fine status distinctions before professional lawyers', in: *Legalism: Rules and Categories*, ed. Paul Dresch and Judith Scheele, Oxford 2015, 129–152.

48 *Lex Ribuaria* 54 (53) (*De eo qui grafionem interfecerit*), ed. Beyerle and Buchner, MGH LL nat. Germ. 3, 2, 103: [1] *Si quis iudicem fiscalem, quem comitem vocant, interfecerit, ter ducenos solidos multetur.* [2] *Quod si regius puer vel ex tabulario ad eum gradum ascenderit, sexies quinquagenos solidos multetur;* (*LSRF*. Translated by Rivers, 191).

specific title, or rather the fact that legal dependency and functional office did not exclude each other, was essential to the formation of the *ministeriales* as a distinguished social class later on. It would be wrong to assume that the comital office and the position of public judges were open to anybody, just because the *leges* take judges and counts of lower decent (*Minderfreie*) into account. The most likely explanation for this phenomenon is that rulers had an interest to staff crucial positions with trusted retainers, whose loyalty counted more than status. This is already attested for the office of the count's deputy called *sacebaron* or *obgrafio* in the *Lex Salica* who appear to have been recruited chiefly among the *pueri regii*.[49] This practice was certainly convenient from the king's point of view but not necessarily appreciated by local elites. In the aftermath of Chlothar II's struggle for control over the Merovingian kingdoms, the twelfth chapter of the Edict of Paris tied the appointment of local *iudices* to the condition of local origin, to ensure that judges be held accountable for any bad judgements with their own landed possessions.[50] While the law certainly was not just a concession to a powerful aristocracy, it does attest to popular opposition against royal appointments in the judiciary. Such friction was probably also the context for the multiple status of different judges in both Salic and Ripuarian law.

Another even more telling example of the distinction between functional and social status is provided by the central title 40 (36) concerning various homicides, which contains a catalogue of wergilds for foreigners and clerics with two additional clauses on commutable goods and silver currency used

49 *Pactus legis Salicae* 54 *De grafione occiso*, ed. Eckhardt, MGH LL nat. Germ. 4, 1, 203–204: [2] *Si quis sacebaronem aut ⟨ob⟩grafionem occiderit, qui puer regius fuerit, ⟨cui fuerit adprobatum⟩, mallobergo le(o)de saccem(i)ther sunt, XIIM denarios qui faciunt solidos CCC culpabilis iudicetur.* [3] *Si quis sacebaronem, qui ingenuus est ⟨et se [uel alium] sacebaronem posuit⟩, occiderit, XXIVM denarios qui faciunt solidos DC culpabilis iudicetur.* — '[2] If anyone kills a *sacebaro* or an *obgrafio*, who is a servant of the king [known in the malberg as *leode saccemither*], let him be held liable, if it can be proven that he did this, for 12,000 denarii, which make 300 solidi. [3] If anyone kills a sacebaro who is a freeman, and he declares himself a sacebaro, or [appoints] another, let him be held liable for 24,000 denarii, which make 600 solidi' (*LSRF*. Translated by Rivers, 101).

50 *Chlotharii II. Edictum* 614 Oct. 8, ed. Boretius, MGH Capit. 1, Hanover 1883, No. 9, 21–23, here 22: c. 12. *Et nullus iudex de aliis provinciis aut regionibus in alia loca ordinetur; ut, si aliquid mali de quibuslibet condicionibus perpetraverit, de suis propriis rebus exinde quod male abstolerit iuxta legis ordine debeat restaurare.* — 'c. 12. Let no judge be appointed from outside the region or province. Thus if he commits any wrong with respect to litigation before him, he will have to make good from his own property, in accordance with the law, that which he wrongfully took away' (Alexander Callander Murray, 'Immunity, Nobility and the Edict of Paris', *Speculum* 69 [1994], 27).

for actual wergild payments.[51] The centrality of title 40 is evident: in assigning wergilds to groups of foreign migrants in Ripuaria, it hints at the so-called principle of the personality of law as much as on the legislator's eagerness to accommodate migrants fit for military service in Ripuaria. The assignment of wergilds to clerics exemplifies the growing importance of the church within the Merovingian kingdoms, as much as it is reflective of the leading role probably played by bishop Kunibert of Cologne as one of two regents for the minor King Sigibert III in the immediate context of the compilation of the *Lex Ribuaria*. By including a table for the conversion of wergilds into material assets, the title sheds some light on the modes of wergild payment in social practice. In referring to the coinage ratio of twelve *denarii* for one *solidus*, title 40.12 is among the earliest written testaments for the introduction of a new silver currency in the Merovingian kingdoms by the end of the sixth century.[52] Here, I shall concentrate on only one particular clause, which is special because the manuscripts transmitting the A and B versions of the *Lex Ribuaria* recorded alternate readings. First among the clerics' wergilds is that provided for clerics of the minor orders, presumably referring to aspirants who had not yet been ordained. In the manuscripts containing the purportedly older A-version, title 40.5 reads: 'If anyone kills a free-born cleric, let him be held liable for twice fifty *solidi*,'[53] thus grouping the lowest orders of the clergy with Romans or persons of inferior legal status. In the manuscripts containing the B-version the same title reads: 'If anyone kills a cleric, whatever [the cleric's] class was at birth, let him be compensated for in this fashion: If [he was] a slave, just as a slave; if a king's man or a churchman, just as another king's man or churchman. If a freedman, just as a freedman. If a freeman, let him be compensated with 200 *solidi*, just as for another freeman.'[54]

51 *Lex Ribuaria* 40 (36) (*De diversis interfectionibus*), ed. Beyerle and Buchner, MGH LL nat. Germ. 3, 2, 92–95.

52 *Lex Ribuaria* 40.5 (*De diversis interfectionibus*), ed. Beyerle and Buchner, MGH LL nat. Germ. 3, 2, 95: *Quod si cum argento solvere contigerit, pro solido duodecim denarios, sicut antiquitus est constitutem;* — 'If he pays with silver, for a solidus [let it be equal to] twelve denarii, just as was decided long ago' (*LSRF*. Translated by Rivers, 186); cf. Mark Blackburn and Philip Grierson, *Medieval European Coinage 1: The Early Middle Ages (5th–10th centuries)*, Cambridge ²1991, 106.

53 *Lex Ribuaria* 40.5 (*De diversis interfectionibus*), ed. Beyerle and Buchner, MGH LL nat. Germ. 3, 2, 93: [A] *Si quis clericum ingenuum interfecerit, bis quinquagenos solid. culpabilis iudicetur*; (*LSRF*. Translated by Rivers, 185).

54 Ibid.: [B] *Si quis clericum interficerit, iuxta quod nativitas eius fuerit, ita conponatur. Si servus, sicut servum. Si regius aut ecclesiasticus, sicut alius regius aut ecclesiasticus. Si litus, sicut litum. Si liber, sicut alium ingenuum cum 200 solid. conponat*; (*LSRF*. Translated by Rivers, 213).

The ecclesiastical hierarchy is mirrored in the wergild valuation of clergymen. While the precise values vary, both manuscript classes agree in only guaranteeing higher legal protection, similar to that of royal office holders, for the clerical *ordines*. For the humblest clergy, their profession did not raise their wergild.[55] The B-reading referring to the birth status is difficult to interpret, however. Perhaps the change resulted from a specific dispute over the wergild of a killed un-ordained clergyman of disputed freedom. The canons prohibited unfree clerics or at least demanded that slaves be manumitted before joining the clergy,[56] which seems to be taken into account by the A-version's provision. *Marculf* 1.19 suggests that, to adopt a church career, even free people had to prove they were not on the tax register.[57] Since cathedral churches were unlikely to transgress these rules and ordain unfree persons, the revised *nativitas* rule did not apply to the higher *ordines*. In the context of so-called proprietary churches, however, unfree clerics were quite common, and their status mattered to anyone claiming or owing their wergild in a local context. Depending on the cleric's birth status, the revised provision of the B-version could benefit both wergild debtors and recipients. Either way, the solution found here is as pragmatic as that of the judge's wergild. Individual status enhancement followed upon clerical ordination, while birth rank continued to matter, at least for the lowest echelons of the clergy.

There is a certain tension between the poles of increased legal protection for royal and ecclesiastical office holders on the one hand, and efforts to maintain the basic categories of social status, especially regarding personal freedom, on

55 Cf. Thomas Faulkner, *Law and Authority in the Early Middle Ages. The Frankish* Leges *in the Carolingian Period*, Cambridge 2016, 158–168.

56 *Concilium Aurelianense* a. 538, c. 29 (26), ed. Friedrich Maassen, MGH Concilia 1, Hanover 1893, 81/82: *Ut nullus servilibus colonariisque conditionibus obligatus iuxta statuta sedis apostolicae ad honores ecclesiastecus admittatur, nisi prius aut testamento aut per tabolas eum legeteme constetirit absolutum*; cf. Edgar Loening, *Geschichte des deutschen Kirchenrechts* 2, Straßburg 1878, 280–284.

57 *Marculfi Formulae* 1.19 *Preceptum de clericatum*, ed. Zeumer, MGH Formulae Merovinigici et Karolini aevi, 55–56: […] *Precipientes ergo iobemus, ut, se memoratus ille de caput suum bene ingenuus esse videtur et in poleptico publico censitus non est, licenciam habeat comam capitis sui tunsorari et ad suprascribta baselica, vel monasterio, deservire vel pro nobis Domini misericordia adtentius exorare.* — '[…] Therefore we command by our order that, if the said A is seen to be of truly free status, and is not counted in the public register as paying dues, he may have the permission to tonsure the hair of his head and go into the service of the church — or: the monastery — written above, and pray vigilantly for God's forgiveness on our behalf' (*The Formularies of Angers and Marculf. Two Merovingian Legal Handbooks*. Translated with an Introduction and Notes by Alice Rio [Translated Texts for Historians 46], Liverpool 2008, 153 [cited as *Formularies of Angers and Marculf*. Translated by Rio]).

the other. The underlying theme of increased legal protection for office holders is the gradual expansion of royal authority. If royal authority were to be respected, the king had to make sure it would not be challenged. The mere fact that counts and bishops had wergilds is more than telling. Stefan Esders has convincingly argued that the *Lex Baiuvariorum*'s title on the *dux* in particular, which includes — among other offenses — sedition against the *dux* (*seditio*), bears the imprint of Roman military law, probably appropriated in Bavaria through Visigothic and Frankish intermediaries now lost.[58] Thus embedded in a military context and framed as penal law, the Bavarian title on the *dux* served as a warning to potentially unruly subjects who were likely to challenge comital, ducal and ultimately royal authority. This and a similar provision in the *Lex Alamannorum* testify to a concerted effort of Merovingian kings to protect their local representatives in the periphery. The Ripuarian provisions assigning higher wergilds to office holders must be interpreted in the same vein.

On the other hand, the maintenance of birth-derived social status categories surely resonates with the desire to stabilise a stratified society. This top-down approach of 'quasi-penal law' was flanked by a bottom-up approach to 'community building' that advertised the 'Ripuarian project' in soft-power terms. Defining and protecting the status of a Ripuarian freeman is a *leitmotif* in the *Lex Ribuaria* as this group was of crucial political and military importance. It was as important to the Austrasian king to have as many Ripuarians under his command as possible, as it was desirable for any free person living in the Austrasian subkingdom to identify with the Ripuarians in order to secure their status.[59] Below the Ripuarian *ingenui* the *Lex Ribuaria* also redefined the rights and obligations of the apparently increasing group of intermediate social status and freedom (*Minderfreie*). Extending royal authority while at the same time redefining the boundaries of the most important status groups was a complex issue. How was the king to protect office holders of various social backgrounds without crashing the wergild scheme as a whole? Distinguishing social from functional status and combining both with 'community building'

58 Stefan Esders, 'Late Roman Military Law in the Bavarian Code', *clio@themis. Revue électronique d'histoire du droit* 10 (2016) (thematic issue *La forge du droit. Naissance des identités juridiques en Europe, IV*[e]*–XIII*[e] *siècles*), 1–24: http://www.cliothemis.com/IMG/pdf/3-_Esders-2.pdf (cited as: Esders, 'Military Law').

59 For this kind of "ethnic engineering" in the *Lex Salica* cf. Patrick Wormald, 'The Leges Barbarorum: Law and Ethnicity in the Post-Roman West', in: *Regna et Gentes. The relationship between Late Antique and Early Medieval Peoples and Kingdoms in the Transformation of the Roman World*, ed. Hans-Werner Goetz, Jörg Jarnut and Walter Pohl, Leiden 2003, 32; cf. also most recently: Karl Ubl, *Sinnstiftungen eines Rechtsbuchs: Die Lex Salica im Frankenreich* (Quellen und Forschungen zum Recht im Mittelalter 9), Ostfildern 2017, 97 (cited as Ubl, *Sinnstiftungen*).

was an avenue already tried by Salic law.[60] Office holders merited higher wergilds but those had to be discernible as multiples of the original wergild pertaining to inherited social status.

A *comes* of Ripuarian descent thus had a wergild of three times 200 *solidi* while the wergild of a *tabularius* who had risen to that office was only three times 100 *solidi*. The logic applied here suggests that the semi-free (*Minderfreie*) could make a career in royal office while they could not as easily claim Ripuarian identity and the social status of freeborn men attached to it. Even though Ripuarian identity remained fairly exclusive, obtainable only by birth or *denaratio*, individual social advancement was still possible through personal achievement. Apparently, legislators could pursue different intentions at the same time. From a military point of view, there was an interest in keeping Ripuarian identity as inclusive as possible for military coherence in the important frontier region of the Rhineland. The duchy laws of Bavaria and Alamannia went further and avoided ethnic terminology altogether to minimise frictions and to compel all *homines* to compulsory military service.[61] In the Ripuarian part of Austrasia, however, it was equally important to strengthen a poised identity shared by the dominant social group. From a wider socio-political point of view, there was thus a desire to keep Ripuarian status as exclusive as possible in order to safeguard the Frankish elite's vested privileges and property rights. Both motifs were considered in the *Lex Ribuaria* and informed its concepts of semi-freedom, functional status and Ripuarian identity. *Romani*, *regii* and *ecclesiastici* were obliged to military service like freemen.[62] Function paved the way for social climbers, but it could not guarantee full participation, which remained reserved for Ripuarians and those manumitted by *denaratio* before the king. Albeit in only two special cases, the comital and clerical wergilds illustrate that the *Lex Ribuaria* defined legal status categories as combinations of social and functional status.

4 Wergild and Royal Authority

Claiming that regular wergild payment was a private affair whereas wergild paid for a slain judge was a public affair would be overly simplistic. Both were at the same time private and public, which is at the heart of the wergild puzzle

60 *Pactus legis Salicae* 54 *De grafione occiso*, ed. Eckhardt, MGH LL nat. Germ. 4, 1, 203–204.
61 Cf. Esders, 'Military Law', 20.
62 *Lex Ribuaria* 68 (*De eo qui bannum non adimplet*), ed. Beyerle and Buchner, MGH LL nat. Germ. 3, 2, 119.

and makes it so difficult to establish its origins.[63] However, it will suffice to recount the importance of the *fredus,* which formed a substantial portion (one third of the total) of all Frankish wergilds, to remind us that the institutionalisation of wergild payment imagined by Simmel was already well underway when the *Lex Salica* was compiled at some point of the late fifth century.[64] The *Lex Ribuaria* documents a later stage of the same process and Simmel's theoretical reflections help to understand the general trend. The remainder of this article will briefly hint at some of the most telling examples for the evolution of monetary fines from royal seizure of the wergild scheme. A case in point is proximity to the king (*Königsnähe*) as a factor for increased legal protection.

> *Lex Ribuaria* 11 [Concerning homicides of those who are in the king's retinue (*trustis*)]
>
> [1] If anyone kills him who is in the king's retinue [*trustis*], let him be held liable for 600 *solidi.* And whatever is done to [the victim], let him be similarly compensated threefold as other Ripuarians [are compensated].
>
> [2] If he denies killing him, let him swear with seventy-two [oathtakers].
>
> [3] If anyone applies force by any means to a king's man or a churchman or forcibly carries him off, let him compensate threefold as other Ripuarians [are compensated].[65]

A group of professional warriors *in truste regia* constituted a military elite at the king's disposal whose members were already referred to as being *in truste dominica* and protected by a threefold wergild in the *Lex Salica. Trustis dominica* and *trustis regia* obviously referred to a group of men in the direct environment of the king and entrusted with the protection of the king and his household.[66] The so-labeled persons have been associated with the king's private retinue,[67] but this notion smacks of the so called Germanic *comitatus*

63 Cf. Siems's contribution in this volume, 38–64.

64 Cf. Ubl. *Sinnstiftungen*, 53–97, esp. 96–97.

65 *Lex Ribuaria* 11 (*De homicidiis eorum qui in truste regis sunt*), ed. Beyerle and Buchner, MGH LL nat. Germ. 3, 2, 78: [1] *Si quis eum interfecerit, qui in truste regia est, sexcentos solid. culpabilis iudicetur. Et quicquid ei fietur, similiter sicut de reliquo Ribvario in triplo conponatur.* [2] *De hoccisione eius si negaverit, cum 70 duobus iuret.* [3] *Si quis regio aut ecclesiastico homine de quacumque rem fortiam fecerit aut per vim tullerit, in triplo sicut reliquo Ribvario conponatur*; (*LSRF*. Translated by Rivers, 174).

66 Heinrich Brunner and Claudius von Schwerin, *Deutsche Rechtsgeschichte* vol. 2, Leipzig ²1928, 143–137, esp. 135.

67 Cf. Gabriele von Olberg-Haverkate, Art. ‚Antrustionen', in: *HRG* 1, Berlin ²2008, col. 253–254; Danielle Annex-Cabanis, Art. ‚Antrustio', *LexMA* 1, Munich and Zurich 1980, col. 735–736.

(*germanisches Gefolgschaftswesen*), which enjoyed a dubious career in twentieth century German historiography.[68] Nevertheless, the relationship between the king and his *antrustiones* was characterised by mutual trust, famously attested in a seventh century weapon oath that survived in the formulary of *Marculf* 1.18:

> Regarding the *antrustion* of the king. It is right that he who promises undying fidelity to us should be protected by our help. And because our faithful follower A, with God's favour having come here to our palace along with his weapons, was seen to swear into our hands military service and fidelity to us, we therefore decide and order by the present order that from now on the said A will be counted among the number of our *antrustions*. And should someone perhaps dare to kill him, let him know that he will be liable [to pay] 600 *solidi* for his wergeld.[69]

The formulary draws a direct connection from the sworn fidelity to the king to the granting of royal protection which is exemplified by the increased wergild. Equally important is the enlistment of the oath taker *in numero antrustionum,* which was a clear reference to a military unit in Roman terms. Rather than part of a loose circle of retainers, the royal *trustis* is very likely to have been a regular military unit that constituted the core of the Frankish army under direct command of the king.[70] Bernard Bachrach assumes that the *antrustiones* regularly fulfilled peacekeeping duties such as 'to quell minor uprisings, deal with unfaithful magnates, and of course to protect the king.'[71] However, the increased wergild of the *antrustiones* obviously resulted from their personal proximity and institutionalised attachment to the king (*Königsnähe*). From the beginnings of Frankish law through to the capitulary legislation of the ninth century, Frankish kings took measures to protect their representatives, their

---

68 Karl Kroeschell, Art. ‚Gefolgschaft', in: *HRG* 1, Berlin ^{2}2008, col. 1991–1995.

69 *Marculfi Formulae* 1.18, ed. Zeumer, MGH Formulae Merovingici et Karolini aevi, 55: *De regis antrustione. Rectum est, ut qui nobis fidem pollicentur inlesam, nostro tuenantur auxilio. Et quia illi fidelis, Deo propitio, noster veniens ibi in palatio nostro una cum arma sua in manu nostra trustem et fidelitatem nobis visus est coniurasse: propterea per presentem preceptum decernemus ac iobemus, ut deinceps memoratus ille inter numero antruscionorum conputetur. Et si quis fortasse eum interficere presumpserit, noverit se wiregildo suo solidos sexcentos esse culpabilem*; (*Formularies of Angers and Marculf.* Translated by Rio, 151–152).

70 Cf. Bernard Bachrach, *Early Carolingian Warfare. Prelude to Empire*, Philadelphia 2001, 68–71; Hims., 'Merovingian Mercenaries and Paid Soldiers in Imperial Perspective', in: *Mercenaries and Paid Men. The Mercenary Identity in the Middle Ages*, ed. John France, Leiden 2008, 180–183.

71 Cf. Bernard Bachrach, *Merovingian Military Organization 481–751*, Minneapolis 1972, 72, see also 13, 32–33.

property and their royal prerogatives.[72] Within the legal framework of *compositio*, royal protection of office holders and military retainers translated as a tripling of their wergilds.

A similar point can be made for royal and ecclesiastical patronage in case of the *homines regii* and *homines ecclesiastici* whom a third provision of the *antrustio* title involves. These labels refer to nominally free *coloni* settled on royal or church estates where they had to render certain services.[73] *Homines regii* were also known as *fiscalini*[74] because of their attachment to the fiscal estates in the tradition of the late Roman Colonate.[75] Since the church had been entrusted with huge chunks of fiscal land, many *fiscalini* had hence become *ecclesiastici*.[76] *Lex Ribuaria* 11.3, however, demands that violent privation of a *homo regius* or *ecclesiasticus* entailed threefold compensation compared to what would be owed to Ripuarian victims. Beyerle believed that the rules concerning royal and church people were added later, as the author allegedly aimed to equate royal and church people with *antrustiones*.[77] However, in fact this provision has little to do with individual status. It rather aims at the protection of royal and church property, misappropriation of which also resulted in threefold compensation.[78]

---

72 E.g. the precedence of royal diplomas in *Lex Ribuaria* 59 (60), ed. Beyerle and Buchner, MGH LL nat. Germ. 3, 2, 106–107; or Charles the Bald's coinage reform in the Edict of Pîtres: *Edictum Pistense*, ed. Alfred Boretius and Viktor Krause, MGH Capitularia regum Francorum 2, Hanover 1897, No. 273, cc. 8–19 and 21–24, 314–318 and 319–320.

73 *Lex Alamannorum* 22 (A), ed. Karl Lehmann, MGH LL nationum Germanicarum 5, 1, Hanover 1962, 83: [1] De *liberis autem ecclesiasticis quod colonus vocant, omnes sicut et coloni regis, ita reddant ad ecclesiam* […] — 'Concerning [freedmen and] church freemen, whom they call *coloni*, let them render all things to a church just as the *coloni* of the king do […]' (*Laws of the Alamans and Bavarians*. Translated with an Introduction by Theodore John Rivers, Philadelphia, Pennsylvania 1977, 73 [cited as *LAB*. Translated by Rivers]).

74 *Capitulare legi Ribuariae additum* 803, c. 2, ed. Boretius, MGH Capit. 1, No. 41, 117: [2] *X cap. Homo regius, id est fiscalinus, et aeclesiasticus vel litus interfectus centum solidis conponatur*; — '[2] Regarding the 10th chapter: A killed king's man, that is a *fiscalinus*, and a churchman or *litus*, shall be compensated for with one 100 *solidi*' (trans. L. B.).

75 For a controversial perspective on the late Roman Colonate, see. Boudewijn Sirks, 'The Colonate in Justinian's Reign', *The Journal of Roman Studies* 98 (2008), 120–143; for the intricacies of ligitimising the Colonate, see Susanna Elm, 'Sold to Sin through Origo: Augustine of Hippo and the late Roman slave trade', *Studia Patristica* 98 (2017), 1–22.

76 Cf. Ian Wood, 'Entrusting Western Europe to the Church, 400–750', *Transactions of the RHS* 23 (2013), 37–73.

77 *Lex Ribuaria*, Sachkommentar 11.3, ed. Beyerle and Buchner, MGH LL nat. Germ. 3, 2, 139.

78 *Lex Ribuaria* [58 c] (60.8), ed. Beyerle and Buchner, MGH LL nat. Germ. 3, 2, 107: *Quod si quis de ecclesia aliquid vim tulerit, cum suprascribta lege in triplum conponat;* — 'If anyone forcibly removes something from a church, let him compensate threefold in accordance with the law written above' (*LSRF*. Translated by Rivers, 194).

The tripling of compensations for robbing royal or church people is thus only partly surprising. Indeed, the wergild of these intermediate status groups was fixed way below that of *antrustiones* at the 100 *solidi* threshold in the two proceeding titles, yet it was supplemented by a general rule according to which only half a Ripuarian's fine was to be claimed from a *homo regius* or *ecclesiasticus* accused of any offense.[79] This first general rule pertaining to *homines regii* and *ecclesiastici* (10.2) is uncontroversial because it appears to consider these groups' economic weakness and suggests proportionality as a guiding principle of the Ripuarian compensation system. In the face of the second general rule (11.3), which put *homines regii* and *ecclesiastici* on a level with *antrustiones* in compensation matters related to robbery, both rules appear to have been more self-interested securities on behalf of king and church as the potential warrantors or recipients of fines owed or claimed by their dependents. When held accountable, king and church paid only half of the amount due, while at the receiving end they claimed thrice as much as everyone else. As a result, ecclesiastical and ultimately royal protection had similar effects on a person's legal status as office or function, because both resulted from special relationships between the king and his protégé, characterised either by hierarchical patronage or by mutual trust. 'Königsnähe' of the *antrustio* and 'Königsschutz' of the *homo regius* granted similar facilities in terms of the compensation system even though the respective persons were of different status mirrored in the substantial wergild difference.

5 From Compensation to Punishment

The penal character of functional wergilds in the *Lex Ribuaria* is obvious. *Iudices* and *antrustiones* earned a threefold wergild by virtue of their functional importance for the king and the public. Clerics' wergilds corresponded to ecclesiastical *ordines*. The king's and the church's *coloni* were pooled with various freedmen, although their powerful patrons were granted certain privileges in the *lex*. Assaults against any of the above-mentioned were assaults against royal interests and, at least regarding *antrustiones* and *iudices,* due compensation by threefold wergild. Such a fine would almost certainly ruin

79 *Lex Ribuaria* 10.2, ed. Beyerle and Buchner, MGH LL nat. Germ. 3, 2, 77: [2] *Sic in reliqua conpositione, unde Ribvarivs 15 solidos culpabilis iudicetur, regius aut ecclesiasticus homo meditate conponat, vel deinceps, quantacumque culpa scenderit;* — 'Thus for remaining recompense, where a Ripuarian is held liable for fifteen solidi, let the accused compensate a king's man or a churchman for half [of this amount], and [let him do so] proportionately as much as the crime is assessed' (*LSRF*. Translated by Rivers, 174); cf. Sachkommentar 10.2, ibid. 138.

the offender and if he was unable to gather the amount with the help of family and friends, his heirs would be indebted for the next three generations.[80] Apart from the symbolic politics involved in wergild tripling, it was indeed a form of punishment with the aim of causing serious harm to the offender. Based on the assumption that wergild and *compositio* were originally means to secure peace and legal security in a society, in which an authoritative and punitive approach to justice was hardly viable,[81] the characteristic tripling of wergilds in the *Lex Ribuaria* appears to be the exception that proves the rule. In Simmel's view, it represents a crucial stage of the development of the monetary fine ('Geldstrafe') from the allegedly purely utilitarian wergild of a 'pre-legal state of indifference'.[82] As triple wergilds were also inflicted for certain capital crimes in the *Lex Ribuaria*,[83] I would even suggest that the *lex* be viewed as an attempt to recover stately responsibility over criminal justice, at least with respect to core crimes such as murder and human trafficking.[84]

A detailed discussion of statehood issues is unrewarding here. Instead, I shall hint at one particularly telling example for the authoritative seizure of the wergild system for the threat of punishment, and that refers to crimes committed on military duty:

> Lex Ribuaria 66 (63) [Concerning killing a man who is in the army]
> 1. If anyone kills a man who is in the army, let him be held liable for three times his wergild.
> 2. Similarly concerning theft.[85]

---

80 *Lex Ribuaria* 12.2 (*De homicidiis mulierum*), ed. Beyerle and Buchner, MGH LL nat. Germ. 3, 2, 78: [2] *Et ubicumque sexcenti solidi accedunt, simili modo cum 72 iuret. Si homo ille ita pauper fuerit, ut insimul solver non possit, per tres decessiones filiorum solvat* — '[2] And whereever the 600 solidi are required, let him swear in similar manner with seventy-two [oathtakers]. If that man is so poor that he cannot pay, let his descendants pay up to three generations [after him]' (*LSRF*. Translated by Rivers, 175).

81 Stefan Esders, '"Eliten" und "Strafrecht" im frühen Mittelalter. Überlegungen zu den Bußen- und Wergeldkatalogen der *Leges barbarorum*', in: *Théories et pratiques des élites au haut Moyen Âge* (Collection Haut Moyen Âge 13), ed. François Bougard, Hans-Werner Goetz and Régine Le Jan, Turnhout 2011, 261–282, esp. 265–269.

82 Simmel, *Philosophie des Geldes*, 483–496.

83 *Lex Ribuaria* 16 (15) (*De homine mordrido*), 17 (16) (*De captivate homine vel femina ingenua*), 18 (17) (*De incendio*), 19 (18) (*De sonesti*), ed. Beyerle and Buchner, MGH LL nat. Germ. 3, 2, 80–82.

84 Cf. Lukas Bothe, 'Mediterranean Homesick Blues. Human Trafficking in the Merovingian Leges', in: *The Merovingian Kingdoms in Mediterranean Perspective: Revisiting the Sources*, ed. Stefan Esders, Yitzak Hen, Pia Lucas and Tamar Rotman, London 2019, 79–92.

85 *Lex Ribuaria* 66 (63) (*De homine in hoste occiso*), ed. Beyerle and Buchner, MGH LL nat. Germ. 3, 2, 118: [1] *Si quis hominem in hoste interfecerit, triplice weregeldum culpabilis iudicetur.* [2] *De texaga similiter*; (*LSRF*. Translated by Rivers, 201).

Both crimes, homicide and theft within the army, are punished by a threefold wergild, or perhaps only by threefold theft compensation (*texaga*) in the latter case. Punishment, rather than compensation, seems to be the appropriate terminology here. Threefold wergild — *triplice weregeldum* — appears to be a vague sanction at first glance. In fact, it reveals a much higher degree of abstraction than the subjective casuistry dominant in other titles. We would expect to find 600 *solidi* for an *ingenuus* killed in the army, 1800 *solidi* for an *antrustio* killed in the army, additionally perhaps 300 *solidi* for a *homo regius* or *ecclesiasticus* killed in the army. And indeed, that is the way in which the same issue is handled in the *Lex Salica*.[86] In omitting this casuistry, the authors of the *Lex Ribuaria* deliberately emphasised the criterion that leads to the multiplication of wergild, i.e. criminal action within the army.

Theft and manslaughter were compensable offenses anyway, but on campaign they were serious offenses against military discipline and a potential threat to the kingdom's defensiveness. After all, the *Lex Ribuaria*'s origin is closely related to an Austrasian subkingdom that was established in reaction to repeated raids in Thuringia and other Austrasian *pagi* in the wake of a disastrous campaign against Samo's Slavs.[87] According to the Chronicle of Fredegar, the subkingdom established by Dagobert for his minor son Sigibert III in 633/34 was provided with substantial means, including a separate *fiscus*, and effectively guarded the Eastern frontier of the Merovingian kingdoms thereafter.[88] Hence, the emphasis on military discipline in what was most likely the legal framework of that new kingdom should not surprise anyone.[89] Pertaining to the above-mentioned tendency to keep the wergild system stable, *Lex Ribuaria* 66 (63) constitutes another deliberate transgression of that same system. The triple wergild inflicted for homicide and theft in the army is thus to be seen in the same punitive vein as the functional wergilds discussed above.

Multiplication of wergilds and fines for legally protected interests of the king or the church appear in other *leges*, too.[90] The phenomenon may be attributed

86 *Pactus legis Salicae* 63 *De hominem in hoste occisum*, ed. Eckhardt, MGH LL nat. Germ. 4, 1, 228–230.

87 *Chronicle of Fredegar* IV, 68, 75, ed. Krusch, MGH SS rer. Merov. 3, 154–155, 158–159.

88 Ibid. 158–159.

89 Cf. Esders, 'Military Law', 5, 10.

90 E.g. *Lex Bauivariorum* III (*De furtis ecclesiae, quomodo conponantur*), ed. Ernst von Schwind, MGH LL nationum Germanicarum 5, 2, Hanover 1926, 270–271: *Si quis res ecclesiae furaverit et exinde probatus fuerit, unamquamque rem niungeldo solvat, id est novem capita restitutat* […] — 'If anyone steals church property and is convicted, let him pay for that property ninefold […]' (*LAB*. Translated by Rivers, 119); cf. *The Laws of Æthelberht of Kent*, ed. and trans. Lisi Oliver, *The Beginnings of English Law*, Toronto 2002, 60–64: [1] *Godes feoh cirican XII gylde*; [10] *Gif frygman cyninge stele, IX gylde forgylde.*

to the monetary logic of compensatory penal systems centered on wergild, which were eventually seized by authority in Simmel's sense. However, since the triple wergild of 600 *solidi* features more prominently and more systematically in the *Lex Ribuaria* than anywhere else in the *leges*,[91] I would like to conclude that the Ripuarian high fine ('Hochbuße'; the triple wergild) cannot readily be compared to regular wergilds. Harald Siems admonishes in this volume that, from the outset, there is no acceptable way to estimate human life in monetary terms because of the uniqueness of human life itself.[92] Yet, the Ripuarian wergild catalogue suggests that human beings were valued quite differently according to social and functional status. Of course, this valuation can be explained by the notion that wergild actually compensated for lost services and obligations that the deceased person owed his family and kin.[93] A different notion is that shame and embodied honour called for atonement.[94] Both explanations have a claim to validity; they can explain distinct wergilds of most status groups, but neither one of them explains the much higher fines for killed functionaries or serious crimes that the *Lex Ribuaria* at times referred to as *triplice weregeldum*.[95] In analogy to the capital crime of murder,[96] the *Lex Ribuaria* demands triple wergilds in various instances, each of which appear to punish relatively severe transgressions of the law. Triple wergilds were preventive measures designed partly to protect the interests of a ruling class and partly to guarantee a minimum of peace and legal security. Social and functional status were tools to balance those competing interests. Far from atoning for damage alone, the allegedly arbitrary tripling of wergilds thus indicates an attempt to regulate society more extensively.

---

91 *Lex Ribuaria* 11; 12; 16 (15); 17 (16); 18 (17), 19 (18); 40.8 (39.8); 54 (53); 66 (63); 67 (64), ed. Beyerle and Buchner, MGH LL nat. Germ. 3, 2, 78; 80–81; 93; 103; 118.

92 Cf. Siems, above, 41.

93 Ibid., 56.

94 Cf. the contributions of Paul Lambert and Han Nijdam to this volume, 133–160 and 161–182.

95 *Lex Ribuaria* 66.1 (63.1) and 67.1 (64.1), ed. Beyerle and Buchner, MGH LL nat. Germ. 3, 2, 118.

96 *Lex Ribuaria* 16 (15) (*De homine mordrido*), ed. Beyerle and Buchner, MGH LL nat. Germ. 3, 2, 80: *Si quis ingenuus Ribvarius ingenuum Ribvarium interfecerit et eum cum rama aut callis vel in puteo seu in aqua quacumque libet loco celare voluerit, quod dicitur mordridus, sexcentos solidos culpabilis iudicetur, aut cum 70 duobus iuret;* — 'If a free Ripuarian kills another free Ripuarian and conceals him with branches or skins either in a well or under water or whatever place he wilfully [does this], which is known as murder [*mordridus*], let him be held liable for 600 solidi, or let him swear with seventy-two [oathtakers]' (*LSRF*. Translated by Rivers, 176).

Bibliography

Primary Sources

Capitulare legi Ribuariae additum a. 803, ed. Alfred Boretius, MGH Capitularia regum Francorum 1, Hanover 1883, No. 41, 117–118.

Chilperici Edictum 561–584, ed. Alfred Boretius, MGH Capitularia regum Francorum 1, Hanover 1883, No. 4, 8–10.

Chlotharii II. Edictum 614 Oct. 8, ed. Alfred Boretius, MGH Capitularia regum Francorum 1, Hanover 1883, No. 9, 20–23.

Chronicle of Fredegar, ed. Bruno Krusch, MGH SS rerum Merovingicarum 3, Hanover 1888, 1–193.

Concilium Aurelianense a. 538, ed. Friedrich Maassen, MGH Concilia 1, Hanover 1893, 72–86.

Edictum Pistense, ed. Alfred Boretius and Viktor Krause, MGH Capitularia regum Francorum 2, Hanover 1897, No. 273, 310–324.

Formulae Salicae Merkeliane, ed. Karl Zeumer, MGH Formulae Merovingici et Karolini aevi, Hanover 1886, 239–263.

Laws of the Alamans and Bavarians. Translated with an Introduction by Theodore John Rivers, Philadelphia, Pennsylvania 1977.

Laws of the Salian and Ripuarian Franks. Translated with an Introduction by Theodore John Rivers, New York 1986.

Lex Alamannorum, ed. Karl Lehmann, MGH LL nationum Germanicarum 5, 1, Hanover 1962.

Lex Bauivariorum, ed. Ernst von Schwind, MGH LL nationum Germanicarum 5, 2, Hanover 1926.

Lex Ribuaria, ed. Franz Beyerle and Rudolf Buchner, MGH LL nationum Germanicarum 3, 2, Hanover 1954.

Marculfi Formulae, ed. Karl Zeumer, MGH Formulae Merowingici et Karolini aevi, Hanover 1886, 32–106.

Pactus legis Salicae, ed. Karl August Eckhardt, MGH LL nationum Germanicarum 4, 1, Hanover 1962.

The Formularies of Angers and Marculf. Two Merovingian Legal Handbooks. Translated with an Introduction and Notes by Alice Rio (Translated Texts for Historians 46), Liverpool 2008.

The Laws of Æthelberht, ed. and trans. Lisi Oliver, *The Beginnings of English Law*, Toronto 2002, 52–116.

Secondary Works

Anderson, Thomas, 'Roman military colonies in Gaul, Salian ethnogenesis and the forgotten meaning of Pactus legis Salicae 59.5', *Early Medieval Europe* 4 (1995), 129–144.

Annex-Cabanis, Danielle, Art. 'Antrustio', *LexMA* 1, Munich and Zurich 1980, col. 735–736.

Bachrach, Bernard, 'Merovingian mercenaries and paid soldiers in imperial perspective', in: *Mercenaries and paid men. The mercenary identity in the middle ages*, ed. John France, Leiden 2008, 167–192.

Bachrach, Bernard, *Early Carolingian Warfare. Prelude to Empire*, Philadelphia 2001.

Bachrach, Bernard, *Merovingian Military Organization 481–751*, Minneapolis 1972.

Bischoff, Bernhard, *Latin Palaeography: Antiquity and the Middle Ages*, trans. Dáibhí ó Cróinín and David Ganz, Cambridge 1990.

Blackburn, Mark and Grierson, Philip, *Medieval European Coinage. With a Catalogue of the Coins in the Fitzwilliam Museum, Cambridge. 1: The Early Middle Ages (5th–10th centuries)*, Cambridge ²1991.

Bothe, Lukas, 'From subordination to integration: Romans in Frankish law', in: *Transformations of Romanness. Early Medieval Regions and Identities* (Millennium Studies 71), ed. Walter Pohl, Clemens Gantner, Cinzia Grifoni and Marianne Pollheimer-Mohaupt, Berlin 2018, 345–369.

Bothe, Lukas, 'Mediterranean Homesick Blues. Human Trafficking in the Merovingian *Leges*', in: *The Merovingian Kingdoms in Mediterranean Perspective: Revisiting the Sources*, ed. Stefan Esders, Yitzak Hen, Pia Lucas and Tamar Rotman, London 2019, 79–92.

Brunner, Heinrich and Schwerin, Claudius von, *Deutsche Rechtsgeschichte* vol. 2, Leipzig ²1928.

Brunner, Heinrich, *Deutsche Rechtsgeschichte* vol. 1, Leipzig ²1906.

Brunner, Heinrich, 'Duodecimalsystem und Decimalsystem in den Busszahlen der fränkischen Volksrechte', *Sitzungsberichte der Preussischen Akademie der Wissenschaften* 2 (1889), 1039–1043.

Brunner, Heinrich, 'Kritische Bemerkungen zur Geschichte des germanischen Weibererbrechts', *ZRG GA* 21 (1900), 1–19.

Ehrhardt, Arnold, 'Rechtsvergleichende Studien zum antiken Sklavenrecht I., Wergeld und Schadensersatz', *ZRG RA* 68 (1951), 74–130.

Elm, Susanna, 'Sold to Sin Through *Origo*: Augustine of Hippo and the Late Roman Slave Trade', *Studia Patristica* 98 (2017), 1-22.

Esders, Stefan, '"Eliten" und "Strafrecht" im frühen Mittelalter. Überlegungen zu den Bußen- und Wergeldkatalogen der *Leges barbarorum*', in: *Théories et pratiques des élites au haut Moyen Âge* (Collection Haut Moyen Âge 13), ed. François Bougard, Hans-Werner Goetz and Régine Le Jan, Turnhout 2011, 261–282.

Esders, Stefan, 'Late Roman Military Law in the Bavarian Code', *clio@themis. Revue électronique d'histoire du droit* 10 (2016) (thematic issue *La forge du droit. Naissance des identités juridiques en Europe, IVᵉ–XIIIᵉ siècles*): http://www.cliothemis.com/IMG/pdf/3-_Esders-2.pdf.

Esders, Stefan, *Die Formierung der Zensualität. Zur kirchlichen Transformation des spätrömischen Patronatswesens im frühen Mittelalter*, Ostfildern 2010.

Faulkner, Thomas, *Law and Authority in the Early Middle Ages. The Frankish Leges in the Carolingian Period*, Cambridge 2016.

Geary, Patrick, 'Ethnic identity as a situational construct', *Mitteilungen der Anthropologischen Gesellschaft in Wien* 113 (1983), 15–26.

Halsall, Guy, *Settlement and Social Organization: the Merovingian Region of Metz*, Cambridge 1995.

Kroeschell, Karl, Art. ‚Gefolgschaft', in: *HRG* 1, Berlin ²2008, col. 1991–1995.

Mordek, Hubert, 'Die Hedenen als politische Kraft im austrasischen Frankenreich', in: *Karl Martell in seiner Zeit*, ed. Jörg Jarnut, Ulrich Nonn and Michael Richter, Sigmaringen 1994, 345–366.

Murray, Alexander Callander, *Germanic Kinship Structure. Studies in Law and Society in Antiquity and the Early Middle Ages*, Toronto 1983.

Murray, Alexander Callander, 'Immunity, Nobility and the Edict of Paris', *Speculum* 69 (1994), 18–39.

Nehlsen, Hermann, *Sklavenrecht zwischen Antike und Mittelalter: germanisches und römisches Recht in den germanischen Rechtsaufzeichnungen*, Frankfurt 1972.

Nelson, Janet, 'The wary widow', in: *Property and Power in Early Medieval Europe*, ed. Wendy Davies and Paul Fouracre, Cambridge 1995, 82–113.

Olberg, Gabriele von, *Die Bezeichnungen für soziale Stände, Schichten und Gruppen in den Leges Barbarorum*, Berlin 1991.

Olberg-Haverkate, Gabriele von, Art. ‚Antrustionen', in: *HRG* 1, Berlin ²2008, col. 253–254.

Oliver, Lisi, *The Body Legal in Barbarian Law*, Toronto 2011.

Rio, Alice, '"Half-free" categories in the early middle ages: Fine status distinctions before professional lawyers', in: *Legalism: Rules and Categories*, ed. Paul Dresch and Judith Scheele, Oxford 2015, 129–152.

Rio, Alice, 'Freedom and Unfreedom in Early Medieval Francia: The Evidence of the Legal *Formulae*', *Past & Present* 193 (2006), 7–40.

Rio, Alice, 'Self-sale and Voluntary Entry into Unfreedom, 300–1100', *Journal of Social History* 23 (2012), 661–685.

Rio, Alice, *Legal Practice and the Written Word in the Early Middle Ages, Frankish Formulae c. 500–1000*, Cambridge 2009.

Schmidt-Wiegand, Ruth, 'Rechtsvorstellungen bei den Franken und Alemannen vor 500', in: *Die Franken und die Alemannen bis zur 'Schlacht bei Zülpich' (496/497)*, ed. Dieter Geuenich, Berlin 1998, 545–557.

Simmel, Georg, *Philosophie des Geldes*, ed. David P. Frisby and Klaus Christian Köhnke (Georg Simmel Gesamtausgabe 6), Frankfurt/Main 1989.

Ubl, Karl, *Sinnstiftungen eines Rechtsbuchs: Die Lex Salica im Frankenreich* (Quellen und Forschungen zum Recht im Mittelalter 9), Ostfildern 2017.

Voss, Wulf-Eckart, 'Der Grundsatz der ärgeren Hand bei Sklaven, Kolonen und Hörigen', in: *Römisches Recht in der europäischen Tradition*, ed. Okko Behrends, Malte Deisselhorst and Wulf-Eckart Voss, Ebelbach 1985, 117–184.

Wood, Ian, 'Entrusting Western Europe to the Church, 400–750', *Transactions of the Royal Historical Society* 23 (2013), 37–73.

Wormald, Patrick, 'The *Leges Barbarorum*: law and ethnicity in the post-Roman West', in: *Regna et Gentes. The Relationship between Late Antique and Early Medieval Peoples and Kingdoms in the Transformation of the Roman World*, ed. Hans-Werner Goetz, Jörg Jarnut and Walter Pohl, Leiden 2003, 21–53.

CHAPTER 9

Penance and Satisfaction: Conflict Settlement and Penitential Practices in the Frankish World in the Early Middle Ages

Rob Meens

This contribution addresses the question of mediation by clerics in violent conflict by looking in particular at books used for confession circulating in Francia in the period from the late sixth to the late ninth centuries, and the way these penitential books include forms of material compensation when assigning penances for sins. Secular law codes contain elaborate rules about the proper financial compensation for particular crimes. Yet, we know very little about the practical implementation of such rules. Nowadays few if any historians would subscribe to Dorothy Whitelock's views that fines and compensations were fixed by the law and applied in courts.[1] More recent studies have established that in the early Middle Ages informal procedures were of major importance in settling disputes.[2] Mediation was an important part of such processes of reconciliation and Edward James and Paul Hyams have both drawn attention to the role of religious and clerical actors in such mediating processes.[3] Laurent Jégou has recently discussed the role of bishops in dispute

1 Dorothy Whitelock, *The Beginnings of English Society*, Harmondsworth 1952, 145–146: 'The amount to be paid for any offence was not left to the discretion of the court; it was for it to pronounce the sentence in accordance with the law-books.'

2 Seminal collections of essays are John Bossy (ed.), *Disputes and Settlements: Law and Human Relations in the West*, Cambridge, 1983 and Wendy Davies and Paul Fouracre (ed.), *The Settlement of Disputes in Early Medieval Europe*, Cambridge 1986. Two Spoleto conferences have been devoted to the subject: *La giustizia nell'alto medieovo (secoli V–VIII)* (Settimane di Studio del Centro Italiano di Studi sull'Alto Medioevo 42), Spoleto 1995, and *La giustizia nell'alto medioevo (secoli IX–XI)* (Settimane di Studio del Centro Italiano di Studi sull'Alto Medioevo 44), Spoleto 1997. More recent useful collections are J. Büchert Netterstrøm and Bjørn Poulsen (ed.), *Feud in Medieval and Early Modern Europe*, Aarhus 2007, Thomas Lambert and David Rollason (ed.), *Peace and Protection in the Middle Ages*, Durham and Toronto 2009; and Per Andersen, Helle Møller Sigh and Helle Vogt (ed.), *Law and Disputing in the Middle Ages. Proceedings of the Ninth Carlsberg Academy Conference on Medieval Legal History 2012*, Copenhagen 2013.

3 Edward James, '"Beati Pacifici": Bishops and the Law in Sixth-Century Gaul', in: *Disputes and Settlements. Law and Human Relations in the West*, ed. John Bossy, Cambridge 1983, 25–46 (cited as James, '"Beati Pacifici"') and Paul Hyams, *Rancor and Reconciliation in Medieval*

 | DOI:10.1163/9789004466128_010

settlement in great detail and with admirable acuity. He has not only stressed formal judgments of bishops, but also their role in more informal ways of conflict resolution, as mediators and intercessors.[4] In his study Jégou has also drawn attention to the fact that legal manuscripts consist often of a compilation including secular laws, ecclesiastical regulations, penitential books and Biblical excerpts.[5] He also touched upon the role of penitential books in the process of conflict resolution. According to him bishops employed penitential books as additional instruments in the arsenal of legal texts at their disposal. Such works were particularly useful because they did not present their rulings as sanctions but as a means for salvation.[6] This provided possibilities for giving in to your opponent without loss of face, which was of major importance when trying to reconcile two parties.

This contribution takes Jégou's approach further focussing on the role of penance in the processes by which conflicting opponents could be reconciled. Jégou stresses the role of bishops, which is logical regarding the focus on bishops in his study, yet I think that penitential books were not exclusively used by these high-ranking officials. They could also be in the hands of a local priest, an abbot or monks providing pastoral care. Involvement of a monk, priest or bishop could entail some form of religious satisfaction by means of penitential acts. The monk and abbot Columbanus, who as we will see provided ample room for ways of secular composition in his penitential book, is a case in point. Particular manuscripts containing such texts, moreover, can be classified as books for simple priests.[7] This would mean that not only bishops could play a mediating role in disputes, but that monks and local priests might act in a similar way. In this contribution I will focus on those penitential rulings in which

---

England, Ithaca and London 2003, 18–19 when discussing Robert Axelrod and game theory: 'It also helps if there exists from the start "a small initial cluster of potential cooperators" [citing Axelrod and Keohane] to seed the peace process in other people's minds. In a medieval European context, the obvious cooperator would be the Church, with its message of peace and its success at influencing at least some of the secular nobility and others. Clerical peacemaking is never certain to succeed — it must be done well — but it clearly enters the equation.'

4 Laurent Jégou, *L'évêque, juge de paix. L'autorité épiscopale et le règlement des conflits* (*VIII*[e]–*XI*[e] *siècle*), Turnhout 2011 (cited as Jégou, *L'évêque, juge de paix*).

5 Ibid., 44.

6 Jégou, *L'évêque, juge de paix*, 46.

7 As I argued in Rob Meens, 'The Frequency and Nature of early Medieval Penance', in: *Handling Sin: Confession in the Middle Ages* (York Studies in Medieval Theology 2), ed. Peter Biller, Alistair J. Minnis, Woodbridge 1998, 35–61. See also Rob Meens, *Penance in Medieval Europe, 600–1200*, Cambridge 2014 (cited as Meens, *Penance*) and the volume by Steffen Patzold and Carine Van Rhijn (ed.), *Men in the Middle. Local Priests in Early Medieval Europe*, Berlin 2016 which discusses the books used by local priests.

room is made for some form of material compensation for the offended party. If paying compensation to the offended party is required as part of a penitential procedure, the priest, monk or bishop must play a mediating role between the two parties. It also indicates that such a form of penitential practice cannot be entirely secret. Some form of publicity must be involved in order for the two parties to acknowledge guilt, agree on financial compensation and to reach reconciliation. Before looking at these aspects of penitential books in more detail, let us first consider one of the most famous feuds of the early Middle Ages, because it describes the intricacies of negotiating and reaching a settlement in case of a violent conflict and accords an interesting role to the bishop involved, who actually recorded the history for posterity. This 'classical feud', as it was related by Gregory of Tours, is generally known as the feud of Sichar and Chramnesind and in the words of a translator of Gregory's *Historiae* it would show 'the Dark Ages at their worst'.[8]

1 Feud in Tours

Although it is generally regarded as a feud, in this context Gregory of Tours speaks of a *bellum civile*.[9] This may be an exaggeration by Gregory, yet its

8 The episode is recounted in two chapters in Gregory of Tours, *Decem Libri Historiarum*, 7.47 and 9.19, ed. Bruno Krusch and Wilhelm Levison, MGH SS rerum Merovingicarum 1, 1, Hanover 1951, 366–368 and 432–434; for the citation see *The history of the Franks by Gregory of Tours*. Translated by Ormonde M. Dalton, vol. 2, Oxford 1927, 572; for comments see Ian Wood, '"The bloodfeud of the Franks": a historiographical myth', *Early Medieval Europe* 14 (2006), 489–504, at 494. The central importance of this episode in historiography is highlighted by Guy Halsall's introduction to his *Violence and Society in the Early Medieval West*, Woodbridge 1998 (cited as Halsall, *Violence*), which starts off with a discussion of this case. Recent expositions of this conflict are to be found in Malte Diesselhorst, 'Die Fehde von Sichar und Chramnesind, erzählt von Gregor von Tours', in: *Libertas: grundrechtliche und rechtsstaatliche Gewährungen in Antike und Gegenwart; Symposion aus Anlass des 80. Geburtstages von Franz Wieacker*, ed. Okko Behrends and Malte Diesselhorst, Ebelsbach 1991, 187–208 (a bit simplistic at times); Phillippe Depreux, 'Une faide exemplaire? À propos des aventures de Sichaire: vengeance et pacification aux temps mérovingiens', in: *La vengeance 400–1200* (Collection de l'École française de Rome 357), ed. Dominique Barthélemy, François Bougard and Régine Le Jan, Rome 2006, 65–85 (cited as Depreux, 'Une faide exemplaire'); Warren Brown, *Violence in Medieval Europe*, Harlow 2011, 38–41 (cited as Brown, *Violence*); Hans-Werner Goetz, 'Spielregeln, politische Rituale und symbolische Kommunikation in der Merowingerzeit', in: *Spielregeln der Mächtigen. Mittelalterliche Politik zwischen Gewohnheit und Konvention*, ed. Claudia Garnier and Hermann Kamp, Darmstadt 2010, 33–59 (cited as Goetz, 'Spielregeln, politische Rituale').

9 The feud-like character of the conflict is exemplified in the title of Michael Wallace-Hadrill, 'The Bloodfeud of the Franks', in: idem, *The Long-Haired Kings*, London 1962, 121–147 (cited as

elaborate description as well as its position in the *Histories* demonstrate the importance Gregory attached to this episode.[10] The story has received quite a lot of attention recently as well as in the past and therefore there is no need to consider it here in every detail. It concerns two *cives* from Tours who ran into a serious conflict with one another after the servant of a priest got killed at a Christmas party, for a reason Gregory does not supply. Sichar came to the aid of the priest whose servant was killed, and, fully armed and with a group of followers, went to a church, probably the church of the priest, to try to kill a man called Austregisel. We may assume that Austregisel was involved in the killing of the priest and may have been regarded as the murderer. In the ensuing fight Sichar was unable to lay his hands on Austregisel and was forced to flee. Austregisel himself killed a number of Sichar's men and took his gold and silver. In a legal procedure before the citizens of Tours, probably the municipal court of the *civitas*, Austregisel was later condemned for his actions. The return of the stolen goods was most probably part of this legal settlement but seems not to have been effected. This must have incited Sichar to attack a certain Auno, together with his son and brother, who were in the possession of the properties that Austregisel had stolen from Sichar. Sichar killed the three men, after which the conflict revolved around Sichar and another son of Auno's by the name of Chramnesind. The latter accepted financial compensation, and this should have been the end of the conflict, but it was not.

When sometime later — Gregory does not specify exactly how much later but apparently the two rivals had in the meantime established a warm relationship[11] — Sichar boasted that Chramnesind owed his riches only to the fact that he had received such a splendid compensation from Sichar for killing his father, Chramnesind felt so insulted that he flared up in anger and drew his sword with which he then split Sichar's skull. After this gruesome act Chramnesind went to a church and threw himself before the king (Childebert II) to plead for his life. The king decided that Chramnesind had acted in a just way and thus he was acquitted. Gregory's story does not provide

Wallace-Hadrill, 'Bloodfeud of the Franks'); but see Peter Sawyer, 'The bloodfeud in fact and fiction', in: *Tradition og historieskrivning. Kilderne til Nordens ældste historie* (Acta Iutlandica 63/2), ed. Kirsten Hastrup and Preben Meulengracht Sørensen, Aarhus 1987, 27–38, who warns not to confuse feud and personal revenge; Erich Auerbach in his critical appraisal of Gregory's command of Latin in this episode even goes as far as to lecture him: 'bella civilia is certainly not the proper term for the disorderly brawls and thefts and killings which he has in mind.', Erich Auerbach, *Mimesis. The Representation of Reality in Western Literature*, trans. Willard R. Trask, Princeton 2003, 94.

10 Martin Heinzelmann, *Gregor von Tours (538–594). 'Zehn Bücher Geschichte'. Historiographie und Gesellschaftskonzept im 6. Jahrhundert*, Darmstadt 1994, 56–57.

11 Depreux, 'Une faide exemplaire', 71 speaks of 'quelques années plus tard'.

all the details that we historians would be interested to hear. It remains unclear, for example, why the priest was killed in the first place, what exactly the relationship between the murdered priest and Sichar was, or that between Austregisel and Auno. Gregory furthermore does not provide any details concerning how the bishop and *iudex* cooperated in this case or whether they used written codes of law in order to decide a case such as this. Yet, although many details are shrouded in historical fog, this remains the best-documented case of a complex conflict between two powerful families in a Merovingian civitas. As such it nicely demonstrates the uses of violence in a conflict in combination with complicated negotiations between the parties to the dispute, the involvement of other parties such as the *iudex* and the bishop, the attempts to resolve the conflict by monetary payments, as well as the honour and shame that such disputes could generate.

There has been ample discussion of this case. Gabriel Monod drew on the *Lex Salica* when discussing it and proposed a 'Germanic reading' of the episode, a reading contested by Fustel de Coulanges.[12] Michael Wallace-Hadrill was interested in the efforts that were put into containing and controlling the violence,[13] an interest that resulted partly from his contacts in Manchester where he was teaching with the anthropologist Max Gluckman, the author of the seminal article 'The Peace in the Feud', published in *Past & Present* in 1955.[14] Guy Halsall sees this 'violent series of events [...] lasting the best part of two years and leading to at least thirteen deaths' as 'an extremely appropriate focus' for the introduction to a book concerned with the role of violence in early medieval society.[15] Philippe Depreux recently revisited this famous case to demonstrate how physical violence and legal procedures were both used in order to try and settle the conflict.[16] Hans-Werner Goetz used Gregory's story to demonstrate the importance of ritual behaviour and symbolic communication in the Merovingian era.[17] Although Edward James has drawn our attention to the role of bishops as mediators in such conflicts, the religious aspects of conflict settlement have not received the attention they deserve and

---

12 Discussed in Patrick Geary, 'Gabriel Monod, Fustel de Coulanges et les "aventures de Sichaire". La naissance de l'histoire scientifique au XIXe siècle', in: *La vengeance 400–1200* (Collection de l'École française de Rome 357), ed. Dominique Barthélemy, François Bougard and Régine Le Jan, Rome 2006, 87–99.

13 Wallace-Hadrill, Bloodfeud of the Franks.

14 Max Gluckman, 'The Peace in the Feud', *Past and Present* 8 (1955), 1–14; for a closer investigation of the contacts between Wallace-Hadrill and Gluckman, see Wood, 'Bloodfeud of the Franks'.

15 Halsall, *Violence*, 2.

16 Depreux, 'Une faide exemplaire'.

17 Goetz, 'Spielregeln, politische Rituale'.

it is such aspects that I would like to discuss in this chapter by looking at the ways in which penitential books circulating in the Latin West deal with violent behaviour.[18]

If we look at this feud, we can see the following aspects that have a religious connection. When Sichar had killed Auno and his relatives, Gregory relates how he, in close cooperation with the local *iudex*, sent messengers with an invitation to (probably) both parties in order to discuss their conflict and to establish peace. When they had come, Gregory addressed them in the presence of their fellow citizens of Tours and incited them to offer proper compensation for their wrongdoing in order to prevent further bloodshed among the 'sons of the church'. Gregory went so far as to offer to pay part of the compensation with money belonging to the church to prevent further bloodshed and the loss of souls, but his offer was declined by the followers of Chramnesind, who demanded satisfaction for the death of their father, brother and uncle. When Chramnesind and Sichar finally came to an agreement, however, half of the compensation was paid by the church, Gregory informs us. When the conflict flared up again and Chramnesind had murdered Sichar because of his insulting remarks, he went to a church to see the king and threw himself at his feet in order to plead for his life, through an act that looks very much like a *deditio*.[19] I do not think that it is an accident that Chramnesind acted thus in this particular place, a church, a place where no blood should be shed. The whole episode, which is generally regarded as a classic feud, reveals a close connection between the rule of law and judicial proceedings on the one hand and social groups taking recourse to violent means in order to obtain their goals on the other. Moreover, we are also able to observe how the local bishop tried hard to mediate between the parties. The bishop cooperated with the local *iudex* and the population of Tours to bring the two parties together to negotiate an agreement. He used the financial reserve of the church to help Sichar pay the compensation owed to his opponent's family. Perhaps Chramnesind relied on clerical mediation, too, when, in order to seek mercy from the king, he finally fled to a church, where he could expect to be protected by the laws of sanctuary, the priest or bishop supervising that building and the saint who was buried there.[20]

18 James, '"Beati Pacifici"'.

19 Not discussed as such by Goetz, 'Spielregeln, politische Rituale'.

20 For the importance of the practice of sanctuary for Gregory of Tours, see Rob Meens, 'The sanctity of the basilica of St. Martin. Gregory of Tours and the practice of sanctuary in the Merovingian period', in: *Texts and Identities in the early Middle Ages*, ed. Richard Corradini, Rob Meens, Christina Pössel and Philip Shaw, Vienna 2006, 277–287 (cited as Meens, 'The sanctity of the basilica of St. Martin').

That mediation by clerics, as transpiring in this case, was not unusual is suggested by a *formula* in Marculf's collection. This late Merovingian collection of formal legal letters, meant as a model book for such documents and remaining in use throughout the Carolingian period as the surviving manuscripts demonstrate, contains one such model letter that should serve to guarantee security for a murderer after peace had been made.[21] This particular *formula* refers explicitly to 'the intervention of priests (*sacerdotes*) and great men (*magnificis viris*)' who arranged the reconciliation between the murderer and the kin of the murdered person. The formulaic character of this source suggests that *sacerdotes* quite frequently played a mediating role in serious conflicts such as murder. In the *Formulae Salicae Lindenbrogianae*, a collection of *formulae* closely related to Marculf's collection, bishops (*pontifices*) appear as partners cooperating with counts in settling a murder case and warranting safety for the culprit who had paid compensation.[22] In a way such clerical interference should not surprise us, since the people taking part in violent actions in sixth-century Gaul were Christians and Christian doctrine in principle condemned bloodshed. Christian shepherds, above all priests and bishops, but also abbots and abbesses, were to uphold Christian doctrine in this respect.[23] Moreover, already in Late Antiquity we see that bishops played a role in adjudicating conflicts in their *audientia episcopalis*.[24] Bishops often came from aristocratic families that were well versed in Roman legal tradition. Their social standing and aristocratic connections, moreover, made them well-suited as mediators in social conflicts. Holy men could also play a mediating role in conflicts because of their religious authority.[25] Gregory's story furthermore indicates

21 *Marculfi Formulae* 2.18, ed. Karl Zeumer, MGH Formulae Merowingici et Karolini aevi, Hanover 1886, 88–89; *The Formularies of Angers and Marculf. Two Merovingian Legal Handbooks*. Translated with an Introduction and Notes by Alice Rio [Translated Texts for Historians 46], Liverpool 2008, 203–204; for a discussion of its date, 110–113 and Alice Rio, *Legal Practice and the Written Word in the Early Middle Ages. Frankish Formulae, c. 500–1000*, Cambridge 2009, 85–88 (cited as Rio, *Legal Practice*). See for further discussion of these sources the contribution by Warren Brown to this volume.

22 *Formulae Salicae Lindenbrogianae* 19, ed. Zeumer, MGH Formulae Merowingici et Karolini aevi, 280–281. For further discussion of this text Rio, *Legal Practice*, 103–104.

23 James, 'Beati Pacifici'.

24 Claudia Rapp, *Holy bishops in Late Antiquity. The Nature of Christian Leadership in an Age of Transition*, Berkeley, Los Angeles and London 2005, 242–253; Kevin Uhalde, *Expectations of Justice in the Age of Augustine*, Philadelphia 2007, 44–76; Caroline Humfress, 'Bishops and law courts in Late Antiquity: How (not) to make sense of the legal evidence', *Journal of Early Christian Studies* 19 (2011), 375–400.

25 The literature on holy men is vast. Seminal is of course Peter Brown, 'The Rise and function of the holy man in Late Antiquity', *Journal of Roman Studies* 61 (1971), 80–101 [repr. in Peter Brown, *Society and the Holy in Late Antiquity*, Berkeley and Los Angeles 1982, 103–152];

that ecclesiastical institutions could dispose of large amounts of capital to help and encourage parties to settle for financial compensation instead of seeking murderous revenge. Churches were places of refuge and this feature pressed clerics to intervene and negotiate when someone had fled to safety in a church.[26] In my opinion, therefore, we should exercise caution when viewing conflict resolution by means of wergild or other forms of compensation in the Frankish world as a purely secular affair. There are many indications that religious attitudes towards violence, religious authority and ecclesiastical institutions played their part in the whole process, and it is to a few of these religious aspects that this chapter is devoted.

2 Penitential Books and Compensation Payments

Books used in the religious sphere of hearing confession and imposing a specific kind of penance resemble legal texts in a number of different ways. Both censure forms of misbehaviour and assign specific acts of satisfaction for this misconduct. They partly treat the same kind of offenses: theft, violence and murder, offenses that constitute major disturbances of the social order. They also both try to assess the weight of a particular offense. There are, however, also significant differences. Whereas legal texts mainly try to restore relations between two conflicting parties, sometimes with an eye for the interests of the ruler, penitential books first of all try to regain divine favour. Penance is first of all a way to make peace with God for a particular sin. It is, however, also a way of regaining the favour of the Christian community, in which there is, in principle, no place for a serious sinner. It is therefore also a way to restore relations with one's neighbours and as such it cannot be completely 'private' in cases where sins had caused a major social upheaval, even if penitential books are often — and wrongly I believe — associated with what historians call 'private penance'.[27] Although law codes and penitential books both try to assess

Brown's reassessment in 'The Rise and Function of the holy man in Late Antiquity, 1971–1997', *Journal of Early Christian Studies* 6 (1998), 463–484; see also James Howard-Johnston and Paul Hayward (ed.), *The Cult of Saints in Late Antiquity and the Middle Ages. Essays on the Contribution of Peter Brown*, Oxford 1999; Albrecht Diem, 'Monks, kings, and the transformation of sanctity: Jonas of Bobbio and the end of the holy man', *Speculum* 82/3 (2007), 521–559.

26 See Meens, 'The sanctity of the basilica of St. Martin'; for the Carolingian age: Rob Meens, 'Sanctuary, penance and dispute settlement under Charlemagne. The conflict between Alcuin and Theodulf of Orléans over a sinful cleric', *Speculum* 82/2 (2007), 277–300.

27 For the social functions of penitential practices, see Meens, *Penance*.

the seriousness of a particular offense by establishing an appropriate form of satisfaction, there is a major difference in that in law codes the social status of the victim or his relationship to the king is of paramount importance. Killing a count was considered to be more serious than killing a freeman. Penitential books in general demonstrate a greater interest in trying to assess the culprit's motives and the circumstances in which a deed was done and attach less importance to the social position of the offended party.

The way penitential texts deal with violence is exemplified in the *Discipulus Umbrensium* version of the penitential of the Archbishop Theodore of Canterbury, composed sometime near the year 700 and well-known in northern Frankish regions in the eighth century.[28] The text contains a chapter on killing, which distinguishes between cases in which a man kills a person for reasons of vengeance (*pro ultione*) or in particular for avenging a brother. It also distinguishes killing someone *odii meditatione*, which we might translate as 'premeditated'. It does make a distinction regarding someone's status in assigning a specific kind of penance for killing a monk or a cleric, while referring someone who killed a priest or a bishop to the judgment of the king. It also assigns a penance for someone who killed someone on the king's orders or for killing *in publico bello*, which I read with Guy Halsall as 'in a battle under banner of the king'.[29] Lastly it distinguishes between killing in anger, by accident, through poisoning or by trickery (*per artem aliquam*) or in a brawl. We also see in this text that the author accounted for a form of settlement with the offended party, when, in the first canon of this section, he advised to assign only half the penance in case someone was willing to pay a certain amount of money to the victim's relatives. The term used here, *pecuniam aestimationis*, the estimated price, clearly refers to a particular scale for measuring a person's value, and therefore to a particular wergild.[30]

---

28 For the penitentials connected to Theodore of Canterbury, see Thomas Charles-Edwards, 'The penitential of Theodore and the *Iudicia Theodori*', in: *Archbishop Theodore. Commemorative Studies on his Life and Influence*, ed. Michael Lapidge, Cambridge 1995, 141–174; Roy Flechner, 'The making of the Canons of Theodore', *Peritia* 17/18 (2003), 121–143; and Meens, *Penance*, 89–96.

29 Guy Halsall, *Warfare and society in the barbarian West, 450–900*, London and New York 2003, 17.

30 *Paenitentiale Theodori Discipulus Umbrensium* version, 1.4, ed. Paul Willem Finsterwalder, *Die Canones Theodori Cantuariensis und ihre Überlieferungsformen. Untersuchungen zu den Bußbüchern des 7., 8. und 9. Jahrhunderts* 1, Weimar 1929, 294–295. Canon 1 reads as follows: *Si quis pro ultione propinqui hominem occiderit, peniteat sicut homicida VII vel X annos; si tamen reddere vult propinquis pecuniam aestimationis, levior erit penitentia, id est dimidio spatio.*

The genre of penitential books was probably introduced in Francia in the period that Sichar and Austregisel started their feud in Tours. In 590 the Irish monk Columbanus arrived in Francia and he probably carried some kind of penitential book with him when he arrived.[31] The penitential book that is attributed to this Irish abbot is clearly linked to his foundation in Bobbio where his literary legacy was well preserved. It is based on the Irish penitential book composed in the sixth century by Finnian; therefore we must suppose that Columbanus took texts of this kind with him on his *peregrinatio*. Columban's work explicitly couples ecclesiastical penance with material forms of compensation to the offended parties, as is demonstrated by those canons in which Columbanus deals with offenses of the laity causing major social disruptions. Take canon B 13 discussing the case of manslaughter: Here the text states that if a layman kills someone, he should do penance for three years in exile on bread and water going without arms. After three years he can return to his home rendering the compensation of filial piety and duty to the relatives of the slain. Only after such a satisfaction has been given can he regain access to the altar.[32] If a layman commits adultery and begets a child by another man's wife, so Columbanus continues, he should do penance for three years and refrain from appetizing food and from sexual relations with his own wife. He should, moreover, pay the 'price of chastity' (*praetium pudititiae*) to the husband of

31 For a discussion of Columbanus's penitential, see Raymund Kottje, 'Überlieferung und Rezeption der irischen Bußbücher auf dem Kontinent', in: *Die Iren und Europa im früheren Mittelalter*, ed. Heinz Löwe, vol. 1, Stuttgart 1982, 511–524; Thomas Charles-Edwards, 'The penitential of Columbanus', in: *Columbanus. Studies on the Latin Writings*, ed. Michael Lapidge, Woodbridge 1997, 217–239; Meens, *Penance*, 52–57 and Rob Meens, 'The Irish contribution to the penitential tradition', in: *The Irish in Early Medieval Europe: Identity, Culture and Religion*, ed. Roy Flechner and Sven Meeder, London and New York 2016, 136–137. Donnchádh Ó Corráin, 'The penitential attributed to Columbanus', in: *L'eredità di san Colombano: memoria e culto attraverso il Medioevo: costruire l'Europa: Colombano e la sua eredità = L'héritage de saint Colomban: mémoire et culte au Moyen Âge: construire l'Europe: Colomban et son héritage = Saint Colombanus' legacy: memory and cult in the Middle Ages: making Europe: Columbanus and his legacy*, ed. Eleonora Destafanis, Rennes 2017, 131-146.

32 *Paenitentiale Columbani* B 13, ed. Ludwig Bieler, *The Irish Penitentials* (Scriptores Latini Hiberniae 5), Dublin 1963, 102: *Quicunque fecerit homicidium, id est proximum suum occiderit, III annis inermis exsul in pane et aqua paeniteat et post III annos revertatur in sua reddens vicem parentibus occisi pietatis et officii; et sic post satisfactionem iudicio sacerdotis iungatur altario*. For the clause prescribing serving the parents of the deceased person (*reddens vicem parentibus occisi pietatis et officii*), see Rob Meens, 'Penance, shame and honour in the early Middle Ages', in: *Shame between Punishment and Penance. The Social Uses of Shame in the Middle Ages and Early Modern Times* (Micrologus Library 54), ed. Jörg Wettlaufer and Bénédicte Sère, Florence 2013, 90 and 92–93 and Stefan Jurasinski, *The Old English Penitentials and Anglo-Saxon Law*, Cambridge 2015, 150–171.

the violated wife.[33] If someone commits fornication with an unmarried girl, Columbanus requires that he should pay the price of her humiliation to her relatives.[34] If someone steals a cow from his neighbour, he should restore the loss and should do penance for three periods of 40 days of fasting. If he does so repeatedly or is unable to restore the goods, he should fast for a longer period.[35] When someone sheds blood in a brawl and wounds or maims his neighbour, he has to pay for the damage that he has done; if he is unable to pay, he has to attend the neighbour's work as long as the latter was unable to do so and should seek a doctor. After his victim's recovery, the culprit should do penance for 40 days on bread and water.[36]

So in the penitential of Columbanus, we can observe a variety of forms of compensation offered to the offended party, ranging from fulfilling particular services or restituting damages to paying a form of financial compensation, probably based on the details of material compensation as found in secular legislation. The fact that in many cases Columbanus required some form of satisfaction for the offended party clearly implies that penitential procedures were part of a wider process of reconciliation between two parties, strongly suggesting that the offended party was somehow implicated in the whole penitential process. This combination of doing penance and offering compensation therefore indicates that the priest hearing confession and assigning a specific penance played an intermediary role in settling a conflict.

33 *Paenitentiale Columbani* B 14, ed. Bieler, 102: *Si quis laicus de alterius uxore filium genuerit, id est adulterium commiserit toro proximi sui violato, III annis paeniteat abstinens se a cybis suculentioribus et a propria uxore, dans insuper praetium pudititiae marito uxoris violatae et sic culpa illius per sacerdotem abstergatur*. The term *praetium pudicitiae* is biblical, see Exodus 21.10; see also Joseph D. Pheifer, 'The Canterbury Bible glosses: facts and problems', in: *Archbishop Theodore. Commemorative Studies on his Life and Influence*, ed. Michael Lapidge, Cambridge 1995, 291.

34 *Paenitentiale Columbani* B 16, ed. Bieler, 102: *Si quis autem fornicaverit de laicis cum mulieribus a coniungio liberis, id est viduis vel puellis, si cum vidua, uno anno; si cum puella, duobus annis, reddito tamen humiliationis eius praetio parentibus eius paeniteat …*

35 *Paenitentiale Columbani* B 19, ed. Bieler, 102–104: *Si quis laicus furtum fecerit, id est bovem aut aequum aut ovem aut aliquod animal proximi sui furaverit, si semel aut bis fecit, reddat primum proximo suo dampnum quod fecit et tribus XLmis in pane et aqua peniteat; si autem saepe furtum facere consuevit et reddere non potuerit, anno et III XLmis peniteat et deinceps nequaquam facere promittat et sic in Pascha alterius anni communicet, id est post duos annos, data tamen ante pauperibus de suo labore helemosina et sacerdoti paenitentiam iudicanti epula et ita abremitatur illi malae consuetudinis culpa.*

36 *Paenitentiale Columbani* B 21, ed. Bieler, 104: *Si quis laicorum per scandalum sanguinem fuderit aut proximum suum vulneravit aut debilitaverit, quantum nocuit tantum reddere cogatur; si autem non habet unde solvat, opera proximi sui primum agat quamdiu ille infirmus est medicumque quaerat et post sanitatem eius XL dies in pane et aqua peniteat.*

According to Columbanus, therefore, the compensation for an offense could consist of a whole bundle of acts, including material compensation and/or rendering particular services to the offended party, but also of more purely religious acts, such as fasting and alms. I would like to propose that these more religious acts were not only a way to propitiate God, but were also seen as part of the compensation paid by the offender. This is perhaps most visible in the case of exile. The fact that the culprit had to leave his home country for a long period of time could through its visibility be seen as part of a punishment. Other visible forms of atonement, such as distributing alms and fasting, might also have been regarded as forms of compensation that somehow helped to satisfy the demand for retaliation on the part of the offended party, or the Christian community at large. To see someone not taking part in public festivities and to see someone distributing part of his possessions to the church or the poor might contribute to someone's perception of justice being done. Columbanus ruled, as we have seen, that the adulterer who had conceived a child by somebody else's wife should not only pay the price of chastity to her husband, but should also refrain from certain kinds of food and from sexual relations with his own wife.[37] One might see this abstinence from some kinds of food and from sex as a kind of 'spiritual emasculation', which could help to satisfy a deceived husband's inclinations for physical forms of revenge.

The *Paenitentiale Oxoniense II*, a text possibly written by Willibrord in the first half of the seventh century for use in the region of Frisia, refers twice to the payment of a financial compensation.[38] The first of these concerns manslaughter in peacetime in cases in which the motive was robbery, although the Latin is not easy to follow. It requires that the killer returns the goods of the victim to his wife or children and that he pays 'the price of the blood according to local custom'.[39] This is again stipulated in canon 18 where the Latin, however, raises some interpretative problems. The canon reads as follows:

37 *Paenitentiale Columbani* B 14, ed. Bieler, 102.

38 As I argued in Rob Meens, 'Willibrords boeteboek?', *Tijdschrift voor Geschiedenis* 106 (1993), 163–78; see also Rob Meens, 'Christentum und Heidentum aus der Sicht Willibrords? Überlegungen zum *Paenitentiale Oxoniense II*', in: *L'évangélisation des régions entre Meuse et Moselle et la fondation de l'abbaye d'Echternach* (*V^e–IXe siècle*). *Actes des 10es Journées Lotharingiennes* (Publications de la Section Historique de l'Institut G.-D. de Luxembourg 117), ed. Michel Polfer, Luxemburg 2000, 415–428; and Meens, *Penance*, 102–106.

39 *Paenitentiale Oxoniense II*, c. 6, ed. Raymund Kottje *et al.*, *Paenitentialia minora Franciae et Italiae saeculi VIII–IX*, CC 156, Turnhout 1994, 192: *De homicidium in pace. Si quis autem occiderit hominem in pace et non fuerit turbatus propter homicidii causam aut occansionem aut avaritiae res eius capiat, ille ieiunet ebdomada* XXVIII. *Sic tamen res eius, que occidit, reddat uxori vel filiis eius et praetium sanguinis eius tantum quantum consuetudo loci*

De eos qui nolendo parentibus occidit hominem. Si aliquis nolendo parentibus occidit hominem, det praetium quantum consuetudo est loci ilius et penitentiam egendo ieiunet ebdomada VII.

It is difficult to see what the phrase means. Does the author by using the words 'nolendo parentibus' mean 'against the wishes of his relatives' and is he therefore referring to problems of collective responsibilities? Or does he here discuss the case of killing someone on behalf of one's relatives, as revenge, although the culprit himself was unwilling to take action?[40] Remarkably, the *Oxoniense II* only requires payment of financial compensation in the case of murder, not in the case of adultery or fornication, as Columbanus had done.

A group of later penitential texts, sometimes associated with Columbanian monasticism, elaborated Columbanus's penitential with the help of Merovingian conciliar legislation. This group must have used a common source that could have originated as early as the first half of the seventh century.[41] That common source must have contained Columbanus's clause suggesting that a killer should serve the family of the slain man in compensation for his loss, since it appears in three texts from that group. It is adopted in the *Paenitentiale Burgundense*, probably an eighth century work, and in the *Paenitentiale Parisiense simplex*, a text surviving in a manuscript written in Chelles around the middle of the eighth century.[42] It is also adopted in a penitential that is transmitted in a manuscript in Düsseldorf, which, as Ludger Körntgen has demonstrated, contains a series of canons that is based upon a text belonging to this group but which has been enriched by material taken from the penitential of Columbanus in a process of *relecture*.[43] *The Paenitentiale Bobbiense*,

est, quem occidit sine causa, qui nihil sic Deus requirit quomodo sanguinem hominis, quia secundum imaginem Dei creatus est homo …

40 *Paenitentiale Oxoniense II*, c. 18, ed. Kottje, 195.

41 Meens, *Penance*, 76.

42 *Paenitentiale Burgundense*, c. 1, ed. Kottje, 5: *Si clericus homicidium fecerit et proximum suum occiderit, decem annis exsul peneteat; post hoc recipiatur in patriam. Si bene egerit penitentiam in pane et aqua, testimonio conprobatus episcopi vel sacerdotes, cum quo penetuit et cui commissus fuit, ut satisfaciat parentes eius, que occidit, uicem filii reddit dicens: Quecumque uultis, faciam vobis.Si autem non satisfaceret parentibus illius, numquam recipiatur in patriam, sed more Cain vacuus et profugus sit super terram.*; *Paenitentiale Parisiense simplex*, c. 3, ed. ibidem, 6. The *Paenitentiale Parisiense simplex* survives in Ms. Paris, BNF, lat. 7193, see Kottje, *Paenitentialia minora*, XXXVI.

43 Ludger Körntgen, *Studien zu den Quellen der frühmittelalterlichen Bußbücher* (Quellen und Forschungen zum Recht im Mittelalter 7), Sigmaringen 1993, 216–232; it concerns ms. Düsseldorf, Universitätsbibliothek, B 111 ff. 78r–81v canon 1, f. 78r: *Si quis clericus homicidium fecerit, decem annos exsul paeniteat; post hos recipiatur in patria sua si bene egerit penitentiam in pane et aquam testimonio conprobetur episcopi uel sacerdotis cum quibus*

preserved in a manuscript possibly written as early as the late seventh century, only retains that the killer should give satisfaction to the relatives of the murdered person, but leaves out the details of how to do so.[44] The other five texts of this group do not refer to any form of compensation to the family of the deceased person.[45] It is probably no coincidence that these texts are only preserved in ninth- or tenth-century manuscripts, suggesting that for the compilers of the later texts secular forms of compensation became less important.[46]

This tendency to leave out the requirement to compensate the offended party is exemplified by a number of so-called tripartite penitentials, a group of texts that were composed with the help of a particular set of sources: the penitentials of Theodore and Cummean, as well as a text belonging to the 'simple Frankish penitentials'. The most influential text from this group, as the number of surviving manuscripts indicates, is a text known as the *Excarpsus Cummeani*.[47] This compilation originated in the monastery of Corbie in the years 725–750 and possibly the influential missionary and church reformer Boniface was somehow implicated in its production.[48] The canon from the simple Frankish penitentials, that contains a reference to a murderer in the

---

penituit et cui commissus fuit; et satisfaciat parentibus eius quem occidit et uicem filii reddens et dicens quecumque uultis faciam uobis. Si autem non satisfecerit parentibus eius, numquam recipiatur in patriam sed moriatur; uagus et profugus sit super terram.

44 *Paenitentiale Bobbiense* 1, ed. Kottje, 5: *Si quis clericus humicidium fecerit et proximum suum occiderit, x annus exsol peneteat; post hoc recipiatur in patriam, cui conmisit, satisfaciat parentibus eius, quem occidit.* This text is preserved in Ms. Paris, BNF, lat. 13246 (the so-called Bobbio Missal). For the date of this ms. see Rosamond McKitterick, 'The scripts of the Bobbio Missal', in: *The Bobbio Missal. Liturgy and Religious Culture in Merovingian Gaul*, ed. Yitzhak Hen and Rob Meens, Cambridge 2004, 19–52.

45 These are the *Paenitentiale Sletstatense, Floriacense, Hubertense* and *Sangallense simplex*, ed. Kottje, *Paenitentialia minora*, 6–8.

46 The *Sletstatense* is preserved in ms. Sélestat, Bibliothèque Humaniste, Ms. 2 (Lake Constance 825–850); the *Oxoniense I* in ms. Oxford, Bodleian Library, Bodl. 311 (Northern France 10th century); the *Floriacense*, in ms. Florence, Biblioteca Medicea-Laurenziana, ms. Ashburnham 82 (32) (Western France, Fleury? 850–875); the *Sangallense simplex* in ms. St. Gall, Stiftsbibliothek, Cod.150 (St. Gall 825–850); the *Hubertense* was first edited by Martène and Durand from a ms. in the monastery of St. Hubert in the Ardennes, but that ms. can no longer be identified.

47 Hermann Joseph Schmitz (ed.), *Die Bussbücher und das kanonische Bussverfahren. Nach handschriftlichen Quellen dargestellt*, Düsseldorf 1898 [repr. Graz 1958], 597–644.

48 Ludger Körntgen, 'Der *Excarpsus Cummeani*, ein Bußbuch aus Corbie', in: *Scientia veritatis. Festschrift für Hubert Mordek zum 65. Geburtstag*, ed. Oliver Münsch and Thomas Zotz, Ostfildern 2004, 59–75; for connections with Boniface, see Rob Meens, 'Aspekte der Christianisierung des Volkes', in: *Bonifatius — Leben und Nachwirken. Die Gestaltung des christlichen Europa im Frühmittelalter*, ed. Franz J. Felten, Jörg Jarnut and Lutz von Padberg, Mainz 2007, 211–229 and Meens, *Penance*, 108–109.

service of the relatives of the slain in order to make up for his misdeed, is adopted in such a way as to leave out this whole clause.[49] The *Excarpsus* moreover, merges the two first canons from Theodore's chapter dealing with feuding into one and postpones them from the beginning to a place near the end of the chapter dealing with murder.[50] The requirement to make up for murder by providing material satisfaction to the relatives of the victim in order to diminish the period of penance is thus mentioned, but receives less emphasis.

The *Excarpsus* was reworked at the end of the eighth century in Salzburg, resulting in a text we now know as the *Paenitentiale Vindobonense B*.[51] In this text the *Excarpsus* with its careful selection of sentences was enriched by material taken from other works, one of which was the insular penitential of Finnian, perhaps the earliest text of this genre, originating in the sixth century. Where the *Excarpsus* had edited out many references to the payment of wergild, financial and other forms of compensation were reintroduced in the Salzburg book through inclusion of material from Finnian's penitential. From this early text the compiler included the clause that a murderer should give satisfaction to the friends of the victim and serve his/her parents.[52]

The *Paenitentiale Sangallense tripartitum* was composed in the Northern part of Francia at the end of the eighth century and contains three series of canons based on the work of Columbanus, Theodore and Cummean, respectively. It is a text that thus carefully distinguishes its sources and mirrors a Carolingian preoccupation with unity, diversity and authority. The *Sangallense tripartitum*, although building on the work of Columbanus (via a simple Frankish penitential) and Theodore, leaves out every reference to the forms of compensation mentioned in these works.[53] It does, however, include a canon from Cummean's penitential which demands the payment of the medical costs

---

49 *Excarpsus Cummeani* 6.12, ed.Schmitz, *Die Bussbücher und das kanonische Bussverfahren*, 623: *Si quis clericus homicidium fecerit, X annos peniteat, III exul in pane et aqua.*

50 *Excarpsus Cummeani* 6.27, ed. Schmitz, *Die Bussbücher und das kanonische Bussverfahren*, 625: *Si per vindictam fratris sui hominem occiderit, III annos peniteat, si conponit, dimidio spacio.*

51 See Meens, Rob, 'Kanonisches Recht in Salzburg am Ende des 8. Jahrhunderts. Das Zeugnis des *Paenitentiale Vindobonense B*', ZRG *KA* 82 (1996), 13–34.

52 *Paenitentiale Vindobonense B*, 33.11, ed. Rob Meens, *Het tripartite boeteboek. Overlevering en betekenis van vroegmiddeleeuwse biechtvoorschriften* (*met editie en vertaling van vier* tripartita), Hilversum 1994, 408: *satisfaciat amicis eius quem occiderat et uicem pietatis et oboedientie reddat patri et matri eius si adhuc in corpore sunt et dicat 'Ecce ego uobis pro filio uestro; quecumque dixeritis mihi faciam'*; cf. *Paenitentiale Vinniani*, c. 23, ed. Bieler, 80–82.

53 *Het tripartite boeteboek*, 326–353, see 1.1 and 2.1, ed. Meens, 328 and 336–338.

of an injury as well as of the price of the injury (*maculae praetium*).[54] If we look at the *Paenitentiale Capitula Iudiciorum*, an influential text composed in the second half of the eighth century on the basis of the *Sangallense tripartitum* as well as on the *Excarpsus Cummeani*, again carefully distinguishing the authorities of its sources, we can see that it retains the clauses from the *Excarpsus* about providing satisfaction to the relatives of a murdered person and those requiring payment for the medical indemnities.[55]

The *Paenitentiale Merseburgense A*, a text written sometime between ca. 750 and 850, perhaps in Francia but mainly disseminated in Northern Italy judging from the three surviving manuscripts, adopts the Columbanian clause on murder prescribing satisfaction for the relatives of the victim, but one of the three remaining manuscripts leaves out this particular regulation.[56] That this was not done by accident is demonstrated by the fact that the same manuscript leaves out the requirement to pay the medical costs in the case of an injury.[57] When dealing with revenge killing, this penitential book adopts the sentence from Theodore that paying composition would diminish the period of penance by half, but two of the three manuscripts leave out this sentence.[58]

When bishop Halitgar of Cambrai composed a penitential book that should adhere to new norms of authority as expressed in Carolingian reform circles, he added a sixth book to his collection which he allegedly took from the Roman archives.[59] This sixth book is known as the *Pseudo-Roman Penitential*, because an analysis of its sources has established that this is not a Roman text, but clearly a Frankish one. In this work that Halitgar added to his collection, there is no reference to forms of financial compensation for the family of a killed person. The text does, however, retain Columbanus's clause regarding adultery and the requirement to pay the 'price of chastity' to the deceived husband.[60] In the case of theft, this text also prescribes the return of the stolen goods in order

---

54 *Paenitentiale Sangallense tripartitum* 3.2a, ed. Meens, 342: *Si quis per rixam iactans debilem ac deformem fecerit hominem, reddat inpensas ad medicos et maculae praetium donec sanetur restituat et dimidium annum peniteat.*

55 *Paenitentiale Capitula Iudiciorum* 1.2c, 2.1–2, ed. Meens, 436–438. For the character of this text, see Meens, *Penance*, 111–112.

56 *Paenitentiale Merseburgense A*, c. 1, ed. Kottje, 126; the ms. leaving out this clause is Vienna, Österreichische Nationalbibliothek, lat. 2225.

57 *Paenitentiale Merseburgense A*, c. 24, 40 and 65, ed. Kottje, 132, 137 and 145.

58 *Paenitentiale Merseburgense A*, c. 113, ed. Kottje, 158.

59 For Halitgar's penitential, see Raymund Kottje, *Die Bussbücher Halitgars von Cambrai und des Hrabanus Maurus. Ihre Überlieferung und ihre Quellen*. (Beiträge zur Geschichte und Quellenkunde des Mittelalters 8), Berlin and New York 1980 (cited as Kottje, *Bussbücher*).

60 *Paenitentiale Halitgarii*, Bk 6 (= *Paenitentiale Pseudo-Romanum*), c. 14, ed. Schmitz, *Die Bussbücher und das kanonische Bussverfahren*, 295 (= P. Columbani B 14, see fn. 22).

to lessen the penance.[61] This does not entail the payment of a wergild-like sum, but still strongly suggests that some form of secular settlement accompanied the penitential procedure.

The *Paenitentiale Pseudo-Gregorii*, another text related to Carolingian reform ideals, does not mention payment of compensation to the offended party, but only requires a thief to return his stolen goods.[62] On the other hand, a penitential known as the penitential of Pseudo-Theodore, on the basis of a rather doubtful eleventh- or twelfth-century ascription in one of its manuscripts, and which is also responding to Carolingian penitential ideals, contains many references to material forms of compensation.[63] It contains a number of references to material forms of compensation that we already encountered. It adopts, for example, the sentence regarding fornication with an unmarried woman (*puella*) and requires payment of the price of humiliation to her parents.[64] Furthermore, it contains four canons prescribing payment of a sum of money as compensation for physical injuries, paying medical costs, paying the price of the wound and compensating for a loss of income during a period of sickness.[65] In the case of theft, the thief should return the stolen goods. In the case of frequent theft, however, our text elaborates on the way the thief and victim should be reconciled. It states that the culprit should do penance for seven years, but that the priest has the possibility to modify this sentence if the thief provides satisfaction — the technical term *componere* is used here — for the victim. Moreover, Pseudo-Theodore stipulates that the thief should always seek reconciliation with the victim and should return what he has stolen.[66] The text here seems to refer to a payment of compensation and explicitly demands a form of reconciliation between culprit and victim. Pseudo-Theodore also speaks about wergild when it discusses how a powerful man should make up for his criminal

61 *Paenitentiale Halitgarii*, Bk 6 (= *Paenitentiale Pseudo-Romanum*), c. 28 and 30, ed. Schmitz, *Die Bussbücher und das kanonische Bussverfahren*, 295–296.

62 *Paenitentiale Pseudo-Gregorii*, c. 9, ed. Franz Kerff, 'Das Paenitentiale Pseudo-Gregorii. Eine kritische Edition', in: *Aus Archiven und Bibliotheken. Festschrift für Raymund Kottje zum 65. Geburtstag*, ed. Hubert Mordek, Frankfurt/Main and Bern et al. 1992, 173. For this text, see Franz, Kerff, 'Das Paenitentiale Pseudo-Gregorii III. Ein Zeugnis karolingischer Reformbestrebungen', *ZRG KA* 69 (1983), 46–63 (cited as Kerff, 'Paenitentiale Pseudo-Gregorii'); Meens, *Penance*, 135–136.

63 See Meens, *Penance*, 136.

64 *Paenitentiale Pseudo-Theodori*, c. 10.12, ed. Carine van Rhijn, *Paenitentiale Pseudo-Theodori*, CC 156B, Turnhout 2009, 12.

65 *Paenitentiale Pseudo-Theodori*, c. 15.23, 26–27, 38 and 41, ed. van Rhijn, 41 and 43.

66 *Paenitentiale Pseudo-Theodori*, c. 17.3–4; c. 4 reads as follows: *Qui sepe furtum fecerit, vii annos peniteat, uel ut sacerdos iudicat iuxta quod componi potest quibus nocuit, et semper debet reconciliare ei quem offendebat, et restituere iuxta quod nocuit ...*, ed. van Rhijn, 48.

sins. Such a person should follow the example of Zacchaeus who gave half of his possessions to the poor and provided fourfold compensation for what he had stolen (Lk 19. 8–9). If, however, it was impossible to return the stolen goods or to give half of his property to the poor, as Zacchaeus had done, the powerful man should give at least his *wera geditii* to the poor and some of his land to the Church and he should release some of his serfs and redeem captives. The term *wera geditii* is remarkable here and the variant readings in other manuscripts indicate that it must stand for the person's wergild. There it is found as *suimet pretium* or *suum ueregeldum* (or *suum uueregildum*).[67] This is an indication that the compiler of this text was familiar with rulings about wergild and did not hesitate to include the practice when judging sins.

The penitential attributed to archbishop Egbert of York may well be an Anglo-Saxon text that was introduced in Francia at the end of the eighth century. When dealing with major forms of theft it states that the culprit should pay 'the price' (*pretium*), or else should do penance twice as long.[68] It is unclear if this is a reference to the value of what was stolen or refers to clauses in law codes demanding payment of a particular sum of money for such a crime. This is the only reference to payment of a secular nature in this text. In cases of killing or maiming someone, as well as in the case of adultery, providing material compensation to the victim or his relatives is not mentioned. The penitential attributed to Egbert was gradually combined with a text attributed to Bede, in a process of which we can still discern a number of intermediate stages.[69] The latter text did contain two clauses demanding, in the case of violent behaviour that resulted in physical harm, payment of a price for the wounds and a compensation for the time someone was unable to function.[70] These clauses were retained in the process by which these two texts were merged finally into a new one, a text we call the *Paenitentiale Pseudo Bedae-Egberti mixtum*.[71] In the case of theft, we find here the interesting addition stating that the thief should

67 *Paenitentiale Pseudo-Theodori*, c. 49.13, ed. van Rhijn, 123.

68 *Paenitentiale Egberti* c. 10.3, ed. Schmitz, *Die Bussbücher und das kanonische Bussverfahren*, 669: *Item si quis furtum capitale comiserit, id est quadrupedia vel domos effregerit, si laici unum annum peniteant et pretium reddant vel duobus annis poeniteat.*

69 Carefully analysed in Reinhold Haggenmüller, *Die Überlieferung der Beda und Egbert zugeschriebenen Bußbücher*, Frankfurt/Main and Bern et al. 1991.

70 *Paenitentiale Pseudo-Bedae*, c. 8, ed. Schmitz, *Die Bussbücher und das kanonische Bussverfahren*, 657: *Qui per rixam ictu debilem vel deformem hominem reddidit, inpensat in medicum et macule pretium et opus eius donec sanetur*; c. 10: *Quod et si eum vulneravit, XL dies, si clericus, annum totum, sed et pecuniam pro modo vulneris cui inflixit tribuat.*

71 *Paenitentiale mixtum Pseudo-Bedae Egberti*, c. 13.1 and 31.1, ed. Schmitz, *Die Bussbücher und das kanonische Bussverfahren*, 690 and 695.

pay 'the price or such as the priest decides', suggesting an intermediary or arbitrating role of the priest in the settlement with the offended party.

The analysis of the clauses demanding a form of material compensation for acts of violence, adultery and theft that we find in penitential books circulating in Francia from the period of Columbanus to the ninth century shows, therefore, a certain tendency, which certainly can be refined through further research. Columbanus's penitential, the earliest text of this kind to be introduced in Francia, is remarkable for its almost systematic inclusion of different techniques of secular dispute settlement in a penitential context. It demanded not only the return of stolen goods or the payment of a 'price of chastity' or a 'price of humiliation' in cases of sexual offenses, but also insisted on the payment of medical costs, a material compensation for the period of illness caused by an injury, and even on providing personal service for the victim's parents. As we have seen, most of these regulations were adopted in later penitential books, but the theme of offering material compensation to a victim or his or her relatives was not further elaborated. On the contrary, we can observe a tendency for these regulations to peter out. As we have seen, the parts demanding forms of material compensation for sinful behaviour that damaged other members of the community are sometimes left out when using such sentences in a new compilation to establish the proper scale of penance. Sometimes, as we have seen with regard to the *Paenitentiale Merseburgense A*, such parts were edited out in the process of copying a text. One can conclude that forms of material compensation became less evident and less important in later penitential books composed in Francia. They certainly did not disappear altogether and we have seen instances of their application throughout the ninth century, but they were no longer as systematically applied in a penitential setting as had been foreseen by Columbanus.

3 Conclusions

How can we explain this fading out of the importance of material forms of compensation that we can observe in penitential books of the later eighth and ninth centuries? There is no evident answer to this question, but some important features of Carolingian religious and social history should be taken into account and may help to explain this change, at a moment when we can observe that terms belonging to the realm of ecclesiastical penance were often used in judicial acts.[72] First of all it should be noticed that penitential books

72 For the employment of penitential language in judicial records, see Jégou, *L'évêque, juge de paix*, 251.

continue to include payments of composition in their rulings, suggesting that confessors continued to play a role in conflict settlement. Further we should note that there is no simple answer to the question why some texts include such features and others leave them out. Penance and confession seem to have changed in character from the time of Columbanus to that of Charlemagne and his successors. In the earlier period, penance was not a regular feature of the life of a Christian layman or woman. It was a means to reconcile oneself with God and the community in cases of serious sins, such as murder or adultery, which threatened the social fabric and could result in major public turmoil. Such a context would very well explain the emphasis on secular forms of compensation that we encounter in the penitential of Columbanus. In the texts from the Carolingian period we come across more sins that have no social repercussions, for example forms of sexual behaviour between spouses that were denounced as sinful. The treatment of such sins suggests that hearing confession and assigning penance increasingly became a part of regular Christian life. In the Carolingian era we see that confessing one's sins was linked to receiving the Eucharist, which Christians did between once and thrice a year, on the major feast days.[73] Such a standardized form of confession was perhaps less appropriate for dealing with critical social problems than a confession that was ignited by a critical situation or a radical personal conversion.

In the early ninth century, penance also became a matter of debate within the Carolingian Church. Two major issues were being raised during Carolingian councils: one concerned the authority of the books used in hearing confession, the other the proper ways of doing penance (in secret or publicly). The latter issue led to a rule stating that secret sins could be absolved in secret, but that public sins should be atoned for in a public penitential ritual.[74] Although one may wonder how effective this rule was in practice and who was to decide what was public and what was not, it does suggest that sins causing major social divisions, could be dealt with in a different way, by bishops using their episcopal authority and insisting on public forms of satisfaction, instead of by clerics mediating in conflicts by requesting material and spiritual forms of compensation. The issue of the questionable authority of penitential books that was raised in some early ninth-century councils might also relate to a greater stress on episcopal authority. The Carolingian reform penitentials written by Halitgar of Cambrai and Hrabanus Maurus or the *Paenitentiale Pseudo-Gregorii*, which is also reckoned among these reform penitentials, do not refer to material forms

73 Meens, *Penance*, 138–139.

74 See the discussion in Meens, *Penance*, 118–123.

of compensation for an offended party.[75] For the authors of these texts only 'proper canon law' counted, that is conciliar decisions, papal letters or texts by the Church Fathers. In such texts, material forms of compensation paid to any offended party are nowhere addressed. The greater emphasis on canon law proper, although such exclusivity could hardly be maintained by the reformers themselves, would explain the diminishing emphasis put on the payment of wergild and similar procedures in the texts related to the Carolingian reforms.

These developments should be seen against the background of Charlemagne and his court making new claims about royal power and its efforts to control private forms of violence within the realm. Charlemagne promoted the need to accept compensation for injuries and prohibited forms of violent self-help in such cases.[76] He thus legislated against *faida*, a term he used for what we might call a feud.[77] By doing so, he emphasized royal authority in settling violent disputes and this attitude might have led to a waning of clerical forms of dispute settlement with the help of penance and confession, if it were not in the hands of royal agents such as bishops. Yet one may wonder on the basis of which legislation or what kind of rules bishops and other magnates settled issues such as adultery or murder. We do not know which texts in particular were used in the context of a judicial case. Were the Lex Salica and royal capitularies the main forms of authority? Were they supplemented by ecclesiastical legislation? If we look at particular tenth-century manuscripts, we see that canon law texts, secular legislation and penitential books are regularly combined in a single codex.[78] We need to study such manuscripts in more detail in order to understand how they were applied and how the different kinds of text that we find in them relate to one another.

75 For the penitentials compiled by Halitgar and Hrabanus Maurus see Kottje, *Bussbücher*; for the pseudo-Gregory penitential, see Kerff, 'Paenitentiale Pseudo-Gregorii'.

76 See in general Brown, *Violence*, chapter 3: 'Charlemagne, God, and the license to kill', 69–96 and Jégou, *L'evêque, juge de paix*, 163.

77 *Capitulare Haristallense*, a. 779, c. 22, ed. Alfred Boretius, MGH Capitularia regum Francorum 1, Hanover 1883, 51; *Admonitio Generalis*, c. 66, ed. Hubert Mordek, Klaus Zechiel-Eckes and Michael Glatthaar, *Die Admonitio generalis Karls des Großen*, MGH Fontes Iuris Germanici Antiqui in usum scholarum separatim editi 16, Hanover 2012, 218; *Capitulare Missorum in Theodonis villa datum*, a. 805, c. 5, ed. Boretius, MGH Capit. 1, 123.

78 For example, Heiligenkreuz, Stiftsbibliothek, Hs. 217 (late 10th century), containing conciliar legislation, the collection of capitularies compiled by Ansegisus, and a number of penitential books; related mss. of a similar kind: Munich, Bayerische Staatsbibliothek, Clm 3853 (2nd half of 10th century); Paris, BnF, lat. 3878 (late 10th century); Münster, Staatsarchiv, Msc. VII 5201(10th century) with a similar content; see also Stuttgart, Württembergische Landesbibliothek, HB VI 112 (10th century). For the heterogeneous composition of legal manuscripts, see Jégou, *L'évêque, juge de paix*, 44.

The Carolingians employed a ritual language of political discourse in which penitential elements were of central importance. We only need to think of Louis the Pious who employed the ritual of public penance twice in two totally different political settings.[79] Gerd Althoff and Geoffrey Koziol have demonstrated the importance of religious elements in rituals of submission and reconciliation for a later period. This strongly suggests that confession and penance were not separated from social and political life in general and that the religious, political and social spheres were closely intertwined. The less systematic use of material forms of compensation in Carolingian penitential books, therefore, was not the result of a greater separation of the religious and secular spheres. Possibly, however, it was the result of an effort to control such processes.

However, although the topic of compensation to the offended party is less prominent in later penitential handbooks, the combination of secular and ecclesiastical legislation and of handbooks for penance in a single manuscript strongly suggests that in the tenth century bishops continued to play a crucial role in conflict settlement, just like their predecessor Gregory of Tours had done in the feud between Sichar and Chramnesind. Whether we can assume priestly or episcopal involvement in conflict resolution also for the late eighth and ninth centuries remains an intriguing puzzle. Yet the fact that penitential books retain clauses demanding other forms of reconciliation besides doing penance, some more emphatically than others, indicates that bishops and priests acted as conflict mediators throughout the early medieval period. At least when reading their penitential handbooks, bishops and priests were incited to think about ways to reconcile their feuding fellow Christians and we can be sure that this will have had some effect on their actual behaviour when they were confronted with such disputes.

Bibliography

Manuscripts

Düsseldorf, Universitätsbibliothek, B 111
Heiligenkreuz, Stiftsbibliothek, Hs. 217
Munich, Bayerische Staatsbibliothek, Clm 3853
Münster, Staatsarchiv, Msc. VII 5201
Paris, BnF, lat. 3878
Stuttgart, Württembergische Landesbibliothek, HB VI 112

79 See Mayke de Jong, *The Penitential State. Authority and Atonement in the Age of Louis the Pious, 814–840*, Cambridge 2009; and Courtney Booker, *Past Convictions. The Penance of Louis the Pious and the Decline of the Carolingians*, Philadelphia 2009.

Primary Sources

Admonitio Generalis, ed. Hubert Mordek, Klaus Zechiel-Eckes and Michael Glatthaar, *Die Admonitio generalis Karls des Großen*, MGH Fontes iuris Germanici antiqui in usum scholarum separatim editi 16, Hanover 2012.

Capitulare Haristallense a. 779, ed. Alfred Boretius, MGH Capitularia regum Francorum 1, Hanover 1883, 46–51.

Capitulare Missorum in Theodonis villa datum, a. 805, c. 5, ed. Alfred Boretius, MGH Capitularia regum Francorum 1, Hanover 1883, 121–126.

Excarpsus Cummeani, ed. Hermann Joseph Schmitz, *Die Bussbücher und das kanonische Bussverfahren. Nach handschriftlichen Quellen dargestellt*, Düsseldorf 1898 [repr. Graz 1958], 597–644.

Formulae Salicae Lindenbrogianae, ed. Karl Zeumer, MGH Formulae Merowingici et Karolini aevi, Hanover 1886, 265–282.

Gregory of Tours, *Decem Libri Historiarum*, ed. Bruno Krusch and Wilhelm Levison, MGH SS rerum Merovingicarum 1, 1, Hanover 1951.

Gregory of Tours, *History of the Franks*. Translated by Ormonde M. Dalton, Oxford 1927.

Marculfi Formulae, ed. Karl Zeumer, MGH Formulae Merowingici et Karolini aevi, Hanover 1886, 32–106.

Paenitentiale Burgundense, ed. Raymund Kottje et al., *Paenitentialia minora Franciae et Italiae saeculi VIII–IX*, CC 156, Turnhout 1994, 61–65.

Paenitentiale Bobbiense, ed. Raymund Kottje et al., *Paenitentialia minora Franciae et Italiae saeculi VIII–IX*, CC 156, Turnhout 1994, 66–71.

Paenitentiale Capitula Iudiciorum, ed. Rob Meens, *Het tripartite boeteboek. Overlevering en betekenis van vroegmiddeleeuwse biechtvoorschriften* (*met editie en vertaling van vier* tripartita), Hilversum 1994, 434–485.

Paenitentiale Columbani, ed. Ludwig Bieler, *The Irish Penitentials* (Scriptores Latini Hiberniae 5), Dublin 1963, 96–107.

Paenitentiale Egberti, ed. Hermann Joseph Schmitz, *Die Bussbücher und das kanonische Bussverfahren. Nach handschriftlichen Quellen dargestellt*, Düsseldorf 1898 [repr. Graz 1958], 661–674.

Paenitentiale Floriacense, ed. Raymund Kottje et al., *Paenitentialia minora Franciae et Italiae saeculi VIII–IX*, CC 156, Turnhout 1994, 95–103.

Paenitentiale Halitgarii, Bk 3–6 (= *Paenitentiale Pseudo-Romanum*), ed. Hermann Joseph Schmitz, *Die Bussbücher und das kanonische Bussverfahren. Nach handschriftlichen Quellen dargestellt*, Düsseldorf 1898 [repr. Graz 1958], 252–300.

Paenitentiale Hubertense, ed. Raymund Kottje et al., *Paenitentialia minora Franciae et Italiae saeculi VIII–IX*, CC 156, Turnhout 1994, 105–115.

Paenitentiale Merseburgense A, ed. Raymund Kottje et al., *Paenitentialia minora Franciae et Italiae saeculi VIII–IX*, CC 156, Turnhout 1994, 123–169.

Paenitentiale Oxoniense I, ed. Raymund Kottje et al., *Paenitentialia minora Franciae et Italiae saeculi VIII–IX*, CC 156, Turnhout 1994, 87–93.

Paenitentiale Oxoniense II, c. 6 ed. Raymund Kottje et al., *Paenitentialia minora Franciae et Italiae saeculi VIII–IX*, CC 156, Turnhout 1994, 179–205.

Paenitentiale Parisiense simplex, ed. Raymund Kottje et al., *Paenitentialia minora Franciae et Italiae saeculi VIII–IX*, CC 156, Turnhout 1994, 73–79.

Paenitentiale Pseudo-Bedae, ed. Hermann Joseph Schmitz, *Die Bussbücher und das kanonische Bussverfahren. Nach handschriftlichen Quellen dargestellt*, Düsseldorf 1898 [repr. Graz 1958], 654–659.

Paenitentiale mixtum Pseudo-Bedae Egberti, ed. Hermann Joseph Schmitz, *Die Bussbücher und das kanonische Bussverfahren. Nach handschriftlichen Quellen dargestellt*, Düsseldorf 1898 [repr. Graz 1958], 679–701.

Paenitentiale Pseudo-Gregorii, c. 9, ed. Franz Kerff, 'Das Paenitentiale Pseudo-Gregorii. Eine kritische Edition', in: *Aus Archiven und Bibliotheken. Festschrift für Raymund Kottje zum 65. Geburtstag*, ed. Hubert Mordek, Frankfurt/Main and Bern et al. 1992, 161–188.

Paenitentiale Pseudo-Theodori, ed. Carine van Rhijn, *Paenitentiale Pseudo-Theodori*, CC 156B, Turnhout 2009.

Paenitentiale Sangallense simplex, ed. Raymund Kottje et al., *Paenitentialia minora Franciae et Italiae saeculi VIII–IX*, CC 156, Turnhout 1994, 117–121.

Paenitentiale Sangallense tripartitum, ed. Rob Meens, *Het tripartite boeteboek. Overlevering en betekenis van vroegmiddeleeuwse biechtvoorschriften* (*met editie en vertaling van vier* tripartita), Hilversum 1994, 326–353.

Paenitentiale Sletstatense, ed. Raymund Kottje et al., *Paenitentialia minora Franciae et Italiae saeculi VIII–IX*, CC 156, Turnhout 1994, 81–85.

Paenitentiale Theodori Discipulus Umbrensium version, ed. Paul Willem Finsterwalder, *Die Canones Theodori Cantuariensis und ihre Überlieferungsformen* (Untersuchungen zu den Bußbüchern des 7., 8. und 9. Jahrhunderts 1), Weimar 1929, 285–334.

Paenitentiale Vindobonense B, 33.11, ed. Rob Meens, *Het tripartite boeteboek. Overlevering en betekenis van vroegmiddeleeuwse biechtvoorschriften* (*met editie en vertaling van vier tripartita*), Hilversum 1994, 354–433.

Paenitentiale Vinniani, ed. Ludwig Bieler, *The Irish Penitentials* (Scriptores Latini Hiberniae 5), Dublin 1963, 74–95.

The Formularies of Angers and Marculf. Two Merovingian Legal Handbooks. Translated by Alice Rio (Translated Texts for Historians 46), Liverpool 2008.

Secondary Works

Andersen, Per, Helle Møller Sigh and Helle Vogt (ed.), *Law and Disputing in the Middle Ages. Proceedings of the Ninth Carlsberg Academy Conference on Medieval Legal History 2012*, Copenhagen 2013.

Auerbach, Erich, *Mimesis. The Representation of Reality in Western Literature*, trans. Willard R. Trask, Princeton 2003.

Barthélemy, Dominique, François Bougard and Régine Le Jan (ed.), *La vengeance 400–1200* (Collection de l'École française de Rome 357), Rome 2006.

Bossy, John (ed.), *Disputes and Settlements: Law and Human Relations in the West*, Cambridge, 1983.

Brown, Peter, 'The Rise and function of the holy man in Late Antiquity', *Journal of Roman Studies* 61 (1971), 80–101 [repr. in Brown, Peter, *Society and the Holy in Late Antiquity*, Berkeley and Los Angeles 1982, 103–152].

Brown, Peter, 'The Rise and Function of the holy man in Late Antiquity, 1971–1997', *Journal of Early Christian Studies* 6 (1998), 463–484.

Charles-Edwards, Thomas, 'The penitential of Theodore and the *Iudicia Theodori*', in: *Archbishop Theodore. Commemorative Studies on his Life and Influence*, ed. Michael Lapidge, Cambridge 1995, 141–174.

Charles-Edwards, Thomas, 'The penitential of Columbanus', in: *Columbanus. Studies on the Latin Writings*, ed. Michael Lapidge, Woodbridge 1997, 217–239.

Davies, Wendy and Paul Fouracre (ed.), *The Settlement of Disputes in Early Medieval Europe*, Cambridge 1986.

Depreux, Phillippe, 'Une faide exemplaire? À propos des aventures de Sichaire: vengeance et pacification aux temps mérovingiens', in: *La vengeance 400–1200* (Collection de l'École française de Rome 357), ed. Dominique Barthélemy, François Bougard and Régine Le Jan, Rome 2006, 65–85.

Diem, Albrecht, 'Monks, kings, and the transformation of sanctity: Jonas of Bobbio and the end of the holy man', *Speculum* 82/3 (2007), 521–559.

Diesselhorst, Malte, 'Die Fehde von Sichar und Chramnesind, erzählt von Gregor von Tours', in: *Libertas: grundrechtliche und rechtsstaatliche Gewährungen in Antike und Gegenwart; Symposion aus Anlass des 80. Geburtstages von Franz Wieacker*, ed. Okko Behrends and Malte Diesselhorst, Ebelsbach 1991, 187–208.

Flechner, Roy, 'The making of the Canons of Theodore', *Peritia* 17/18 (2003), 121–143.

Garnier, Claudia and Hermann Kamp (ed.), *Spielregeln der Mächtigen. Mittelalterliche Politik zwischen Gewohnheit und Konvention*, Darmstadt 2010.

Geary, Patrick, 'Gabriel Monod, Fustel de Coulanges et les "aventures de Sichaire". La naissance de l'histoire scientifique au XIXe siècle', in: *La vengeance 400–1200* (Collection de l'École française de Rome 357), ed. Dominique Barthélemy, François Bougard and Régine Le Jan, Rome 2006, 87–99.

Gluckman, Max, 'The Peace in the Feud', *Past and Present* 8 (1955), 1–14.

Goetz, Hans-Werner, 'Spielregeln, politische Rituale und symbolische Kommunikation in der Merowingerzeit', in: *Spielregeln der Mächtigen. Mittelalterliche Politik zwischen Gewohnheit und Konvention*, ed. Claudia Garnier and Hermann Kamp, Darmstadt 2010, 33–59.

Haggenmüller, Reinhold, *Die Überlieferung der Beda und Egbert zugeschriebenen Bußbücher*, Frankfurt/Main and Bern et al. 1991.

Halsall, Guy, *Violence and Society in the Early Medieval West*, Woodbridge 1998.

Heinzelmann, Martin, *Gregor von Tours (538–594). 'Zehn Bücher Geschichte'. Historiographie und Gesellschaftskonzept im 6. Jahrhundert*, Darmstadt 1994.

Howard-Johnston, James and Hayward, Paul (ed.), *The Cult of Saints in Late Antiquity and the Middle Ages. Essays on the Contribution of Peter Brown*, Oxford 1999.

Humfress, Caroline, 'Bishops and law courts in Late Antiquity: How (not) to make sense of the legal evidence', *Journal of Early Christian Studies* 19 (2011), 375–400.

Hyams, Paul, *Rancor and Reconciliation in Medieval England*, Ithaca and London 2003.

James, Edward, '"Beati Pacifici": Bishops and the Law in Sixth-Century Gaul', in: *Disputes and Settlements. Law and Human Relations in the West*, ed. John Bossy, Cambridge 1983, 25–46.

Jégou, Laurent, *L'évêque, juge de paix. L'autorité épiscopale et le règlement des conflits (VIIIe–XIe siècle)*, Turnhout 2011.

Jong, Mayke de, *The Penitential State. Authority and Atonement in the Age of Louis the Pious, 814–840*, Cambridge 2009.

Jurasinski, Stefan, *The Old English Penitentials and Anglo-Saxon Law*, Cambridge 2015.

Kerff, Franz, 'Das Paenitentiale Pseudo-Gregorii III. Ein Zeugnis karolingischer Reformbestrebungen', *ZRG KA* 69 (1983), 46–63.

Körntgen, Ludger, *Studien zu den Quellen der frühmittelalterlichen Bußbücher* (Quellen und Forschungen zum Recht im Mittelalter 7), Sigmaringen 1993.

Körntgen, Ludger, 'Der *Excarpsus Cummeani*, ein Bußbuch aus Corbie', in: *Scientia veritatis. Festschrift für Hubert Mordek zum 65. Geburtstag*, ed. Oliver Münsch and Thomas Zotz, Ostfildern 2004, 59–75.

Kottje, Raymund, *Die Bussbücher Halitgars von Cambrai und des Hrabanus Maurus. Ihre Überlieferung und ihre Quellen* (Beiträge zur Geschichte und Quellenkunde des Mitttelalters 8), Berlin and New York 1980.

Kottje, Raymund, 'Überlieferung und Rezeption der irischen Bußbücher auf dem Kontinent', in: *Die Iren und Europa im früheren Mittelalter* 1, ed. Heinz Löwe, Stuttgart 1982, 511–524.

La giustizia nell'alto medieovo (secoli V–VIII) (Settimane di Studio del Centro Italiano di Studi sull'Alto Medioevo 42), Spoleto 1995.

La giustizia nell'alto medioevo (secoli IX–XI) (Settimane di Studio del Centro Italiano di Studi sull'Alto Medioevo 44), Spoleto 1997.

Lambert, Thomas and Rollason, David (ed.), *Peace and Protection in the Middle Ages*, Durham and Toronto 2009.

McKitterick, Rosamond, 'The scripts of the Bobbio Missal', in: *The Bobbio Missal. Liturgy and Religious Culture in Merovingian Gaul*, ed. Yitzhak Hen and Rob Meens, Cambridge 2004, 19–52.

Meens, Rob, 'Willibrords boeteboek?', *Tijdschrift voor Geschiedenis* 106 (1993), 163–78.

Meens, Rob, 'Kanonisches Recht in Salzburg am Ende des 8. Jahrhunderts. Das Zeugnis des *Paenitentiale Vindobonense B*', ZRG KA 82 (1996), 13–34.

Meens, Rob, 'The Frequency and Nature of early Medieval Penance', in: *Handling Sin: Confession in the Middle Ages* (York Studies in Medieval Theology 2), ed. Peter Biller, Alistair J. Minnis, Woodbridge, 1998, 35–61.

Meens, Rob, 'Christentum und Heidentum aus der Sicht Willibrords? Überlegungen zum *Paenitentiale Oxoniense II*', in: *L'évangélisation des régions entre Meuse et Moselle et la fondation de l'abbaye d'Echternach* (*V*^e^–*IX*^e^ *siècle*). Actes des 10es Journées Lotharingiennes (Publications de la Section Historique de l'Institut G.-D. de Luxembourg 117), ed. Michel Polfer, Luxemburg 2000, 415–428.

Meens, Rob, 'Aspekte der Christianisierung des Volkes', in: *Bonifatius — Leben und Nachwirken. Die Gestaltung des christlichen Europa im Frühmittelalter*, ed. Franz J. Felten, Jörg Jarnut and Lutz von Padberg, Mainz 2007, 211–229.

Meens, Rob, 'The sanctity of the basilica of St. Martin. Gregory of Tours and the practice of sanctuary in the Merovingian period', in: *Texts and Identities in the early Middle Ages*, ed. Richard Corradini, Rob Meens, Christina Pössel and Philip Shaw, Vienna 2006, 277–287.

Meens, Rob, 'Sanctuary, penance and dispute settlement under Charlemagne. The conflict between Alcuin and Theodulf of Orléans over a sinful cleric', *Speculum* 82/2 (2007), 277–300.

Meens, Rob, 'Penance, shame and honour in the early Middle Ages', in: *Shame between Punishment and Penance. The Social Uses of Shame in the Middle Ages and Early Modern Times* (Micrologus Library 54), ed. Bénédicte Sère and Jörg Wettlaufer, Florence 2013, 89–102.

Meens, Rob, *Penance in Medieval Europe, 600–1200*, Cambridge 2014.

Meens, Rob, 'The Irish contribution to the penitential tradition', in: *The Irish in Early Medieval Europe: Identity, Culture and Religion*, ed. Roy Flechner and Sven Meeder, London and New York 2016, 131–145.

Netterstrøm, J. Büchert and Bjørn Poulsen (ed.), *Feud in Medieval and Early Modern Europe*, Aarhus 2007.

Patzold, Steffen and Carine Van Rhijn (ed.), *Men in the Middle. Local Priests in Early Medieval Europe*, Berlin 2016.

Pheifer, Joseph D., 'The Canterbury Bible glosses: facts and problems', in: *Archbishop Theodore. Commemorative Studies on his Life and Influence*, ed. Michael Lapidge, Cambridge 1995, 281–333.

Rapp, Claudia, *Holy bishops in Late Antiquity. The Nature of Christian Leadership in an Age of Transition*, Berkeley, Los Angeles and London 2005.

Rio, Alice, *Legal Practice and the Written Word in the Early Middle Ages. Frankish Formulae, c. 500–1000*, Cambridge 2009.

Sawyer, Peter, 'The bloodfeud in fact and fiction', in: *Tradition og historieskrivning. Kilderne til Nordens ældste historie* (Acta Iutlandica 63/2), ed. Kirsten Hastrup and Preben Meulengracht Sørensen, Aarhus 1987, 27–38.

Uhalde, Kevin, *Expectations of Justice in the Age of Augustine*, Philadelphia 2007.

Wallace-Hadrill, Michael, 'The Bloodfeud of the Franks', in: idem, *The Long-Haired Kings*, London 1962, 121–147.

Whitelock, Dorothy, *The Beginnings of English Society*, Harmondsworth 1952.

Wood, Ian, '"The bloodfeud of the Franks": a historiographical myth', *Early Medieval Europe* 14 (2006), 489–504.

CHAPTER 10

The Limits of Government: Wergild and Legal Reforms under Charlemagne

Karl Ubl

The anniversary of Charlemagne's death has set off an avalanche of new studies on the history of his reign.[1] Considering the dominant role of Germany in the politics of the European Union in the present day, it is only fitting that this avalanche took place mainly in Germany.[2] It is here that Charlemagne was widely celebrated as a founding father of European History. If I had to identify a dominant trait of these new studies of Charlemagne, I would point to the narratives of heroization which still structure the characterization of his greatness. A fitting example is Johannes Fried's book on 'Karl der Große. Glaube und Gewalt'.[3] Fried claims that the existence of the Frankish empire was rendered possible solely by the combination of violence and fanatic religious belief anchored in the personality of Charlemagne — a corollary being that his empire fell as soon as his incompetent and lenient son came to power. Fried also claims that Charlemagne shaped the literary culture and theological debates taking place in his court, impressing his personal opinions on his contemporaries in most respects.

A similar heroization is present in Stefan Weinfurter's book 'Karl der Große. Heiliger und Barbar'.[4] In his view, Charlemagne is not (as with Fried) a tragic warrior in the timeless battle between violence and morality, but rather a proponent of a whole new theory of power, based on the idea of 'unambiguousness' (*Eindeutigkeit*), which he brought to bear on every aspect of life: culture, education, law-giving, religion, and politics. The idea of unambiguousness was obstructed by his unwilling and resentful aristocracy, but then became — according to Weinfurter — one of the corner-stones of European modernity

---

1 I would like to thank Courtney Booker and Jennifer Davis for helpful comments and suggestions on drafts of this essay. The paper was completed in 2016. Publications after this date are included only occasionally.

2 For a survey of the activities during the anniversary cf. Karl Ubl, 'Karl der Große und die Rückkehr des Gottesstaates. Narrative der Heroisierung für das Jahr 2014', *Historische Zeitschrift* 301 (2015), 374–390.

3 Johannes Fried, *Karl der Große: Gewalt und Glaube. Eine Biographie*, Munich 2013.

4 Stefan Weinfurter, *Karl der Große: Der Heilige Barbar*, Munich 2013.

 | DOI:10.1163/9789004466128_011

and rationality. Horst Bredekamp's book on 'Der schwimmende Souverän'[5] follows a similar trajectory. Bredekamp also detects a new theory of power in Charlemagne's actions, based on the idea of 'fluidity', which he traces through the works of art still present in the Aachener Marienkirche, and which supposedly lies at the core of the emperor's idea of power and domination.

Unambiguousness and fluidity — it is hard to conceive of more opposed ideas of power. In these heroic narratives, we hear nothing of competing power brokers at court, nothing of anticipations and expectations shaping the actions of Charlemagne's peers, nothing of the rivalry between nobles and royal offspring influencing the decisions of the emperor, nothing of traditions and local customs that Charlemagne had to respect and honour, nothing of favourable circumstances which were out of his control, but decisive for his success. Reading these new studies is like looking into a magnifying glass: the centre is enlarged and distinctly visible, while its surroundings are blurred and overlapping.

This magnified image of Charlemagne, however, does not fit well with what we know about the implementation of his legal reforms. Einhard already had some difficulties in matching Charlemagne's greatness with the failure he diagnosed regarding his attempt at legal reforms. Einhard famously wrote:

> After he received the imperial name, he realized that his people's laws were deficient in many ways, for the Franks had two laws, which differed sharply in many respects. He resolved to supply whatever was lacking, to reconcile the differences, and to correct whatever was badly or even falsely promulgated. But of this plan nothing else was done by him except that he added a few chapters to the laws, and these were incomplete. Still, he did command that the unwritten laws of all the peoples under his authority be written down.[6]

The subject of law apparently does not lend itself easily to the narratives of heroization. It therefore comes as no surprise that Charlemagne's legal reforms do not figure prominently in the new biographies of the anniversary of 2014.

5 Horst Bredekamp, *Der schwimmende Souverän: Karl der Große und die Bildpolitik des Körpers. Eine Studie zum schematischen Bildakt* (Kleine Kulturwissenschaftliche Bibliothek 86), Berlin 2014.

6 Einhard, *Vita Karoli Magni* 29, ed. Oswald Holder-Egger, MGH SS rerum Germanicarum in usum scholarum separatim editi 25, Hanover and Leipzig 1911, 33; Thomas F. X. Noble., *Charlemagne and Louis the Pious. Lives by Einhard, Notker, Ermoldus, Thegan, and the Astronomer. Translated, with Introductions and Annotations*, University Park 2009, 44.

The seminal studies of the great François Louis Ganshof are conspicuously absent from the bibliography of these books.

In her new magisterial book on 'Charlemagne's Practice of Empire' Jennifer Davis demonstrates that the fuzziness of legal sources seems compatible with a narrative of heroization.[7] Davis follows the footsteps of Ganshof and acknowledges the heterogeneous and often chaotic nature of the Carolingian capitularies, pointing to their contradictory instructions on military service and to the unclear and overlapping deployment of functionaries. Yet, she does not consider these issues as deficiencies on the part of Charlemagne, but rather as a 'pragmatic approach to governance' which created a feeling of unpredictability among his subjects and hence was instrumental in fostering a constant reassurance of royal control. According to Davis, Charlemagne did not aim at unification or regularity. He pursued generic goals like the salvation of his subjects, royal dominance, community-building and the restructuring of power networks.[8] In order to achieve these goals, he resorted to improvisation and experimentation. Davis arrives at a narrative of heroization in a surprising volte-face: 'inconsistency', 'inefficiency', and 'unpredictability'[9] are seen as a product of a clever governing mind firmly in control. In conclusion, she claims that Charlemagne 'invented medieval rulership'.[10]

In the following paper, I will attempt to reappraise the subject of Charlemagne's governmental strategy by focusing on the payment of wergild. There is no doubt about the fact that the payment of wergild was of central importance to the emperor. His very first capitulary, issued in 779 at the royal palace in Herstal, included the provision that nobody should refuse to settle a feud by the payment of wergild lest he be sent into exile.[11] In 802, Charlemagne reiterated the ban on homicides (*homicidia*), taking the opportunity to add a long sermon on the perilous consequences of feuds for the soul of the perpetrators. Among other admonitions, the sermon warns: 'How can anyone confide in a placable God, who kills his neighbour who is God's son? How can anyone think Christ the Lord to be well-disposed towards him, who murders his brother? It is a great danger before God and Christ, the ruler of heaven

7 Jennifer R. Davis, *Charlemagne's Practice of Empire*, Cambridge 2015 (cited as Davis, *Practice of Empire*).

8 Davis, *Practice of Empire*, 396–403.

9 Davis, *Practice of Empire*, 48, 79, 154, 434.

10 Davis, *Practice of Empire*, 431.

11 *Capitulare Haristallense*, a. 779, c. 22, ed. Alfred Boretius, MGH Capitularia regum Francorum 1, Hanover 1883, 51.

and earth, to provoke hatred and enmity among men.'[12] In order to stop the cycle of violence, Charlemagne ordered that the perpetrators should immediately pay the wergild to the relatives of the victim and that the relatives should on their part immediately accept the compensation and give surety for the pacification.[13] Other capitularies touch on the same topic.[14]

Wergild, thus, was an essential means of conflict resolution.[15] However, Charlemagne did not address consistently and coherently the amount of wergild due for compensation and the currency of the payment. In the following pages I want to discuss what this discrepancy tells us about the leading principles of Charlemagne's government and legal reform. In studying the *leges* emanating from his reign and comparing their approach to the wergild systems I want to bring into focus the tensions among tradition, local custom, and royal

---

12 *Capitulare missorum generale*, a. 802, c. 32, ed. Boretius, MGH Capit. 1, 97: *Quomodo enim secum Deum placatum fore confidit, qui filium suum proximum sibi occiderit? Qualiter vero Christum dominum sibi propitium esse arbitretur, qui fratrem suum interficerit? Magnum quoque et inhabitaculum* [sic!] *periculum est cum deo patre et Christo coeli terrae dominatore inimicitias movere*. 'Inhabitaculum' (a substantive meaning habitation: Thesaurus linguae latinae 7, 1, 1584), is a scribal error.

13 *Capitulare missorum generale*, a. 802, c. 32, ed. Boretius, MGH Capit. 1, 97. The nature of this capitulary is disputed: Steffen Patzold, 'Normen im Buch. Überlegungen zu Geltungsansprüchen so genannter "Kapitularien"', *Frühmittelalterliche Studien* 41 (2007), 331–350; Rosamond McKitterick, 'Charlemagne's missi and their Books', in: *Early Medieval Studies in Memory of Patrick Wormald*, ed. Stephen Baxter, Catherine E. Karkov, Janet Nelson and David Pelteret, Farnham 2009, 253–267, here 261; Matthew Innes, 'Charlemagne, Justice and Written Law', in: *Law, Custom and Justice in Late Antiquity and the Early Middle Ages*, ed. Alice Rio, London 2011, 155–203; Michael Glatthaar, 'Subjektiver und indirekter Stil in den Kapitularien Karls des Großen. Ein Beitrag zur Frage ihrer Entstehung', *Deutsches Archiv* 70 (2014), 1–42, here 20.

14 *Capitulare missorum specialia*, a. 803, c. 8, ed. Boretius, MGH Capit. 1, 100; *Capitulare missorum in Theodonis villa datum secundum generale*, a. 805, c. 5 ed. Boretius, MGH Capit. 1, 123; *Caroli Magni capitulare generale*, a. 813, c. 23, ed. Hubert Mordek, *Bibliotheca capitularium regum Francorum manuscripta. Überlieferung und Traditionszusammenhang der fränkischen Herrschererlasse* (MGH Hilfsmittel 15), Munich 1995, 993. Cf. Philippe Depreux, "Wergeld, composition et rachat dans les capitulaires des rois francs", in: *La victime 2: La réparation du dommage*, ed. Jacqueline Hoareau-Dodinau, Guillaume Métairie and Pascal Texier (Cahiers de l'Institut d'Anthropologie Juridique 22), Limoges 2009, 345–362.

15 In general cf. Stefan Esders, 'Wergeld und soziale Netzwerke im Frankenreich', in: *Verwandtschaft, Name und soziale Ordnung (300–1100)* (Ergänzungsbände zum Reallexikon der Germanischen Altertumskunde 90), ed. Steffen Patzold and Karl Ubl, Berlin and New York 2014, 141–160; Stefan Esders, '"Eliten" und "Strafrecht" im frühen Mittelalter. Überlegungen zu den Bußen- und Wergeldkatalogen der Leges barbarorum', in: *Théorie et pratiques des élites au Haut Moyen Age. Conception, perception et réalisation sociale* (Collection Haut Moyen Age 13), ed. François Bougard, Hans-Werner Goetz and Régine Le Jan, Turnhout 2011, 261–282.

law-giving. What should emerge at the end of my paper is a wide-angle image of Charlemagne, one that includes the spaces beside, above and beneath him.

Let me begin by presenting the evidence from the *Lex Salica*, the Frankish law code drafted in the late fifth century.[16] The *Lex Salica* stands out among all law codes of the early middle ages because of its monetary system. The compensations are numbered in solidi and in denarii, based upon the relation of one solidus equaling 40 denarii. I do not want to enter into the debate about the origins and meaning of this double currency, but it seems that the compensations were first recorded in the silver currency of denarii and later converted to the gold currency of solidi.[17] The later additions to the *Lex Salica* tell us that during the sixth century the silver currency was gradually eliminated.[18] Since the middle of the sixth century, compensations were charged only in solidi as in all the other barbarian law codes of the fifth and sixth centuries. When the Carolingians decided to rework the text of the *Lex Salica* two centuries later, the monetary system had changed profoundly. On the one hand, the gold currency vanished in favor of silver coins, making solidi a mere unit of account; on the other hand, the relation between solidi and denarii was fixed already in the seventh century to be one solidus equal to 12 denarii.[19]

Despite these changes, the first redaction of the *Lex Salica* issued in the middle of the eighth century under Pippin the Younger preserves both currencies with the old relation of 1:40. Or at least so it seemed to the critical editor of the text. In fact, only one out of three manuscripts has the old double currency system, while two mention only solidi.[20] The next redaction of the *Lex Salica*,

16 Cf. Karl Ubl, *Sinnstiftungen eines Rechtsbuchs. Die Lex Salica im Frankenreich* (Quellen und Forschungen zum Recht im Mittelalter 9), Ostfildern 2017 (cited as Ubl, *Sinnstiftungen*).

17 Philip Grierson and Mark Blackburn, *Medieval European Coinage I. The Early Middle Ages (5th–10th Centuries)*, Cambridge 1986, reprinted Cambridge 2006, 105–106 (cited as Grierson and Blackburn, *Coinage*); Michael McCormick, 'Coins and the Economic History of Post-Roman Gaul: Testing the Standard Model in the Moselle, ca. 400–750', in: *Die Merowingischen Monetarmünzen als Quelle zum Verständnis des 7. Jahrhunderts in Gallien* (Mittelalterstudien 27), ed. Jörg Jarnut and Jürgen Strothmann, Paderborn 2013, 337–376, here 349.

18 The oldest additional capitulary (*Capitulare quintum*) retains the double standard, whereas the next addition (*Capitulare primum*) omits the denarius: *Pactus legis Salicae*, 117–133 and 66–78, ed. Karl August Eckhardt, MGH LL nationum Germanicarum 4, 1, Hanover 1962, 263–267 and 238–250. My chronology differs from Eckhardt's: Ubl, *Sinnstiftungen*.

19 Grierson and Blackburn, *Coinage*; Bernd Kluge, *Am Beginn des Mittelalters. Die Münzen des karolingischen Reiches 751 bis 814. Pippin, Karlmann, Karl der Große* (Das Kabinett 15), Berlin 2014.

20 D7 (Montpellier, Bibliothèque Interuniversitaire, H 136) and D9 (St. Gallen, Stiftsbibliothek, 731) mention only solidi, whereas D8 (Paris, BNF, lat. 4627) offers both currencies. Cf. *Lex Salica*, ed. Eckhardt, who gives denarii in angle brackets.

which took place around the year 788 under Charlemagne, simplifies the text in many respects, removing the old Frankish glosses as well as the old currency system. This so-called E-version, extant in six manuscripts, mentions only compensations in solidi.[21] After his imperial coronation, Charlemagne ordered a new redaction of *Lex Salica,* which became the most widely transmitted version of the text, with over 60 manuscripts and many fragments. This redaction, known as the *Lex Salica Karolina* apparently restored the old currency system. The compiler of the *Karolina* assembled his text from copies of nearly every older version and tried to preserve the old and authentic text exhaustively.[22] Even though he omitted the old Frankish glosses, he decided to retain the old monetary system, mentioning in every compensation clause the double currency of solidi and denarii.[23]

The ratio of 1:40 is therefore upheld by the compiler, prompting Charlemagne to react to this in his *Capitulare legibus addendum* from the year 803 by confirming this exceptional payment of the *Lex Salica.* In chapter 9, he declared: 'Every obligation owed to the king should be paid in solidi worth 12 deniers, except the fine for breaking the peace which is mentioned in the Lex Salica; this should be paid in the same solidi with which other compensations are settled'.[24] The precise meaning of this clause is not at all clear, but it seems to tell us that the ratio of solidi and denarii can differ according to different law codes. If this reading is true, then it is at odds with our understanding of Charlemagne's monetary reform of the 790s when he issued new, heavier coins and supposedly determined the ratio of pound, solidi and denarii once and for all. The *Capitulare legibus addendum* allows for a surprising fuzziness regarding the currency of payment. What is even more surprising: this text, transmitted in more than 50 manuscripts (not counting the transmission via the capitulary collection of Ansegis) is Charlemagne's most widely distributed normative text. In contrast, the Frankfurt capitulary of 794, which prescribed the new currency,[25] is only known by a single manuscript from Rheims (Paris, BN, lat. 10758) and its direct descendants.

---

21 Cf. Karl Ubl, 'Die erste Leges-Reform Karls des Großen', in: *Das Gesetz — The Law — La Loi* (Miscellanea mediaevalia 38), ed. Guy Guldentops and Andreas Speer, Berlin 2014, 75–92.

22 Ubl, *Sinnstiftungen*, 176–181.

23 *Pactus legis Salicae* 14.4, ed. Eckhardt, MGH LL nat. Germ. 4, 1, 65: *Si vero Francus Romanum expoliaverit, MCC denariis qui faciunt solidos XXX culpabilis iudicetur.*

24 *Capitulare legibus additum*, a. 803, c. 9, ed. Boretius, MGH Capit. 1, 114: *Omnia debita quae ad partem regis solvere debent, solidis duodecim denariorum solvent, excepto freda quae in lege Saliga scripta est; illa eodem solido quo caeterae compositiones solvi debent componatur.*

25 *Synodus Franconofurtensis*, a. 794, c. 5, ed. Boretius, MGH Capit. 1, 74.

Eventually, tradition was stronger than concerns over unambiguousness or unification. Charlemagne, promising to his subjects in several capitularies to preserve their law untouched and to respect their legal traditions, had to give in to these expectations, even though in his first redaction of the *Lex Salica* he had tried to simplify the text. Later, his bishops noticed that this exceptional status of the Franks provoked discontent and was difficult to maintain in a Christian empire. At a synod in Rheims (813), they submitted a request to the emperor asking to take back his monetary privilege for the Franks, because 'many perjuries and wrong testimonies happened on this account'.[26] We do not hear of any reaction on the part of Charlemagne, but his successor Louis the Pious somehow attenuated the privilege of the Franks a couple of years later.[27]

Should we see this as an isolated case? What about those law-codes which Charlemagne first arranged to be written down for the *gentes* in the north-east provinces of his realm? Did he intend to enforce the Frankish wergild and monetary system in the law-codes of the Thuringians, Frisians, Saxons, and Franks of the lower Rhine valley? In the remaining part of this paper I will turn to these new codifications from the time of Charlemagne. Einhard tells us in the above-mentioned text that 'Charlemagne did command that the unwritten laws of all the peoples under his authority be written down'.[28] Four law codes seem to be the product of this legislative, textualizing initiative: the *Lex Saxonum*, the *Lex Thuringorum*, the *Lex Frisionum,* and the *Notitia vel commemoratio de illa ewa, quae se ad Amorem habet*, which was issued for the Franks of the Rhine delta,[29] but is commonly and wrongly known as *Lex Francorum Chamavorum*. Moreover, two other law codes might be added to this list: first, the *Lex Suavorum*, whose text is now lost, but which is known from a table of contents in a legal compilation assembled during the age of Charlemagne. Considering that the beginning of the *Lex Suavorum* mentions

---

26 *Concilium Remense*, a. 813, c. 41, ed. Albert Werminghoff, MGH Concilia 2, 1, Leipzig 1906, 257: *Ut dominus imperator secundum statutum bonae memoriae domni Pippini misericordiam faciat, ne solidi, qui in lege habentur, per quadragenos denarios discurrant, quoniam propter eos multa periuria multaque falsa testimonia repperiuntur.*

27 *Capitula legi addita*, a. 816, c. 3, ed. Boretius, MGH Capit. 1, 268; *Item Capitula legi addita*, a. 816, c. 2, ed. Boretius, MGH Capit. 1, 269. Cf. Ubl, *Sinnstiftungen*, 186–188.

28 Confirmed by the *Annales Laureshamenses* a. 802, ed. Georg Heinrich Pertz, MGH SS 1, Hanover 1826, 39.

29 Cf. Jan Frederik Niermeyer, 'Het Midden-Nederlands rivierengebied in de Frankische tijd', *Tijdschrift voor Geschiedenis* 66 (1953), 145–169; Peter Hoppenbrouwers, 'Leges nationum and Ethnic Personality of Law in Charlemagne's Empire', in: *Law and Empire: Ideas, Practices, Actors* (Rulers & Elites 3), ed. Jeroen Duindam, Jill D. Harries, Caroline Humfress and Nimrod Hurvitz, Leiden and Boston 2013, 251–274 (cited as Hoppenbrouwers, 'Leges nationum').

a *homo nobilis*, this law code of the Swabians might very well have originated under Charlemagne, since the law codes from the early ninth century are characterized by the recognition of a separate nobility.[30] The second law code that might be added to the list is known as *Capitula Remedii*. According to Reinhold Kaiser, this text might have originated as a statute of bishop Remedius of Chur under the authority of one of Charlemagne's missi.[31]

The most conspicuous common denominator of these law codes is the recognition of a separate nobility with a higher wergild.[32] The details, however, vary considerably. Whereas the *Ewa ad Amorem* and the law code of the Thuringians value the life of a noble man with 600 solidi, that is, three times higher than that of a free-born man, the *Lex Saxonum* more than doubles the amount with 1440 solidi, while the Frisian law fixes the wergild of a noble at the meagre amount of just 80 to 106 solidi.[33] The amount and its relation to the wergild of the free-born man therefore differ, as does the terminology. The *Ewa ad Amorem* speaks of the *Francus homo*, the law of the Thuringians employs the Germanic word *adalingus*, whereas the Saxon and Frisian laws use the Latin concept of *nobilis*. Behind this terminological variance lies a more fundamental conceptual criterion of selection. The *francus homo* and the *adalingus* of the *Ewa ad Amorem* and the Thuringian law are strictly gendered

30 Karl Ubl, 'Recht in der Region. Die Rezeption von leges und capitula im karolingischen Alemannien', in: *817 — Die urkundliche Ersterwähnung von Villingen und Schwenningen. Alemannien und das Reich in der Zeit Kaiser Ludwigs des Frommen* (Veröffentlichungen des Alemannischen Instituts 83), ed. Jürgen Dendorfer, Heinrich Maulhardt, R. Johanna Regnath and Thomas Zotz, Ostfildern 2016, 207–223 (cited as Ubl, 'Recht in der Region').

31 As argued by Reinhold Kaiser, 'Die "Capitula Remidii": Veranlassung, Autorschaft und Geltungsgrund, Verbreitung und Wirkung', in: *Schrift, Schriftgebrauch und Textsorten im frühmittelalterlichen Churrätien: Vorträge des internationalen Kolloquiums vom 18. bis 20. Mai 2006 im Rätischen Museum in Chur. Eine Publikation des Instituts für Kulturforschung Graubünden in Chur*, ed. Heidi Eisenhut, Karin Fuchs, Martin Hannes Graf and Hannes Steiner, Basel 2008, 146–182; more cautious: Harald Siems, 'Recht in Rätien zur Zeit Karls des Großen — Ein Beitrag zu den Capitula Remedii', in: *Wandel und Konstanz zwischen Bodensee und Lombardei zur Zeit Karls des Grossen: Kloster St. Johann in Müstair und Churrätien. Tagung 13.–16. Juni 2012 in Müstair* (Acta Müstair, Kloster St. Johann 3), ed. Katrin Roth-Rubi, Eckart Kühne and Hans Rudolf Sennhauser, Zurich 2013, 199–238.

32 Harald Siems, *Studien zur Lex Frisionum* (Abhandlungen zur rechtswissenschaftlichen Grundlagenforschung 42), Ebelsbach 1980, 281 (cited as Siems, *Studien*).

33 *Ewa ad Amorem* 3, ed. Rudolph Sohm, MGH Fontes iuris Germanici antiqui in usum scholarum separatim editi 6, Hanover 1883, 117; *Lex Thuringorum* 1, ed. Claudius Freiherr von Schwerin, MGH Fontes iuris Germanici antiqui in usum scholarum separatim editi 4, Hanover and Leipzig 1918, 57; *Lex Saxonum* 14, ed. von Schwerin, MGH Fontes iurius 4, 21; *Lex Frisionum*, 1.1 and 1.10, ed. Karl August Eckhardt, MGH Fontes iuris Germanici antiqui in usum scholarum separatim editi 12, Hanover 1928, 34 and 36.

notions, because they only apply to men, not to women.[34] A *franca femina* is not mentioned in the *Ewa ad Amorem*, and women are not called *adalinga*, but *nobilis* in the Thuringian law. This conceptual distinction points to the fact that in both codes the law of inheritance favours the male offspring regarding the devolution of land. The Thuringian law even begins with the rubric *de alodibus* and the explicit provision that the son and not the daughter should receive the inheritance of a deceased person.[35] Only if there is no male heir up to the fifth generation, can a daughter be considered a legitimate heir to landed property. The *Ewa ad Amorem* also denies the inheritance of land and wood owned by a *Francus homo* to daughters.[36] That this exclusion suggests a military context is clearly visible in the case of the *Ewa ad Amorem*, large parts of which read like military law – regulating the military bans, local guards, public roads, bridges and watergates and so forth.[37] Contrary to this martial, functional view of the nobility, the Saxon law — as has been noticed by many historians — conceives of its *nobiles* as a separate and stratified caste.[38]

---

34 Heike Grahn-Hoek, 'Das Recht der Thüringer und die Frage ihrer ethnischen Identität: mit einer Bemerkung zur Entstehung von Begriff und Institution "Adel"', in: *Die Frühzeit der Thüringer: Archäologie, Sprache, Geschichte* (Ergänzungsbände zum Reallexikon der germanischen Altertumskunde 63), ed. Helmut Castritius, Berlin and New York 2009, 415–456, here 421–428 (cited as Gran-Hoek, 'Das Recht der Thüringer'). An English version of the same paper: Heike Grahn-Hoek, 'The Thuringi, the Peculiarities of Their Law, and Their Legal Relations to the Gentes of Their Time, Chiefly According to the Lex (Angliorum et Werinorum hoc est) Thuringorum and the Other Leges barbarorum of the Early Middle Ages', in: *The Baiuvarii and Thuringi. An Ethnographic Perspective* (Studies in Historical Archaeoethnology 9), ed. Janine Fries-Knoblach and Heiko Steuer, Woodbridge 2014, 289–315. I disagree, however, with her refusal of using the concept of nobility. Cf. Hans-Werner Goetz, '"Nobilis". Der Adel im Selbstverständnis der Karolingerzeit', *Vierteljahrschrift für Sozial- und Wirtschaftsgeschichte* 70 (1983), 53–191.

35 *Lex Thuringorum* 26–27, ed. von Schwerin, MGH Fontes iuris 4, 60–61. Cf. Peter Landau, 'Die Lex Thuringorum — Karls des Großen Gesetz für die Thüringer', *ZRG GA* 118 (2001), 23–57, here 41–46.

36 *Ewa ad Amorem* 42, ed. Sohm, MGH Fontes iuris 6, 122.

37 *Ewa ad Amorem* 34–39, ed. Sohm, MGH Fontes iuris 6, 121. The military context is elucidated by Hoppenbrouwers, 'Leges nationum'. The nobility still seems to have been hereditary, cf. Ernst von Moeller, 'Der Homo Francus der Ewa Chamavorum', *Mitteilungen des Instituts für Österreichische Geschichtsforschung* 23 (1902), 217–230, here 227. Thomas Faulkner, *Law and Authority in the Early Middle Ages. The Frankish leges in the Carolingian Period* (Cambridge studies in medieval life and thought, fourth series 104), Cambridge 2016, 29–45, argues unconvincingly that the law book is a reaction to the "monasticisation of the frontier zone", negating royal sponsorship.

38 Martin Lintzel, *Ausgewählte Schriften* 1, Berlin 1961, 376 (cited as Lintzel, *Ausgewählte Schriften*); more cautious Matthias Springer, *Die Sachsen* (Kohlhammer-Urban-Taschenbücher 59), Stuttgart 2004, 242–250 (cited as Springer, *Die Sachsen*).

The status and function of the nobility therefore vary significantly in each of these law codes. But is it at least possible to claim that the recognition of a separate nobility can be traced back to the initiative of Charlemagne himself? Even this suggestion is difficult to substantiate. As we all know, the Frankish law-codes ignore a separate noble class, only allowing for a higher wergild of royal functionaries like the *comites* or the *antrustiones*.[39] Similarly, the capitularies of Charlemagne employ the concept of *nobilis* only once,[40] and never do so regarding the wergild. Indeed, Charlemagne had the quite clear intention of protecting the class of free-born men from being subjected to seniors because of the heavy burden of being called to arms or before court.[41] In another famous statement in his capitularies, he stated that there was no recognized status other than free and unfree.[42] Whatever motives we impute to Charlemagne, he does not seem to be especially sympathetic to the aspirations of the elite in its claim to legal privileges. In contrast to this, from the time of his first capitulary for Saxony, issued in a period of bitter war and with the intention of utter humiliation, Charlemagne accepted the exceptional position of the Saxon nobility. This may or may not be considered to be an attempt at outreach on Charlemagne's part to forge an alliance in this specific case against the free-born and half-free population of Saxony.[43] Regarding the other three law codes, such acceptance of the nobility's status was definitely not part of a governmental strategy, but rather the recognition of expectations from the regional elite and a corollary to what Charlemagne had approved of for the Saxons.

We arrive at a similar conclusion if we take into account the different monetary systems of the four law codes. They are in stark contrast to everything that numismatists tell us about the unequaled achievements of Charlemagne. The numismatic evidence gives the impression that Charlemagne succeeded in establishing a degree of uniformity throughout the Frankish kingdom that had previously only existed during the rule of the Roman Empire. After the monetary reform of 793/794, a single currency with a uniform appearance

39 Grahn-Hoek, *Die fränkische Oberschicht*, 46–54; Olberg, *Die Bezeichnungen*, 124–133. A noble class is unknown as well in *Capitula Remedii*.

40 *Capitula de rebus ecclesiasticis*, a. ante 813, c. 2, ed. Boretius, MGH Capit. 1, 186.

41 Cf. Johannes Schmitt, *Untersuchungen zu den Liberi Homines der Karolingerzeit* (Europäische Hochschulschriften 3/83), Frankfurt/Main 1977; Timothy Reuter, 'The End of Carolingian Military Expansion', in: *Charlemagne's heir. New perspectives on the reign of Louis the Pious 814–840*, ed. Roger Collins and Peter Godman, Oxford 1990, 391–405.

42 *Responsio misso cuidam data*, a. 802/813, c. 1, ed. Boretius, MGH Capit. 1, 145: [...] *quia non est amplius nisi liber et servus.*

43 Springer, *Die Sachsen*, 242–250, contra Lintzel, *Ausgewählte Schriften*, 334.

circulated east and west of the Rhine as well as in Italy, and the production of coinage was gradually constricted to royal sites, monasteries and episcopal mints playing a smaller and smaller role during Charlemagne's reign. Simon Coupland asserts: 'Was Charles the Great — Charlemagne, really great? On the basis of the numismatic evidence, the answer is resoundingly positive.'[44]

The evidence of the four law codes tells a quite different story. The *Ewa ad Amorem* counts in *solidi* and *unciae*, the law of the Thuringians in *solidi* and *tremisses*, whereas both the Saxon and the Frisian law codes operate with two entirely different monetary systems. The Saxon law employs a *solidus maior* which is worth two *tremisses*, and a *solidus minor* which is worth three *tremisses*.[45] How these monetary units relate to the actual coins, the *denarii*, is unspecified. The Frisian law, in turn, uses the equation of one pound to 20 solidi so dear to Charlemagne, but the solidus is not worth 12 denarii as was widely the case since the seventh century, but 3 denarii. Moreover, the Frisian law employs the notions of *tremissis*, *semissis,* and *uncia*, as well as *denarii fresonici* or *denarii veteres* and *denarii novae monetae*, presumably meaning Charlemagne's deniers of 793/794. However, the solidus is worth only two and half new deniers in West Frisia and two in East Frisia. Taking into account this utter chaos, it comes as no surprise that the scholarship of the late 19th and early 20th century witnessed heated debates about the respective value and dissemination of Charlemagne's coins in the north-east provinces of the empire.[46] No definitive conclusion has ever been reached in this debate — but in my view this monetary chaos smacks of local custom and tradition and does not suggest a strong governmental regime.

I wish to turn now to the presence of the royal *fredus* and *bannus* in the four law codes of the north-east provinces. Both are owed to the king, the *fredus* being a pacification fine due in most compensation payments, whereas the *bannus* was meant to circumscribe a special sphere of royal protection whose breach lead to the automatic fine of 60 solidi. The *Ewa ad Amorem* is the most explicit code on these fees owed to the king. Chapter 2 asserts that 'concerning the royal ban, we have it the same way as the other Franks'.[47] In spite of this

---

44 Simon Coupland, 'Charlemagne's Coinage: Ideology and Economy', in: *Charlemagne: Empire and Society*, ed. Joanna Story, Manchester 2005, 211–229, here 211.

45 Lintzel, *Ausgewählte Schriften*, 333–341.

46 Analyzed in detail by Siems, *Studien*, 232–265.

47 *Ewa ad Amorem* 2, ed. Sohm, MGH Fontes iuris 6, 117: *De banno dominico similiter habemus, sicut et alii Franci habent.* On the royal ban cf. Felix Grollmann, *Vom bayerischen Stammesrecht zur karolingischen Rechtsreform. Zur Integration Bayerns in das Frankenreich* (Abhandlungen zur rechtswissenschaftlichen Grundlagenforschung 98), Berlin 2018, 248–322.

vague, sweeping clause, the royal ban of sixty solidi is only mentioned twice, in the first instance regarding the release of a robber (not handing him over to the count) and in the second concerning the breach of a betrothal.[48] In contrast to this, the refusal of a military summons is not sanctioned by the royal ban of 60 solidi, as we would expect from Frankish sources, but rather by the minor sum of 4 solidi.[49] The fine for peace-breaking or *fredus* is consistently mentioned throughout the *Ewa ad Amorem*. In cases of wergild payment, it amounts to a third of the compensation, in cases of perjury to a fourth of the compensation, and in several other cases there is a kind of flat-rate of 4 solidi.[50] The expression *in dominico*, also present in the capitularies,[51] clarifies that this fee is owed to the king. The *Ewa ad Amorem* therefore clearly links the local dispensation of justice to the substantial participation of the king and his functionaries.

The law code of the Thuringians lies at the other side of the spectrum. Royal influence in local peace-keeping is rarely mentioned. The royal ban is due for payment in three cases: traffic in human beings, gang assault, and arson.[52] The *fredus* is only demanded in two instances: seven solidi for stealing six pigs and a boar, and 12 solidi for stealing female jewelry.[53] Whether we should assume that the *fredus* is implied in the other compensation payments is open to question. Frankly, I am skeptical — given that this law code never mentions any royal functionary nor does it refer to any felony regarding the king.[54] Royal interests seem to be conspicuously absent from this law code. This is astonishing considering the fact that the Thuringians were conquered by the Franks in the sixth century, received a Frankish duke in the seventh, and were fully integrated in the secular and religious administration of Carolingian rule during the eighth century.[55] However, this detail should not be seen as evidence for an earlier date of the Thuringian law-book, which H. Grahn-Hoek proposed

48 *Ewa ad Amorem* 30 and 47, ed. Sohm, MGH Fontes iuris 6, 120 and 122.

49 *Ewa ad Amorem* 34–35, ed. Sohm, MGH Fontes iuris 6, 121.

50 E.g. *Ewa ad Amorem* 40, ed. Sohm, MGH Fontes iuris 6, 121. This is significantly lower than the 15 sol. required in *Pactus legis Salicae* 1, ed. Eckhardt, MGH LL nat. Germ. 4, 1, 18; *Lex Ribuaria* 36.1, ed. Franz Beyerle and Rudolf Buchner, MGH LL nationum Germanicarum 3, 2, Hanover 1954, 88.

51 Siems, *Studien*, 282.

52 *Lex Thuringorum* 38, 41 and 54, ed. von Schwerin, MGH Fontes iuris 4, 63 and 66.

53 *Lex Thuringorum* 34–37, ed. von Schwerin, MGH Fontes iuris 4, 62–63.

54 The *Ewa ad Amorem*, in contrast, mentions the *missus*, the *comes*, and the *centenarius*.

55 Cf. Mathias Kälble, 'Ethnogenese und Herzogtum: Thüringen im Frankenreich (6.–9. Jahrhundert)', in: *Die Frühzeit der Thüringer: Archäologie, Sprache, Geschichte* (Ergänzungsbände zum Reallexikon der germanischen Altertumskunde 63), ed. Helmut Castritius, Berlin and New York 2009, 329–413.

in a series of recent articles.[56] The absence of royal interference rather demonstrates the fact that the drafting of the law-book was guided by central authority only in very general terms. The regional elites were in charge to determine the specific contents of the *Lex Thuringorum*.

The Saxon law seems to be comparable to the Thuringian law code. No royal functionaries are mentioned, the royal ban is also non-existent, and the *fredus* is only demanded in one chapter on the theft of things worth less than three solidi.[57] However, the *lex Saxonum* does touch on royal felonies like treason and obstruction of travel to the army or to the palace. In addition, one could argue very convincingly that the two capitularies destined for Saxony (*Capitulatio de partibus Saxoniae* and *Capitulare Saxonicum*) themselves convey the royal interests exhaustively, and that these two texts remained in force alongside the *Lex Saxonum*.[58]

A still different picture of royal fees is visible in the *Lex Frisionum*. The law code devotes a chapter heading to the royal ban: *Hic bannus est*.[59] The content of the chapter, however, does not resemble what we know about the eight cases of the royal ban from the capitularies of Charlemagne.[60] The payment of 30 solidi is due ninefold in the following instances: a fight within the army, murder in the church or in the palace of the duke, and murder of the royal or ducal missus. The *fredus* amounts to the sum of the wergild in the case of group assault or human trafficking with the pagans.[61] In several more instances (e.g. for every theft, perjury and violence), the *fredus* is equated with the wergild throughout the law code, which is a rather peculiar regulation.[62] Beside this exceptionally high *fredus*, the *Lex Frisionum* also operates with the smaller amounts of 2, 4, and 12 solidi as *fredus*. This law code therefore is, on the one hand, quite similar to the *Ewa ad Amorem* in the frequency with which the royal fees are mentioned; on the other hand, it never alludes to royal functionaries at the local level, only mentioning the king and a duke. The identity of the duke is still open to discussion.[63]

To sum up: Diversity reigns in the law books of the north-east provinces of the Frankish Empire. We can still render this messy picture messier by adding

56 Grahn-Hoek, 'Das Recht der Thüringer', 417.
57 *Lex Saxonum* 36, ed. von Schwerin, MGH Fontes iurius 4, 27.
58 Lintzel, *Ausgewählte Schriften*, 395; Theuerkauf, *Lex*, 53–54.
59 *Lex Frisionum* 14, ed. Eckhardt, MGH Fontes iurius 12, 60. Cf. Siems, *Studien*, 282.
60 *Summula de bannis*, ed. Boretius, MGH Capit. 1, 224.
61 *Lex Frisionum* 17.4–5, ed. Eckhardt, MGH Fontes iurius 12, 62.
62 *Lex Frisionum* 3.8, 5.2, 5.8 and 10, ed. Eckhardt, MGH Fontes iurius 12, 44, 46, 48 and 52; *Lex Frisionum Additio* 3.76 and 3.78, ed. Eckhardt, MGH Fontes iurius 12, 96.
63 Cf. Siems, *Studien*, 324.

details about the varying amount of compensation payments. For example: to constrain someone by chains without authority or reason leads to 30 solidi for a noble and 10 solidi for a freeman in Thuringia, 12 solidi plus 4 solidi *fredus* for a homo Francus *ad Amorem*, and 15 solidi plus 12 solidi *fredus* in the Frisian code.[64] None of these regulations squares neatly and evenly with the 32 solidi demanded for a free-born man in the *Lex Salica* or 30 in the *Lex Ribuaria*.[65] Such differences are partly due to the fact that the four law books of the north-east provinces use different patterns for assembling legal cases: the Frisian law draws on the *Lex Alamannorum*, the *Ewa ad Amorem* most closely resembles the Bavarian law book, and both the Saxon and the Thuringian *lex* are dependent on the *Lex Ribuaria*.[66] There is no convincing explanation for this difference of template.

In my opinion, what this difference and variety imply is the absence of a governmental strategy of unification,[67] even less of 'unambiguousness'. As I have argued with respect to the status of the nobility: the terminology, the amount of wergild and its relation to the other ranks of society, all mirror local custom and meet the expectations of those taking part in the compilations of the law

64 *Lex Thuringorum* 39, ed. von Schwerin, MGH Fontes iuris 4, 63; *Ewa ad Amorem* 17, ed. Sohm, MGH Fontes iuris 6, 119; *Lex Frisionum* 22.82, ed. Eckhardt, MGH Fontes iurius 12, 78. Cf. Siems, *Studien*, 230.

65 *Pactus legis Salicae* 32.1, ed. Eckhardt, MGH LL nat. Germ. 4, 1, 122; *Lex Ribuaria* 45.1, ed. Beyerle and Buchner, MGH LL nat. Germ. 3, 2, 97.

66 Cf. Siems, *Studien*, 355–360; Heinrich Brunner, *Deutsche Rechtsgeschichte* vol. 1, [2]Leipzig 1906, 465, 471, 474; Grahn-Hoek, 'Das Recht der Thüringer', 418.

67 The debate is of long standing: Raymund Kottje, 'Einheit und Vielfalt des kirchlichen Lebens in der Karolingerzeit', *Zeitschrift für Kirchengeschichte* 76 (1965), 323–342; Janet Nelson, 'On the Limits of the Carolingian Renaissance', *Studies in Church History* 14 (1977), 51–69; Hubert Mordek, 'Kirchenrechtliche Autoritäten im Frühmittelalter', in: *Recht und Schrift im Mittelalter* (Vorträge und Forschungen 23), ed. Peter Classen, Sigmaringen 1977, 237–255, here 245–247; Roger E. Reynolds, 'Unity and Diversity in Carolingian Canon Law Collections: The Case of the Collectio Hibernensis and Its Derivatives', in: *Carolingian Essays: Andrew W. Mellon Lectures in Early Christian Studies*, ed. Uta-Renate Blumenthal, Washington 1983, 99–135; Rosamond McKitterick, 'Unity and Diversity in the Carolingian Church', *Studies in Church History* 32 (1996), 145–169; Steffen Patzold, 'Eine Hierarchie im Wandel: Die Ausbildung einer Metropolitanordnung im Frankenreich des 8. und 9. Jahrhunderts', in: *Hiérarchie et stratification sociale dans l'Occident médiéval 400–1100* (Collection Haut Moyen Âge 6), ed. Dominique Iogna-Prat, François Bougard and Régine Le Jan, Turnhout 2008, 161–184; Rob Meens, *Penance in Medieval Europe, 600–1200*, Cambridge 2014, 111–118; Davis, *Practice of Empire*, 298–303; Steffen Patzold, 'Prozesse der Vereinheitlichung? Unitas, concordia und pax in der karolingischen Welt', in: *Entscheiden und Regieren. Konsens als Element vormoderner Entscheidungsfindung in transkultureller Perspektive* (Macht und Herrschaft 9), ed. Linda Dohmen and Tilmann Trausch, Göttingen 2019, 197–220.

code at the local level. The same relationship has to be true for the varying monetary systems which are so conspicuously at odds with the reform policy of Charlemagne. The involvement of royal agents is most clearly visible in the *Ewa ad Amorem*, which is not surprising considering the Frankish population of the Rhine delta. Conquered by the Pippinids in the early eighth century, Frisia ranks second in terms of royal involvement, even though no Frankish functionaries seem to have operated on the ground. The Saxon law is ambivalent on this point, since we have to factor into the equation the capitularies which were already issued very early in Charlemagne's Saxon war. Thuringia, in contrast, while being a part of the Frankish kingdom since the middle of the sixth century, had only been marginally affected by the import of Frankish legal institutions. Even such generic goals like the assertion of 'royal dominance' or the 'restructuring of power-networks' are not present in the law codes.

When we take all this together, we can hardly detect any governmental strategy. Even to assert that Charlemagne was undertaking, in the words of Patrick Wormald, a kind of 'ethnic engineering'[68] is, in my opinion, only partly true. On the one hand, the legal reform of 802 clearly aims at the implementation of the idea of providing every ethnic community with its own law-book. There is no other reason why Charlemagne would have equipped the Frisians, Thuringians, Swabians and Saxons with written codification even though written law in itself was of limited use east of the Rhine. On the other hand, our four law codes do not presuppose clear ethnic distinction. The *Ewa ad Amorem* is more like a regional *coutumier* of the thirteenth century, destined for the Franks living on the border to the Saxons and Frisians. The *Lex Thuringorum* embraces *Angli* and *Warni* in its title, the *Lex Saxonum* distinguishes between the customs of Eastphalians, Westphalians, and Engern, and the *Lex Frisionum* divides Frisia into three regions with different legal customs. Separate law books for *Alamanni* and Swabians are equally difficult to make sense of, given that both *gentes* are frequently identified as being one and the same.[69]

What remains of a governmental strategy can be summed up in the following way: Charlemagne intended to put the wergild system into a written form and to gather information about local customs at the royal court. The idea, that Frankish kings are responsible for pacifying feuds and for punishing

68 Patrick Wormald, 'The "leges barbarorum": Law and Ethnicity in the Post-Roman West', in: *Regna and gentes. The Relationship between Late Antique and Early Medieval Peoples and Kingdoms in the Transformation of the Roman World* (The Transformation of the Roman World 13), ed. Hans-Werner Goetz, Jörg Jarnut and Walter Pohl, Leiden and Boston 2003, 32 (referring to *Lex Salica*).

69 Ubl, 'Recht in der Region'.

recalcitrant subjects, was rooted in Merovingian precedent.[70] Charlemagne reasserted this idea in his capitularies and extended his peace-keeping ambitions to the whole Frankish empire — contrary to Merovingian rule which was rarely felt in the periphery. Still, he stopped short of unifying the amounts of compensation, the social differences in wergild, the involvement of his functionaries or the currency of the payment. This disorder did not reflect a sophisticated hidden agenda.

Finally let me return to our view of Charlemagne 1200 years after his death in Aachen. In my opinion, the pendulum of his biographical narrative has swung in the wrong direction. We should be cautious about attributing every achievement of the years around 800 to the emperor himself. It is evident that the relatively high level of learning and culture distinguishes his era as one of profound renewal and regeneration. The exhibition in Aachen, remembering the anniversary of his death in 2014, made this achievement strikingly clear in its lavish presentation of manuscripts. Still, the duty of the historian consists of balancing personal efforts and social structures, royal initiatives and local expectations, individual mindsets and the weight of tradition. What the four law codes of the north-east provinces tell us is that we owe their existence to the imperial program of Charlemagne. Their contents, however, mirror local traditions and the expectations of the regional elite, and only peripherally reflect a governmental strategy.

Bibliography

Primary Sources

Annales et chronica aevi Carolini, ed. Georg Heinrich Pertz, MGH SS in Folio 1, Hanover, 1826.

Capitularia regum Francorum 1, ed. Alfred Boretius, MGH Capitularia regum Francorum 1, Hanover, 1883.

Capitula Remedii, ed. Elisabeth Meyer-Marthaler, Die Rechtsquellen des Kantons Graubünden A,1: Lex Romana Curiensis, Aarau ^{2}1966.

70 Cf. Alexander Callander Murray, '"Pax et disciplina" in Roman Public Law and the Merovingian State', in: *Proceedings of the Tenth International Congress of Medieval Canon Law* (Monumenta Iuris Canonici Series C, Subsidia), ed. Kenneth Pennington, Vatikan 2001, 269–285; Jürgen Weitzel, 'Strafe und Strafverfahren in der Merowingerzeit', *ZRG GA* 111 (1994), 66–147; Warren Brown, *Violence in Medieval Europe*, Harlow 2011, 33–68. Concerning ideology cf. Paul Kershaw, *Peaceful Kings: Peace, Power and the Early Medieval Political Imagination*, Oxford 2011, 119–128.

Caroli Magni capitulare generale, ed. Hubert Mordek, Bibliotheca capitularium regum Francorum manuscripta. Überlieferung und Traditionszusammenhang der fränkischen Herrschererlasse (MGH Hilfsmittel 15), Munich 1995, 990–994.

Concilia aevi Karolini [742–842]. Part 1 [742–817], ed. Albert Werminghoff, MGH Concilia 2, 1, Leipzig, 1906.

Einhard, *Vita Karoli Magni*, ed. Oswald Holder-Egger, MGH SS rerum Germanicarum in usum scholarum separatim editi 25, Hanover and Leipzig, 1911.

Leges Saxonum und Lex Thuringorum, ed. Clauduis Freiherr von Schwerin, MGH Fontes iuris Germanici antiqui in usum scholarum separatim editi 4, Hanover and Leipzig, 1918.

Lex Ribuaria, ed. Franz Beyerle and Rudolf Buchner, MGH LL nationum Germanicarum 3, 2, Hanover, 1954.

Lex Ribuaria et Lex Francorum Chamavorum, ed. Rudolph Sohm, MGH Fontes iuris Germanici antiqui in usum scholarum separatim editi 6, Hanover, 1883.

Lex Frisionum, ed. Karl August Eckhardt and Albrecht Eckhardt, MGH Fontes iuris Germanici antiqui in usum scholarum separatim editi 12, Hanover, 1982.

Noble, Thomas F. X., *Charlemagne and Louis the Pious. Lives by Einhard, Notker, Ermoldus, Thegan, and the Astronomer. Translated, with Introductions and Annotations*, University Park, 2009.

Pactus legis Salicae, ed. Karl August Eckhardt, MGH LL nationum Germanicarum 4, 1, Hanover, 1962.

Secondary Works

Bredekamp, Horst, *Der schwimmende Souverän: Karl der Große und die Bildpolitik des Körpers. Eine Studie zum schematischen Bildakt* (Kleine Kulturwissenschaftliche Bibliothek 86), Berlin 2014.

Brown, Warren, *Violence in Medieval Europe*, Harlow 2011.

Brunner, Heinrich, *Deutsche Rechtsgeschichte* vol. 1, ²Leipzig 1906.

Coupland, Simon, 'Charlemagne's Coinage: Ideology and Economy', in: *Charlemagne: Empire and Society*, ed. Joanna Story, Manchester 2005, 211–229.

Davis, Jennifer R., *Charlemagne's Practice of Empire*, Cambridge 2015.

Depreux, Philippe, 'Wergeld, composition et rachat dans les capitulaires des rois francs', in: *La victime 2: La réparation du dommage.* (Cahiers de l'Institut d'Anthropologie Juridique 22), ed. Jaqueline Hoareau-Dodinau, Guillaume Métairie and Pascal Texier, Limoges 2009, 345–362.

Esders, Stefan, '"Eliten" und "Strafrecht" im frühen Mittelalter. Überlegungen zu den Bußen- und Wergeldkatalogen der Leges barbarorum', in: *Théorie et pratiques des élites au Haut Moyen Age. Conception, perception et réalisation sociale* (Collection Haut Moyen Age 13), ed. François Bougard, Hans-Werner Goetz and Régine Le Jan, Turnhout 2011, 261–282.

Esders, Stefan, 'Wergeld und soziale Netzwerke im Frankenreich', in: *Verwandtschaft, Name und soziale Ordnung (300–1100)* (Ergänzungsbände zum Reallexikon der Germanischen Altertumskunde 90), ed. Steffen Patzold and Karl Ubl, Berlin and New York 2014, 141–160.

Faulkner, Thomas, 'Carolingian Kings and the leges barbarorum', *Historical Research* 86 (2013), 443–464.

Faulkner, Thomas, *Law and Authority in the Early Middle Ages. The Frankish leges in the Carolingian Period* (Cambridge studies in medieval life and thought, fourth series 104), Cambridge 2016.

Fried, Johannes, *Karl der Große: Gewalt und Glaube. Eine Biographie*, Munich 2013.

Glatthaar, Michael, 'Subjektiver und indirekter Stil in den Kapitularien Karls des Großen. Ein Beitrag zur Frage ihrer Entstehung', *Deutsches Archiv* 70 (2014), 1–42.

Goetz, Hans-Werner, '"Nobilis". Der Adel im Selbstverständnis der Karolingerzeit', *Vierteljahrschrift für Sozial- und Wirtschaftsgeschichte* 70 (1983), 53–191.

Grahn-Hoek, Heike, 'Das Recht der Thüringer und die Frage ihrer ethnischen Identität: mit einer Bemerkung zur Entstehung von Begriff und Institution "Adel"', in: *Die Frühzeit der Thüringer: Archäologie, Sprache, Geschichte* (Ergänzungsbände zum Reallexikon der germanischen Altertumskunde 63), ed. Helmut Castritius, Berlin and New York 2009, 415–456.

Grahn-Hoek, Heike, 'The Thuringi, the Peculiarities of Their Law, and Their Legal Relations to the Gentes of Their Time, Chiefly According to the Lex (Angliorum et Werinorum hoc est) Thuringorum and the Other Leges barbarorum of the Early Middle Ages', in: *The Baiuvarii and Thuringi. An Ethnographic Perspective* (Studies in Historical Archaeoethnology 9), ed. Janine Fries-Knoblach and Heiko Steuer, Woodbridge 2014, 289–315.

Grierson, Philip and Mark Blackburn, *Medieval European Coinage I. The Early Middle Ages (5th–10th Centuries)*, Cambridge 1986, reprinted Cambridge 2006.

Grollmann, Felix, *Vom bayerischen Stammesrecht zur karolingischen Rechtsreform. Zur Integration Bayerns in das Frankenreich* (Abhandlungen zur rechtswissenschaftlichen Grundlagenforschung 98), Berlin 2018.

Hoppenbrouwers, Peter, 'Leges nationum and Ethnic Personality of Law in Charlemagne's Empire', in: *Law and Empire: Ideas, Practices, Actors* (Rulers & Elites 3), ed. Jeroen Duindam, Jill D. Harries, Caroline Humfress and Nimrod Hurvitz, Leiden and Boston 2013, 251–274.

Innes, Matthew, 'Charlemagne, Justice and Written Law', in: *Law, Custom and Justice in Late Antiquity and the Early Middle Ages*, ed. Alice Rio, London 2011, 155–203.

Kälble, Mathias, 'Ethnogenese und Herzogtum: Thüringen im Frankenreich (6.–9. Jahrhundert)', in: *Die Frühzeit der Thüringer: Archäologie, Sprache, Geschichte* (Ergänzungsbände zum Reallexikon der germanischen Altertumskunde 63), ed. Helmut Castritius, Berlin and New York 2009, 329–413.

Kaiser, Reinhold, 'Die "Capitula Remidii": Veranlassung, Autorschaft und Geltungsgrund, Verbreitung und Wirkung', in: *Schrift, Schriftgebrauch und Textsorten im frühmittelalterlichen Churrätien: Vorträge des internationalen Kolloquiums vom 18. bis 20. Mai 2006 im Rätischen Museum in Chur. Eine Publikation des Instituts für Kulturforschung Graubünden in Chur*, ed. Heidi Eisenhut, Karin Fuchs, Martin Hannes Graf and Hannes Steiner, Basel 2008, 146–182.

Kershaw, Paul, *Peaceful Kings: Peace, Power and the Early Medieval Political Imagination*, Oxford 2011.

Kluge, Bernd, *Am Beginn des Mittelalters. Die Münzen des karolingischen Reiches 751 bis 814. Pippin, Karlmann, Karl der Große* (Das Kabinett 15), Berlin 2014.

Kottje, Raymund, 'Einheit und Vielfalt des kirchlichen Lebens in der Karolingerzeit', *Zeitschrift für Kirchengeschichte* 76 (1965), 323–342.

Landau, Peter, 'Die Lex Thuringorum — Karls des Großen Gesetz für die Thüringer', *ZRG GA* 118 (2001), 23–57.

Lintzel, Martin, *Ausgewählte Schriften* 1, Berlin 1961.

Lück, Heiner, 'Der wilde Osten. Fränkische Herrschaftsstrukturen im Geltungsbereich der "Lex Saxonum" und "Lex Thuringorum" um 800', in: *Von den leges barbarorum bis zum ius barbarum des Nationalsozialismus. Festschrift für Hermann Nehlsen zum 70. Geburtstag*, ed. Hans-Georg Hermann, Thomas Gutmann, Joachim Rückert, Mathias Schmoeckel and Harald Siems, Cologne 2008, 118–131.

McCormick, Michael, 'Coins and the Economic History of Post-Roman Gaul: Testing the Standard Model in the Moselle, ca. 400–750', in: *Die Merowingischen Monetarmünzen als Quelle zum Verständnis des 7. Jahrhunderts in Gallien* (Mittelalterstudien 27), ed. Jörg Jarnut and Jürgen Strothmann, Paderborn 2013, 337–376.

McKitterick, Rosamond, 'Unity and Diversity in the Carolingian Church', *Studies in Church History* 32 (1996), 145–169.

McKitterick, Rosamond, 'Charlemagne's missi and their Books', in: *Early Medieval Studies in Memory of Patrick Wormald*, ed. Stephen Baxter, Catherine E. Karkov, Janet Nelson, and David Pelteret, Farnham 2009, 253–267.

Meens, Rob, *Penance in Medieval Europe, 600–1200*, Cambridge 2014.

Moeller, Ernst von, 'Der Homo Francus der Ewa Chamavorum', *Mitteilungen des Instituts für Österreichische Geschichtsforschung* 23 (1902), 217–230.

Mordek, Hubert, 'Kirchenrechtliche Autoritäten im Frühmittelalter', in: *Recht und Schrift im Mittelalter* (Vorträge und Forschungen 23), ed. Peter Classen, Sigmaringen 1977, 237–255.

Murray, Alexander Callander, '"Pax et diciplina" in Roman Public Law and the Merovingian State', in: *Proceedings of the Tenth International Congress of Medieval Canon Law* (Monumenta Iuris Canonici Series C, Subsidia), ed. Kenneth Pennington, Vatikan 2001, 269–285.

Nelson, Janet, 'On the Limits of the Carolingian Renaissance', in: *Studies in Church History* 14 (1977) 51–69.

Niermeyer, Jan Frederik, 'Het Midden-Nederlands rivierengebied in de Frankische tijd', *Tijdschrift voor Geschiedenis* 66 (1953), 145–169.

Patzold, Steffen, 'Normen im Buch. Überlegungen zu Geltungsansprüchen so genannter "Kapitularien"', *Frühmittelalterliche Studien* 41 (2007), 331–350.

Patzold, Steffen, 'Eine Hierarchie im Wandel: Die Ausbildung einer Metropolitanordnung im Frankenreich des 8. und 9. Jahrhunderts', in: *Hiérarchie et stratification sociale dans l'Occident médiéval 400–1100* (Collection Haut Moyen Âge 6), ed. Dominique Iogna-Prat, François Bougard, and Régine Le Jan, Turnhout 2008, 161–184.

Patzold, Steffen, 'Prozesse der Vereinheitlichung? Unitas, concordia und pax in der karolingischen Welt', in: *Entscheiden und Regieren. Konsens als Element vormoderner Entscheidungsfindung in transkultureller Perspektive* (Macht und Herrschaft 9), ed. Linda Dohmen and Tilmann Trausch, Göttingen 2019, 197–220.

Reuter, Timothy, 'The End of Carolingian Military Expansion', in: *Charlemagne's heir. New perspectives on the reign of Louis the Pious 814–840*, ed. Roger Collins and Peter Godman, Peter, Oxford 1990, 391–405.

Reynolds, Roger E., 'Unity and Diversity in Carolingian Canon Law Collections: The Case of the Collectio Hibernensis and Its Derivatives', in: *Carolingian Essays: Andrew W. Mellon Lectures in Early Christian Studies*, ed. Uta-Renate Blumenthal, Washington 1983, 99–135.

Schmitt, Johannes, *Untersuchungen zu den Liberi Homines der Karolingerzeit* (Europäische Hochschulschriften 3/83), Frankfurt/Main 1977.

Siems, Harald, *Studien zur Lex Frisionum* (Abhandlungen zur rechtswissenschaftlichen Grundlagenforschung 42), Ebelsbach 1980.

Siems, Harald, 'Recht in Rätien zur Zeit Karls des Großen — Ein Beitrag zu den Capitula Remedii', in: *Wandel und Konstanz zwischen Bodensee und Lombardei zur Zeit Karls des Grossen: Kloster St. Johann in Müstair und Churrätien. Tagung 13.–16. Juni 2012 in Müstair* (Acta Müstair, Kloster St. Johann 3), ed. Katrin Roth-Rubi, Eckart Kühne and Hans Rudolf Sennhauser, Zurich 2013, 199–238.

Springer, Matthias, *Die Sachsen* (Kohlhammer-Urban-Taschenbücher 59), Stuttgart 2004.

Theuerkauf, Gerhard, *Lex, Speculum, Compendium juris. Rechtsaufzeichnung und Rechtsbewußtsein in Norddeutschland vom 8. bis zum 16. Jahrhundert* (Forschungen zur deutschen Rechtsgeschichte 6), Cologne and Graz 1968.

Ubl, Karl, 'Die erste Leges-Reform Karls des Großen', in: *Das Gesetz — The Law — La Loi* (Miscellanea mediaevalia 38), ed. Guy Guldentops and Andreas Speer, Berlin 2014, 75–92.

Ubl, Karl, "Karl der Große und die Rückkehr des Gottesstaates. Narrative der Heroisierung für das Jahr 2014", *Historische Zeitschrift* 301 (2015), 374–390.

Ubl, Karl, *Sinnstiftungen eines Rechtsbuchs. Die Lex Salica im Frankenreich* (Quellen und Forschungen zum Recht im Mittelalter 9), Ostfildern 2016 (in print).

Ubl, Karl, 'Recht in der Region. Die Rezeption von leges und capitula im karolingischen Alemannien', in: *817 — Die urkundliche Ersterwähnung von Villingen und Schwenningen. Alemannien und das Reich in der Zeit Kaiser Ludwigs des Frommen* (Veröffentlichungen des Alemannischen Instituts 83), ed. Dendorfer Jürgen et al., Ostfildern 2016, 207–223.

Weinfurter, Stefan, *Karl der Große: Der Heilige Barbar*, Munich 2013.

Weitzel, Jürgen, 'Strafe und Strafverfahren in der Merowingerzeit', *ZRG GA* 111 (1994), 66–147.

Wormald, Patrick, 'The "leges barbarorum": Law and Ethnicity in the Post-Roman West', in: *Regna und gentes. The Relationship between Late Antique and Early Medieval Peoples and Kingdoms in the Transformation of the Roman World* (The Transformation of the Roman World 13), ed. Hans-Werner Goetz, Jörg Jarnut and Walter Pohl, Leiden and Boston 2003, 21–53.

CHAPTER 11

Wergild in the Carolingian Formula Collections

Warren Brown

The most visible and commonly used sources on wergild in early medieval disputes are normative and prescriptive: law codes, and to a lesser extent capitularies.[1] From these sources, older scholarship in particular tended to draw pictures of ideal legal worlds, in which defined acts of violence brought equally defined and carefully graduated payments that culminated in the blood-price or wergild.[2] Other more recent work, however, and especially the essays in this volume, have abandoned the anachronistic assumptions about what law means and how it was used that underlay these pictures; they have thus opened up new ways of understanding early medieval laws and what they say about the role played by money payments in resolving conflicts.[3] The essays in this volume do refer to other kinds of sources, such as saints' lives and other works of literature, penitentials, diplomas and legal formulas. Nevertheless, the normative sources and in particular the *leges* have stood clearly at the center; we are still working over the same ground as our predecessors.

---

1 I have for the most part followed the text of the original conference paper; I have made some small changes and added some material in response to the discussion.

2 See e.g. Andreas Roth, Art. 'Wergeld. I. Germanisches und Deutsches Recht', in: *LexMA* 8, Munich 1997, 2199–2201; Heinrich Brunner, *Deutsche Rechtsgeschichte* vol. 1, Leipzig 1906, 221–231; Franz Beyerle, 'Das Entwicklungsproblem im germanischen Rechtsgang, I. Sühne, Rache und Preisgabe in ihrer Beziehung zum Strafprozess der Volksrechte', *Deutschrechtliche Beiträge* 10, 2 (1915), 195–602, esp. 326–345.

3 See, for example, in addition to the work of the scholars contributing to this volume: William Ian Miller, *Eye for an Eye*, Cambridge 2006, esp. 104–108; Régine Le Jan, 'Justice royale et pratiques sociales dans le royaume Franc au IXe siècle', in: *La giustizia nell'alto medioevo (secoli IX–XI), 11–17 Aprile 1996*, Spoleto 1997, 47–90 (cited as Le Jan, 'Justice royale'), esp. 64–69; Philippe Depreux, 'Une faide exemplaire? À propos des aventures de Sichaire: vengeance et pacification aux temps Mérovingiens', in: *La vengeance 400–1200* (Collection de l'École française de Rome 357), ed. Dominique Barthélemy, François Bougard and Régine Le Jan, Rome 2006, 65–85 (cited as Depreux, 'Une faide exemplaire'); Paul R. Hyams, *Rancor and Reconciliation in Medieval England*, Ithaca 2003, 78–79, 83–89. See also in general on the development of the scholarship on vengeance and compensation Jean-Marie Moeglin, 'Le "droit de vengeance" chez les historiens du droit au moyen âge (XIXe–XXe siècles)', in: *La vengeance 400–1200* (Collection de l'École française de Rome 357), ed. Dominique Barthélemy, François Bougard and Régine Le Jan, Rome 2006, 102–148.

 | DOI:10.1163/9789004466128_012

We do have documents of practice, however, that can help us understand the role played by wergild in early medieval disputes. Some are royal or imperial diplomas, some are letters. Some are charters, or copies of charters copied into cartularies. Perhaps the most important, in my opinion, are the model charter and letter texts contained in the Frankish formula collections. These collections stem from across the Frankish world in the eighth, ninth and tenth centuries, mostly the ninth. They contain examples of documents and letters that served as models or sources for language, or as examples with which to train students.[4]

The formulas offer a number of advantages. They describe what people might do or, in the very many formula texts that were drawn from real documents, what people had already done. The manuscripts that contain them tell us, through the ways that their compilers copied, arranged, modified, and corrected them, that the people who put the collections together saw the formulas as documents that they might actually need to use at some point in the future, or from which they could draw useful language as they drafted documents for their own use and for the people who lived around them.

The formulas also capture the actions of people below the level of kings. Moreover, they bring us closer to the laity. The real charters that refer to wergild all stem from churches and monasteries; they therefore depict the actions of people as they interacted with churches and monasteries. In contrast, many (in fact more than half) of the formulas represent documents that involve only the laity.[5] The information they give us adds an important dimension to our picture of who paid money compensations as part of dispute settlements, and how and in what context they paid. They also show us things that ecclesiastical and monastic charters do not.

Finally, while most if not all of the surviving real charters and cartularies come from east of the Rhine, a great many (though again not all) of the formulas and the manuscripts into which they were copied are western. The formulas therefore fill in our image of wergild in practice in those western areas from which many of our normative sources come.

---

4 Edition: *Formulae Merowingici et Karolini aevi*, ed. Karl Zeumer, MGH Formulae Merowingici et Karolini aevi, Hanover 1886. Basic literature: Rudolf Buchner, *Deutschlands Geschichtsquellen im Mittelalter. Vorzeit und Karolinger. Beiheft: Die Rechtsquellen*, Weimar 1953, 49–55 (cited as Buchner, *Rechtsquellen*); Alice Rio, *Legal Practice and the Written Word in the Early Middle Ages: Frankish Formulae, c. 500–1000*, Cambridge 2009 (cited as Rio, *Legal Practice*); Sarah Patt, *Studien zu den 'Formulae imperiales'. Urkundenkonzeption und Formulargebrauch in der Kanzlei Ludwigs des Frommen (814–40)*, Wiesbaden 2016, esp. 10–46.

5 See Warren C. Brown, *Beyond the Monastery Walls: Lay Men and Women in Early Medieval Legal Formularies*, Cambridge, forthcoming.

The formulas use two words to describe blood-price: wergild, and *leodis*. I am going to treat these two words as essentially synonymous, since they both stem from Germanic words for 'man' or 'person'.[6] I will skip over the more general term 'compensation', expressed in Latin in the noun *compositio* or in the verb *componere*. These words appear quite often in the formulas, but they usually refer to some sort of compensation given to settle a number of different kinds of disputes, not just violent ones. *Componere* may refer to the handing over of money or valuables; it often, however, does not. In only one case, that I will mention below, does *compositio* explicitly refer to blood price.[7]

The first thing that we get out of the formulas is a set of securities for the payment of blood-price, or, as I like to call them, 'wergild-receipts' or 'Wergeldquittungen.'[8] These are by far the most common wergild formulas. According to Karl Zeumer's numbering in his edition of the formulas for the *Monumenta Germaniae Historica*[9] there are eight of them; some exist in multiple copies.[10] They all stem from cases of violent homicide. Here is one example, from a collection from Sens that has been dated to the mid-eighth century:

6 See the essay by Wolfgang Haubrichs in this volume, 92–112.

7 See below at note 12.

8 These are discussed briefly in Le Jan, 'Justice royale', 67 and Depreux, 'Une faide exemplaire', 80.

9 See note 4 above.

10 *Cartae Senonicae* 11 and 51, ed. Zeumer, MGH Formulae Merowingici et Karolini aevi, 189 and 207: Paris, BNF, lat. 4627 (Francia 9th century, shortly after 818?); *Formulae Salicae Bignonianae* 8, ed. Zeumer, MGH Formulae Merowingici et Karolini aevi, 230–231: Paris, BNF, lat. 13686 (Francia 9th century); *Formulae Salicae Merkelianae* 39, ed. Zeumer, MGH Formulae Merowingici et Karolini aevi, 256: Vatican City, Biblioteca Apostolica Vaticana, Reg. Lat. 612 (Francia [Northern?] late 9th century); *Formulae Extravagantes* I/8, ed. Zeumer, MGH Formulae Merowingici et Karolini aevi, 537–538: Wolfenbüttel, Herzog August Bibliothek, Cod. Guelf. 97 Weiss. (North or East Francia 2nd half of the 8th century); *Formulae Salicae Lindenbrogianae* 19, ed. Zeumer, MGH Formulae Merowingici et Karolini aevi, 280–281: Munich, Bayerische Staatsbibliothek, Clm 4650 (Salzburg? late 9th century), Copenhagen, Kongelige Bibliotek, GKS 1943 (Francia [East?] late 9th century), Munich, Bayerische Staatsbibliothek, Clm 29095 (Bavaria [St. Emmeram?] 1st half of the 9th century), lost 'Liber traditionum' copied in the 18th century by Frobenius Forster; *Marculfi Formulae* 2.18, ed. Zeumer, MGH Formulae Merowingici et Karolini aevi, 88–89: Leiden, Universiteitsbibliotheek Leiden, BPL 114 (Bourges? 8th/9th century), Paris, BNF, lat. 4627 (Francia 9th century), lat. 10756, (Francia 9th century), lat. 2123 (Flavigny late 8th or early 9th century), Copenhagen, Kongelige Bibliotek, Fabr. 84 (Francia mid 9th century); *Formulae Salicae Bignonianae* 9, ed. Zeumer, MGH Formulae Merowingici et Karolini aevi, 231: Paris, BNF, lat. 13686 (Francia 9th century); *Formulae Andecavenses* 6, ed. Zeumer, MGH Formulae Merowingici et Karolini aevi, 6–7: Fulda, Hochschul- und Landesbibliothek, D1 represents a similar security that deals with a quarrel and assault. See Rio, *Legal Practice*, 241–271 and her discussions of the individual collections and manuscripts throughout.

> Security
>
> Not a little but rather the greatest discord was exchanged between A and B. Coming before N and N, A raised a complaint against B, namely that he had in an evil manner slain his father, *or* his brother, C. It was asked of that person (B) by those men [N and N] if he had carried out and perpetrated this offence or not; he should say immediately. But that B was not able to deny this offence. It was thus judged by those men, that he ought to pay compensation, as was the law; and he did so at once. And I have asked this security to be made and affirmed for this B, that we ought not, neither I myself or any of my heirs nor anyone whomsoever, bring or raise any malicious actions or claims at any time concerning the death just discussed nor concerning that compensation. If we should attempt this, let it have no effect, and moreover let us pay to you as a penalty, together with a share for the fisc, so-and-so many ounces of gold, and let this present security remain firm for all time.[11]

In another one, again from the middle of the eighth century but this time from Tours, a man writes a letter to another man, saying that he had killed his brother — or some other relative. In the presence of a judge, the accused agreed to pay compensation. His accuser then acknowledges that the killer

> [...] gave to me so-and-so many silver *solidi*, as was acceptable to me, as complete compensation for the above-named relative of mine for his death. Therefore I have ordered this letter of security concerning this to be given to you, so that you need not fear any calumny or repetition concerning the above-mentioned homicide either from me or my heirs or any other outside person or representative, neither you nor anyone from

---

11 *Cartae Senonicae* 11, ed. Zeumer, MGH Formulae Merowingici et Karolini aevi, 189: *Securitas. Non minima, sed maxima vertetur discordia inter illos et illos. Venientes ante illo et illo, repedivit ipse ille adversus ipsius lui, eo quod genitore suo, aut germano suo, illo mala ordine interfecisset. Interrogatum fuit ad ipsos viros ipsius lui, se hac causa hacta vel perpetrata fuisset, anon, sed ipse in presente edicere deberet. Sed ipse ille hanc causam minime potuit denegare. Sic ab ipsis viris fuit iudicatum, ut illa leodem,* [*cum*] *lex erat, desolvere deberet; quod ita in presente et fecit. Et ego hanc securitate in ipso illo fieri et adfirmare rogavi, ut nullunquam tempore de iam dicta morte nec de ipsa leude nec ego ipse nec ullus de heredibus meis nec quislibet ullas calumnias nec repeditionis agere nec repedire non debeamus. Quod quia adtemptaverimus, nullum obteneat effectum, et insuper inferamus tibi una cum sotio fisco auri untias tantas esse multando, et presens securitas omni tempore firma permaneat.* See Karl Zeumer, 'Über die älteren fränkischen Formelsammlungen', *Neues Archiv der Gesellschaft für ältere deutsche Geschichtskunde*, 6 (1880), 9–115, here 69–79; Rio, *Legal Practice*, 121–126.

> your party, who lives with you, but that you be able to live henceforward free and clear in all things.[12]

This is the one case where the formula uses the word composition (*compositio*) rather than *leodis* or wergild.

The wergild receipts are all different from each other; they did not come from one old formula that kept getting copied over and over. They therefore tell us about a variety of different situations that could produce wergild payments. Some of the disputes they describe were settled by adjudication, at courts. In a Frankish formula that probably comes from the later eighth century, a man killed another man belonging to a bishop or an abbot and was therefore in danger of his life.[13] The killer came before a bishop and a count and other 'magnificent men', admitted his crime, and was told to pay the wergild with a pledge; he did so. The bishop and count then ordered the security to be written to secure the killer from any further trouble about the matter.

Other cases were handled outside of courts, and produced negotiated settlements that avoided bloodshed. In a formula from the famous seventh century collection compiled by the monk Marculf, a man writes to another man who has killed his brother.[14] Because of the killing, the man had come in danger of his life. He was saved, however, when 'priests and magnificent men' (*sacerdotes et magnificis viris*) brought them back to peace and concord, on the condition that the killer pay compensation. The letter represents security that he had done so.

One formula lets us a see a dispute move from one kind of process to another. It tells us that one man charged another with having killed his brother.[15] While

12 *Formulae Turonenses* 38, ed. Zeumer, MGH Formulae Merowingici et Karolini aevi, 156: [...] *et pro integra conpositione pro iam dicto parente meo pro ipsa morte, sicut mihi bene conplacuit, argentum soledos tantos dedisti: ideo hanc epistolam securitatis tibi ex hoc emittendam decrevi, ut neque a me neque ab heredibus meis neque a quolibet opposita vel emissa persona nullam calumniam neque repetitionem de iam dicto homicidio habere non pertimescas, neque tu neque ullus de parte tua, qui tecum commorantur, sed ducti atque securi in omnibus exinde valeatis residere.* See Depreux, 'La tradition manuscrite des 'Formules de Tours' et la diffusion des modèles d'actes aux VIIIe et IXe siècles', *Annales de Bretagne et des Pays de l'Ouest* 111, 3 (2004), 55–71, here 55; Rio, *Legal Practice*, 112–117.

13 *Formulae Salicae Lindenbrogianae* 19, ed. Zeumer, MGH Formulae Merowingici et Karolini aevi, 280–281; Buchner, *Rechtsquellen*, 53–54; Rio, *Legal Practice*, 101–110.

14 *Marculfi Formulae* 2.18, ed. Zeumer, MGH Formulae Merowingici et Karolini aevi, 88–89; Rio, *Legal Practice*, 81–101 and *The Formularies of Angers and Marculf. Two Merovingian Legal Handbooks*, Liverpool 2008, 104–123.

15 *Formulae Extravagantes* I/8, ed. Zeumer, MGH Formulae Merowingici et Karolini aevi, 537–538; Rio, *Legal Practice*, 162–64.

they 'thus contended with each other in another manner' (*dum sic inter se alius modis intenderunt*), good men stepped between them and recalled them to concord. An agreement was reached whereby the accused paid the *leodis*. I would very much like to know what 'in another manner' means. Perhaps it means that they were fighting, but it could as well mean that they were arguing before a court.

The method of killing described by these formulas can vary. Usually, they say that one man was accused of a killing, but sometimes the killing was carried out by a group. A formula that survives in a ninth century Frankish manuscript says that a man with his following (*in contubernium*) had assaulted and killed another man.[16] The relatives and friends of the dead man sued him before a count. The accused was not able to deny it; he was ordered to pay compensation to the relatives, who were then required to give him this security.

The most outrageous of these wergild receipts tells us that not only men, but women too both killed and paid compensation. In this formula from Sens, a woman is accused at a judicial assembly of a rather remarkable act of violence:

> Not a little, but a great deal of discord took place between A and B. Coming to the place N before good men, he related in his suit or rather in that of his wife C against the accused, saying that she (B) had struck her (C) knees and moreover their daughter named D had fled and there she (B) had killed her. But she B was not able to deny this suit.[17]

The accused woman is ordered to pay compensation. This security indemnifies her from further trouble.

As in the law codes, the wergild receipts portray blood price payments as a matter for families and kin.[18] People accuse others of having killed their father, brother, or some other relative, or having attacked their wife and killed their

16 *Formulae Salicae Bignonianae* 8, ed. Zeumer, MGH Formulae Merowingici et Karolini aevi, 230–231; Paris, BNF, lat. 13686 (Francia 9th century); Rio, *Legal Practice*, 126–132.

17 *Cartae Senonicae* 51, ed. Zeumer, MGH Formulae Merowingici et Karolini aevi, 207: *Non minima, sed maxima verteretur discordia inter illo et ill. Venientes in loco illo ante bonis hominibus, repedebat ipse in causa sua vel in coniugia sua illa adversus ipsius lue, dum diceret, eo quod ipsa genua sua inpinxit et super filia eorum nomen illa cessisset et ipsa ibidem occisit. Sed ipsa illa hac causa minime potuit denegare.*

18 See e.g. *Pactus Legis Salicae* 62, ed. Karl August Eckhardt, MGH LL nationum Germanicarum 4, 1, Hanover 1962, 227–28, and, for example, the so-called 'Systematic Version' of the *Lex Salica Karolina*: *Lex Salica* 14, ed. Karl August Eckhardt, MGH LL nationum Germanicarum 4, 2, Hanover 1969, 204–05. See also *Pactus Legis Salicae* 68, ed. Eckhardt, MGH LL nat. Germ. 4, 1, 239; Lisi Oliver, *The Body Legal in Barbarian Law*, Toronto 2011, 46.

daughter, and are compensated for them. None of these formulas say that kings or any other constituted authority were directly involved (though in the penalty clauses they sometimes mention part of a penalty going to the royal fisc).[19] The only exception is the wergild receipt from the later eighth century mentioned above, in which a man is accused of having killed a dependent of a bishop or an abbot.[20] The man admits his crime and is ordered to pay the *leodis*. The two men heading the judicial assembly, a bishop and a count, issue this security saying that he had paid. In the absence of any explicit statement, I can only conclude that the wergild was paid to the dead man's lord: the bishop or abbot. If this is true, then the formula not only tells us that ecclesiastical or monastic dependents had wergilds; it appears that an ecclesiastical *familia* could serve as an ersatz kindred.

One final wergild receipt makes clear the etymological connection between *leodis* as man price and *leodis* as man in the most physical possible way; *leodis* means man, or body, and man-price in the same document. A man comes before a public court, or *mallus,* headed by a count.[21] There he charges another with having assaulted his man on the road and killed him, and taken all of his goods. Moreover,

> [...] he had buried the corpse (*leodis*) against the law; but that N was seen to stand up at once and he was in no way able to deny this charge, but he professed, that at the instigation of the enemy [i.e., the devil] he had killed and slain that man. But they in that court declared to him thus, that he should thereupon pay that man (*ipsum hominem*) or rather that compensation (*leodis*) according to the laws; and he therefore did this.[22]

In the penalty clause, it says that if someone should presume to raise any further trouble, he was to pay double the amount of the *leodis*.

These wergild securities tell us not only that wergild was a consequence of homicide, but also that it was actually paid. It was paid in a variety of real-life

---

19 See e.g. *Cartae Senonicae* 11, ed. Zeumer, MGH Formulae Merowingici et Karolini aevi, 189.

20 *Formulae Salicae Lindenbrogianae* 19, ed. Zeumer, MGH Formulae Merowingici et Karolini aevi, 280–281.

21 *Formulae Salicae Bignonianae* 9, ed. Zeumer, MGH Formulae Merowingici et Karolini aevi, 231.

22 *Formulae Salicae Bignonianae* 9, ed. Zeumer, MGH Formulae Merowingici et Karolini aevi, 231: [...] *vel leode contra legem ibi burisset; sed ipsi illi de praesente adstare videbatur et hac causa nullatenus potuit denegare, sed taliter fuit professus, quod faciente inimicum ipsum hominem occidisset vel interfecisset. Sed taliter in ipso mallo ei iudicaverunt, ut ipsum hominem vel ipsa leode legibus exinde trassolvere deberet; quod ita et fecit.*

situations. It was assigned to and paid not only by free men but also dependents and women. The payments were worked out in courts as well as outside them.

But there are other formulas besides the securities that refer to blood price. Some of these show us wergild being paid in still other situations from those I have just discussed, and being used in still different ways.

A formula from the Bavarian diocese of Passau highlights the role played by patron/client relationships, by sanctuary, and by intercession in settling disputes. In it, we see a man pleading to be able to pay wergild. The formula represents a letter from a bishop, probably in the original letter from which the formula was drawn the bishop of Passau.[23] The first part of the letter deals with some stolen cows. The second part of the formula reads:

> A certain man of yours N came before the altar of St. Stephen and there sought aid, because he, compelled by necessity, had killed another of your men, just as he reported [the events] to us in their proper order (*ex ordine*), and he asked, that he be allowed to pay his wergild for him. Therefore I pray, that, since he sought help in this place, that your mercy not recede from him, and that he make good his transgressions.[24]

The killer was apparently trying to escape harsher consequences, that is, corporal punishment or death, at the hands of the dead man's family or at the hands of the count; there is no way to tell.

In all of the cases we have looked at so far, wergild is compensation paid for homicide. There is one case, however, in which it is not. Here wergild is instead a unit of measurement, that is, a way of measuring compensation in other kinds of transactions.[25] The formula represents a gift of property to a monastery, in which the donor, his wife, and his heirs retained use rights to the property in exchange for a census.[26] If he or his heirs ever wanted to

---

23 *Collectio Pataviensis* 2, ed. Zeumer, MGH Formulae Merowingici et Karolini aevi, 457; Rio, *Legal Practice*, 137–139; Franz Brunhoelzl, *Studien zum geistigen Leben in Passau im achten und neunten Jahrhundert*, Munich 2000.

24 *Collectio Pataviensis* 2, ed. Zeumer, MGH Formulae Merowingici et Karolini aevi, 457: *Quidam homo vester N. ante altare sancti Stefani venit et ibi querebat auxilium, eo quod occideret alium hominem vestrum necessitate conpulsus, sicut iste nobis referebat ex ordine, petivitque, ut sibi wergeltum eius conponere licuisset. Ideo precamur, ut, quia auxilium ab isto loco quesierat, misericordia vestra ab eo non recedat, et delicta peremendet.*

25 Cf. the essay by Lisi Oliver in this volume, 127–128.

26 *Formulae Sangallenses* 2/21, ed. Zeumer, MGH Formulae Merowingici et Karolini aevi, 407–408.

redeem the property, it says, 'let him or his heirs redeem [it] with a third part of [their] wergild.'[27]

According to the law codes, wergild amounts were fixed. As is well known, for example, the wergild for a freeman in the *Lex Salica* is 200 solidi.[28] I have always, however, tended to think that in reality, blood-price payments were negotiable. I have been influenced in particular by Bishop Gregory of Tours' account in his *Ten Books of Histories* of the dispute involving Austregisel, Sichar, and Chramnesind that played out in the late sixth century, in and around the city of Tours.[29] The dispute produced a great deal of violence and a number of killings, most importantly the killing of Chramnesind's father and brother by Sichar. Chramnesind refused to accept compensation, and plundered and burned Sichar's house and the houses of some of Sichar's neighbors. A judge intervened, and with the help of Bishop Gregory himself brokered a settlement. The terms of the settlement were as follows: Chramnesind, by refusing compensation, had forfeited his right to be compensated. Nevertheless, he would be compensated, but with only half of the amount he would have received previously. Gregory tells us explicitly that this settlement was against the letter of the law[30] (the settlement did not stick, by the way; Chramnesind ended up killing Sichar anyway).

The formulas do not help us much. Some suggest that wergild was indeed fixed. Several say that *leodis* was to be paid according the law (*cum lex erat*, or simply *legibus*).[31] In addition, a formula from Book I of Marculf's collection states that when a man became a sworn follower of the king, or *antrustio*, his wergild was set at 600 *solidi*; this matches what the Salic Law says.[32] The property gift discussed above specifies that if the donor or his heirs wanted to

27 *Formulae Sangallenses* 2/21, ed. Zeumer, MGH Formulae Merowingici et Karolini aevi, 408: [...] *cum tercia parte weregeldi redimat ipse vel heres eius.*

28 *Pactus Legis Salicae* 15.1 and 41.1, ed. Eckhardt, MGH LL nat. Germ. 4, 1, 70 and 154; *Lex Salica* 11.1, ed. Eckhardt, MGH LL nat. Germ. 4, 2, 203.

29 Gregory of Tours, *Decem Libri Historiarum* 7.47 and 9.19, vol. 2, ed. Rudolf Buchner, 2 vols., Darmstadt 1967–1970, 152–157, and 256–259; Warren C. Brown, *Violence in Medieval Europe*, Abingdon 2011, 39–41 (cited as Brown, *Violence*); Depreux, 'Une faide exemplaire'.

30 Gregory of Tours, *Decem Libri Historiarum* 7.47, ed. Buchner, 156: [...] *et hoc contra legis actum.*

31 *Cartae Senonicae* 11, ed. Zeumer, MGH Formulae Merowingici et Karolini aevi, 189; *Formulae Salicae Bignonianae* 8 and 9, ed. Zeumer, MGH Formulae Merowingici et Karolini aevi, 230–231 and 231.

32 *Marculfi Formulae* 1.18, ed. Zeumer, MGH Formulae Merowingici et Karolini aevi, 55; *Pactus Legis Salicae* 41.5, ed. Eckhardt, MGH LL nat. Germ. 4, 1, 156; *Lex Salica* 11.4, ed. Eckhardt, MGH LL nat. Germ. 4, 2, 204.

redeem the property they had to pay one third of their wergild; this implies that their wergild was a fixed, known amount.[33]

Other formulas, however, suggest that wergild might have been negotiable by leaving the amount of the payment blank. The formula discussed above, in which the parties 'contended with each other in another manner' before a settlement was reached, says that the accused killer agreed to pay 'so-and-so many *solidi* as a *leodis*' (*solidus de leodum tantus* [sic]).[34] A similar formula in Marculf's collection, for a case in which one man was accused of killing another's brother, likewise says that the accused would pay 'so-and-so many solidi' (*solidus tantus* [sic]).[35]

It is nevertheless possible that these formulas left the amount of the payments blank not because wergilds were negotiable but rather because they fluctuated according to the specifics of each individual case. The *leges* certainly tell us that in legal theory, wergild amounts were supposed to vary quite a bit, depending on the condition or status of the people involved or the nature of their killing.[36] To draw once more on the Salic Law, the wergild for free men goes up or down depending on, for example, whether they are adult freemen or boys,[37] whether they are Roman or Frank,[38] whether they are in their homes or in the army.[39] That for women depends on whether they are of childbearing age or not, or pregnant.[40] Killing in secret or drowning someone raised the wergild dramatically.[41] Status, too, mattered. Wergild amounts change depending on whether a slain man is (at the upper end) a royal follower, agent, or

33 *Formulae Sangallenses*, 2/21, ed. Zeumer, MGH Formulae Merowingici et Karolini aevi, 407–408.

34 *Formulae Extravagantes* I/8, ed. Zeumer, MGH Formulae Merowingici et Karolini aevi, 537–538.

35 *Marculfi Formulae* 2.18, ed. Zeumer, MGH Formulae Merowingici et Karolini aevi, 88–89. See also e.g. *Formulae Salicae Lindenbrogianae* 19, ed. Zeumer, MGH Formulae Merowingici et Karolini aevi, 280–281.

36 See Brown, *Violence*, 49–52; Oliver, *The Body Legal*, esp. 203–226 on variations according to rank and status.

37 *Pactus Legis Salicae* 15.1 and 41.1, ed. Eckhardt, MGH LL nat. Germ. 4, 1, 70 and 154; *Lex Salica* 11.1, ed. Eckhardt, MGH LL nat. Germ. 4, 2, 203.

38 *Pactus Legis Salicae* 41.8–10, ed. Eckhardt, MGH LL nat. Germ. 4, 1, 157; *Lex Salica* 11.6–8, ed. Eckhardt, MGH LL nat. Germ. 4, 2, 203.

39 *Pactus Legis Salicae* 41.21, 42.1 and 43.1, ed. Eckhardt, MGH LL nat. Germ. 4, 1, 161, 162, and 164–166; *Lex Salica* 8.1 and 12.1, ed. Eckhardt, MGH LL nat. Germ. 4, 2, 202 and 204.

40 *Pactus Legis Salicae* 24.5, 24.8–9, 41.15–17, 41.19, and 65e.1–4, ed. Eckhardt, MGH LL nat. Germ. 4, 1, 91, 92, 160, 160 and 235; *Lex Salica* 33.4 and 33.6–8, ed. Eckhardt, MGH LL nat. Germ. 4, 2, 213.

41 *Pactus Legis Salicae* 41.2–4 and 41.6–7, ed. Eckhardt, MGH LL nat. Germ. 4, 1, 155–156; *Lex Salica* 11.2 and 11.5, ed. Eckhardt, MGH LL nat. Germ. 4, 2, 203.

companion,[42] or (at the lower end) a particular kind of servant, such as an ironsmith, goldsmith, swineherd, vintner, or stablehand.[43] The Carolingian revision of the Salic Law, the Lex Salica Karolina, provides for religious status: deacons were to be compensated with a higher wergild than ordinary freemen, and priests with twice the wergild of a deacon.[44]

The formulas do not tell us whether these categories, with their corresponding wergild amounts, were applied in practice. They do cover people of different status. Some parties to homicide cases were plainly of high status. They had access to counts' courts attended by very powerful people; one places its case in a court headed by a count, a bishop, and 'many magnificent men.'[45] One accused killer was important enough to have an armed following.[46] In contrast, other cases were handled at courts headed only by *boni homines*. One specifies that the people involved were subordinate to someone more important or powerful than they.[47] But regardless of the status of the people involved, the formulas do not say anything about whether wergild amounts varied accordingly.

The only conclusion I can draw is that in some cases — most likely depending on the politics surrounding particular situations — wergild amounts were possibly, even probably, negotiated. In cases where political considerations did not apply and settlements were therefore more straightforward, they may have been fixed. The formulas do not let us say for sure. But the fact that they leave wergild amounts blank does allow them to cover the full range of possibilities.

Do the formulas tell us anything about what wergild was intended to accomplish, and why it was levied? Was it, as the older scholarship often presents it, a punishment to deter violence and to reinforce a general peace, which was legally required for all homicides? That is, was it a fine? Was it compensation for a wrong incurred by the victim's kin, that satisfied both the physical loss and the loss of honor, and that could replace violent vengeance but did not always do so? Was it simply the killer buying himself (or herself) out of a blood feud? I am dubious about the first suggestion, that is, that wergild was a fine. It is very

---

42 *Pactus Legis Salicae* 41.5, 41.8–10, 42.1, 54.1–3 and 63.2, ed. Eckhardt, MGH LL nat. Germ. 4, 1, 156–157, 162, 203–204, and 230; *Lex Salica* 11.4, 11.6–8, 12.2, 7.1–3, and 8.2, ed. Eckhardt, MGH LL nat. Germ. 4, 2, 203-204, and 202.

43 *Pactus Legis Salicae* 35.9, ed. Eckhardt, MGH LL nat. Germ. 4, 1, 132; not in the *Lex Salica*.

44 *Lex Salica* 6.3–4, ed. Eckhardt, MGH LL nat. Germ. 4, 2, 202.

45 *Formulae Salicae Lindenbrogianae* 19, ed. Zeumer, MGH Formulae Merowingici et Karolini aevi, 280–281.

46 *Formulae Salicae Bignonianae* 8, ed. Zeumer, MGH Formulae Merowingici et Karolini aevi, 230–231.

47 *Collectio Pataviensis* 2, ed. Zeumer, MGH Formulae Merowingici et Karolini aevi, 457.

clear that early medieval society tolerated both laws and courts and the right to vengeance killings side by side, and that the law worked with, not against the culture of personal violence.[48] Unfortunately, the formulas do not tell us much more. The wergild securities make it clear that once wergild was paid, it was supposed to end a dispute by threatening anyone who tried to revive it with reprisal from the victim's family. But beyond this I can see no evidence for how the people who paid wergild understood what they were doing. The best I can say is that when violent conflict reached a point where one party, or outside mediators, brought it to the law, then it was paid, and paid to the victim's kin or the head of his *familia*.

A few of the formulas tell us that despite how the law codes might make things look, wergild was not always required. People did not have to settle a dispute by compensation or risk legal sanction; they could choose the path of violence. Two of our formulas state that someone who had killed another was in danger of being killed himself until the community intervened.[49] These suggest that if mediators had not intervened, the victim's kin would indeed have tried to take violent revenge on the perpetrator. The formulas do not say anything to suggest that they would then be acting against the law. This is of course very weak evidence, but it does raise the possibility that some disputes were not governed by the law as we see it in the written law codes, but rather by the norms of vengeance.

So what do we get out of all this? The formulas show us that in the wake of violent disputes among laymen, wergild was actually paid, though it is not clear whether the amounts fit what our normative sources say or not. It was paid as the result of judgments in courts, and in settlements outside of court. It was paid by freemen, but also by women and dependents. It was paid after homicides carried out in a variety of situations and in a variety of ways. The formulas show us wergild being paid in a process that generated a parchment trail; the person who had paid wergild received a document protecting him from further trouble. This adds an important piece to a general argument that I and others have made, that laypeople used documents, some of which at least they would have wanted to keep and store.[50]

Formulas of course are not only the evidence for wergild in practice: as I mentioned at the beginning, we do have diplomas, charters, and letters that

48 Brown, *Violence*, 33–67.

49 *Marculfi Formulae* 2.18, ed. Zeumer, MGH Formulae Merowingici et Karolini aevi, 88–89; *Formulae Salicae Lindenbrogianae* 19, ed. Zeumer, MGH Formulae Merowingici et Karolini aevi, 280–281.

50 Warren C. Brown et al., *Documentary Culture and the Laity in the Early Middle Ages*, Cambridge 2013.

refer to it. I want to go through some of these briefly and compare them to the formulas.

These sources for the most part confirm what the formulas say. Because they are mostly ecclesiastical and monastic, they tell us about killings in which clerics or ecclesiastical/monastic dependents were involved. These people were killed, and they also killed; abbots and bishops both received and paid wergild. A charter from the Bavarian diocese of Freising from 814 has a man named Hleopehrt giving property *pro wergeldum* for the priest Hroadolf.[51] In a diploma of Lothar I. from 855, the emperor agrees to pay the abbot of Prüm wergild for a cleric that had been killed by men of the fisc.[52] In Freising once again, the *sculdhaisus* Isanhart works out with Bishop Erchanbert and his advocate Odolt the *wergaldum* [sic] of his *barscalti* and accepts from the bishop a *colonica* in exchange for a census; this implies that it was one of the bishop's men (possibly a cleric?) who had carried out the killing.[53] One example that does not concern the church implies that in this particular case, the applicable wergild amounts were fixed and known. A fragment of an imperial judgment, dated sometime to the reign of Charlemagne, concerns a man who had seized a *servus* and forced him to kill his lords, who were children.[54] Once the *servus* had carried out his commission, he himself was thrown into a pit, where he died. The man in charge of the whole operation was caught and brought before Charlemagne. The king ordered that he pay a triple wergild for the younger boy and a double wergild for the older. In addition, he was to pay a triple wergild for the *servus* and on top of everything the royal ban (60 solidi).

Here too we see people seeking sanctuary and intercession from powerful people in order to be able to pay wergild and avoid the anger and vengeance of their victim's kin or lord. A letter from Archbishop Hincmar of Reims to the west Frankish king Charles the Bald asks the king to allow a man to pay wergild.[55] In a letter of the Carolingian courtier and intellectual Einhard, Einhard writes to his friend the *vicedominus* Marchrad. Two *servi* had fled

51 *Die Traditionen des Hochstifts Freising*, a. 814, nr. 318b, ed. Theodor Bitterauf, vol. 1, Munich 1905–1909, 273.

52 *Die Urkunden Lothars I. und Lothars II.*, a. 854 or 855, nr. 132, ed. Theodor Schieffer, MGH DD Lo I / Lo II, Berlin 1966, 295–296; 'Concessio Lotharii imperatoris de Gozhelino interfecto', nr. 88, in: *Urkundenbuch zur Geschichte der, jetzt die Preussischen Regierungsbezirke Coblenz und Trier bildenden mittelrheinischen Territorien*, ed. Heinrich Beyer, Coblenz 1860, 93.

53 *Die Traditionen des Hochstifts Freising*, a. 846, nr. 679, ed. Bitterauf, 571–572.

54 *Capitularia Regum Francorum* I, nr. 129, ed. Alfred Boretius, MGH Capitularia regum Francorum 1, Hanover 1883, 257; Brown, *Violence*, 81.

55 Hincmar of Reims, *Ad Carolum Regem*, Epistola XV, ed. Jacques-Paul Migne, Patrologia Latina, vol. 126, Paris 1852, 96–97.

within the boundaries of Einhard's monastery of Saints Marcellinus and Peter at Seligenstadt. It seems that their brother had killed one of his companions. They begged Einhard to intercede with Marchrad on their behalf; they asked that they be allowed to pay the wergild for their brother, so that 'his members not be lost to him.'[56]

But interestingly, by far the most numerous examples of wergild outside the formulas are charters that use wergild as a unit of measurement, or as an amount to pay in a penalty clause. In a St. Gall charter of 779, a man gives property to St. Gall but keeps it for life in exchange for a census. If he has no children, any relatives who shall wish to redeem it can do so in exchange for a payment of the donor's wergild (*cum meo wirigeldo*).[57] A second St. Gall charter tells us that in 786, Count Gerold gave property to St. Gall and received it back for his lifetime in exchange for a census. If he wanted to redeem it, he could, for a payment of three times his wergild.[58] Farther north, in Fulda in 788, a man gives property to Fulda on the condition that he, or his legitimate children, could redeem it by paying twice their wergild.[59] Finally, in Freising in 755, one Starcholf gives property to Freising *post obitum*. The penalty clause says that anyone who tried to act against the gift would pay his wergild to a judge *ut mos est*.[60]

The formulas nevertheless give us a greater variety of images of homicide that led to wergild payments than these charters and letters do. This very variety should reassure us that the formulas are not just conservative models, carried forward by generations of copyists, that had no relation to reality in the times and places they were copied. They are all independent traditions, based on very different situations and describing different ways of resolving disputes. The details of the stories they tell, suggest that most if not all of them were derived from real documents. We see violence between kindreds, killings carried out by armed followings, killings carried out by women. They were resolved in courts, by judgment, or by mediation and negotiation. It is not quite clear in the formulas (or elsewhere for that matter) how the law figured into anything, that is whether people in conflict thought that wergild amounts were fixed by law, varied according to the status and condition of the parties involved, and applied in every case, as the laws imply, or that the amounts

56 *Einharti Epistolae*, a. 828–840, nr. 48, ed. Karl Hampe, MGH EE 5, Epistolae Karolini aevi III, Berlin 1899, 133–134: [...] *ut ei membra perdonentur*.

57 *Urkundenbuch der Abtei Sanct Gallen*, a. 779, nr. 88, ed. Hermann Wartmann, vol. 1, Zürich 1863, 84.

58 *Urkundenbuch der Abtei Sanct Gallen*, a. 786, nr. 108, ed. Wartmann, 102.

59 *Codex Diplomaticus Fuldensis*, a. 788, nr. 89, ed. Ernst F. J. Dronke, Cassel 1850, 54–55.

60 *Die Traditionen des Hochstifts Freising*, a. 755, nr. 8, ed. Bitterauf, 34–35.

could be negotiable. Trace evidence in the formulas suggest that it could go either way depending on the situation. Finally, some formulas do suggest that the payment of wergild after a homicide was not automatic, that in some situations people assumed the right to pursue their enemies with violence.

Bibliography

Primary Sources

Capitularia Regum Francorum 1, ed. Alfred Boretius, MGH Capitularia regum Francorum 1, Hanover 1883.

Codex Diplomaticus Fuldensis, ed. Ernst F. J. Dronke, Cassel 1850.

Die Traditionen des Hochstifts Freising, ed. Theodor Bitterauf, vol. 1, Munich 1905–1909.

Die Urkunden Lothars I. und Lothars II., ed. Theodor Schieffer, MGH Diplomata Lo I / Lo II, Berlin 1966.

Einharti Epistolae, ed. Karl Hampe, MGH EE 5, Epistolae Karolini aevi III, Berlin 1899.

Formulae Merowingici et Karolini aevi, ed. Karl Zeumer, MGH Formulae Merowingici et Karolini aevi, Hanover 1886.

Gregory of Tours, *Decem Libri Historiarum*, ed. Rudolf Buchner, 2 vols., Darmstadt 1967–1970.

Hincmar of Reims, *Ad Carolum Regem*, ed. Jacques-Paul Migne, Patrologia Latina, vol. 126, Epistola XV, Paris 1852, 94–99.

Lex Salica, ed. Karl August Eckhardt, MGH LL nationum Germanicarum 4, 2, Hanover 1969.

Pactus Legis Salicae, ed. Karl August Eckhardt, MGH LL nationum Germanicarum 4, 1, Hanover 1962.

Urkundenbuch der Abtei Sanct Gallen, ed. Hermann Wartmann, vol. 1, Zürich 1863.

Urkundenbuch zur Geschichte der jetzt die Preussischen Regierungsbezirke Coblenz und Trier bildenden mittelrheinischen Territorien, ed. Heinrich Beyer, Coblenz 1860.

Secondary Works

Beyerle, Franz, 'Das Entwicklungsproblem im germanischen Rechtsgang, I. Sühne, Rache und Preisgabe in ihrer Beziehung zum Strafprozess der Volksrechte', *Deutschrechtliche Beiträge* 10, 2 (1915), 195–602.

Brown, Warren C., *Violence in Medieval Europe*, Abingdon 2011.

Brown, Warren C., *Beyond the Monastery Walls: Lay Men and Women in Early Medieval Legal Formularies*, Cambridge, forthcoming.

Brown, Warren C., Marios Costambeys, Matthew Innes and Adam J. Kosto (ed.), *Documentary Culture and the Laity in the Early Middle Ages*, Cambridge 2013.

Brunhoelzl, Franz, *Studien zum geistigen Leben in Passau im achten und neunten Jahrhundert*, Munich 2000.

Brunner, Heinrich, *Deutsche Rechtsgeschichte* vol. 1, Leipzig ²1906.

Buchner, Rudolf, *Deutschlands Geschichtsquellen im Mittelalter. Vorzeit und Karolinger. Beiheft: Die Rechtsquellen*, Weimar 1953.

Depreux, Philippe, 'La tradition manuscrite des "formules de Tours" et la diffusion des modèles d'actes aux VIIIᵉ et IXᵉ siècles', *Annales de Bretagne et des Pays de l'Ouest* 111, 3 (2004), 55–71.

Depreux, Philippe, 'Une faide exemplaire? À propos des aventures de Sichaire: vengeance et pacification aux temps Mérovingiens', in: *La vengeance 400–1200* (Collection de l'École française de Rome 357), ed. Dominique Barthélemy, François Bougard and Régine Le Jan, Rome 2006, 65–85.

Hyams, Paul R., *Rancor and Reconciliation in Medieval England*, Ithaca 2003.

Le Jan, Régine, 'Justice royale et pratiques sociales dans le royaume Franc au IXᵉ siècle', in: *La giustizia nell'alto medioevo (secoli IX–XI), 11–17 Aprile 1996*, Spoleto 1997, 47–90.

Miller, William Ian, *Eye for an Eye*, Cambridge 2006.

Moeglin, Jean-Marie, 'Le "droit de vengeance" chez les historiens du droit au moyen âge (XIXᵉ–XXᵉ siècles)', in: *La vengeance 400–1200* (Collection de l'École française de Rome 357), ed. Dominique Barthélemy, François Bougard and Régine Le Jan, Rome 2006, 101–148.

Oliver, Lisi, *The Body Legal in Barbarian Law*, Toronto 2011.

Patt, Sarah, *Studien zu den 'Formulae imperiales'. Urkundenkonzeption und Formulargebrauch in der Kanzlei Ludwigs des Frommen (814–40)*, Wiesbaden 2016.

Rio, Alice, *Legal Practice and the Written Word in the Early Middle Ages: Frankish Formulae, c. 500–1000*, Cambridge 2009.

Rio, Alice, *The Formularies of Angers and Marculf. Two Merovingian Legal Handbooks*, Liverpool 2008.

Roth, Andreas, Art. 'Wergeld. I. Germanisches und Deutsches Recht', in: *LexMA* 8, Munich 1997, 2199–2201.

Zeumer, Karl, 'Über die älteren fränkischen Formelsammlungen', *Neues Archiv der Gesellschaft für ältere deutsche Geschichtskunde* 6 (1880), 9–115.

CHAPTER 12

The Kin's Collective Responsibility for the Payment of Man's Compensation in Medieval Denmark

Helle Vogt

In 1537 the Danish king Christian III and the Council of the Realm issued the Recess of Copenhagen, the first in a line of penal laws coming in the wave of the Lutheran Reformation that had taken place in the preceding year.[1] Article 7 of the Recess stated that because the kinsmen's collective payment of wergild, or man's compensation as it is called here,[2] together with the killer was a source of frequent killings, from now on all non-nobles who committed an intentional homicide should pay 'a life for a life', the killer's possessions should be confiscated, and his kinsmen should be free of all obligations.[3] One might imagine that the Danes would be happy that they no longer had to pay for their kinsmen's misbehaviour, but that was certainly not the case. The royal chancellery's letter-books from the sixteenth century are full of petitions from widows or kinsmen of killed persons who ask permission to have the killer's life spared and receive man's compensation instead.[4] It is quite clear that the Danes had difficulty accepting that it was more just to take a man's life than to let him and his kin pay compensation, especially to the widow, children or parents of the

1 Thanks to Kate Gilbert, Hans Jacob Orning, and Stephen D. White for valuable help and comments. Wherever possible, references are made to literature in English. References to the discussion in Danish can be found in the English literature.

2 In this article, the term 'man's compensation' is used for wergild: see the next page for an explanation.

3 *Den danske rigslovgivning 1523–1558*, 'Kong Christian 3.s anden københavnske reces 24. august 1537', ed. Aage Andersen, Copenhagen 2015, 198–199. The killer's possessions were to be divided between the king and the killed man's heirs. If there were no heirs of the body, the inheritance after the killed man went back to his family, and since the widow did not take inheritance, she was left with nothing. If the killer was poor, the heirs would not receive any compensation.

4 *Kancelliets Brevbøger vedrørende Danmarks indre Forhold i Uddrag*, ed. Carl F. Bricka et al., 39 vols., Copenhagen 1885–2005; Ole Fenger, *Fejde og mandebod — Studier over slægtsansvaret i germansk og gammeldansk ret*, Copenhagen 1971, 510–524 (cited as Fenger, *Fejde og mandebod*); Jeppe B. Netterstrøm, 'Bondefejder i Danmark 1450–1650', in: *Feider og fred i nordisk middelalder*, ed. Erik Opsahl, Unipub 2007, 35–72; Jeppe B. Netterstrøm, 'Criminalization of Homicide in Early Modern Denmark (16th–17th centuries)'. *Scandinavian Journal of History* 42, 4 (2017), 459–475.

 | DOI:10.1163/9789004466128_013

deceased who were left without a breadwinner and had therefore become the responsibility of their kinsmen.

How is it that the collective payment of man's compensation functioned so relatively well in Denmark during the Middle Ages, and that it took both a reformation and a couple of generations of schooling in Lutheran doctrines to get the Danes to fully accept that the price for a life was a life, and not something that could be measured in money? In that respect Denmark differed from the other Nordic countries, where the kin's collective payment of man's compensation was abolished with the introduction of national laws in Norway in 1274 and heavily reduced in Sweden in 1350.[5] In Sweden a killer caught red-handed had to pay 'a life for a life'. Otherwise, he had to pay a fine to the king and compensation to the killed person's heir. If the killer died before fines and compensation were paid, his heirs had to pay the compensation.[6] During the later Middle Ages capital punishment also became more used if the killer was convicted.

This paper falls into four parts. First comes a presentation of the Danish rules of man's compensation. This section addresses the question of why a new and strict regulation of collective paying and receiving of man's compensation was introduced around 1200 and explains why the rules we find in the Danish laws were not a reflection of customary dispute resolution, but the product of royal legislation to secure the peace and avoid feuds. The second part of this paper focuses on the relationship between compensation to the kinsmen of the killed person, the fine to the king for breaking the peace, and the distinction between intentional and unintentional killings. Thirdly, I will turn to the relationship between peace, kinship and the Church's doctrine on individual guilt and penance. In the conclusion a few words will be said about the relationship between legislation and practice with regard to payment of man's compensation.

It will be noted that in this paper the term 'man's compensation' is used in preference to 'wergild', a choice also made in the English translation of the

---

5 For Norway see *Norges gamle Love indtil 1387*, Retterböder 2, ed. Rudolf Keyser and Peter A. Munch, vol. 2, Christiania 1848, 176. The collective responsibility in Norway had already been reduced in the north-eastern Frosta Law province by 1260: *Norges gamle Love indtil 1387* 1.1–1.2, ed. Keyser and Munch, vol. 1, Christiania 1846, 121. An English translation is found in *The Earlist Norwegian Laws, Being the Gulathing and the Frostathing Law*, ed. and trans. Laurence Marcellus Larson, New York 1935, 213. For Sweden see *Konung Magnus Erikssons Landslag Samling af Sweriges Gamla Lagar*, Drapæ Balken meÞ vilia 2, 23 and 26, ed. Carl J. Schlyter, vol. 10, Lund 1862, 286, 298 and 299.

6 Helle Vogt, 'Danish Penal Law in the Middle Ages — Cases of Homicide and Woundings', in: *Scandinavian Provincial Laws — Between Local Customs and European Traditions*, ed. Stefan Brink and Lisa Collinson, Turnhout 2014, 185–200.

Danish medieval laws.[7] In Old Danish we find the word *manbot* (plur. *mannæ bøter*) — from *man*: man and *bot:* worth or compensation — used for the compensation the killer and his kinsmen had to pay to the relatives of the killed person. The Old English word *manbot* is also found in the *Leges Henrici Primi* from around 1115, the English law closest in time to the Danish provincial laws, but in the English context *manbot* was a fine paid to the lord of the killed person and not to his kinsmen. The payment to the kinsmen was called *were* — the root of the word 'wergild'.[8] To avoid any misunderstanding or confusion between the Old Danish *manbot* and Old English *manbot* and *were*, I have chosen to translate *manbot* as 'man's compensation'.

The Danish laws were written down in the period from the 1170s to the mid-thirteenth century.[9] We know very little about how the laws were constructed, by whose initiative they were written down, and to what degree royal power took part in or initiated the process. But since the laws remained in force until a national law was given in 1683, we can probably assume that for the most part they must have been in accord with the interests of royal power, the Church and the magnates. Parts of the laws were based upon royal legislation, as for instance the rules on payment of man's compensation; and the rules concerning succession and donations seem to have been developed as part of the negotiations relating to paying the bishop's tithe in around 1170.[10] Other provisions more likely had their origin in the provincial assemblies or the teachings of the Church.

The Danish realm was divided into three legal provinces, each with its own law or laws: Scania in the east, Zealand in the middle, and Jutland to the west. There were differences between the laws and in what they regulated, but in general the same legal system was found all over the kingdom. Even though there were some substantial differences, especially within the procedural law, most of the provisions in the laws are more or less the same and, apart from the procedural system, many of the variations were due to adaption to changes in canon law. For example, whereas the Law of Jutland reflects the change in the

7 *The Danish Medieval Laws — The Laws of Scania, Zealand and Jutland*, ed. Ditlev Tamm and Helle Vogt, London/New York 2016.

8 *Leges Henrici Primi* 87.4, ed. and trans. Leslie J. Downer, Oxford 1972, 266.

9 For further information on the writing down and the contents of the Danish laws see Helle Vogt, *The Function of Kinship in Nordic Medieval Legislation*, Leiden and Boston 2010 (cited as Vogt, *The Function of Kinship*), and Helle Vogt and Ditlev Tamm, 'Introduction', in: *The Danish Medieval Laws*, ed. Ditley Tamm and Helle Vogt, 3–42 (cited as Vogt and Tamm, 'Introduction').

10 These negotiations resulted in Church laws for Scania and Zealand from around 1171. The laws are almost identical.

church's definition of consanguinity after the Fourth Lateran Council (1215), the Law of Scania does not.

The oldest law was probably the Law of Scania, which can be dated to the first decades of the thirteenth century. Large parts of that law were copied directly or indirectly into the other laws. It is generally accepted that the Law of Scania was written down by men closely attached to the archbishop of Lund, and to the provincial assembly there. In Zealand two laws were used, Valdemar's Law, which very likely was written down in the 1220s and was closely related to the Law of Scania, and Erik's Law, which probably was in force before 1248. The prologue to the Law of Jutland states that the law was given by the king with the consensus of all the best men in the kingdom in 1241.[11]

Whereas the Danish as well as the other Nordic laws were written in the vernacular, all the Danish charters and narratives and even the royal ordinances were written in Latin. Most likely a written Danish language with Latin letters was developed in the second half of the twelfth century as a tool for the writing down of the laws.[12]

1 The Danish Rules of Man's Compensation

The Danish laws distinguished between two kinds of crimes, including killings: non-compensable and compensable.[13] A murder was non-compensable if the peace was broken when it was committed, i.e. if it took place in the church, at the assembly, at the victim's home, or as revenge after man's compensation was received. The punishment for non-compensable crimes was outlawry and confiscation of the killer's possessions.[14] Normal honourable killing that did

11 On the dating of the Danish laws in general see Per Andersen, *Legal Procedure and Practice in Medieval Denmark*, Leiden and Boston 2011, 71–83, and Vogt and Tamm, 'Introduction', where Andersen's theories are discussed. On the dating of Erik's Law see Vogt, *The Function of Kinship*, 68–71.

12 Denmark was one of the last places in Europe where Latin was replaced by the vernacular, a reform introduced in around 1425. Anders L. Knudsen, 'Testimonia Placiti — Private Charters as Public Instruments: A Study in Medieval Danish Diplomatics', *Archiv für Diplomatik, Schriftgeschichte, Siegel- und Wappenkunde* 57 (2011), 147–179.

13 The Old Danish word was *Orbotemal*, from *or* — non, *bot* — compensation and *mal* — case or crime.

14 In his learned Latin version of the Law of Scania, the *Liber legis Scaniae* (c. 1202–1215), the archbishop Anders Sunesen adds the kidnapping of women, arson murder and killing either a host or a guest to the list of non-compensable crimes. *Danmarks gamle Landskabslove med Kirkelovene* 61, ed. Erik Kroman et al., vol 1.2, Copenhagen, 1933–1961, 552 (cited as *DgL*). Despite the use of the term 'non-compensable', it was actually possible

not break the peace was punished by the payment of man's compensation, the paying and receiving of which was regulated in a royal ordinance on homicide from 1200 known as Knud VI's Ordinance on Homicide.[15] The prologue to this ordinance informs us that its purpose was to abolish the abuse that often took place when man's compensation was paid:

> Even though no one should find support doing evil, those who sink to committing homicide — a deed that should make them poor — become rich, as by openly taking their goods or by rapine they force those whom they count as kinsmen, even if they are not, to pay fines with them, as much as they demand.[16]

The prologue to the Ordinance shows that collective payment of man's compensation was an established practice in twelfth-century Denmark, but that no written rules regulated the process, which could lead to abuse. Now strict rules were laid down for the process. Only men related by blood should participate.[17] The father's side of the family was to pay a third of the compensation, called an instalment (*sal*), the mother's side another third, and the killer the remaining third. The kinsmen were to hand over their instalments directly to the dead person's kinsmen and not to the killer, removing the risk of his running away with the money or spending it and thereby forcing his kinsmen to pay again if they wanted to avoid revenge. In addition a fine to the king should be paid for the breaking of the peace.[18] After the compensation was paid, levelling oaths were exchanged, and the peace restored. The rules found in the royal ordinance laid the foundation for the system of paying man's compensation

---

with this type of crime to buy back the peace from the king. See Vogt, *The Function of Kinship*, 127–132.

15 The Ordinance was given for the province of Scania, but the same regulations were found all over the realm.

16 *Diplomatarium Danicum* (*DD*), ser. 4, no. 24, ed. Niels Skyum-Nielsen, vol. 1, Copenhagen 1958, 45: *Quippe cum nemini deberet sua malicia suffragari in homicidium corruentes efficiuntur unde depauperari debuerant locuplete quos sibi consanguineos annumerant licet extraneos rapinis et depredacionibus uiolentis ad satisfaciendum secum quantum exigunt compellentes.* (Translation is taken from *The Danish Medieval Laws*, ed. Tamm and Vogt).

17 The Ordinance did not mention how kinship was determined, but from other law texts we can see that kinship was calculated using the canonical measurement, i.e. before the Fourth Lateran Council in 1215 to the seventh degree removed and after the Council to the fourth degree.

18 One advantage to the crown of the collective payment of man's compensation was that the fines could be much higher than if only one person had to pay. In Norway the amount of the fine to the king was reduced considerably in 1274 when the National Law abolished collective payment.

in all the Danish provincial laws. The only difference among the various laws was that the instalments were valued at 15 marks in Scania and Zealand and 18 marks in Jutland.

Somewhere between 1202 and 1241 Knud's Ordinance was replaced by a new royal ordinance, the Ordinance on Offering Compensation.[19] Here the killer's personal responsibility was tightened: the killer himself would have to pay the total amount of man's compensation if none of his kin offered to help him. At first glance it seems to free the kinsmen of responsibility, but a more thorough reading gives another impression. If the killer did not pay the full amount, he was outlawed and had to flee. Given the amount of money involved, there must have been very, very few killers who could afford to stay and pay a full man's compensation. Yet outlawing the killer did not close the case; the compensation still had to be paid. The killer's third was considered to have fled with him, but the killer's kinsmen were obligated to paid the remaining two instalments, just as the ordinance of 1200 had prescribed, with the mother's and the father's side each paying one-third. If the killer's kinsmen did not pay they might be subject to revenge, and 'they can blame themselves that they did not offer compensation', as the Ordinance states.[20] In the later Erik's Law, the closest kinsman inherited the case and could himself be outlawed if the compensation was not paid. After that the responsibility went over to the next of kin, and so on.[21] Thus, in practical terms the killer's personal responsibility remained only partial, and the kin might just as well help the killer with the payment in the first instance, since their ultimate liability remained the same. The Ordinance was probably first and foremost intended to send a political message about royal authority, rather than being a genuine reform effort.[22]

It should also be emphasized that the man's compensation was the same for all free men. In the laws there were only two categories of persons — free and

---

19 The Ordinance was given by Valdemar II (r. 1202–1241), but is not easy to date more precisely. It is printed in Old Danish in *DgL*, supplements to the Law of Scania, text 2, ed. Kroman et al., vol. 1.2, 735; and an English translation is found in *The Danish Medieval Laws*, ed. Tamm and Vogt.

20 *DgL*, supplement to the Law of Scania, text 2, ed. Kroman et al., vol. 1.2, 735: *Oc kunnj sic sialua yuir. at the buthu ai botar.*

21 *DgL* 3, ed. Kroman et al., vol. 5.3, 295–298.

22 The Ordinance on Offering Compensation found its way into the legislation for the rest of the kingdom. The same principle is seen in Thord's Articles, a supplement to the Law of Jutland from the beginning of the fourteenth century (*DgL*, Thords Artikler, Text 6A, no. 61, ed. Kroman et al., vol. 4, 184), and in Erik V's Helsingborg Ordinance from 1283 (*Den danske rigslovgivning indtil år 1400*, 'Lex Erici regis Danorum 4', ed. Aage Andersen, Copenhagen 1991, 106) which was in force throughout the kingdom.

slaves — and the value of all free persons, male as well as female was, at least in the laws, the same.

Elsewhere I have argued that the way kinship was defined in the Nordic laws was copied from the Church's teaching on consanguinity. This 'canonical kinship' informed the way in which many of the provisions affecting transfer of property, inheritance and killing compensation were structured in the laws.[23] The canonical kinship replaced an older system, which I have called the 'elective- and alliance-based kinship' because there was no strict definition of who your relatives were, i.e. those whom you were obligated to love and support, and personal choice played a central role. Blood was definitely an important factor, but the absence of fixed norms for how kinship functioned made it possible that 'within these groups [the bilateral kinship group] one could hand-pick one's "relatives" and deselect persons, which for different reasons one would not want to belong to the kin',[24] as the Swedish historian Lars Hermanson explains it. Other 'family' constructions such as foster-brother-hood and godfather-hood could replace relationships based on blood. Canonical kinship did not offer that possibility, however: here kinship was not a choice but an obligation. In addition, the Church preached that one should love and support one's kinsmen because of the 'bond of blood', as the archbishop Anders Sunesen of Lund put it at the beginning of the thirteenth century.[25]

By creating an ideology in which solidarity and obligations toward kinsmen was a Christian virtue, canonical kinship became a way in which people were able to escape the primacy of the self and concentrate on others instead, thereby bringing themselves closer to their own salvation. It is therefore untenable to claim that the Church opposed collective responsibility on the grounds that it might distract from personal guilt and salvation.[26] The theological context was much more complex.

Theological arguments in favour of forgiveness and against taking revenge, which was driven by anger (*ira* — a deadly sin), can be used to understand why the offended party would agree to accept man's compensation instead of taking revenge in the period when revenge and feud were still viable options.

23 Vogt, *The Function of Kinship*.

24 Lars Hermanson, *Släkt, vänner och makt. En studie av elitens politiska kultur i 1100-talets Danmark*, Gothenburgh, 2010, 10: *Inom dessa sammanslutningar kunde man handplocka sina "slaktingar" och valja bort personer, vilka man av olika anledninger inte ville skulle hore til släkten.*

25 *DgL* 45, ed. Kroman et al., vol. 1.2, 524: *Obligatum autem coniunccione sanguinis.*

26 This is a dominant interpretation in Danish legal history, best expressed in the classical work of Ole Fenger, which is still frequently quoted: Fenger, *Fejde og mandebod*, 183–202.

It cannot be questioned that honour was an important factor when settlements were negotiated, and that rituals were needed to re-establish the honour of the wronged party, something that could not be bought with money. Hence the kinsmen of the killer, when they paid the man's compensation, were expected to swear that they would do the same, i.e. receive payment if the situation had been reversed, and that it was their kinsman who had been killed. The logic behind this so-called levelling oath is explained by the archbishop Anders Sunesen:

> But the oath of equality is always enforced all the more diligently because by making those who are harmed equivalent to those who have harmed, the contempt appears to be taken away which is customarily stirred up by one who has suffered injury from oppression against those who have inflicted it. For prudent men always value the integrity of their reputation and the restoration of the honour due to them more than pecuniary compensation.[27]

---

27 Quotations from the *Liber legis Scaniae* have been translated by Kate Gilbert. I thank her for her help. After this paper was written *Liber legis Scaniae* has been published in an English version, *The Liber legis Scaniae. The Latin text with introduction, translation and commentaries*, ed. Ditlev Tamm, London and New York, 2017, the translations in this paper differ some places from this translation. *DgL* 46, ed. Kroman et al., vol. 1.2, 530: *Equalitatis autem tanto diligencius semper exigitur juramentum, quod per ipsum, lesis ledentibus adequatis, auferri videatur contemptus, qui perpessis iniuriam ex oppressione solet inferencium suscitari; pluris enim semper prvdentes faciunt integritatem fame et honoris debiti restitucionem quam pecuniariam satisfactionem.* On the sacred oath of surety and the levelling oath Anders Sunesen wrote in the same chapter: *Statim post exhibitam emendacionis terciam exhiberi debet pariter et tercia juratorie caucionis, quam lingua patria* thryd *appellat, jn qua tantum 4*[or] *nominati de consanguineis interfecti jurant de hiis, qui satisfecerint, vindictam de cetero cessaturam; nam plenam et integram caucionem xii constituunt nominati, habituram tunc demum locum, cum postremam emendacionis terciam reus exhibuerit principalis; quam caucionem semper debet precedere sacramentum, quod* jafhnethe [eth] *in lingua patria nominatur, virorum xii nominatorum de consanguineis occisoris, qui, non sacris reliquiis, sed sacro coram posito tacto libro, jurant in suas animas, et sic sibi deum futurum propicium deprecantur, quod pro consimili delicto consimilem ad interuentum consanguineorum et amicorum ab aduersariis suis sumerent satisfaccionem; quando vero tantum 4*[or] *admittuntur ad juratoriam caucionem, ad equalitatis quoque juramentum tantum sunt 4*[or] *admittendi.* — 'Immediately after the third [payment] of compensation has been produced, the third oath of surety must in like manner be given which in the language of the land is called *thryd*, in which only four men nominated from the victim's kinsmen swear that with respect to those who have given compensation, revenge will cease thereafter; for 12 nominated men constitute a full and entire surety, which will not be valid until the time when the main defendant will have produced the final third of the compensation. That surety must always precede the oath (which in the language of the land is called *jafhnethe* [*eth*]) of the 12 nominated men from the kinsmen of the killer, who,

It is difficult to translate the value of the man's compensation in the laws. The amount of the compensation was counted in marks, but the mark was not coined; it was a unit of account. A mark was divided into eight *øre*, each of which in turn was divided into three *ørtugh*. Ten *pænning* made an *ørtug*, and only *pænning* circulated as coin. It is uncertain how much a mark was worth in the thirteenth century, but a cautious guess is that it represented the value of a cow. Thus, the full man's compensation would be around 54 cows in Jutland and 45 cows in Scania and Zealand (three times eighteen or fifteen marks). We must imagine that it would be very difficult and also inconvenient to amass the huge number of coins needed to pay even one of the three instalments of the compensation. More likely the compensation was paid in kind. There are no traces of such a practice in the very scattered Danish sources, but in the Icelandic law book *Grágás*, written down in the version we know it in the 1260s, we find a quite interesting conversion list: 'in accordance with General Assembly regulations it is standard value that in one ounce-unit there shall be six ells of valid homespun, new and unused. A trade-cloak is worth two ounce-units'.[28] The list goes on and on like this for three full pages, valuing everything from cloth and fur to domestic animals and implements. This list is very interesting in part because it shows how things were valuated against each other, for instance how many billy-goats equal a cow and so on. But it is also of note because both the Icelandic and the Danish laws were written at a time when few coins were minted[29] and in the context of what to a large extent were barter economies, and yet money is nevertheless the measure for all kinds of compensations, fines and taxes.

2 Intentional Killings and Fines to the King

Knud VI's Ordinance from 1200 seems to suggest that revenge was still an alternative to compensation. This option is not found in the later legislation,

not on sacred relics but in the presence of the holy book on which their touch has been placed, swear on their souls, and thus pray God for a propitious future for themselves, that for an entirely similar crime they would take compensation from their adversaries upon the entirely similar intervention of their kinsmen and friends; but when only four are permitted for the oath of surety, only four are also to be permitted for the levelling oath'.

28 *Laws of Early Iceland: Grágás, The Codex Regius of Grágás with Material from Other Manuscripts* 246, vols. 1–2, ed. and trans. Andrew Dennis, Peter Foote, and Richard Perkins, Winnipeg 2000, 207.

29 About the shortage of silver and the monetary economy see Niels Hybel and Bjørn Poulsen, *The Danish Resources c. 1000–1550: Growth and Recessions*, Leiden and Boston 2007, 330–334.

however. And whereas in this ordinance the paying, receiving and exchange of levelling oaths were to a large degree a private matter that did not necessarily need the involvement of the assembly or the king's official, this too changed during the first half of the thirteenth century. According to the laws, killings were to be made public at the assembly. In return for the promise of paying man's compensation, the killer would be granted his peace. The king also claimed a right to a fine. The usual fine for an intentional criminal act that did not violate the peace was three marks, while an unintentional action was not fined. The archbishop of Lund, Anders Sunesen, explained it this way in writing about wounds, but the argument can easily be applied to killing cases as well:

> If anyone shall have inflicted a wound on someone, not voluntarily but accidentally, the wounded person — whose pain an accident can no more mitigate than can the intention to strike — should not on that account receive less than the entire compensation, nor does it make much difference to him to have been wounded by accident rather than on purpose; from an accident, however, this benefit is offered to its author: that nothing is owed on that account to the king or to the archbishop, who are not to find fault with an unexpected accident — which no man can foresee — but rather punish an injurious disposition, since from fear of punishment illicit and injurious acts may thereafter be avoided.[30]

In a society without insurance, pension or child benefit, the logic is clear. The loss of a breadwinner for the family was not changed by the fact that the wounding or killing was unintended. This is exactly the same logic that we find in the petitions to the king after the 1537 Recess: only economic compensation, and not the death of the killer, would benefit the family.

30 *DgL* 67, ed. Kroman et al., vol. 1.2, 562: *Siquis non voluntarie, sed casualiter cuiquam wlnus infllixerit, non jdcirco minus integram wlneratus recipiet emendacionem, cuius dolorem lenire non nouit casus pocius quam propositum infligendi, nec ipsius multum interest ex casu pocius quam ex proposito lesum esse; ex casu tamen hoc beneficium prestatur auctori, vt nihil eo nomine regi vel antistiti debeatur, quorum non est casum inopinum, quem nullus potest hominum preuidere, in aliquo castigare, sed iniquam punire pocius voluntatem, quatenus metu pene jllicita et iniqua decetero caueantur.* Clearly the exemption of fines to the king with regard to accidents made it tempting to disguise intentional deeds as accidents, something the chapter goes on to discuss.

3 Law and Legal Practice

The laws prescribed that killings should be redressed by man's compensation. But theory was one thing and practice was another. While there is no doubt that payment of man's compensation was the official form of punishment for killings, the documented cases involving compromise show that the size, content and form of the man's compensation were negotiable, and that the rules prescribed by the laws could be negotiated; and in many cases the laws were probably only followed literally if the parties could not or would not enter into an agreement. Sources about settlements following bloodshed are almost absent in the Danish material up to around 1300. Only a few sources are preserved from the fourteenth century as well. However, from the fifteenth century a few more sources about compromises following killings are known, all of them charters relating to the absolute top level of society.

The compensation found in the charters primarily consisted of two parts: 1) religious gifts for the soul of the departed and 2) symbolic humiliation. Paying of man's compensation as it is described in the laws is seldom found in the charters, but that is probably because they mention only cases from the absolute top of society, and because most of the surviving documents concern transfer of landed property, where the owners' title could be disputed for generations. The logic behind the laws was that the regulations were something you could fall back on if a compromise could not be obtained.[31] After all, compromise was to be preferred to judgment, and as long as the king got his fines for the breaking of the peace, private agreements were no problem. This was probably not only the case for the magnates. Settlements were presumably something that were entered into in all layers of society, but for the common people the monetary element very likely played a very important role. Unfortunately, no sources are preserved to strengthen the argument.[32]

One of the very earliest sources we have about killing compensation among private parties is from 1345, the year in which the brother and other kinsmen of the deceased murderer Niels Thygesen promised to establish a chantry in Roskilde.[33] The chantry was to be finely equipped and endowed with enough

31 Jørn Øyrehagen Sunde, *Speculum legale — rettsspegel en. Ein introduksjon til den norske rettskulturen si historie i ett europeisk perspektiv*, Bergen 2005, 53–86.

32 Further on Danish killing compromises see Helle Vogt, 'How to be remembered. Securing the *memoria* of a slain person in medieval Denmark', in: *Emotion, Violence, Vengeance and Law in the Middle Ages: Essays in Honour of William Ian Miller*, ed. Kate Gilbert and Stephen D. White, Boston and Leiden, forthcoming 2018.

33 The earlier charters are almost exclusively about cases in which a town was the paying party, because travellers or tradesmen had been killed in riots.

land to provide income for three masses to be said every week for the soul of the victim; and for the sake of his sins a pilgrim was to be sent to Rome to pray at saints' graves.[34] A letter of donation for the chantry from 1348[35] reveals that the Bishop of Roskilde had acted as mediator when the compromise was obtained. There is no evidence that the brother or other kinsmen of the murderer had to humiliate themselves. This is not surprising, since they did not have personal responsibly for the killing, but had simply 'inherited' the conflict from their late kinsman. Nevertheless, examples of massive rituals of humiliation and enormous gifts to the church are to be found in other documents, especially from the fifteenth century.[36]

In 1310 King Erik VI witnessed a compromise between the townsmen in Lund and the brothers and kinsmen of the knight Josef Magnussen, who had been killed there.[37] Like many of the settlements known from the charters, the agreement was between the townspeople and kinsmen of a person killed in the town. It was reached with the archbishop of Lund and the bishop of Roskilde as mediators, among others. The charter includes a long list of acts of penance that the inhabitants of Lund were supposed to undergo as part of the compromise. The penance comprised religious gifts for the soul of the departed, and symbolic humiliation of the townsmen. The townsmen promised to establish three new altars, two in Lund and one in Roskilde, where masses would be sung for the soul of the departed. The altars were to be finely equipped and endowed with enough land to provide enough income to support priests who could serve them in perpetuity. Yearly gifts were to be given to the poor. Additional money was allocated to vigils and donations were made to a long list of churches and to send two pilgrims to Rome. As a sign of their penitence some of the mayors and city council members were expected to carry a litter around town in a procession from church to church, followed by the barefooted townsmen, male as well as female. The townsmen were also required to appear at the provincial assembly in Lund and, on their knees, ask the departed's brothers and kinsmen for forgiveness and follow the procedure with security and levelling oaths and kisses as prescribed in the Law of Scania. The only mention of personal gain for the heirs was to the effect that one of the brothers, Juris, who was a canon in Lund, should have the profit from two of the altars during his lifetime.

---

34 *DD*. ser. 2, no. 193 (23 November 1345), ed. Carl A. Christensen, vol. 3.
35 *DD*. ser. 3, no. 60 (26 September 1348), ed. Carl A. Christensen, vol. 3.
36 http://diplomatarium.dk/search?from_date=&to_date=&search=drab.
37 *DD*. ser. 6, no. 305 (20 September 1310), ed. Franz Blatt, vol. 2.

However it was not only townsfolk that could be forced to perform humiliating rituals as part of the compromises, as we can see in this example from 1405 in which the knight Jens Nielsen entered a compromise with another knight, Jens Andersen, and his grandsons.[38] Jens Nielsen had killed Jens Andersen's son, Jens Jensen. There is no mention of paying man's compensation in the charter. Instead of paying a compensation, Jens Nielsen was to endow perpetual masses for the dead man's soul in three churches, give gifts to the poor, pay the costs for six pilgrims to travel to different holy places such as Jerusalem and Santiago de Compostela, and pay for nine pilgrims to travel to different holy places in the Nordic kingdoms. Witnessed by 200 knights and squires, Jens Nielsen had to beg forgiveness of the father and sons of the dead man on his knees, and say these words: 'Were I the best and the mightiest knight in Denmark, and had you killed my son or my father in such a way, then would I enter a similar reconciliation with you.'[39] This was the same formulary as the levelling oath used when man's compensation was paid. The widow and the daughters of the deceased were each to have a precious gift, in the form of jewels, and again on his knees Jens Nielsen was to give a sword or a knife to the killed man's father and to his sons while asking their forgiveness, and beg that they would not start a feud. All this was promised by Jens Nielsen on behalf of all his kinsmen, both on his mother's and his father's side, born as well as unborn, and Jens Jensen's father and sons promised the same for their kin. The compromise charter was witnessed by a large number of men from both the kin groups. The compromise was entered into in the presence of Margrethe, first lady and lord of Denmark, the de facto ruling queen. In this respect it follows the pattern found in the later Middle Ages, when the crown or its representatives begin to play a much greater role as mediators at the expense of the church.

The general picture is that, in the few killing cases we know about from the sources that almost exclusively concerned the elite, financial compensation came mostly in the form of gifts for the soul of the departed, while any gifts to the kinsmen were more of symbolic importance than of tangible value. The compromise also included an element of humiliation of the killer and his kinsmen.[40] As we have seen, however, the royal Letter Books show that for

---

38 http://diplomatarium.dk/dd/diplomer/05–017.html, no. 29 (24 February 1405).

39 *Denn beste och mechtigste riddere y Danmarck, och hafde de slagidt min sønn eller min fader y saadan maade, da ville ieg hafve saadann en læghe och saadan en saane af dem der for.*

40 In his studies of feud and peace-making in Western France in the eleventh century Stephen White makes a very convincing argument that the offended party actually had a very good economic reason for agreeing to a compromise. When a nobleman died,

common people most of the settlements were made according to the letter of the law, or at least in those cases the paying of man's compensation was the central transaction. After the Lutheran reformation the nobility maintained the right to receive man's compensation and make private compromises, even if the religious argument for the donations for the soul of the departed was gone. The religious element did not, however, disappear. Instead, a practise developed where noble criminals were sent to fight against the Turks to redeem their breach of the divine law.[41]

4 Concluding Remarks

In some of the papers in this volume we will read that the wergild system worked well because the threat of feud and revenge lay behind it. Yet that explanation cannot be applied to medieval Denmark, where blood revenge was prohibited in the first half of the thirteenth century. My claim is that feud and revenge do not necessarily need to be the underlying explanation for why compensation was effectual. In twelfth- and thirteenth-century Denmark, as elsewhere in western Europe, the king was depicted as the protector of the peace. We can also see that in this period the king starts to take an interest in the administration of justice — as, for instance, by the introduction of outlawry and non-compensable crimes. In other words, the fear of revenge is replaced by the fear of the king, and man's compensation can be attributed to factors other than the absence of public institutions and administration of law.

This does not mean that kin solidarity and honour did not play an important part. They did, and especially for the elite the upholding of their honour was very important. Even so, making the killer's kin responsible for making large gifts to the church for the killed person's soul meant that the killed person's kin saved a fortune on the masses, burial and other gifts that society expected in order to ensure his salvation. Even for the elite, money was an important factor in deciding on a compromise. However, this is not the same as saying that

whether peacefully or violently, his family was expected to donate large gifts to the church to pray for his soul. This was a very costly affair, but through a compromise it would be the offender, possibly helped by his family, who would pay for the donations. Stephen D. White, 'Feuding and Peace-Making in the Touraine around the Year 1100', *Traditio, Studies in Ancient and Medieval History, Thought, and Religion* 42 (1986), 195–265, here 238.

41 Morten Kjær and Helle Vogt, 'Udi krigen at lade sig bruge — Straf og forvisning i det efterreformatoriske Danmark-Norge', in: *Reformationen i Danmark*, ed. Ole Hørris and Per Ingesman, Aarhus Universitet Forlag 2017, 393–412.

honour and religious teachings about not taking revenge and having to forgive your neighbour had no impact on the system. My claim is that man's compensation must be understood as an interaction among all three elements: money, honour and religion.

Bibliography

Primary Sources

Danmarks gamle Landskabslove med Kirkelovene (*DgL*), ed. Erik Kroman et al., 8 vols., Det danske Sprog- og Litteraturselskab og Selskabet, Copenhagen 1933–1961.

Den danske Rigslovgivning indtil år 1400, ed. Aage Andersen, Det danske Sprog- og Litteraturselskab og Selskabet, Copenhagen 1991.

Den danske Rigslovgivning 1523–1558, ed. Aage Andersen, Det Danske Sprog- og Litteraturselskab og Selskabet, Copenhagen 2015.

Diplomatarium Danicum (*DD*), ed. Niels Skyum-Nielsen, Carl A. Christensen, Franz Blatt et al., vols. 1–3, Det danske Sprog- og Litteraturselskab, Copenhagen 1938–1990.

Kancelliets Brevbøger vedrørende Danmarks indre Forhold i Uddrag, ed. Carl F. Bricka et al., 39 vols., Copenhagen 1885–2005.

Konung Magnus Erikssons Landslag Samling af Sweriges Gamla Lagar, ed. Carl J. Schlyter, vol. 10, Lund 1862.

Laws of Early Iceland: Grágás, The Codex Regius of Grágás with material from other manuscripts, vols. 1–2, trans. and ed. Andrew Dennis, Peter Foote, and Richard Perkins, Winnipeg 2000.

Leges Henrici Primi, trans. and ed. Leslie J. Downer, Oxford 1972.

Norges gamle Love indtil 1387, ed. R. Keyser and P. A. Munch, vols. 1–2, Christiania 1846–1848.

Samling af gamle danske Love. Danske Recesser og Ordinancer af Kongerne af den Oldenborgske Stamme med Indledning og Anmærkninger, ed. Janus L. A. Kolderup-Rosenvinge, Copenhagen 1824.

The Danish medieval laws — the laws of Scania, Zealand and Jutland, ed. Ditlev Tamm and Helle Vogt, London and New York 2016.

The Earliest Norwegian Laws, being the Gulathing and the Frostathing Law, trans. and ed. Marcellus Larson, New York 1935.

The Liber legis Scaniae. The Latin text with introduction, translation and commentaries, ed. Ditlev Tamm, London and New York 2017.

Secondary Works

Andersen, Per, *Legal Procedure and Practice in Medieval Denmark* (Medieval Law and its Practice 11), Leiden and Boston 2011.

Fenger, Ole, *Fejde og mandebod — Studier over slægtsansvaret i germansk og gammeldansk ret*, Copenhagen 1971.

Hermanson, Lars, *Släkt, vänner och makt. En studie av elitens politiska kultur i 1100-talets Danmark*, Avhandlinger från Historiska Institutionen i Göteborg, Gothenburgh 2010.

Hybel, Niels and Bjørn Poulsen, *The Danish Resources c. 1000–1550: Growth and Recessions*. Leiden and Boston 2007.

Kjær, Morten and Helle Vogt, 'Udi krigen at lade sig bruge — Straf og forvisning i det efterreformatoriske Danmark-Norge', in: *Reformationen i Danmark*, ed. Ole Hørris and Per Ingesman, Aarhus Universitet Forlag 2017, 393–412.

Knudsen, Anders L., 'Testimonia Placiti — Private Charters as Public Instruments: A Study in Medieval Danish Diplomatics', *Archiv für Diplomatik, Schriftgeschichte, Siegel- und Wappenkunde* 57 (2011), 147–179.

Netterstrøm, Jeppe Büchert, 'Bondefejder i Danmark 1450–1650', in: *Feider og fred i nordisk middelalder*, ed. Erik Opsahl, Unipub 2007, 35–72.

Netterstrøm, Jeppe Büchert, 'Criminalization of Homicide in Early Modern Denmark (16th–17th centuries)', *Scandinavian Journal of History* 42, 4 (2017), 459–475.

Sunde, Jørn Ø., *Speculum legale — rettsspegelen. Ein introduksjon til den norske rettskulturen si historie i ett europeisk perspektiv*, Bergen 2005.

Tamm, Ditlev, and Vogt, Helle, 'Introduction', in: *The Danish medieval laws — the laws of Scania, Zealand and Jutland*, ed. Ditlev Tamm and Helle Vogt, Abingdon 2016, 3–42.

Vogt, Helle, *The Function of Kinship in Nordic Medieval Legislation* (Medieval Law and its Practice 9), Leiden and Boston 2010.

Vogt, Helle, 'Danish Penal Law in the Middle Ages — Cases of Homicide and Woundings', in: *Scandinavian Provincial Laws — between local customs and European traditions*, ed. Stefan Brink and Lisa Collinson, Turnhout 2014, 185–200.

Vogt, Helle, 'How to be remembered. Securing the *memoria* of a slain person in medieval Denmark', in: *Emotion, Violence, Vengeance and Law in the Middle Ages: Essays in Honour of William Ian Miller*, ed. Kate Gilbert and Stephen D. White, Boston and Leiden 2018.

White, Stephen D., 'Feuding and Peace-Making in the Touraine around the Year 1100', *Traditio, Studies in Ancient and Medieval History, Thought, and Religion* 42 (1986), 195–265.

CHAPTER 13

Concluding Thoughts from England and the 'Western Legal Tradition'

Paul Hyams

These thoughts will be something of a 'trespasser's reconnaissance report' from one who has mostly worked on England in later periods when wergild was moribund there.[1] They are derived in part from my own speculations since the conference on early medieval English law and its European context. These concern the watershed of the Church's great reform movement from the later eleventh century and the not coincidentally contemporaneous 'legal revolution', with its revival of Roman law and the creation of the new law schools that gave European law a fresh start. I use the resulting 'Western Legal Tradition' (WLT), emerging with difficulty over the next centuries, as a base from which to pose a few questions of my own on wergild. In doing so, I take a position somewhat differing from the very persuasive current trend on Anglo-Saxon law that argues for the exclusion, pro tempore, of evidence from outside the time and place under examination, seeking to approach the evidence in more strictly chronological order and without much (initial) reference to the rest of Europe. The aim is to clarify concepts and issues towards a future synthesis more closely in accord with strictly contemporary *mores* and mindset.[2]

I deliberately contrast Anglo-Saxon practice against ideas from the centuries after 1066 to identify challenges in law and order which the early English either handled differently or simply did not see and understand the same way as later generations. My strategy here is to model the later system of the WLT in its English form of the 'Common Law', so that I can better understand the context within which wergild had formerly operated. I am not suggesting that England was typical of the areas covered by this volume, simply that it too can suggest hypotheses worth testing.

1 The quoted phrase comes from James C. Scott.

2 Tom Lambert (author of chap. 6, above) carefully explains his reasons in his *Law and Order in Anglo-Saxon England*, Oxford 2017, 7–12 (cited as Lambert, *Law and Order*) and Alice Taylor, *The Shape of the State in Medieval Scotland, 1124–1290*, Oxford 2016, adopts a similar strategy. I accept Dr. Lambert's criticisms of his predecessors, including myself, and offer these thoughts as a supplement only.

 | DOI:10.1163/9789004466128_014

I start from a 1984 book which argued that the WLT, that great achievement on which we Westerners have so congratulated ourselves over the centuries, cannot have been assembled in anything like its lasting form until after the transformation of its attitudes to and organisation of law over the eleventh to thirteenth centuries. To Harold Berman, this constituted the first of three major revolutions in Western law.[3] Historian reviewers were less kind than lawyer colleagues. As a result the book has made little impact on the historiography of the period. This may be a mistake. All interested in the culture of medieval Christendom need to give serious consideration to Berman's contentions that the WLT was born out of the way Roman law was understood and deployed in the schools and courtrooms of the twelfth- and thirteenth-centuries, that it has strong claims to be considered revolutionary, and that the circumstances out of which it emerged were very influential on Western culture at the time in ways that are still discernible today. It would follow from this that we should beware of approaching early medieval law and dispute resolution by way of ideas largely invented during the revolution itself.[4]

I would offer a summary draft model of the WLT that differs somewhat from Berman's. It rests on two premises. First, the establishment by Gregorian Reform of a much sharper distinction between temporal and sacred matters was an indispensable part of the movement towards a more human-centred approach to law as well as government. Second, that the Twelfth-Century Renaissance and especially the revival of legal studies in schools dedicated to written (hence learned) laws, including the Church's own canons, served to lead secular (i.e. less learned) law towards many of the same standards. The resulting raised level of literacy and logical skills transformed law not just by introducing new ideas from Rome but by subjecting older ones to argument round closely reasoned conceptual distinctions and definitions to identify distinguishable categories of wrong, their remedies and causes of action. Courts were to be expected to deliver similar treatment to similar wrongs, to be consistent within the legal system, in a way that eventually led to the generation of doctrines of precedent and a *system* of appeals to higher authorities able to over-rule and correct their inferiors. Litigants and their advisers could now criticize verdicts without needing to accuse the judges of acting fraudulently, unjustly, or corruptly. Previously independent and largely untrained court

3 Harold J. Berman, *Law and Revolution: The Formation of the Western Legal Tradition*, Cambridge, Massachusetts 1983, was followed by later volumes on the other two revolutions. Berman was a leading specialist in Soviet law not previously known for his interest in the middle ages.

4 Of course, many elements of the WLT come from the previous situation. I consider one likely illustration of this, rights theory, below in my Coda.

assemblies would then develop towards becoming parts of a *system*, with its own discrete (legal) discourses adapted to the different realms and polities. Courts acquired the power to routinely enforce appearance before them (mesne process), and control their trials and procedure. Without this, such characteristic features of the WLT as the Rule of Law, Due Process, and the provision of equal justice to 'all' through widely accessible standard procedures could hardly have emerged.

One might describe the thrust of the whole process as a diminution of divine influence over conflict resolution, moving away from various kinds of proof by God's Judgment towards a more human use of human means, from oaths, ordeals, and judicial battle to evidence, strict construction of documents, and jury trial.[5] None of this was as quick or automatic as they seem in hindsight. Nobody directly questioned the ability of an omniscient God to detect falsehood and reveal truth. Yet ideas of 'evidence' (itself now become a substantive, hence a recognisable entity) soon led to procedures for testing the authenticity of the writings litigants produced and, less surely, the tales they told in court. Sometimes, judges were able to reach decisive conclusions in contested matters. More often, their efforts to control the suits that reached their courts were less successful, but it is the principle of the rational trial that matters here, constrained though this was by both contemporary Christian and Roman notions of law and reason.[6] One particularly relevant by-product of all this rationalization is the criminalization of vengeance and the separation of forceful self-help including formal feud from lawsuits within the court system.[7]

I shall proceed to look now at wergild as a practice or institution that flourished in England as elsewhere but was perhaps incompatible with an WLT which never granted it entry. I start with a model of how lawsuits might have functioned before the WLT, and then go on to examine a few aspects of this wergild, in and out of law, to reveal a little of the kind of *imaginaire* whose presence it required and without which it perhaps ceased to make sense to lawmakers.

---

5 I first expressed my views in 'Trial by Ordeal: the Key to Proof in the Early Common Law', in: *Of the Laws and Customs of England: Essays in Honor of Samuel E. Thorne*, ed. Thomas A. Green et al., Chapel Hill 1981, 90–126. I should now emphasize more strongly my disbelief in that simple opposition between early medieval 'superstition' and modern 'rationality', which was then still to be found in the literature.

6 Roman law notions of rationality, despite exerting a profound influence on western views in the middle ages and beyond, should not be confused with modern choices. Consider torture for illustration.

7 I return to this point below.

1 Model

We must start from homicide, for the taking of a life is the act that gives wergild its name, etymologically meaning the 'payment for a (hu)man (life)'. It was payable to the deceased's relicts to compensate them for their loss by the death. The deceased's lord would also receive a payment, under the name of *mann-bot* or '(hu)man compensation'. Each payment was an alternative to facing the feud; the perpetrators must 'buy the lance from the flank, or bear it', as a late text put it.[8] Recipients were forgoing the near-universal urge to avenge the victim's blood with some flowing from the perpetrator or some close 'friend'. Similar compensation might be exacted for other lesser wrongs, where the question was almost always one of the proper level of pecuniary compensation only, a subject which took up much of the early *leges*. Yet public interest, as measured perhaps by references to payments that went not to the victim's friends but to the king or other ruler, focuses largely on homicide, which raises a question of balance.

Though homicide is primarily a wrong against another human being and his community, it also offends God. The perpetrator needs both His forgiveness and that of his (or her) victim, Mt. v. 23; Mc. xi. 25. Since the deceased is unavailable to show mercy,[9] this can only come from his (or her) close friends, a group expanding outwards from the closest blood kin (OE *healsfang*) to allies, neighbours and plain-vanilla friends. The first challenge after a killing was thus to decide on the composition of a support group for the deceased, to press for and receive apologies and peace-making inquiries, and also decide who should get the money if and when it arrived. This must often have been an awkward matter for friends of both parties, also, since un-peace was everybody's problem, for more remote local residents all of whom had a view. All the same, homicide was primarily a matter for the principals and their supporters

---

8 The twelfth-century *Leges Edwardi Confessoris*, 12.6, that quotes this saying, has just dealt with *manbot*, ibid., 3–5 (ed. Bruce R. O'Brien, *God's Peace and King's Peace*, Philadelphia, Pennsylvania 1999, 170–171). Cf. Joseph Bosworth and Thomas N. Toller, *An Anglo-Saxon Dictionary*, Oxford 1921, reprinted 1976 (consulted online at http://www.bosworthtoller.com/) s.vv. mann-bot, wer-gild, 669, 1206 (cited as BT). Whether we ought to call these payments compensation, penalty, or fine is important. As others have noted above, translation of individual Old English or Latin texts can be controversial. I hedge my bets on the gender of the deceased here, since both OE *mann* and Latin *homo* can on occasion denote women, as hinted at by Esders, above, 17, cf. Haubrichs, above, 98.

9 It is noteworthy how very secondary pardon and forgiveness generally are in wergild texts. The Jewish rabbis treated this as a problem. It raised for them the uncomfortable difficulty that killings might be viewed by God as literally unforgiveable. So far as I can tell, their sources are all post-biblical.

to handle. Non-compensable (bootless) offences are not found in English laws much before the eleventh century and even then did not include all homicides.[10]

These facts shaped the consultations that followed a killing. The immediate aftermath saw a lot of activity and much questioning on how best to proceed. If the deed was premeditated, the perpetrators would continue a process already begun. They may even have publicly declared their act and whether they stood ready to negotiate a settlement or defend themselves.[11] Failure to declare themselves made matters more serious and transferred the initiative, or rather burden of choice, to the victim's party.

This had three basic options to consider. First, there was direct action, initially as the threat of taking a life for a life.[12] This might lead to counteraction, or even the tit-for-tat of feud. For a while, nobody could be sure. If this reaction was common, something we cannot ever know, it helps to explain why homicide was, in England, so slow to become like theft a capital offence.[13] Self-help was most attractive to those who could be confident that they had the resources to contain the dispute and achieve a sustainable result without too much outside participation. When a victim's friends feared that more violence was still to come, even that all their lives were in danger, they may have felt they had little alternative but to turn and fight.

Secondly, some close kin of the victim might call out (or appeal, as the French put it) the killer in public, most obviously at the *gemot*, assembly.[14] Though scholars almost unanimously treat this as litigating, contemporaries need not have agreed. They might well have seen the assembly more like one particularly good place to publicize one's injury or name those they held responsible. OE *talu* (from which our word 'tale' developed) meant something like today's

10 Opinions differ as to whether III Atr 1; VII Atr 1. 1 represent innovations or merely record rules for the first time. I have cited Anglo-Saxon laws (leges) by the standard method with the sigla of Felix Liebermann, *Gesetze der Angelsachsen*, 3 vols., Halle 1903–1916, as listed at vol. 1, xi.; Cf. John G. Hudson, *The Oxford History of the Laws of England* 2, Oxford 2012, 181–184 (cited as Hudson, *The Oxford History of the Laws of England*); and my *Rancor and Reconciliation in Medieval England: Wrong and its Redress from the Tenth to Thirteenth Centuries*, Ithaca, New York 2003, 84–86 (cited as *Rancor and Reconciliation*). Cf. above Bothe, 205; and Vogt, 281–82.

11 The declaration itself signalled a willingness to come to terms, Siems, above, 41.

12 Vogt, above, 277.

13 Cf. Tom Lambert, 'Theft, Homicide and Crime in Late Anglo-Saxon England', *Past and Present* 214 (2013), 3–43.

14 Where Old French used a noun, *apel*, the English appear to have used verbs like *beclipian*; *Dictionary of Old English*, ed. Ashley C. Amos, Angus Cameron and Antonette di Paolo, Toronto 1986 (consulted online at http://doe.utoronto.ca/pages/in-dex.html), s.v. *beclipian* (cited as 'DOE'). My phrase, 'calling out' is taken from Frank Herbert's series of Dune novels. I follow current practice in writing of 'assemblies' rather than courts.

'statement of claim'. They could use it to publicize their story and challenge the opposition to engage with them, admit the wrong, and accept the consequences, or to stand up and prove their innocence and credibility in whatever manner public opinion required. One can imagine rituals to dramatize their choice, although I know of no clear contemporary evidence.[15] Either of these two options could, perhaps should, lead toward arrangements for payment of the wergild for which the victim's friends were perhaps hoping.

The third option, in contrast, abandons that hope and with it much chance of saving face through some visible form of reconciliation. Some call this 'lumping it', which means accepting both the injury and its accompanying insult, possibly also abandoning a neighbourhood which would not soon forget a shaming. There is no way to assess the relative frequency of the three options, but it is by no means impossible that this third one could be in certain places and times at the top of the list.[16] Certainly the factors involved in this choice must be as important as any to placing wergild in context.

2 Imaginaire

Wergild in context must always have provoked strong passions, literally issues of life and death. This emotional side to our topic reaches to the core of the practice. There is more than enough fear and sorrow, anger, envy and competitive urges to delight any novelist. The snag, of course, is that the stories we possess focus far more frequently on blood than peacemaking. Yet both derive from the same efforts to establish a new peace and mend psychological damage on terms satisfactory to those most concerned. Any artificial dichotomy between feud and its settlement could distort our whole understanding of the early medieval law and order.

I have but a few questions to suggest and still fewer answers. But perhaps these may encourage us to seek out hints of the thoughts and feelings which

15 Later analogues include the throwing down of a token glove and the formal defiance, for which see my 'Homage and Feudalism: A Judicious Separation', in: *Die Gegenwart des Feudalismus*, ed. Natalie Fryde, Pierre Monnet and Otto Gerhard Oexle, Göttingen 2003, 13–49. The well publicized taking of some object from the opposition, which became distraint procedure, is another possibility.

16 Though both Warren Brown, *Violence in Medieval Europe*, Harlow 2011, and Bothe, most recently in his 'From Debt to Sin? Wergild Liability and the evolution of individual guilt in Frankish law (c. 6th–c. 9th)', at the Conference on *Law and Legal Agreement*, Cambridge in January 2018 (unpublished), make good use of contemporary letters and formularies to flesh out the pre-history of wergild. I am not personally aware of much comparable English materials.

surround attempts to handle the killings of an age when violence was never far removed from the stage on which actors acted, friendships and enmities were forged and destroyed, relationships crafted and dissolved. This is what the term *imaginaire* conjures up in me.[17] Let us seek a context for the way that early medieval people attempted to stave off chaos and ensure the survival of their collective life in the perspective of wergild its values and symbols. Here to set the conversation going are three themes that emerged from our conference and are taken up in some of the foregoing chapters. First comes the tacit but broad consensus that wergild, evidenced so largely from codes of law, must be a 'legal' matter, and so one where the leading, and often also the last, word goes to legal historians. Next, the role of honour and its compatibility with the pecuniary valuation of human lives and social peace. And thirdly, the meaning of the tariff figures in the *leges* and how to understand their role. Then in my Coda I use the question of whether wergild was a right, to sum up some of the points at issue.

If one accepts that most contemporaries saw feud and law as part of a single integral approach to the settlement of serious disputes, this law has to have been different in kind from that of the WLT, with its Roman-derived distinction between public and private law. We may more usefully associate wergild with a wider group of issues that end up treated within the later Common Law, but were in Anglo-Saxon England largely open to political negotiation, especially when they involved the rich and powerful, and likely as often as not to be dealt with outside the local 'public' assemblies of shire, hundred and borough.[18] Though some homicide accusations are likely to have been brought to such assemblies, there is, surprisingly little evidence that this was where wergild business was normally transacted.[19]

We naturally associate homicide with the criminal law, and crime words are liberally utilised in this volume despite the fact that the familiar distinction

17 If I were myself about to begin researching the literature, I should probably start from Charles Taylor, *Modern Social Imaginaries*, Durham/North Carolina and London 2004, and John B. Thompson, *Studies in the Theory of Ideology*, Cambridge 1984.

18 Some matters seldom reached a court trial. I have suggested in my 'Servitude in Anglo-Saxon England; Searching for the Serfs', in: *Languages of the Law in Early Medieval England: Essays in Memory of Lisi Oliver*, ed. Andrew Rabin and Stefan Jurasinski, Leuven, Paris and Bristol 2019, 127–154 (cited as 'Servitude in Anglo-Saxon England'), that this may include most disputes concerning free and unfree status.

19 Few legal narratives record disputes that would be classified as criminal later. Even so, a moot hearing may yet have been the default. We cannot to my knowledge show a homicide suit in a local assembly, or an award of wergild in a local assembly. Nor do any of the plethora of enactments in the *leges* concerning wergild rules explicitly prescribe that suits or oaths etc. be held there.

between civil and criminal law like the opposition of 'crime' to tort is an innovation of the WLT, and largely absent from early medieval secular texts.[20] True we all are aware of one important way in which early lawsuits resemble the later actions in tort (called 'trespass' in medieval England): they are primarily organized to compensate the victim and/or his friends. They must be initiated by those damaged, yet do not seek full restitution of the *status quo ante*. That tends to make questions of punishment in any *public* interest secondary, even fines payable to the ruler, however important these may be in the wider picture.[21] Although thieves were customarily hanged with little in the way of trial, and other afflictive sanctions were frequently imposed on wrongdoers, such acts never provoked explanatory theory or much written law. I therefore prefer to reserve the criminal vocabulary for later occasions when there is an explicit opposition between the prosecution of 'crime' and a non-criminal treatment of civil wrongs, tort. Lexicographers can always find Latin *crimen* in their texts, partly because the Latin language remained so deeply infused with the vocabulary of Roman law that the association with a punitive, public notion of wrongs was automatic. And *crimen* often denotes 'sin', that is wrong viewed as offending God not man.[22] Roman law's closest equivalent to tort, *delictum*, likewise often means 'sin'.[23] It took time before the vernacular equivalents of these words were sharpened into lawyerly terms of art.[24] Old English does not possess a general word for 'crime' as distinct from delict, tort,

---

20 *Rancor and Reconciliation*, xvii–xviii. Siems, above, 54, is the only contributor to mention tort.

21 Esders discusses the question of whether the context for wergild involves a Roman type of public law of crime in his chapter above, especially but not exclusively in his section 3.1 (above, 15–17, 20–21) and I shall not try to cover the same ground.

22 *Mediae Latinitatis Lexicon Minus*, ed. Jan F. Niermeyer et al., Leiden ²1993, 282 (cited as Niermeyer); *Dictionary of medieval Latin from British sources*, ed. Ronald E. Latham et al., Oxford,2018 (consulted online at https://logeion.uchicago.edu/), s.v. *crimen*, (cited as DMLBS).

23 Niermeyer, 317, s.v.; DMLBS, s.v. *derelinquere*. But since *delictum* retained a penal connotation for lawyers, as did OFr *trespas* for a century and more. Cf. also Isidore, *Etymologiae*, 5.26.1 for *crimen* and 5.26.24 for *talio*: Isidore of Seville, *Etymologiae*. Translated by Stephen A. Barney et al., *The Etymologies of Isidore of Seville*, Cambridge 2006, 122–124.

24 For OE *hearm*, cf. DOE s.v. *hearm* 2, sense 1, also II Atr 6.1, which enacted that the current truce should cover matters which would (presumably) normally be left for vengeance or compensation. This rather strengthens my guess, in *Rancor and Reconciliation*, 108, that OE *hearm*, which never acquired the status of a legal term of art, might have served as an English alternative to trespass. It would be good to have some expert study this word and its cognates.

or claims for compensation,[25] and it would be interesting to know when the other European vernaculars gained theirs.[26]

There is no good reason to suppose that the criteria for bringing homicide before an assembly differed much from any other wrongs or, indeed, the justification for forceful self-help. The essential thing was for a complainant to be able to tell himself, his friends and supporters, and the rest of their community, that he had suffered harm in some way, to tell his story (*talu*) and seek the restoration of his previous standing by appropriate compensation for both the direct loss and the accompanying shame and affront to his honour. I cannot see that he was expected to use any special vocabulary beyond what was needed to make his claim persuasive. His *talu* may not even have sounded specially legal at all.[27]

Once again, I take my cue from practices normal under the WLT but absent from Anglo-Saxon sources. There is good evidence from the first century after 1066 for the hypothesis that like morality the law dealt initially less in labelled categories than some broad notion of wrong, which would then be narrowed down in the detailed exposition of the specific circumstances of the conflict. Twelfth-century litigants still sought their redress without feeling the need to define or name the remedy they were seeking, in the WLT way swiftly introduced by the early Common Law. It seems best to talk of an 'undifferentiated' procedure before the invention of the common-law actions including that of trespass.[28] There is no good evidence for the existence of discrete 'forms of action' before the reign of Henry II, but plenty once regular plea rolls begin to

25 William the Conqueror's early ordinance (*Lad*) on exculpation singles out for coverage theft and homicide (*mansliht*), and then goes on to mention other 'things', using OE *þing*, Latin *res*, Felix Liebermann, *Gesetze der Angelsachsen*, Halle 1903–1916, vol. 1, 483–484 (cited as Liebermann, *Gesetze*); and cf. 1060. This surely represents his advisers' best shot to define previous practice.

26 They did possess from very early on in the middle ages terms for most offences serious enough to merit special treatment as reserved to kings and the few great men, favoured with the Carolingian *vicariae*. Many of these offences became crimes under the WLT while retaining their ancient names. Something similar holds also for most serious offence words in Old English.

27 I leave the search for proof of an Old English 'legal register' to others more comfortable within the Old English prose corpus.

28 *Rancor and Reconciliation*, xviii, 144–145. Henry G. Richardson and George O. Sayles (ed.), *Select Cases of Procedure without writ*, London 1941, cviii–cxxxiv, at cxxxiii, the first work to make this point, talk — in my view inaccurately — of 'a single undifferentiated *action*' (my emphasis) both before and after the invention of what they more defensibly understand as an actual *action* of trespass in the decades around 1200. Such Roman-inspired standard 'forms of action' should be seen as a WLT innovation.

appear in the 1190s.[29] Until the last third of the twelfth century, there appears to have been no call to frame complaints in specific ways for particular kinds of wrongs, even before royal justices. And since the Norman Conquest cannot be seen to have introduced much change in litigation forms, the onus is on anybody who wishes to argue for differentiated lawsuits before Henry II's time. The terminology of crime and wrong seems to point in the same direction. Much later law derives from the effort to justify the use of one legal remedy rather than another. Without this, the style and language of litigants' pleas will likely have been much more akin to that of political dispute or routine conversation than was the case in the thirteenth century, when the emerging Common Law was generating an unmistakeable legal register in plea roll Latin, pleaders' French, and perhaps also in (Middle) English.

There is thus a strong if largely inferential case that in pre-Conquest England, litigation proceeded in much less differentiated fashion than later, and was argued in something close to normal language. Certainly, Anglo-Saxon sources disclose few signs of the kinds of procedural choices required later.[30] Litigants and others very probably pleaded and suitors framed judgments using 'conceptual categories of a more fuzzy-edged sort'.[31] The durable names for the various serious offences imply that these figured in oral argument both within assemblies and outside them. Those involved knew what they meant and how to argue for and against them. But they pass little of this knowledge on to us.

All of this, including the unknowns, known and unknown, is essential context for wergild. We cannot simplify matters by regarding its workings as 'legal' in anything like the modern sense. My preliminary conclusion is that we should start as we would when pondering direct action and feud, from questions about right and wrong as understood by lay people at the time. One might perhaps view wergild decisions as quasi-legal, made in the (distant) shadow of feud as well as law. I find this suggestive of the eleventh-century world of archbishop Wulfstan of York (d. 1023), master homilist in both Latin and the vernacular,

29 Just when and how the 'forms of action' came into existence, and what that means in practice, is not yet clear to me. The plea rolls of the 1190s are the first to survive, but certainly not the first to exist.

30 Confirmation of this point could come from close readings of extant dispute narratives, as listed by Patrick Wormald, *Legal Culture in the Medieval West*, London 1999, 252–287. Investigation should include source material about feud, occurring outside assemblies and presumably therefore less 'legal'. This could suggest the kinds of argument used in local assemblies. The known absence of direct references to the *leges* themselves in the case narratives of the successful litigants tells us something about their general attitude towards law.

31 Lambert, *Law and Order*, 8, n. 24.

and the dominant figure in royal law-making throughout his lifetime. Where scholars once studied his homiletic and theological writings quite separately from his legislative work, they now approach the whole corpus as the integral product of a single, largely uncompartmentalized mind, which adopted the language and style appropriate to the particular purposes of each work. Wergild should be understood within this mostly moral discourse — Wulfstan never lost sight of the ultimate goal of salvation — through peacemaking that operated on lay people moved by an overlapping but distinctive discursive ethos from a culture of feud and secular social control.[32] How far any such hypotheses might hold elsewhere in northern Europe is another matter.

•••

I now turn to consider some questions about honour, a subject which has over the past generation been summoned to explain a great deal of early medieval culture. Most scholars accept that it was a prime mover in efforts to respond to killings and repair the resulting rifts in the social fabric.[33] One may wonder if we ask the notion to do too much work; contemporary sources mention honour in connection with killings and other assaults rather less frequently than modern commentators. By emphasizing first the comparative power and wealth of perpetrators and their victims, we might be better placed to assess honour's influence on the choices behind wergild, on when and how to seek to make peace and at how high a cost. Honour may at some times be a visceral prime motivator, at others a rhetorical trope useful when striving to recruit allies; it will not always be both at the same time. After all it cuts in more than one direction. One may fight to defend or restore one's honour and remove shame, but to do so effectively, it is necessary to act in an honourable manner. Style matters as much in the negative reciprocity relationships of feud and wergild, as it does in the gift exchange around which so much of early medieval social relations turned. To confirm or restore his reputation, a man must stand up for his truth in person and in due form. We know that the heroic ethos authorised the goading of sons and others deemed too slow to go for blood.[34]

32 Newcomers can enter Wulfstan's ideas through Andrew Rabin, *The Political Writings Of Archbishop Wulfstan of York*, Manchester 2015, and idem, *Archbishop Wulfstan of York: Old English Legal Writings.* (Dumbarton Oaks Medieval Library 66), Cambridge 2020.

33 Siems, above, 56 n. 81, is the only contributor to this volume I have noticed to make explicit criticism of the way we talk about early medieval honour.

34 William Ian Miller, *Bloodtaking and Peacemaking*, Chicago and London 1990, 212–214 remains a good place to start the study of goading. One wonders how often it was tried and how effective it proved. Cf. also chap. 3 on the nature of saga trade.

How then can medieval men and their womenfolk have faced the slur that instead of seeking blood vengeance for the killing of a loved one, openly and in good time, a life for a life, they were prepared to set a money value on him, as if they were selling him like cattle or a slave?

All lives matter! Yet even in our own days the fact that right-thinking people condemn the sale of human lives and bodies does not prevent our putting a price on them in many ways, suppressing meanwhile any cognitive dissonance in the words we choose. Respectable nobles in the early middle ages acutely sensitive to public reputation, as we believe them to have been, saw nothing questionable about the sale of slaves. They also blithely transferred many men and women who considered themselves free without consulting them,[35] and routinely traded sons and daughters for dowries.

Did nobody ever see any contradictions here? Perhaps not. Yet we have stories that, years after men had peacefully settled homicide disputes, companions in their cups might deride them for their veniality.[36] And the condemnation of taking money for (noble) blood was very clear in the written sources. The Romans, with their deeply entrenched slave culture embedded in their highly civilized legal system, wholeheartedly rejected in principle any *aestimatio* of a freeman's life, since *libertas inestimabilis est*,[37] and also declared that *iudex non calculat*.[38] The Franks and their neighbours said less about calculation than about the need to take a life for a life.[39] Secular nobles imbibed these vengeance norms with their mothers' milk, and felt an affront to honour almost as deeply as the loss of their kinsman or friend.

35 I display some evidence on non-consensual transfer of free men and women in my 'Servitude in Anglo-Saxon England' (above, n. 18).

36 The favourite supportive anecdote has long been that of Sichar and Chramnesind, referred to above by Esders, Siems, Meens and Brown; see the index s.v. [Sichar] The considerable literature on this shortish passage from Gregory of Tours does not specify the original wergild price.

37 Digest, 3.7, quoted by Siems, n. 20 and commented on by Esders, 'Wergild and Social Practice in the Early Middle Ages', in: *Entre texte et histoire, Mélanges en honneur de Shoichi Sato*, ed. Jean-Loup Lemaitre and Osamu Kano, Paris 2015, 10 (cited as Esders, 'Wergild and Social Practice'). The maxim *libertas inaestimabilis res*, is at Digest, 50.17.106. For *pecuniam aestimatio*, cf. Meens, above, 220.

38 Esders, 'Wergild and Social Practice', 10, and further above, 30.

39 Evidence cited above includes Childebert at one end of period (Siems, 57 at n. 87) and the Danish 'levelling oath' used into the sixteenth century to commit the victim's friends to keep their word (Vogt, 284–86 and at n. 27). The principle was very widely known, and appears, for example, in *Magna Carta*, cl. 38. King Alfred had pertinently paraphrased Hillel's Golden Rule, Mt., 7.12: 'All things therefore whatsoever you would that men should do to you, do you also to them.' as Af El 49. 6 (Liebermann, *Gesetze* 1, 44–45).

Their clerical brothers and cousins often shared this sentiment. If pressed by colleagues with a more New Testament view of peace and the turning of cheeks, some likely cited in their defence the most famous of all betrayals in sacred history, the Crucifixion of God become Man after the kiss of Judas.[40] All ambitious preachers needed to tell this tale to capture the attention of their flock around Eastertime. One possible reading of the story could make it seem very close to peacemaking and wergild. Judas's tragedy was that he realized only after the evil deed was done that his 'blood price' (*pretium sanguinis*) of 30 'silvers' (*argentei*) was not *iustum sanguis*, which is why he had himself to pay the further price of his own life and blood. This capital sin of humankind came over as a supreme act of betrayal of its Lord and King. Many surely understood it through their personal memories of similar acts against some earthly lord or kinsman. And their abhorrence of the one sin would feed into emotions about the other.[41] This must have cast doubt on the probity of accepting a price for the life of their own loved ones too.[42] Was not the human being — at least when he or she was Christian — made in God's own image and therefore to be preserved at all costs?[43]

I cannot myself document this line of argument from the ecclesiastical writings of the eleventh century and before, still less prove that it was voiced during the social drinking in the halls of great lords and elsewhere.[44] It seem quite probable not just that some would think such thoughts but that their teachings would reach lay members of their flocks. One wonders all the same if influential players might not experience special qualms over the acceptance of mere silver as adequate redress for the taking of a life. Such sentiments would

40 Mt. 26.14–16; 27.3, 9; Mc. 14.10–11; Lc. 22.3–6; Io. 13.2; and also Zach. 11.12–13; Ierem. 32.6–9.

41 In an unpublished paper, T.D. Hill, 'Satan, Judas, and the Foundation of the West Saxon State: Myth and Exegesis in the Prologue to Alfred's Laws' analyses the pseudo-history of the origins of a composition system in Af El 49.7, noting with Af 1. 1 that nobody should keep a treasonable oath to kill any lord. He cites Old English texts that present lord-slaying (*hlafordsearwe*) as the bootless exception to the rule of wergild composition. (Cf. DOE, s.v.).

42 Analogies between human relations with God and more ordinary human social relations with each other help to explain the long persistence of the Ransom theory of atonement. I discuss the doctrine of the Atonement a little further in my 'Three-cornered Dynamics of Redemption in the Long Thirteenth Century', *Anglo-Norman Studies* 26 (2013), 1–15.

43 Wulfstan's opinion on this induced him to advise against capital punishment in principle for any but serious offences, V Atr 3; VI Atr 10; II Cn 2. 1, since God had paid His own stiff price for humankind, as Wulfstan made clear in I Cn 18. 3. I see nothing idiosyncratic about these views, nothing distinctively English.

44 In my coda below I suggest that contemporaries comprehended wergild as a kind of entitlement, less than a right but part of their value and status. This might be one way to soften ambivalent feelings if anyone raised them.

certainly complicate peace negotiations. Perhaps this is why so many of the early *leges* consist so largely of tariffs in relation to non-lethal offences,[45] and may be why theft attracted capital penalties so much more readily than homicide. But all this adds speculation to speculation.

We should still ask why wergilds continued to be paid and accepted so long, into the twelfth century in England, even longer elsewhere. Much of the answer is perhaps the lack of a convenient alternative, also no doubt the financial interest of the victim's friends. We have in any case no way of knowing how frequent homicides were, and how often the victim's friends chose the wergild option. Money was always a convenient metric by which to measure the damage suffered to life, limb, and collective honour, a highly complex and otherwise unquantifiable entity. Scholars more or less agree that the real key was to tie the social value of a deceased's life to his status level assessed in amounts of coin much larger than 30 pieces of silver. This value was used as a shorthand mnemonic for the men (and presumably also 'their' womenfolk), so everyone understood what it meant to be a *twyhyndman* (two-hundred-shilling man), and thus as free and honourable as all others of similar social rank.[46] There will be more on this below.

The potential for ambivalence over honour and wergild is one example of the cognitive dissonance which all cultures must on occasion face and attempt to deal with. All peace settlements, as human artefacts, are imperfect. Effective negotiators must accept this, and factor the uncertainties into their approach. Complete forgiveness, meaning the deletion of fault and restoration of warm and friendly relations, is a very different matter than pardon, which merely removes the penalty. It is perhaps too hard to expect this of human beings, especially in killings where the principal victim is unavailable to grant it, than for an omnipotent and all-knowing God.[47]

•••

A little more discussion on the fixed amounts of compensation recorded in the *leges* might provide an appropriate ending to our wergild volume. It is well known that early medieval 'lawcodes' look more similar to modern legislation

45 See next note for two early English law codes that do *not* specify a status link for the composition payments they lay down.

46 I remain a little troubled by the fact that the *leges* of Æthelberht and Alfred (Abt and Af) each list the prices of a whole string of lesser offences without explicitly linking them to the wergild metric.

47 But since the underlying theory of wergild in a Christian society seems to allot victim status to whole kindreds, there is certainly more to say on this subject.

than they really are. We have to resist any temptation to read *leges* as a mandatory statement of actual law. When modern penal legislation enacts a new penalty for some crime, the intention is to bind the courts. Were the compositions Anglo-Saxon and other codes prescribed for non-lethal offences genuinely intended to be followed to the letter? If compositions for killings, wergild, were similarly fixed, it might follow that the price due for killing a 200-shilling man should indeed be two hundred shillings-worth of 2,400 silver pennies, total value 200/-, no more, no less.[48]

Most scholars quietly assume that negotiation on the amount of compensation set a tone for the whole business of settling homicide disputes that permitted far more flexibility than that. I shall now supply some possibly superfluous justifications for this position, and see how this might enhance our understanding of wergild and its overall importance. I shall be on the lookout for signs of a communal interest in the process, as the initiative is not known to have come initially from either kings or moot assemblies.

The difficulty of any fixed penalty view is that it really could encourage people to regard wergild as a mere sale price, one that if it were freely offered after the event should entitle them to have taken an enemy's life for that of a slaughtered friend, possibly even after non-lethal but shaming offences. The idea that payment of fines entitles one to have committed a wrong, that you have thereby bought the act is not totally unknown in our own day, but has been largely confined to the sphere of minor matters, like breaking china on display in a store or parking a car in a banned area. It can tempt perpetrators to regard a fine as a licence fee to act at will.[49] True, this devalues the wrongness of wrongs in general, with potentially damaging consequences to public order, but that is somebody else's problem. Our distant ancestors sometimes felt this way too, as at least one apposite late antique anecdote illustrates.[50] The silence of other early medieval sources is no proof that it never happened. By

48 This is one possible reading of 'tantum quantum consuetudo loci est' from a penitential quoted by Meens, 223, n. 39, but not the only one.

49 An even better illustration comes from the history of 'professional' fouls in football and other professional sports. Time was when this kind of conscious and deliberate act of flouting the rules of the game was rare and generally disapproved. Hence the adjective once implied (in my British youth!) that such behaviour was wrong because unsporting. But as so-called 'sports, and especially basketball in the US, became fully monetized, approving euphemisms such as 'taking one for the team' have become common. (Cf. also applause for a player who can 'draw a foul' from the opposition.) Young onlookers do not miss the obvious lessons.

50 Siems, above, 44, and Esders orally at the conference. But Aulus Gellius surely expected his sophisticated Roman readers to read his tale as a *reductio ad absurdum* and to disapprove the behaviour he described.

emphasizing how hard it was to attain heavenly salvation, clerical preachers and confessors may sometimes have had the unintended effect of moving lay people to feel that their chances were hopelessly remote. This in itself could make them more not less cynical towards legal and moral rules.

Peace-making is never simple. It does not happen of its own accord; it has to be made to happen. Diplomatic interventions first, to close off the original violence and prevent escalation by, for example, separating the warring parties, then to create conditions in which minds might meet and come to terms. Then truces and damage limitation, to buy time for negotiation first at a distance, then later, perhaps, at closer quarters with a search for some new basis for coexistence and a gradual restoration of relations that might one day lead on to fresh friendship. The genocide option (to destroy all potential avengers) is always in the air, as an alternative resolution method to serve as an inducement to come to terms. And so is the third option mentioned above, by which some must swallow pride, 'lump' the loss of their loved one and seek neither vengeance nor compensation.

Some sort of third-party mediation (or possibly arbitration) might help to prevent those most closely involved from facing off against each other once more.[51] Negotiations may have been three-sided or even community-wide and so approximate to a public conversation not just on the rights and wrongs of the specific case but also about the customary canons of local peace-making. My own guesses about the form this took and the general character of the negotiations would start from some early medieval version of the modern legal trope of bargains made 'in the shadow of the law',[52] or rather, in the present context, 'in the shadow of law *and* feud'.

If the actual numbers in the *leges* did figure in discussion,[53] they were perhaps treated a little like those quoted for second-hand cars on dealers' websites,[54] that is, as rough markers from which the haggling started. In matters quite literally of life and death, some early medieval negotiators must have

51 Cf. below 310.

52 Robert H. Mnookin and Lewis Kornhauser, 'Bargaining in the Shadow of the Law: The Case of Divorce', *The Yale Law Journal* 88 (1979), 950–997 seems to have originated this useful formula. How much attention today's lawyers and their paying clients actually pay to the law in their negotiations has been the subject of much contention among legal scholars.

53 They are not in the *Vita Wulfstani* anecdote, cited below [n. 66]. But back before 1066, most families perhaps had some sense of whether they were 200-, 600-, or 1200-shilling men.

54 A suggestion I first heard from the late Tim Reuter, which has won a measure of approval among scholars.

approached the process in a quite instrumental frame of mind.[55] Naturally, the flavour of the bargain process on feud settlements was otherwise very different from deals made on commercial car lots. The most easily accessible hints of its character are accounts of actual or even fictional feuds, including those from the literary culture of Icelandic saga. The wergild tariff is presumably premised on the differential position, reputation and honour ascribed to the men (and their women) at each different social level.[56] When we seek to re-imagine the actual circumstances when the wergild price changed hands and the parties demonstrated publicly that their enmity was now ended, it is tempting to read it in terms of secular honour and other epic values, with killings understood as much as affronts to families as to individuals. But there is something circular about this relationship.

And other considerations claim their due place. Possibly the most important of these is the ethos of peace itself. This is not the place to review the substantial Latin literature on theories of peace from the period.[57] But mention must be made of the kinds of idea current in the circles round the king and his legislating churchmen.[58] During the century or so before 1066, English kings all swore at the very start of their reigns to ensure that God's Church and the whole Christian people preserve the true peace for all time.[59] Exactly what this peace consisted in is hard to say, for Old English possessed several separate words for 'peace', where Latin and modern English use just the one. It did not commit the new king to meet some vision of God's perfect, eternal peace, just some distant, imperfect human simulacrum, yet even this was always under threat down here on earth, most often from theft and violence. It was nevertheless basic both to existing law and to the *leges* by which kings and their advisers increasingly sought to supplement this.

---

55 There have been attempts to demonstrate the value of rational choice theory to the study of conflict in Icelandic sagas that pay special attention to the allegedly rational thinking of their protagonists. But that kind of writing style is specific to saga literature.

56 'Wer' 2 gives the principle as *swa hw geboren sy* (Quad: *sicut natalis eius*); and cf. 'Wer' 7: *ðe him to gebyreð* (Quad. *secundum mensuram que pertinet ei*), which may mean the same.

57 The secondary literature is vast. Readers limited to English could make a sensible start from the works cited by Lambert, *Law and Order*, 207, n. 12 plus Geoffrey Koziol, *The Peace of God*, Leeds 2018, and other works cited at the beginning of Kiril Petkov, *The Kiss of Peace: Ritual, Self, and Society in the High and Late Medieval West*, Leiden and Boston, Massachusetts 2003.

58 Most of what follows is based on the imaginative and evidence-based analyses of Lambert, *Law and Order*, esp. chap. 5, but cf. also above, 135–141.

59 The 'first ordo' of the English coronation liturgy was already old by the tenth century.

The most often cited *Leges* accord surprisingly well with the way one imagines wergild had to work. The code known as II Edmund (*II Em*) is particularly instructive. Its prologue tells us that it had emerged from discussions between king and *witan* (council) on the best way to promote the Christian religion. Most of those who spoke on this will have been churchmen, some of whom knew their Latin texts, but their counsels had to be acceptable to their secular colleagues. The right policy, *II Em* held, was to maintain peace and concord (*gesibsumnesse 7 geþwærnesse*) throughout the land under royal control. The phrase has been judged to imply that they sought a peace 'rooted in ideas of shared kinship', one whose earthly standards human kings must reach through the standard social structures of their day.[60] They could do God's work effectively by repressing the many acts of wrongful violence they saw around them. Among these were exactly those kinds of homicides for which men sought vengeance. Not all violent acts were necessarily wrongful, note, for the draftsman consciously chose language that could warn individuals (and their friends) against attacking each other within the kingdom in time of what should otherwise be peace.[61] The main target of the whole code is to regulate feud (*fǣhþ*) and in so doing to proscribe wrongful violence (especially, perhaps, killings) while permitting rightful vengeance.[62] This message was clear to the learned, for them to pass on as follows: blood vengeance, when proper procedures were followed, was as compatible as non-violent wergild itself with a peace of the nation-qua-family. Thus both forms of direct action against killers, were licit, whether by reciprocal violence or by money payments, that is, by either option 1 or 2 from my model above.[63] How similar this policy was to Continental ones I do not know. There were certainly differences, for the retention of a third of the wergild (under the name of *fredus*) that acknowledged the Frankish king's loan of royal power to compel settlement was unknown in England.[64]

I now turn to consider, as best as one can, the mechanics of reaching this peace in real-life situations. There are four stages. First, both perpetrators and victim's friends had to get through the first week or so. This is when the danger of escalation was at its highest, and also when each side was pondering its basic strategy. Will the perpetrators publicly 'claim responsibility' (in the modern

60 Lambert, *Law and Order*, 225. Cf. BT, 441, 1113 s.v. *ge-sibsumnes* and its antonym.

61 This is II Em prol. 1–2 which bemoans *unrihtlican ... gefeoht*, on which cf. DOE s.v. *ge-feoht*, and distinguish *feoht*, whose usage seems restricted to (external) warfare; and also BT, 1125, for *unrihtlic*.

62 DOE, s.v. *fǣhþ*, *fǣhþu*.

63 Lambert, *Law and Order*, 225–226.

64 See index, s.v. *fredus* for treatments above by esp. Haubrichs above, 100–101, but also Esders, above, 21, and Bothe, above, 189.

phrase) for their deed? This would signal that they were open to negotiation, and challenge the opposition to declare its preferences. Meanwhile both parties must locate, refresh, and if possible supplement their support groups. There will be much persuading to do, and no little pressure and cajoling.[65] Everybody knew both the risks and the chances of profit or expense, for most outside the immediate household had their price. There were, too, always a few with close links to both sides. These 'hinge-men' could lead the way towards peaceful resolution, but they might also become the subjects of a bidding war, which could swiftly turn nasty.

In the second stage, each side must prepare themselves for their chosen options. Each should display its readiness to 'go to the mattresses', as mafiosi say, whether the victim's friends preferred blood, or merely hoped to defend themselves against further violence, canvassing the possibilities for peace while preparing for war in case their overtures were rejected. The very first step, to open up communication channels with the other side, might prove impossible. Bishops, holy men, and local secular powers might or might not offer their services as willing mediators and peacemakers. They had their prices too. For the peace-seekers, the bargaining process was now under way, strengths were trumpeted and weakness concealed. There would be preliminary meetings between proxies, but as yet without the dangerous presence of principals still hot with anger. Peacemakers had somehow to open up the road-map they needed, to discover what the victim's friends would accept by way of money (which is where wergild tariffs come in) or public apology and humiliation, and what the perpetrators were prepared to say, do, and pay. It might take a deal of moral pressure as well as more worldly threats just to bring angry victims to the negotiating table. It helped to bring them into favourable situations and places, the hall of some prelate or nobleman, perhaps, or a moot assembly, or to some convenient religious event like a church dedication that put people in a mood to fear God over earthly interests.[66] In many areas of Western Christendom, but not apparently England, Peace of God meetings were virtually purpose built for the job. I am sure the parties' representatives were in touch much more often than the sources ever show, but doubt that we will ever know much about the details of this third logical stage of the process. The second-hand car dealer analogy is just one possible hypothesis, welcome

65 The killer might need to persuade even his own kin to support him, II Em 1–1. 2.

66 The victim's funeral was an unpromising choice; holidays in honour of a local saint were a better bet. My interest was aroused by a revealing early twelfth-century account of a church dedication from the last third of the eleventh century, *The Vita Wulfstani of William of Malmesbury* 2.15, ed. Reginald R. Darlington (Camden third series 40), London 1928, 38–40.

especially because it makes use of our main source as to quantum of compensation, the wergild tariffs. We actually learn rather more about the non-pecuniary terms of settlements.

The fourth stage is the event itself, when wergild and other payments were to be made. Only now that the results of the negotiations were in, could anyone estimate how closely payments approached the tariff prices. There were commonly a series of occasions, comprising not merely the paying over of the wergild instalments,[67] but also separate public acts of the perpetrators to reassure the victim's party. But I have space here only for the simplest and probably atypical case where payment of the wergild and all public ceremonial took place together on a single occasion.

Most of the arrangements were better made in advance. This too can be illustrated by Edmund's second law-code, which together with an associated treatise provides the fullest single account of wergild procedure.[68] It seeks to regulate and optimize the customary settlement procedures without too much interference. Its goals are durability and the minimizing of collateral damage. To these ends it required safe-conducts for the perpetrators, set time-limits for their compliance with the agreements, and extracted pledges of obedience to the rules.

Since the ending of unpeace was everybody's concern, a crowd was desirable and expected, especially no doubt in towns and substantial villages. There were good reasons to want full publicity, the largest possible future witness, to remember the terms and conditions of the settlement and possibly also stand ready to defend them. Before the WLT, such witness was perhaps not validated by individual oaths but envisaged as a single entity[69] to be assessed and

---

67 Payment by instalments is taken for granted in II Em 7. 3; Wer 6, whose term *frumgyld* for the first instalment seems invented to describe this, DOE, s.v.

68 Patrick Wormald, *The Making of English Law: King Alfred to the Twelfth Century. Volume 1: Legislation and its Limits, Oxford 1999*, 31–32, 374–378, places II Em and the treatise 'Wer' into context.

69 The main evidence is the total absence of any direct interrogation of witnesses. Eleventh-century diplomas as well as dispute narratives commonly precede their list of those present at a land grant with words such as *Ðises is to gewitnesse* ..., S 1473 (1044/8) in the singular. Oaths usually aim to verify the character of those swearing as much as or more than their precise words. Cf. BT, 731, s.v. *ofercyþan*. In England, Latin *testimonium* seems to be used similarly. Lexicographers and editors often conceal the nature of the process by changing the number of the verb from singular to plural. For illustration, cf. BT, 470 s.v. *gewitnes* etc.; DMLBS, s.v. *testimonium*. Since this suggestion flies in the face of all the literature, I offer it with some hesitation.

(almost literally) weighed.[70] The principals and their supporters obviously had to attend in force. Whether they brought with them their arms or their womenfolk was some measure of their confidence that the safe-conducts would hold. The availability of refreshments, especially alcohol, might make a real difference to the outcome! Yet there is evidence neither of open invitations to the general public nor of active efforts to exclude them.

Even among neighbours who know they must continue to deal with each other on a daily basis, peace-making is inevitably an edgy process that demands tactful and patient handling over a protracted period. We cannot easily learn how central wergild was to this process. Non-legal sources rarely declare any fixed price.[71] Its enforcement would be difficult without some authority able to call out a local posse, as may have been done for the small but growing group of bootless offences where money composition was not allowed. Possibly, something of this kind was already moving the handling of law-and-order questions in general in the direction of the WLT, but if so it has left little sign in the sources.

The payment of wergild was meant to hurt perpetrators almost as much as they had hurt their victims. It should stretch their financial resources to the limit, compel the actual killer and his closest kin to take on moral and financial debts to more distant kin, established allies, plain-vanilla friends and neutral neighbours, even sometimes to men of money outside their circle. Perpetrators can seldom have been able to raise the amounts needed from their personal resources in the time allowed. Many potential creditors would take some persuading, some would require heavy pressure, and all could name a price that sometimes included submission to their lordship. Some fair-weather friends may already have distanced themselves and joined the opposition for their own share of the silver. And if wergild suits were at all common, the prudent would be aware that next time they might be the ones pleading for allies, whether to seek vengeance, or a defensible but costly peace.[72]

So, what kinds of things happened on the day? It is notable that we have no liturgical *ordo* to trigger our imagination. Wergild remains essentially a secular

70 My own suspicion is that the primary target of Af 1, Liebermann, *Gesetze* 1, 46, was to bind men to their 'oath and pledge' on everyday matters as much as (or more) than to create a Carolingian-style fidelity oath to the king. The public oath must in some sense grow out of private practice.

71 Among the rare English illustrations are *Bede's Ecclesiastical History of the English People* 4.21, ed. Bertram Colgrave and Roger A. B. Mynors, Oxford 1992, 401, *Anglo-Saxon Chronicle*, s.a. 694, and *Beowulf*. Translated by Seamus Heaney, *Beowulf: A New Verse Translation*, New York 1999, 30–33 (ll. 456–472).

72 Esders has also discussed these questions, above, 13–14 and 23.

matter. Proper procedure would mostly be governed by the parties themselves along lines set on previous occasions. It differed according to areas and over time. Let us start with the payments. Even though, the money was paid in instalments, the scene must have been impressive, with more wealth in one place than many present might ever see again. There was more to see than silver pennies. To make up the full amounts, most perpetrators would produce precious vessels and other bullion, animal livestock (for whose use here texts sometimes note equivalent coin values) and quite possibly even human stock, slaves; they might even offer land.[73] Even so there were likely too many coins for easy handling. The *leges* specified what was due in shillings, but there was no shilling coin. Thus a 200 shilling man owed 2,400 silver pennies and a nobler *twelfhyndman* nearly fourteen and a half thousand, an amount that if transferred on a single occasion could temporarily affect the whole local economy.[74]

Counting such large sums and keeping an agreed account could be a challenge. It might be better to weigh the silver out.[75] This reduced the danger that of adversaries coming to blows over how to count cut, debased, forged, and foreign coins.[76] This was not the only difficulty. Even assuming the exercise was performed indoors, there was plenty of opportunity for individual coins to go missing, accidentally or otherwise.[77] They had to be laid out where everybody could see them to satisfy themselves that there was no cheating. There is rich potential here for some good old English muddle with violent and tragic consequences. The principals and their friends will have been very relieved at the end of the day to have got through it all without further trouble. What a

---

73 See Abt 30 (livestock) and my *Rancor and Reconciliation*, 89 (a princely wergild provides land for a religious house). The use of human stock makes best sense if England possessed a genuine slave culture, a notion I have questioned in my 'Servitude in Anglo-Saxon England' [248–249 above n. 18]. The fascinating illustration at the start of Esders' chapter, above, 2 is sadly too schematic to be much help with visualizing the scene. He cites Frankish documentation of a kind lacking in England, above, 11.

74 I am assuming 12 pennies to the shilling, but the ratio varied by area: Peter Spufford, *Money and its use in Medieval Europe*, Cambridge 1988, 33, 77.

75 Wer 1–1.1 (Quad) a 12th-century Latin translation hints as much, by adding shilling equivalents in terms of pounds, clearly a unit of weight. See next note for half-pounds.

76 I owe to Prof. David Johnson the full references of the notice in BT Suppl., 697 to the Old English translation of Grégoire le Grand, *Dialogues* 2.27, ed. Adalbert de Vogüé, Sources chrétiennes no. 251, 260, 265, Paris 1978–1980 = Hans Hecht (ed.), *Bischofs Wærferth von Worcester Übersetzung der Dialoge Gregors des Grossen* (Bibliothek der angelsächen Prosa v), Leipzig 1900 (rpt. Darmstadt 1965), 157–159. What Gregory had called *argentei*, bishop Wærferth translated as shillings, those undefined 'silver pieces' of the Judas story.

77 I imagine piles with a dozen pennies in each, something for which the sources give a few suggestive hints. But what if they toppled over, and got mixed together?!

spectacle for the locals with so much to see and so much hanging on efficient and speedy dispatch of the business!

There was, of course, more to the day than this. To many the more important part of the action was to hammer home the moral lessons of peace and its breaches. Yet, if we trust the *leges,* these ritual add-ons were just an optional extra.[78] The king was not about to get embroiled in the details of injured egos and friendships gone sour. The parties had to sort these matters out for themselves. The perpetrators' highly visible prostration in the dirt before the opposition, or similar but more finely calibrated acts of self-abasement could mollify shame, restore honour and help a little to recalibrate the balance between the parties. If that seemed over the top, beyond a helpful *mesure,* as the French would say later, the victim's friends might be satisfied with multiple acts of peace homage by perpetrators and friends. Size and weight matter as greatly here as they did with witness. The number as well as the social rank of those who performed the hand-having ritual to the deceased's next of kin did *not* create new lordship but served instead to signal the end of an enmity. However, there is no early evidence of peace homage in pre-Conquest England.[79] Other propitiatory acts that might in due course convert a shaky truce into a lasting peace include a pilgrim's oath and investiture, to get the killer out of the way and aid the deceased's soul, and a peace-weaving marriage to generate a fresh generation of common kindred.

Though so much happened on the big day, then, the wergild process was much more than a single event when a known sum of money changed hands and ended an enmity. It could convert local life for a period into quite a new rhythm, full of political negotiation and tension touching many lives. None of the middle ranks of local society — those who administered and lived off manors — could avoid being drawn in by this to some degree. Their superiors might be so too, for when faced by opponents who outgunned them, the weaker party might plead with a greater man to take over the feud so that he became the wergild principal and perhaps also their new lord. Not even the unfree *weorcmen* or *laboratores* were immune, whether they scented the threat of more intensive exploitation or merely gawped at the brief display of wealth

78 II Em has no equivalent to Wer 6. 1, which holds that should it be wanted, one could go *mid lufe* for *fulle freondrædne,* presumably meaning an affective restoration of social relations. I Em 3; II Em 4 tend in the same direction, by delegating to churchmen decisions as to when penances were complete and the newly penitent might once more be admitted to the king's presence.

79 My account in *Rancor and Reconciliation* expands a little on the fuller discussion in my 'Homage and Feudalism', 247, see n. 15 above. One wonders what roles the homage kiss and the Christian kiss of peace played in each other's story.

and power in the neighbourhood. And afterwards, there was much for everybody to talk about in and around the hall, at church and market, in the very countryside itself, embedding what had happened in memories where it might be recalled much later and possibly rekindle the embers of conflict.

3 Coda: Right Against Wrongs

It seems only proper to end with some brief consideration of how we should categorize wergild. Was it perhaps a *right* for the relicts of the deceased, with a corresponding *duty* for the killer and his supporters? Scholars who deny that 'legal' rights of the WLT kind existed before the twelfth century imply a negative answer to the question. Anglo-Saxon England nevertheless has something to contribute to the pre-history of WLT subjective rights, for it undeniably provided the sources from which some later common-law forms developed.

Brian Tierney moved the history of natural rights back into the twelfth-century schools but no further. Their origin he places with the canon lawyers, especially the decretists of the second half of the century, plumb centre of the WLT's birth pangs.[80] Since his interest like that of all who come to the subject from the direction of the immensely influential Western theories of natural rights is of rights within Western law as we know it, he is little concerned by the fact that the vernacular terms for 'right' in a variety of European vernaculars are all firmly evidenced before 1100. The Old English term *riht*, for example, though it could mean a number of different things linked with a particular status, was sometimes definable as 'that which is straight in a metaphorical sense, right, law, canon, rule', and 'what properly belongs to a person, what may justly be claimed, a right, due'.[81] What is different about OE *riht* is that unlike the Latin equivalents and later 'right' words, it apparently had no antonym meaning 'duty'. Indeed, OE *riht* itself could itself sometimes convey this sense.[82] If it is true that the same word could mean both what is due ***to*** an individual and also what is due *from* him, an obligation, it must have been almost impossible

80 Brian L. Tierney, *The Idea of Natural Rights* (Emory University Studies in Law and Religion 5), Atlanta, Georgia 1997, esp. 48–54 (cited as Tierney, *The Idea of Natural Rights*).

81 BT, 796, senses II and IV. And cf. *Oxford English Dictionary*, Oxford 2010, s.v. *right*, senses 2, 9f.

82 BT, loc. cit., sense V. Thus one word can mean both right and duty, what is due *to* an individual and also what is due *from* him, an obligation. If the same is true of other vernaculars in the eleventh century and earlier, this probably indicates a distinctive feature of the nature of law before the WLT.

to talk of rights and duties in the later manner. *Riht* though clearly part of the pre-history of rights was not at all the finished object.

But Old English has another means of expressing something very similar, the valuation or worth that entitles free individuals to the privileges and responsibilities of their status. A man — and possibly a woman too, I know no direct evidence — is worthy (*wyrðig*) of moot, oath, and *fyrd* (ie fighting with the army), which together may be summarised as full participation in public life, and thus virtually synonymous with the fullest of freedoms.[83] Notably, some of these privileges might also be seen as burdens. The landed wealth and good blood of the free also commits them to pay their geld and risk their lives in the *fyrd*.[84] Its noun, *weorþ* generally covers human values of a highly positive kind but also, however, ransom and compensation prices of the free, who can among other things be *weres wyrðe*, 'worthy of their wergild',[85] but also the economic value of goods and animal stock, both alive and dead, including the human variety (OE *mann, ðeow*).[86]

There is, then, something slightly jarring to a modern sensibility about the Old English notion of worth. It appears at first sight to be intrinsic and unchanging, closely associated with honour inherited from one's forebears. Yet it can be affected by the actions of ourselves and our friends. It may rise and fall according to whether one behaves with generosity and courage or in a cowardly and shameful fashion. And it has a cash value. All of this must have been apparent in the way men and women talked about wergild, whose prices represented a man's worth as then understood,[87] symbolic not market capital. What Anglo-Saxon legislators had in mind was more like a gold standard of honour than a sale price,[88] but how far those closest to the killings understood this is unknowable.

---

83 II Cn 20. The freedom vocabulary has even more possible meanings than that of right. I argue my positions a little less summarily in my 'Servitude in Anglo-Saxon England', 35–37, text at ns. 77–79, 84.

84 E.g. II Cn 79, discussed in my 'Property Talk: Did Anglo-Saxon England know the Concept of Seisin?', in: *Texts and Contexts in Legal History: Essays in Honor of Charles Donahue*, ed. John Witte, Sara McDougall and Anna di Robilant, Berkeley, California 2017, 37–59; 55.

85 Af 32; II As 19; VI As 6.2; II Atr 1. 9 = II Cn 30. 8.

86 BT, 1199 s.v. *weorþ*, with various alternative spellings, senses II–III, e.g. Abt 32.

87 Recidivist troublemakers might be expelled from their kindred: *Rancor and Reconciliation*, 81–82. One may suppose that any really outrageous behaviour (eg. lord-slaying) that led to outlawry or being named a *nithing* might be similarly sanctioned, though I know no supporting evidence.

88 The distant etymology of OE *scilling* from Latin *solidus*, the classic Roman gold coin, may just be relevant here.

We moderns may attempt to categorize wergild within our own schemas. Claims to it do not jibe with later notions of subjective rights, if only because they are never precisely defined. Wergild has the air of a vernacular notion only analysed orally. We should therefore be cautious before assigning it a WLT-type 'legal' context, or trying to map out the road by which it might have been transformed into formal law later.

Wergild is never assigned a divine origin and had no Roman precedents.[89] The nascent Common Law declined to recognize either vengeance or wergild in its courts, because these went unapproved by the *ius scriptum* that set the standards for legal rationality. It was therefore a poor candidate for incorporation into the WLT. To forego licit vengeance for other less visceral forms of satisfaction was patently a choice often open to criticism. Few would see it as 'natural', except in the attenuated sense that it required no permission from prince or law. While its 'neutral sphere of personal choice' may have helped to redefine self-defence in terms of a 'right' of self-preservation,[90] neither of these fit easily into the emerging categories of the twelfth century.[91]

How then should we classify wergild? It certainly did some of the work of the later right. I suggest we might borrow from some lawyers and social scientists their notion of 'entitlement'. They use this for various claims and obligations based on public sentiment which do not meet legal or philosophical definitions of a right, but may have some consequences in or just outside the law. The term has been used to treat a variety of situations without an agreed definition.[92] All of us may feel entitled to such generalities as our share of happiness, our own opinions and tastes. Closer to the present point is the minimum duty we owe our neighbour to not harm him or her, perhaps also to give

89 Since there are analogues in the Old Testament, someone should study early medieval and twelfth-century commentary on bible passages concerning vengeance and homicide.

90 Tierney, *The Idea of Natural Rights*, 45–48, 67, 85–86.

91 Wergild could not be classed as 'permissive' (because non-obligatory) natural law, since the peaceful settlement of disputes was hardly a matter about which people ought to be 'morally indifferent', Brian L. Tierney, *Liberty and the Law: The Idea of Permissive Natural Law, 1100–1800* (Studies in Medieval and Early Modern Canon Law 12), Washington DC 2014.

92 Amartya Sen, *The Idea of Justice*, Cambridge, Massachusetts 2009, introduced me to the notion. Cf. among others Michael J. Sandel, *Justice: What's the Right Thing to do?*, Cambridge, Massachusetts 2009, 160–164. In my 'Medieval Attitudes to Poverty: Amartya Sen and Serfdom Without Strings', in: *Emotions, Communities, and Difference in Medieval Europe*, ed. Maureen C. Miller and Edward Wheatley, London and New York 2017, 180–206, at 182–184 (cited as 'Serfdom Without Strings'), I failed to grasp Sandel's point.

them love and aid.[93] Such good intentions lack enforceability. Under the WLT, courts eventually gained in principle the power to execute their judgments against losing defendants. But this required some definitional pruning, for an entitlement may be either due *to* us or expected *from* us. The same term works in both directions, without the kind of antonym that 'duty' can provide for 'right'. This has the advantage that it places fewer incumbrances in the way of pressing one's claims in the quasi-political ways permitted by early medieval assemblies, but it will not, in principle, do for the WLT with its novel attitude to the definitions and distinctions of the schools.

A nice medieval example is the supposed right of a starving man to take what he needs from his neighbours developed in the decades around 1200 by theologians and by canonists (with, by then, a precise definition of right). But this was late in wergild's day, and no legal system in England or elsewhere took the idea up legally.[94] Other practices contemporary to wergild seem quite closely analogous. Custom had given a grantor's kin and lord a power of veto (sometimes called the *laudatio parentum*) over dispositions which threatened their residual claims to benefit from land. But such entitlements as these were never adopted into the English Common Law after the early thirteenth century, though they were in some other parts of western Europe.[95] Potential litigants had always had the power to solve many of their difficulties by the kind of self-help that the nobility always like to wield. This power did not exactly disappear under the Common Law, but was greatly reined in by the requirements of the WLT, whose central theoretical concern was the maintenance of order. The minority of cases that survived this winnowing process would, I imagine, qualify as legal rights. In England, vengeance was not among them, which goes far to explain why wergild disappeared there but not elsewhere.[96]

• • •

93 Jeremy Waldron, 'Who is my Neighbor? Humanity and Proximity', *The Monist* 86 (2003), 333–354, is rich in suggestions to follow up in medieval bible commentary on the parable of the Good Samaritan and elsewhere.

94 Cf. my 'Serfdom without Strings', 191–192.

95 Stroud F. C. Milsom, *The Legal Framework of English Feudalism*, Cambridge 1976, chap. 4, esp. 121 sq.; Hudson, *The Oxford History of the Laws of England* 2, 171–175; Stephen D. White, *Custom, Kinship, and Gifts to Saints*, Chapel Hill, North Carolina and London 1988, treats the *laudatio parentum* and its successor, the two kinds of *retrait*.

96 Sir Frederick Pollock and Frederic W. Maitland, *The History of English Law before the Time of Edward I*, Cambridge [2]1898, vol. 2, 574–578, may be compared with Hudson, *Oxford History of The Laws of England* 2, 171–175.

The thesis that has emerged from these trespassory thoughts suggests that wergild could not long survive the onset of the WLT, and the manifold changes in sensibility and mental outlook which produced this. Wergild cannot have disappeared with 'marvellous suddenness' as the great Maitland once asserted.[97] Changes of this magnitude took generations and occurred at a pace that differed according to where and when they began. These ones should be studied within the renaissance of the 'long' twelfth century and its accompanying legal revolution. In these the judicialization of wrong and its redress played a larger role than has been allowed. To drive a straight Roman road through the ancient tanglewood logic of dispute resolution entailed much pruning of dead wood, and selection of which entitlements should survive as rights. Where the disempowered once suffered from their lack of political clout, they now lost out because they could not pay for the entry tickets to the legal forums of freedom. The proportion doomed to 'lump' the killings of loved ones is unlikely to have fallen much, but the opposition's expensive lawyers now had an appropriate Latin description; it was *dampnum sine iniuria*. Here is material for a new conference. I hope that it will find better answers to my questions here posed, and better questions too, and that I am still around to join in and learn from it.

Bibliography

Primary Sources

Bede, *Historia ecclesiastica gentis Anglorum*, ed. Bertram Colgrave and Roger A. B. Mynors, *Bede's Ecclesiastical History of the English People*, Oxford 1992.

Beowulf. Translated by Seamus Heaney, *Beowulf: A New Verse Translation*, New York 1999.

Die Gesetze der Angelsachsen, ed. Felix Liebermann, 3 vols., Halle 1903–1916.

Gregory the Great, *Dialogorum libri quattuor seu De miraculis patrum italicorum*, ed. Adalbert de Vogüé, Sources chrétiennes 251, 260, 265, Paris 1978–1980.

Isidore of Seville, *Etymologiae*. Translated by Stephen A. Barney et al., *The Etymologies of Isidore of Seville*, Cambridge 2006.

Leges Edwardi Confessoris, ed. Bruce R. O'Brien, *God's Peace and King's Peace*, Philadelphia, Pennsylvania 1999.

Wærferth of Worcester, *Translation of Gregory the Great's Dialogues*, ed. Hans Hecht, *Bischofs Wærferth von Worcester Übersetzung der Dialoge Gregors des Grossen* (Bibliothek der angelsächen Prosa V), (rpt.) Darmstadt 1965.

---

97 Maitland's judgment on England, *History of English Law* 2, 458, may be compared with my *Rancor and Reconciliation*, chap. 4, esp. 147–148.

William of Malmesbury, *Vita Wulfstani*, ed. Reginald R. Darlington, *The Vita Wulfstani of William of Malmesbury. To which are added the extant abridgments of this work and the miracles and translation of St. Wulfstan*, London 1928.

William the Conqueror's early ordinance (*Lad*), ed. Felix Liebermann, *Gesetze der Angelsachsen*, Halle 1903–1916.

Secondary Works

Amos, Ashley C., Angus Cameron and Antonette di Paolo (ed.), *Dictionary of Old English*, Toronto 1986 (consulted online at http://doe.utoronto.ca/pages/in-dex.html).

Berman, Harold J., *Law and Revolution: The Formation of the Western Legal Tradition*, Cambridge, Massachusetts 1983.

Bosworth, Joseph, and Thomas N. Toller, *An Anglo-Saxon Dictionary*, Oxford 1921 (consulted online at http://www.bosworthtoller.com/).

Brown, Warren, *Violence in Medieval Europe*, New York 2011.

Cameron, Angus, et al. (ed.), *Dictionary of Old English*, Toronto 1986– (hereafter 'DOE').

Esders, Stefan, 'Wergild and Social Practice in the Early Middle Ages', in: *Entre texte et histoire, Mélanges en honneur de Shoichi Sato*, ed. Jean-Loup Lemaitre and Osamu Kano, Paris 2015.

Hill, T. D., 'Satan, Judas, and the Foundation of the West Saxon State: Myth and Exegesis in the Prologue to Alfred's Laws' (unpublished paper).

Hudson, John G., *The Oxford History of the Laws of England* 2, Oxford 2012.

Hyams, Paul, 'Trial by Ordeal: the Key to Proof in the Early Common Law', in: *Of the Laws and Customs of England: Essays in Honor of Samuel E. Thorne*, ed. Thomas A. Green et al., Chapel Hill, North Carolina 1981, 90–126.

Hyams, Paul, 'Homage and Feudalism: A Judicious Separation', in *Die Gegenwart des Feudalismus*, ed. Natalie Fryde, Pierre Monnet and Otto Gerhard Oexle, Göttingen, 2003, 13–49.

Hyams, Paul, *Rancor and Reconciliation in Medieval England: Wrong and its Redress from the Tenth to Thirteenth Centuries*, Ithaca, New York 2003.

Hyams, Paul, 'Three-cornered Dynamics of Redemption in the Long Thirteenth Century', *Anglo-Norman Studies* 26 (2013), 1–15.

Hyams, Paul, 'Property Talk: Did Anglo-Saxon England know the Concept of Seisin?', in: *Texts and Contexts in Legal History: Essays in Honor of Charles Donahue*, ed. John Witte, Sara McDougall, and Anna di Robilant, Berkeley, California 2017, 37–59.

Hyams, Paul, 'Medieval Attitudes to Poverty: Amartya Sen and Serfdom Without Strings', in: *Emotions, Communities, and Difference in Medieval Europe*, ed. Maureen C. Miller and Edward Wheatley, London and New York 2017, 180–206.

Hyams, Paul, 'Servitude in Anglo-Saxon England; Searching for the Serfs', in: *Languages of the Law in Early Medieval England: Essays in Memory of Lisi Oliver*, ed. Stefan Jurasinski and Andrew Rabin, Leuven, Paris and Bristol 2019, 127–154.

Koziol, Geoffrey, *The Peace of God*, Leeds 2018.

Lambert, Tom, 'Theft, Homicide and Crime in Late Anglo-Saxon England', *Past and Present* 214 (2013), 3–43.

Lambert, Tom, *Law and Order in Anglo-Saxon England*, Oxford 2017.

Latham, Ronald E. et al. (ed.), *Dictionary of medieval Latin from British sources*, Oxford 2018, (consulted online at https://logeion.uchicago.edu/).

Miller, William Ian, *Bloodtaking and Peacemaking. Feud, Law, and Society in Saga Iceland*, Chicago and London 1990.

Milsom, Stroud F. C., *The Legal Framework of English Feudalism*, Cambridge 1976.

Mnookin, Robert H., and Lewis Kornhauser, 'Bargaining in the Shadow of the Law: The Case of Divorce', *The Yale Law Journal* 88 (1979), 950–997.

Niermeyer, Jan F., *Mediae Latinitatis Lexicon Minus. Lexique Latin médiéval — Francais/Anglais. A Medieval Latin-French/English Dictionary*, Leiden, New York and Cologne 1993.

Petkov, Kiril, *The Kiss of Peace: Ritual, Self, and Society in the High and Late Medieval West*, Leiden and Boston, Massachusetts 2003.

Pollock, Frederick, and Frederic W. Maitland, *The History of English Law before the Time of Edward I*, 2 vols., Cambridge ²1898.

Rabin, Andrew, *The Political Writings Of Archbishop Wulfstan of York*, Manchester 2015.

Rabin, Andrew, *Archbishop Wulfstan of York: Old English Legal Writings* (Dumbarton Oaks Medieval Library 66), Cambridge 2020.

Richardson, Henry G., and George O. Sayles (ed.), *Select Cases of Procedure without writ*, London 1941.

Sandel, Michael J., *Justice: What's the Right Thing to do?*, Cambridge, Massachusetts 2009.

Sen, Amartya, *The Idea of Justice*, Cambridge, Massachusetts 2009.

Spufford, Peter, *Money and its use in Medieval Europe*, Cambridge 1988.

Taylor, Alice, *The Shape of the State in Medieval Scotland, 1124–1290*, Oxford 2016.

Taylor, Charles, *Modern Social Imaginaries*, Durham, North Carolina and London 2004.

Thompson, John B., *Studies in the Theory of Ideology*, Cambridge 1984.

Tierney, Brian L., *Liberty and the Law: The Idea of Permissive Natural Law, 1100–1800* (Studies in Medieval and Early Modern Canon Law 12), Washington DC 2014.

Tierney, Brian L., *The Idea of Natural Rights* (Emory University Studies in Law and Religion 5), Atlanta, Georgia 1997.

Waldron, Jeremy, 'Who is my Neighbor? Humanity and Proximity', *The Monist* 86 (2003), 333–354.

White, Stephen D., *Custom, Kinship, and Gifts to Saints*, Chapel Hill, North Carolina and London 1988.

Wormald, Patrick, *Legal Culture in the Medieval West*, London 1999.

Wormald, Patrick, *The Making of English Law: King Alfred to the Twelfth Century. Volume 1: Legislation and its Limits*, Oxford 1999.

Index

www.ingramcontent.com/pod-product-compliance
Lightning Source LLC
LaVergne TN
LVHW010543300926
849162LV00002B/219